REVOLUTIONS

Theoretical, Comparative, and Historical Studies

THIRD EDITION

Edited by
JACK A. GOLDSTONE
University of California, Davis

WADSWORTH

Australia • Canada • Mexico • Singapore • Spain
United Kingdom • United States

THOMSON
™
WADSWORTH

Executive Editor: David Tatom
Development Editor: Christine Caperton
Editorial Assistant: Dianna Long
Technology Project Manager: Melinda Newfarmer
Marketing Manager: Caroline Croley
Project Manager, Editorial Production:
 Belinda Krohmer
Print/Media Buyer: Robert King

Permissions Editor: Elizabeth Zuber
Production Service: G&S Typesetters
Copy Editor: Donald Pharr
Cover Designer: Brian Salisbury
Cover Image: Photodisk
Cover Printer: Thomson/West
Compositor: G&S Typesetters
Printer: Thomson/West

For more information about our products, contact us at:
Thomson Learning Academic Resource Center
1-800-423-0563
For permission to use material from this text, contact us by:
Phone: 1-800-730-2214
Fax: 1-800-730-2215
Web: http://www.thomsonrights.com

Library of Congress Control Number: 2002103733
ISBN-13: 978-0-155-06679-3
ISBN-10: 0-155-06679-X

Wadsworth/Thomson Learning
10 Davis Drive
Belmont, CA 94002-3098
USA

Asia
Thomson Learning
60 Albert Street, #15-01
Albert Complex
Singapore 189969

Australia
Nelson Thomson Learning
102 Dodds Street
South Melbourne, Victoria 3205
Australia

Canada
Nelson Thomson Learning
1120 Birchmount Road
Toronto, Ontario M1K 5G4
Canada

Europe/Middle East/Africa
Thomson Learning
Berkshire House
168-173 High Holborn
London WC1V 7AA
United Kingdom

Latin America
Thomson Learning
Seneca, 53
Colonia Polanco
11560 Mexico D.F.
Mexico

Spain
Paraninfo Thomson Learning
Calle/Magallanes, 25
28015 Madrid, Spain

BRIEF CONTENTS

DETAILED CONTENTS

PREFACE

This book was developed for courses on revolution and social change. The readings were chosen to stimulate students to think about revolution in terms of social theory, historical events, and contemporary politics. This book will guide students to the key issues in thinking about revolutions — the problems of democracy and dictatorship, of popular mobilization and conflict — and introduce them to the main episodes of revolutionary struggles in the past and in the present.

The first part of this volume provides both classic statements and the latest approaches to the theoretical understanding of revolutions and revolutionary movements, including structural models, studies of revolutionary ideology and leadership, the role of gender issues, and the outcomes of revolutionary struggles. The second part provides brief accounts of the major revolutionary episodes in modern history. These are grouped according to various types of revolution: the republican revolutions of England (1640), France (1789), and the United States (1776); the major communist revolutions of Russia (1917), China (1949), and Cuba (1959); the anti-dictatorial revolutions in Mexico (1910), Nicaragua (1979), Iran (1979), and the Philippines (1986); the anti-communist revolutions of Eastern Europe (1989), the U.S.S.R. (1991), and China's Tiananmen student revolt (1989); the guerrilla revolutions of Latin America (since the 1950s); and the "ethnic conflict" revolutions of South Africa (1994), Palestine/Israel (1987–), and Afghanistan (1973–).

These groupings are designed so that readings from Part One can be easily paired with readings from Part Two. Thus, Chapter 1 — classic approaches — can be paired with Chapter 5, on the republican revolutions that inspired the classic thinkers. Chapter 2 can similarly be paired with Chapter 6, and Chapter 3 with Chapter 7. Chapter 4, which is a bit longer, can be split into two parts to be paired with chapters 8 and 9. In this way, students can grasp the global development of revolutionary struggles while studying the growth of theoretical reflections on those events.

This volume is addressed primarily to students who have some prior course work in history or social science. All the essays appear with introductory comments to highlight the major points of each selection. The essays are analytical and thought provoking, as well as descriptive, and encourage students to seek further reading (an extensive list of further readings on particular revolutions and personalities is provided at the back of the book).

This third edition covers more revolutions, with more attention to the Third World, than earlier editions. Therefore, the book can be used alone as a text for a survey course designed to introduce students to the remarkably varied and global characteristics of revolutions. This book can also be used to provide a solid theoretical foundation for courses that focus on revolutions in a particular time period or region of the world, in which the instructor will wish to combine this volume with more detailed readings on those events.

All of these selections have appeared in books or scholarly journals; however, the versions in this volume have been edited for brevity and clarity, and most footnotes and citations have been omitted except for direct quotations. I owe thanks to the authors who have worked with me and allowed me to edit their works. Readers who wish more detailed information and citations should consult the original sources, listed on the opening page of each selection.

In teaching and learning about revolutions, I am sharing the gifts I have received from many outstanding scholars. The list of teachers, colleagues, and students who have helped me in understanding revolutions is far too long to print; the following list only hints at my many debts. Daniel Chirot, Robert K. Merton, and Judith Stacy were instrumental in setting this volume in motion; I greatly appreciate their support and advice. Much of what I have learned about revolutions I have drawn from outstanding scholars who I have been fortunate to have as teachers and colleagues: Ron Aminzade, Rod Aya, Craig Calhoun, Randall Collins, S. N. Eisenstadt, John Foran, William Gamson, Jeffrey Goodwin, Roger Gould, John Hall, Gary Hamilton, Michael Hechter, George Homans, Nathan Keyfitz, John Markoff, Doug McAdam, Liz Perry, Charles Ragin, William Sewell Jr., Theda Skocpol, David Snow, Arthur Stinchcombe, Sid Tarrow, Charles Tilly, Mark Traugott, and John Walton. Over the years, many brilliant graduate students have helped me shape the materials and ideas that found their way into this volume. I owe thanks to two in particular: Paul Burke helped me in reviewing the second edition to identify what needed to be changed. Jaime Becker did an outstanding job working with me to select, edit, proofread, and prepare the essays in this edition; her assistance was invaluable.

At various times, work on this and previous editions was supported by Northwestern University, the University of California at Davis, the Center for Advanced Study in the Behavioral Sciences at Stanford University, the American Council of Learned Societies, and National Science Foundation Grant SES-9022192. I am grateful for their support.

My work on the revision for this edition also benefited from the valuable feedback of these reviewers: Valerie Bunce, Cornell University; Michael P. Gabriel, Kutztown University; William M. LeoGrande, American University; Paul Monod, Middlebury College; Darius Rejali, Reed College; A. H. Rifai, Berea College; and Mitchell Smith, University of Oklahoma.

The editorial staff at Harcourt College Publishers, many of whom still are involved with this book now as employees of Wadsworth, has been instrumental to the continued improvement of this text. I owe special thanks to David Tatom for his patience and perseverance in bringing the second and now third editions of this book into being; without him, this volume would not have continued to develop and improve. Thanks also to Marcus Boggs, my original editor, to Nancy Lombardi, who was project editor of the second edition, and to Christine Caperton, who encouraged and sustained me through the third. My appreciation also goes to Gene Carter Lettau, Eleanor Garner, Ruth Cornell, and Jayne Tindall Ponceti, Dianna Long, and Belinda Krohmer from Harcourt/Wadsworth for their enormous effort in turning piles of edited manuscripts into a finished text.

Finally, my own world has changed enormously since the first edition of this text, thanks to my wife of ten years, Gina, and two wonderful children—Alex and Simone—who are engaged with this tumultuous world. May future revolutions help make this a better world for them and for their peers.

Jack A. Goldstone

INTRODUCTION

The Comparative and Historical Study of Revolutions

> The laws are put out of doors. Men walk on them in the streets. . . . The king
> has been deposed by the rabble. . . . The people have reached the position of
> the highest divine court. . . . Every town saith: Let us drive out the powerful
> from our midst.
>
> *The Lament of Ipuwer*

This excerpt from 2100 B.C. describes the fall of Pepi II, pharaoh of the Old Kingdom of
Egypt. Written observations on revolution stretch back over 4,000 years. Why have certain
governments fallen at the hands of their own people? This question has fascinated students
of politics for almost as long as governments have existed. Yet explaining why revolutions
occur is not an easy task. Revolutions are complex events and originate in long and complicated causal processes. Ideas about how and why revolutions occur are widespread, but observers must constantly check those ideas against the evidence that actual revolutions have
left. Over the centuries, Plato, Aristotle, Machiavelli, de Tocqueville, Marx, and many others have added to the observations of Ipuwer. And the study of revolutions has been one of
the most active areas of modern social science. Consequently, people have learned a great
deal about revolutions. But testing and refining our understanding by studying the history of
revolutions still continues, and new insights often emerge from new events.

THEORIES OF REVOLUTION: THE BASIC PROBLEMS

The basic problems in building a theory of revolution become clear if we consider some
common notions of why revolutions occur. One view widely held among lay people is that
"misery breeds revolt." In other words, when oppression becomes too much to bear, the
masses will rise up against their oppressors. Although this view has an element of truth, it
does not explain why revolutions have occurred in some countries but not in others. Revolt
is only one of several paths the oppressed may take. The downtrodden may be so divided and
powerless that they may be unable to organize an effective revolt, or they may simply hope
for a better life in the hereafter. Oppression and misery have been widespread throughout

---

history, yet revolutions have been rare. Therefore, a theorist of revolution must address this question: Does all oppression stir revolt? Or are there conditions under which people, no matter how oppressed, are unlikely to mount a revolution?

Another common view is that revolutions occur when a state faces an unmanageable accumulation of difficulties. When a number of severe problems occur together—a royal bankruptcy, a famine, a conflict within the ruling family, a war—the state collapses, opening the floodgates of revolution. Again, this view has an element of truth, but it also fails to explain where and how revolutions have occurred. The great empires of Rome and Charlemagne faced such difficulties, yet they first crumbled at the edges and then fell into parts, which minor lords ruled or external enemies conquered. These empires died with a whimper, not a bang. So the theorist of revolution must examine this problem: When do pressures on a government lead to revolution, rather than a break-up into lesser states or conquest by external enemies?

A third view is that revolutions arise when new, radical ideas shake people out of their accustomed lives. This idea also has merit, for people generally fight great revolutions under the banner of radical ideas. Yet what causes such ideas to take root and to lead men and women to revolt? Many ideals of a happier existence take the form of religious movements focused on a better life in the next world. And many radical ideas stimulate people to behave in different ways in different times and cultures. The ideas of democracy and citizenship were current among Greeks and Romans; we must wonder why they became revolutionary ideas in Europe 2,000 years later.

In sum, common observations about revolution, though not totally inaccurate, do not provide a full understanding of the historical pattern of revolution. Popular revolts, the process of the collapse of states, and the role of ideologies all need closer scrutiny.

The scientific, comparative study of revolutions began in earnest after the Russian Revolution of 1917–1921. Since that time, theories of revolution have moved through three generations of scholarship, each adding to our understanding: the *natural histories* of the 1920s and 1930s, the *general theories of political violence* of the 1960s and early 1970s, and the *structural theories* of the late 1970s and 1980s. As we begin the twenty-first century and grapple with events such as the collapse of communist states in the U.S.S.R. and Eastern Europe, a fourth generation of revolutionary theory is beginning to develop.

THE NATURAL HISTORY OF REVOLUTIONS

In the 1920s and 1930s, a number of historians and sociologists surveyed the most famous revolutions of the West: the English Revolution of 1640, the American Revolution of 1776, the French Revolution of 1789, and the Russian Revolution of 1917.[1] These writers wanted to identify common patterns of events in the major revolutions. They succeeded in finding a remarkable correspondence among the major events in each of these revolutions. Several of their observations on the "natural history" of revolutions have proven valid so often that they appear to be law-like empirical generalizations:

1. *Prior to a revolution, the bulk of the "intellectuals"—journalists, poets, playwrights, essayists, teachers, members of the clergy, lawyers, and trained members of the bureaucracy—cease to support the regime, write condemnations, and demand major reforms.* These attacks on the old regime even attract the attention of the regime's natural supporters. French aristocrats applauded the plays of Voltaire and Beaumarchais, English lords supported Puritan preachers, and Russian nobles demanded local parliaments and other democratic reforms.

Why is the mass desertion of the intellectuals so important? Primarily for what it portends. When hereditary nobles, high officials, and professionals countenance such public criticism, the regime must be failing to provide services such as security of property and rank, high-level positions for the children of prominent people, and victories and spoils in war. The desertion of the intellectuals on a vast scale thus implies an unusually widespread and pervasive dissatisfaction with regime performance. This dissatisfaction extends even to the highest ranks of government and society. Such uneasiness often presages a reluctance of elite leaders to suppress popular uprisings and even more often portends elite revolts against the regime.

2. *Just prior to the fall of the old regime, the state attempts to meet criticism by undertaking major reforms.* Examples from the past have included the reforms of Louis XVI in France, the Stolypin reforms in Russia, and the Boxer reforms in China. Such reforms often attempt to absorb additional groups into the regime without giving them any real influence by adding parliaments or councils with strictly advisory powers. However, such reforms generally serve to further undermine the regime. They act both as an admission that the regime is flawed and as an encouragement to others to pressure the government for further changes. This pattern bears out Machiavelli's warning to rulers: "If the necessity for [reforms] comes in troubled times, you are too late for harsh measures; and mild ones will not help you, for they will be considered as forced from you, and no one will be under any obligation to you for them."[2]

3. *The actual fall of the regime begins with an acute political crisis brought on by the government's inability to deal with some economic, military, or political problem rather than by the action of a revolutionary opposition.* The crisis may take the form of a state bankruptcy or a weakening command of the armed forces. Revolutionary leaders, who may have been active but relatively powerless for a long time, suddenly find themselves with the upper hand, due to the incapacity of the old regime. The sudden onset of revolution thus stems from a weakening or paralysis of the state rather than from a sudden gain in the strength of revolutionaries.

4. *Even where revolutionaries have united solidly against the old regime, following its collapse their internal conflicts eventually cause problems.* After enjoying a brief euphoria over the fall of the old regime, the revolutionary opposition becomes rapidly disunited. The revolutionaries usually divide into three factions: conservatives, who seek to minimize change (many of whom eventually call for the return of the ousted regime); radicals, who seek rapid and widespread change; and moderates, who try to steer a middle course. The results of such disunity among revolutionaries range from coups to civil war.

5. *The first group to seize the reins of state are moderate reformers.* This axiom, observed in major revolutions a century and more ago, again proved accurate twenty years ago in Iran, where Bazargan, the moderate critic, first took power after revolutionaries forced the Shah's government out.

6. *While the moderates seek to reconstruct rule on the basis of moderate reform and often employ organizational forms left over from the old regime, alternative, more radical centers of mass mobilization spring up with new forms of organization.* In France, the moderate Girondin assembly faced the radical Jacobin clubs; in America, the moderate critics of King George III were pushed into revolutionary war by the radical Sons of Liberty; in modern Iran, the moderates of the executive branch (Bazargan, Bani-Sadr, Gotzbadeh) competed in their attempt to rule the country with the radical, mass-mobilizing Islamic theologians.

7. *The great changes in the organization and ruling ideology of a society that follow successful revolutions occur not when the old regime first falls, but when the radical, alternative, mass-mobilizing organizations succeed in supplanting the moderates.* This step generally occurs because the moderates, seeking continuity, do not rid the government of the liabilities that caused the old regime to fail. Hence, they inherit the same inability to deal with urgent economic and military problems. The success of the radicals generally comes from their willingness to take extreme measures, both in dealing with pressing problems and in securing their rule.

However, as the American Revolution shows, the triumph of the radicals, though common, is not inevitable. Yet only to the extent that the moderates repudiate and dissociate themselves from the old regime—a task in which they are unlikely to equal the radicals—are they likely to succeed. Only in a war of colonial liberation—where the old regime enemy is clearly external—are moderates likely to have a chance for survival. For example, in Indonesia in 1945, in Algeria in 1962, and in Guinea in 1958, as in America in 1787, relatively moderate regimes were able to stay in power because in fighting colonial forces, the moderates could maintain unity with other factions. On the other hand, in Nicaragua and Iran, where the enemy of the revolutionaries was an internal regime, radical leaders supplanted the moderates.

8. *The disorder brought by the revolution and the implementation of radical control usually results in forced imposition of order by coercive rule.* This is the stage of "terror," familiar from the guillotine days of the French Revolution and known to later generations through Stalin's *gulag* and Mao's cultural revolution.

9. *The struggles between radicals and moderates and between defenders of the revolution and external enemies frequently allow military leaders to move from obscurity to commanding, even absolute, leadership.* The long roster of national leaders who emerged in this fashion includes Washington, Cromwell, Napoleon, Ataturk, Mao, Tito, Boumedienne, and Mugabe.

10. *The radical phase of the revolution eventually gives way to a phase of pragmatism and moderate pursuit of progress within the new status quo.* In this phase, the radicals are defeated or have died, and moderates return to power. They condemn the "excesses" of the radicals and shift the emphasis from political change to economic progress within a framework of stable institutions. This phase began with the fall of Robespierre in France, Khrushchev's repudiation of Stalin in Russia, and the fall of Mao's allies, the "gang of four," in China.

These ten propositions, the legacy of the natural historians of revolution, provided a valuable guide to understanding the pattern of events that commonly unfolds in revolutions. However, using this approach alone left many basic questions unanswered. Chief of these was the question of causes: Why did revolutions arise? What were the sources of opposition to the old regime? These issues became the focus of a second generation of analysts who were adherents of the general-theory school.

2nd GENERAL THEORIES OF POLITICAL VIOLENCE

In the 1950s and 1960s, the emergence of new nations captured the attention of scholars. Political changes were clearly part of the process by which traditional societies, as their economies grew and their people became more educated, developed into modern states. Yet the widespread violence that accompanied these changes was striking: Revolutions, coups, riots, and civil wars suddenly seemed to arise everywhere. Some scholars developed general theories to explain all these kinds of political violence.

General theories of political violence took several forms. The psychological approach, as set forth by Davies and further refined by Gurr,[3] attempted to improve the "misery breeds revolt" approach by identifying precisely the kinds of misery likely to lead to political disorders. These authors argued that people generally accept high levels of oppression and misery if they expect such discomforts to be their natural lot in life. Only when people expect a better life, and have their expectations frustrated, are they likely to develop feelings of aggression and resentment. Therefore, any change in a society that raises people's expectations for a better life without providing the means of meeting those expectations can be politically destabilizing. Such expectations may include cultural contacts with more economically advanced societies or rapid but uneven economic growth. Davies argued that one combination of events in particular, a period of growing prosperity that raises people's expectations for a better life, followed by a sharp economic downturn that dashes those expectations (the "J-curve" of economic growth), would yield exceptionally sharp feelings of deprivation and aggression.

A second general-theory approach, developed largely by Smelser and Johnson,[4] argued that instead of focusing mainly on popular discontent, scholars should examine social institutions. These authors stressed that when the various subsystems of a society—the economy, the political system, and the training of young people for new positions—grow at roughly the same rate, the government will remain stable. However, if one subsystem starts to change independently, the resulting imbalance will leave people disoriented and open to considering new values. When such imbalance becomes severe, radical ideologies that challenge the legitimacy of the status quo will become widespread. During such periods, a war, a government bankruptcy, or a famine may bring the government down.

In an influential work, Huntington[5] synthesized these two approaches. He argued that modernization led to institutional imbalance because the resulting education and economic growth would increase people's desire to participate in politics faster than political institutions could change to accommodate this desire. This gap between desire for change and accomplished change would create frustrated expectations about political life, which in turn could lead to riot, rebellion, and revolution.

The psychological and the system-disequilibrium theories of revolution tried to explain why popular discontent and opposition to the regime arose. Tilly[6] developed a third general-theory approach focusing on resource mobilization. Tilly pointed out that discontent alone is unlikely to lead to revolution if the discontented remain unorganized and lack resources. Arguing that discontent and conflict are a normal part of politics, he stressed that political violence is likely to occur only when aggrieved parties have the means to make such violence count—namely, when they have the resources and the organization to take significant actions. In this view, although modernization may bring discontent, it does not necessarily lead to revolution. Instead, revolution will probably occur only when opponents are able to mobilize the massive resources needed to take command of a geographical area and effectively challenge the old regime.

General theories thus moved from (1) approaches stressing relative deprivation and frustration to (2) approaches stressing institutional imbalance to (3) Tilly's approach, stressing resource mobilization by challengers. This work led scholars to study not merely individual discontent but also changes in institutions and resource mobilization by organized groups. Still, *all* the general theory approaches had certain problems in explaining where and how revolutions occurred.

First, the general theories viewed revolutions as the result of actions by an opposition movement that sought to wrest control of the state. They explained revolutions mainly by analyzing the origins of the opposition and its recourse to violence. Yet revolutions often began not from the acts of a powerful revolutionary opposition but from the internal breakdown and paralysis of state administrations, a condition that rendered states incapable of managing normally routine problems. The general theories of revolution and collective violence provided no help in understanding the conditions behind the internal breakdown of states.

Second, during the period when theorists of revolution debated whether modernization engendered revolutions by raising expectations, by disequilibrating the sectors of society, or by shifting resources from authorities to regime opponents, our view of modernization greatly changed. Scholars recognized that the notion that all societies would face the same general process of modernization was too simple. Moore[7] argued that different kinds of societies experienced different kinds of social change. For example, Moore demonstrated that whether or not modernization led to revolution and what *kind* of revolution occurred depended on the relationship between peasants and landlords, a relationship that was very different in England than in France or Germany, and different again in Russia and China. Scholars recognized that in order to explain why revolutions occurred in some countries but not in others and to understand their outcomes, they needed to study the *differences* among political structures and agrarian relationships. The general theories of revolution overlooked these differences.

Therefore, scholars in their search for the bases for revolutions turned from general theories of political violence to historical and comparative studies of the structure of different kinds of states and agrarian relationships. These studies have led to structural theories of revolution.

STRUCTURAL THEORIES OF REVOLUTION

Structural theories argue that states vary in structure and are thus vulnerable to different kinds of revolution. They further contend that revolutions begin from some combination of state weakness, conflicts between states and elites, and popular uprisings.

STATES AND ELITES

Structural theories of revolution start from a few straightforward observations about states: (1) all states are organizations that gather resources from their society; (2) states are in competition—for territory, for military strength, for trade—with other states; and (3) some kinds of state organizations are likely to fare badly in such competition and experience severe political crises.

Therefore, structural theorists ask this question: What kinds of state organizations are apt to experience fiscal or military crises in competition with other states? Scholars have found several answers.

States with relatively backward and unproductive economies, compared to the states with which they are competing, may face overwhelming outside pressures. The extreme case of this is Russia in World War I. The Russian state collapsed under defeats by the more advanced Germany; these defeats ushered in the Russian Revolution. Other countries have faced similar, if less severe pressures: France fought the more economically advanced England in the eighteenth century, and Japan, China, and Turkey fought the more advanced Western powers in the nineteenth and twentieth centuries.

Yet states sometimes do collapse without defeat in war. The probability of an internal collapse generally depends on the relationship of the state to members of the elite, whether they are hereditary nobles, local landlords, or clergy. Skocpol[8] has pointed out that attempts by the state to meet international competitive pressures by increasing government income or authority often run counter to elite interests, for state goals may require suspension of traditional elite privileges and may threaten the resources of elites. The vulnerability of the state to a political crisis then depends on the extent to which elites can influence the state and use their resources against it.

For example, the eighteenth-century French monarchy required the cooperation of noble-controlled *parlements,* independent judicial bodies that could block and challenge the directives that the Crown issued. More recently, the Iranian clergy, because of their financial supporters in the bazaar economy, their role in the traditional courts, and their network of influence in the mosques and schools, retained control of resources with which to mount a challenge to the Shah. Thus, when conflicts between the monarchy and elites arose—in France over the state bankruptcies arising from the Anglo–French wars of the eighteenth century and in Iran over the Shah's rapid modernization plans—the elite's opposition was able to cripple and paralyze the central government.

The loyalty of the army is also crucial. Where the government openly recruits officers from all classes, provides extensive training for the rank and file, and keeps troops isolated from civilians, the army is usually a reliable tool for suppressing domestic disorders. Yet where army officers come primarily from a landed elite, they may sympathize with their own class in a conflict between the central government and elites. Where troops are recently recruited and fraternize with the populace, their sympathy for civilians may override their allegiance to their officers. In either of the last two cases, the unreliability of the army increases the vulnerability of the state to revolution.[9]

In sum, if a powerful elite outside the state bureaucracy has the resources to paralyze the state in times of conflict and if outside allegiances weaken the army, severe political crises are liable to occur when states attempt to increase their authority or resources. This kind of conflict became crucial during the French, English, Chinese, and Iranian revolutions.

However, two other kinds of societal structure are also prone to state breakdown. And again, the relationship between states and elites is the key factor. First, even if there is no strong independent elite outside the state bureaucracy, conflicts between states and elites may still occur. Trimberger[10] has argued that this is likely when officials who lack great personal landholdings or ties to landlord classes but who share a tradition of state service and elite training hold positions *within* the bureaucracy or armed forces. This situation may occur when a state provides certain civil or military officials with special status and/or elite training. If exceptional military or economic pressures from abroad threaten the state and this elite decides the state is failing to meet those pressures, the elite is likely to initiate what Trimberger calls an "elite revolution." Powerful civil or military officials may seize control of the central administrative apparatus and reshape the pattern of resource distribution and extraction in an effort to solve the military and economic difficulties that threaten the nation. Lacking a vested interest in the current economic structure, such officials are free to respond to international pressures by implementing radical reforms—including land reform, abolition or attenuation of traditional status distinctions, and rapid industrialization. Examples include the Meiji restoration in 1868 in Japan, Ataturk's takeover of Turkey in 1923, and Nasser's revolutionary coup in 1952. The anti-communist revolution in the U.S.S.R. also began in this fashion, with current and former communist bureaucrats leading the attack on the communist regime.

Second, certain states (labeled "neo-patrimonial" by Eisenstadt[11]) have a structure characterized by a high degree of patronage. In such states, the government is extremely personal. The chief executive maintains his or her position not with a strong bureaucracy that enforces the law but with the support of elites and bureaucrats secured through an extensive and informal system of personal rewards. In such a state, the leader may keep the bureaucracy and armed forces weak and divided, while he or she may encourage corruption to keep military and civil officials dependent on the patronage of the chief executive.

This kind of state is particularly vulnerable to economic downturns or military pressures. A period of economic stability and growth provides the executive with the resources to build an extended patronage network; however, a sharp economic downturn or military setback may then deprive the executive of the means to continue to reward his or her followers. In this event, the patronage network may begin to crumble, and the competition once encouraged within the bureaucracy may reduce the loyalty of the followers. If at this juncture even a limited popular uprising occurs, the internal divisions and corruption of the bureaucracy and armed forces may limit the state's ability to suppress it quickly, and this failure may lead to the fall of the state.

This type of revolution is distinct from other revolutions in that its leaders' first aim is overthrowing the personal rule of the discredited chief executive, not changing the system of government. Indeed, the chief executive is often attacked for betraying an already existing democratic constitution, which the regime's opponents promise to restore. Nonetheless, because the government is bound up with the person of the chief executive, the crumbling of the patronage network combined with even a limited popular uprising can bring the collapse of the entire regime. The reconstruction of the state may then bring far-reaching changes in government and social organization. Such a revolution at first generally lacks a strong ideological component, and considerable time may pass before the revolutionaries decide what form of government should replace the old personal state. Examples include the Mexican Revolution, the Cuban Revolution, the Nicaraguan Revolution, and the Philippines "people power" Revolution.

In all these cases, revolution depends on elites with independent resources who have substantial grievances against the state over taxation, corruption, attacks on the elite, or the state's failure to stand up to foreign pressures. More than 2,000 years ago, Plato observed that "All political changes originate in divisions of the actual governing power; a government which is united . . . cannot be moved" (*Republic,* Book VII). This observation is no less true today: Precisely those states that are structurally prone to internal conflicts between the state and elites are most vulnerable to revolution.

Yet the paralysis of the state is only one component of revolution. Elite opposition may disable a state and open it to coups or elite revolution, but a full-scale revolution occurs only through the conjunction of such opposition with widespread popular uprisings.

Popular Uprisings

Popular uprisings range from traditional food riots to modern industrial strikes. For convenience, we may divide them into two kinds of uprisings that have been critical in actual revolutions: peasant revolts and urban workers' uprisings.

Peasant Revolts   Peasants the world over have a long history of oppression. Their control over the land they farm is often weak, and they frequently must pay one-third to one-half of their crop to landlords and to the state as rents and taxes. In agrarian societies, outbreaks of peasant protest over the terms of these payments and over control of land have been as common as factory strikes in industrial societies. However, most peasant revolts are small, local, and easily suppressed. A successful peasant revolt is likely only when several key relationships exist simultaneously: peasant solidarity, peasant capacity, and landlord vulnerability.[12]

Peasant revolts generally stem from obvious grievances such as landlords taking over peasant lands, major increases in state taxation or in rents, or famines and military disasters. As Scott has remarked, "The great majority of peasant movements historically, far from being affairs of rising expectations, have rather been defensive efforts to preserve customary rights or to restore them once they have been lost."[13]

Yet what appears to be important is not merely the level of grievances but whether such grievances are widely shared and widely directed at the same target. When the state sharply increases taxes or landlords raise the dues of whole villages or seek to take over village lands, entire villages share common grievances toward obvious targets. But when villages have few or no communal lands, or when each family holds land under different obligations to landlords, some families may suffer great hardships, yet whole villages will not rise in revolt.

Peasants also must have the organizational capacity to plan and act in common before revolts can be successful. This is readily possible where self-governing village councils traditionally exist. Such councils played an important role in the peasant villages of Old Regime France and Tsarist Russia and in the Indian communal villages of rural Mexico. Where peasants have no traditional self-government but are under the close supervision of local landlords or their agents as in England after 1500, in Eastern Germany after 1600, and in Latin American haciendas, major revolts are extremely rare.

The vulnerability of landlords is also a factor. Landlords who have their own means of coercion and strong local governing bodies able to deal with food shortages and local disturbances can generally stand firm against the early stages of peasant uprisings without relying on aid from the state. Such landlords can maintain their authority even if the central government is temporarily disabled. Such landlords may even tolerate or promote peasant protests against higher taxes or other intrusions of the central government. But landlords who must rely almost entirely on central government troops to maintain local order are extremely vulnerable when war or economic distress incapacitates the state. Russian landlords during World War I and French landlords during the Crown's bankruptcy in 1788–1789 had to face peasant uprisings without state protection and had no other means to defend themselves. In these cases, peasant revolts spread rapidly through the countryside.

Still, the transformation of peasant revolts into peasant revolutions requires the action of groups outside the peasantry. Peasants tend to be very local in their outlook and goals. Without national leadership or actions by other groups, peasant revolts tend to dissolve into numerous unconnected local uprisings. But if other efforts join with peasant protest, the rural groups can contribute to a national revolution in two ways. In some cases, an urban elite leaves the cities to work with the peasantry and forge links between peasant groups. Building peasant guerrilla armies and peasant organizations, these elites can provide both organizational capacity and national goals. This is particularly important where peasants lack their own self-government free of landlord control. This pattern occurred in varying degrees in the Chinese, Cuban, Vietnamese, and Nicaraguan revolutions.

A second pattern, found in the French and Russian revolutions, is for peasant revolts to coincide with urban revolts. Urban revolts have often provided the first "shock troops" of revolution by combining with elite protests to paralyze the state. Where appropriate conditions prevailed in the countryside, such as peasant solidarity and landlord vulnerability, the paralysis of the state then allowed peasant revolts to spread and to undermine rural landlords.

Peasant grievances do play a role in peasant movements. But usually the peasants who have suffered the most are *not* those who undertake major revolts. Instead, it is peasants with substantial grievances who also have strong solidarity and organizational capacity, and who face vulnerable landlords, who have been the major actors in social revolutions.

Urban Uprisings   In the countryside, major uprisings have depended on key relationships among peasants, landlords, and the state. In urban settings, such relational factors are less important. The concentration of large masses of workers and the presence of obvious targets for violence such as state buildings and palaces in capital cities provide revolutionary crowds with ready access to potential supporters and targets. The chief factors in urban uprisings are the level of workers' grievances and such physical factors as the scale and layout of cities and the size and effectiveness of urban police forces.

In seeking the roots of urban uprisings, we must first discard some old myths. Whether we look at the residents of growing cities in eighteenth-century France or twentieth-century Mexico, we find they are *not* isolated, ignorant, disoriented masses. Instead, urban migrants tend to be better educated and more highly skilled than the compatriots they leave behind in the countryside, generally have friends or family already in the city, and maintain frequent contacts, through circular migration, with rural kin. Moreover, when we examine the backgrounds of the participants in riots and revolutionary tumults, whether in eighteenth-century European towns or in twentieth-century American ghettos, we find that the rioters tend to be among the better educated residents of their communities and are more likely to be long-term residents than recent arrivals.[14] These urban rioters are generally workers for whom swings in prices and employment have a powerful impact, rather than the poorest, hard-core unemployed. In short, they are people who are responding to current grievances and not criminals or rabble.

Two grievances stand out as the chief causes of revolutionary urban tumults: the cost of food and the availability of employment. Food riots have occurred in sixteenth-century England and twentieth-century Poland while urban rioting has accompanied unusually high levels of unemployment from the French Revolution to twentieth-century Britain and the United States. In the great revolutions of France, England, Russia, and China, and throughout Europe in 1848, high unemployment and sharp jumps in food prices combined to drive the laboring poor into large-scale anti-government protests.

In the absence of such grievances, the mere rapid growth of cities or increases in rural-to-urban migration are not necessarily politically destabilizing. Indeed, if the urban economy is expanding and providing jobs and better conditions for underemployed rural residents, urban expansion may increase political stability. Only when urban growth is combined with food shortages and outpaces the availability of jobs do grievances grow that may stimulate political violence.

Of course, riots are not always successful. The outcome of urban revolts depends on the extent to which crises and elite opposition have weakened the state. The size and discipline of police forces and the layout of cities (narrow streets and strongly cohesive neighborhoods make good bases for revolts) also affect the likelihood of success.

We must add a final word about the interaction of urban and rural revolt. Urban riots alone do not make a revolution. Though urban disorders have often been at the leading edge of revolution—in Paris in 1789, in Petersburg in 1917, in Tehran in 1980—no revolution has succeeded solely on the basis of rioting and seizure of the political capital by the populace. The state can isolate and defeat revolutionaries in the capital city if they do not have support in the provinces and the countryside, as members of the Paris Commune in 1792 and the Chinese Communists of the 1920s discovered. Even where urban revolts in the capital city played a dominant role, as in the Iranian, Philippines, and anti-communist revolutions, they were supported by anti-regime actions throughout the country, often in the form of general strikes, or opposition by critical groups such as miners or oil workers. Still, the enormous growth of urban populations in Third World countries since World War II has created a situation in which urban discontent and opposition may play the primary role in giving rise to social revolutions; rural uprisings may play a lesser role.[15]

In summary, popular uprisings grow from specific grievances that threaten the livelihoods of peasants and workers. In the countryside, these are grievances that peasants share widely and direct at landlords or the state; in the city, grievances center on high food prices and unemployment. When such grievances combine with conducive structural conditions—peasant autonomy and landlord vulnerability in the countryside and weakly policed and isolated enclaves in the cities—the conditions for popular uprisings exist. When such popular uprisings also coincide with conflicts between states and powerful independent elites, all the ingredients for a full-scale revolution are at hand.

4Tu   TOWARD A FOURTH GENERATION: AGENCY, IDEOLOGY, AND THE REVOLUTIONARY PROCESS

Although understanding the factors that make a state vulnerable to revolution is a major first step in explaining why some countries have revolutions and other do not, it is only the first step. To explain why a revolution occurs at a particular time and why a revolution has particular characteristics—certain participants, goals, and outcomes—we need to examine the revolutionary *process*. Fourth-generation theories argue that we need to pay close attention to what happens as revolutionary conflicts develop and unfold.[16]

A focus on revolutionary processes helps us to understand what social scientists call the "agency" and "path dependency" characteristics of revolutions. "Agency" implies that not all aspects of a revolution are predetermined by macro-social, structural factors. The decisions of key actors (or "agents") make a difference in whether a revolution will be successful and how it evolves. "Path dependency" implies that events and actions that occur during the revolutionary process affect later outcomes. If actors had made different decisions, or if a war or popular uprising had occurred at a different time or had not occurred at all, then the eventual outcome might have been very different. For example, in the French Revolution the fact that revolutionary leaders faced both war abroad and peasant uprisings at home led them to dismantle certain old-regime institutions far more completely than they had initially imagined. In Iran and Nicaragua, the particular leaders and coalitions that emerged, and the internal and international conflicts that developed, led to outcomes that were the opposite of what many observers had anticipated. In Iran, the broad-based opposition to the Shah's dictatorship had promised democracy, while many feared that Nicaragua's guerrilla leaders would impose a Castro-style communist dictatorship, yet neither outcome came to pass. Instead, the flow of events produced a harsh religious tyranny in Iran and a free electoral process in Nicaragua that voted the Sandinistas out of power.

The flow chart for revolutions shown below helps to clarify the distinctions among revolutionary origins, processes, and outcomes, and how they are related.

Revolutionary Origins

The origins of a revolutionary situation are usually found in social, economic, and policy changes that bring setbacks for various sectors of society. Typically, the ruler—whether a monarch, an emperor, a dictator, a military junta, or even a democratic regime—suffers from failures to maintain the *effectiveness* and *justice* of the regime. Failures of effectiveness may be demonstrated by problems of excessive state debt, fiscal emergencies, economic mismanagement (high inflation or low or negative economic growth), or military (international or domestic) defeats. Failures of justice may arise if the state is seen as overly dependent on foreign powers, as antagonistic to national religious beliefs or interests, as compromised by

A Flow Chart for Revolutions

	STATE AND INTERNATIONAL CONDITIONS	ELITE CONDITIONS	POPULAR CONDITIONS

ORIGINS	*Development of Crisis*
	Effectiveness
	    Military defeat
	    Financial/debt problems
	Justice
	    Nationalist/religious
	        failures
	    Welfare/corruption failures
		Alienation and Divisions
		Social mobility problems
		Political exclusion
		Economic losses
		State exactions
		Arbitrary and excessive
		    state violence
			Grievances
			Real wage declines
			Un- and underemployment
			Land scarcity/rising rents
			Arbitrary and excessive
			    state violence

PROCESSES	State attempts reforms,
	    and/or repression
	International support or
	    pressures
	State breakdown or civil war
	Possible external interventions
	    or wars
	Persecution of ethnic, religious,
	    or political minorities,
	    "terror"
		Elites become polarized
		    and seek to mobilize
		    supporters
		"Ideologies of opposition"
		    unite elite factions and
		    popular groups (e.g.,
		    nationalism, democracy,
		    communism, religious
		    fundamentalism)
		Elite struggles for power,
		    counter-revolution
			Popular mobilization by
			    local or elite leadership
			Shifts in support may be
			    triggered by state actions
			    that emphasize state
			    weakness or continuing
			    threats from the regime,
			    leading to radicalism and
			    counter-revolution

OUTCOMES	Stronger, more centralized
	    and bureaucratic state
	State efforts to lead economic
	    growth and/or
	    industrialization
		Possible revolutionary
		    innovations in bases of
		    authority and status
			Populist dictatorship or
			    democracy, depending
			    on character of leaders
			Up to decades of efforts
			    to reconstruct and
			    consolidate new
			    institutions

corruption, as creating unfair inequality by favoring certain groups (cronyism), or as committing acts of excessive or arbitrary violence. Such conditions can lead to a "state crisis" in which state leaders, nonstate elites, and popular groups all feel a need for changes to remedy these failures.

However, a state crisis can be resolved by peaceful reforms if elites are united and the general population remains restrained. For a revolutionary situation to develop, it is necessary that elites become divided and polarized, disagreeing sharply on whether the current government should be saved or radically changed. Elite divisions and alienation from the regime can arise from problems of contested social mobility, with certain groups seeing themselves as "squeezed out," or barred from positions of high status and authority; from outright political exclusion of major groups by the government; from sharp economic losses or increased state burdens on elites (new taxation, land seizures, restrictive or ruinous economic policies); or from arbitrary or excessive violence aimed at elites.

Once elites are polarized, with some groups seeking to radically change or overturn the regime, these radical elites may seek popular support. Efforts to forge elite-popular alliances against the government are aided by popular grievances against the regime. These can stem from declines in real wages, in employment, or in access to food or land; from rising rents or other fees extracted by elites or rising taxes imposed by the government; or from arbitrary or excessive violence aimed at popular groups.

The conjunction of these elements—a state crisis, elite divisions and alienation, and popular grievances—sets the stage for revolution, creating severe vulnerability for the existing regime. These were the key findings of structural theories of revolution. Yet what happens next is crucial to whether or not a revolutionary movement builds and succeeds, and what it will accomplish.

REVOLUTIONARY PROCESSES

The state may respond to the perceived need for change with reforms, repression, or both. Whether such reforms are seen as adequate solutions to current problems or as mere window dressing, and whether such repression is seen as limited and justified or as further evidence of arbitrary and excessive action by the regime, determines whether the government is able to quiet—or instead inflames—demands for change. One of the key paradoxes of revolution is that a state's efforts to avoid revolution by reform or repression often make the situation worse, spurring demands for greater change or creating more outrage at the state's unjust actions.[17]

Foreign powers can also have a considerable impact. War or threats of war can further polarize elites and mobilize the masses. Substantial foreign aid to the government can help sustain it, but if such aid comes with tight restrictions, or is seen as simply demonstrating the dependence of the regime on foreign powers, the intervention can further undermine the government. Foreign aid to the opposition can also increase the resources, organization, and effectiveness of the opposition, or similarly lead the opposition to be perceived as a pawn of foreign interests. The response to foreign intervention thus depends not only on the particular actions taken but also on how they appear to contending groups.

How actions appear to various actors depends on how particular ideologies frame the motivations of the state, as well as the aims of international powers and domestic groups. Ideologies form a crucial bridge from grievances to actions. When elites seek to mobilize popular support, they need an ideological framework that will appeal to peasants and urban workers. Such "ideologies of opposition" are crucial to creating the broad, multi-class coalition that is generally necessary to topple a regime.[18] National elites need to connect with local leaders and across a wide range of elite groups (religious, labor, business, government, military) to build a sufficiently powerful opposition to effectively challenge the state for power. Tapping into some broad ideal—nationalism, democracy, communism, or religious beliefs—provides the "glue" to hold a diverse multi-class and inter-elite coalition together. An inspiring ideological framework also leads opposition supporters to believe in the justice of their cause and to believe that they will eventually prevail.

As the authority of the state starts to break down, and the allegiance of elites and popular groups begins to shift, a further rapid expansion of the opposition, or a sharp decline in elite support for the regime, can be triggered by specific events or state actions. For example, in the Philippines and Nicaragua, assassinations of popular opposition leaders led to a massive outpouring of elite and mass support for the revolutionary opposition. In Cuba and Iran, the governments' wild and inconsistent swings between conciliation and harsh repression undermined support for these regimes.

State actions and resources also determine the shape of the revolutionary struggle. Where the state remains strong and the opposition is anchored mainly in rural areas, one may see a drawn-out guerrilla war. Where the state weakens rapidly, many elites abandon it, and urban groups actively support the opposition, one may see a fairly rapid overthrow of the central authorities. Either way, once revolutionary forces manage to seize control of the central government, the revolution can be said to have succeeded in overthrowing the old regime. However, the struggle to shape revolutionary outcomes has then only just begun.

REVOLUTIONARY OUTCOMES

The fall of the old regime and the taking of power by the revolutionary opposition rarely, if ever, marks the end of the revolution. Rather, it marks a new stage in the revolution: the struggle to shape the revolution's outcome. This is a struggle that may take many years, even decades, as revolutionary leaders strive to build lasting political and economic institutions.

If counterrevolutionary forces are strong, particularly if they gain foreign support, the new revolutionary regime may then face a severe test through civil war; such conflicts may also spill over into international military battles. Fears of counterrevolution may also spur "terror" campaigns against suspected enemies of the revolution and are especially likely to target religious, regional, or ethnic minorities.

Within the revolutionary coalition itself, there are often further struggles for power once the old regime has fallen. As Crane Brinton pointed out, radical and moderate regime opponents may fight to shape the course of the revolution. If moderate groups prevail, the result may be a democratic outcome; such was the case in the American Revolution and in the Philippines "People Power" Revolution. But if more radical groups come to the fore, particularly if they are committed to reshaping society regardless of the cost, the outcome is likely to be authoritarian and extremely bloody, as in the Russian Bolshevik, Chinese Communist, and Cambodian Khmer Rouge revolutions.

The ideological beliefs of particular leaders can go far toward shaping revolutionary outcomes, from Mao's belief in continuing revolution, to Nelson Mandela's insistence on a multiracial South Africa, to the traditional beliefs regarding women's roles held by the leaders of the French and Iranian revolutions. Yet such ideologies are often tested in revolutionary struggles with both internal and external enemies; thus, the ideologies that appear dominant at the beginning of a revolution—in particular, those that characterize the broad anti-regime coalition—may differ substantially from the ideology that prevails with the emergence of particular leaders or dominant groups later in the course of the revolution. No ideology at a given point in time can be taken as a certain road map to future revolutionary developments.

Indeed, as particular leaders and factions aim to shift the revolution's outcome, new ideological and institutional innovations may emerge. In the French Revolution, the seizure of Church lands to pay the bills of the revolutionary regime, in the Chinese revolution, the shift to "market socialism," and in the Russian revolution, the cult of Stalinism all emerged rather unexpectedly as revolutionary leaders sought to secure their position or attain certain goals in the face of unexpected obstacles. Thus, the combination of actions, decisions, and responses by a host of revolutionary, opposition, and foreign actors combine to create a particular path from revolutionary origins to revolutionary outcomes that is often difficult, or even impossible, to foresee.

The course of a particular revolution is thus variously shaped by (1) the state crisis, elite divisions, and popular grievances that constituted its origins; (2) the ideologies, coalitions, and conflicts that develop in the unfolding of the revolutionary process; and (3) the struggle among various leaders, factions, and foreign powers to shape revolutionary outcomes.

Yet despite the twists and turns that can arise in these revolutionary processes, two particular elements have been so widely important that they deserve additional scrutiny: the role of nationalism and the development of revolutionary conjunctures.

NATIONALISM AND REVOLUTIONARY CONJUNCTURES

NATIONALISM

Nationalism has been a persistent force in revolutions. From the seventeenth century through the nineteenth century, revolutions against European monarchs used the "nation" as an alternative focus for loyalty, replacing the person of the king. Nationalism thus became the basis for anti-monarchical coalitions in the English and French revolutions, and in the European revolutions of 1848. In the nineteenth and twentieth centuries, the desire to liberate "the nation" from foreign domination was a key factor in anti-colonial revolutions from Algeria and Vietnam to Angola and Mozambique. In recent years, the belief that certain rulers—the Shah of Iran, Marcos in the Philippines, Somoza in Nicaragua—were too dependent on U.S. aid, and hence were following foreign interests, rather than their own nations' interests, played a major role in building support for movements to topple those leaders. Finally, in the 1980s and 1990s, the belief that communist systems had become corrupt and that the people's interest would be better served by "national" governments rather than Soviet rule was crucial to the collapse of central authority in the U.S.S.R. and Yugoslavia.

While the passions aroused by nationalism are obvious, the actual definition and construction of nationalism are often problematic. Who belongs to the "nation"? How is membership defined—by territory, ancestry, or claims of allegiance? Different groups may construct "nationalism" quite differently.[19] Often in times of revolutionary crisis, the struggle to dominate the nationalist issue pits different groups against one another and brings persecution to minorities. The revolutionary faction that is most successful in presenting itself as embodying the true interests of the "nation" is generally the faction that is also most successful in mobilizing supporters, and thus the one that prevails in revolutionary struggles.

It is interesting to note that despite the variety of ideologies that have been offered as the basis for revolutionary mobilization—democracy, communism, pan-Arabism, anti-colonialism, Islamic fundamentalism—all of them rest on the basic argument that this ideology will provide a superior guide to fulfilling the material and spiritual needs of the "nation." Thus, nationalism, either by itself—as the idea that a particular national people are being oppressed—or tied to some other ideological goal, generally plays a central role in revolutionary politics.

Yet as Eisenstadt has pointed out,[20] ideologies are not merely sources of revolutions; ideologies are the products of revolution as well. Most revolutions have begun with ideals that were thought to be universal: the rights of man and citizen in the French Revolution, the superiority of communism in the Russian Revolution, and the intrinsic values of Islam in the Iranian Revolution were believed to hold globally, well beyond the borders of their particular nations. This univeralism gave these revolutions a missionary zeal and contributed to the anxieties regarding the spread of revolution on the part of other countries. Yet in practice, the appeals of nationalism generally triumphed over universalism; French republicanism, Russian communism, and Iranian Islam developed into strongly nationalist systems of governance, and no other countries adopted their revolutionary programs in their entirety. When republican ideals spread throughout the world, inciting a wave of democratic revolutions in the eighteenth and nineteenth centuries, and communist ideals spread and inspired a wave of revolutions in the twentieth century, these ideologies were still molded to the nationalist aspirations of states wherever they were adopted. Thus, the communism of Marxist revolutions was not merely drawn from the ideas of Karl Marx: In Russia, it was the product of Leninism; in China, it was the product of Maoism; and in Yugoslavia and Hungary, it was something slightly different again. In each case, the ideology under which the revolution consolidated developed out of a collision between the initial ideas and the actual experience of particular revolutionaries who struggled for power and built post-revolutionary regimes.[21]

THE PROBLEM OF CONJUNCTURE

If the availability of an appropriate ideology helps to explain the coalescence of extant grievances across various social groups into a coherent revolutionary movement, it does little to explain why at certain times the grounds for state crisis, increased state/elite conflict, and popular uprisings should arise simultaneously.

Experts have often suggested that the pressures of defeat in war are what bring diverse social problems to a head and that these pressures precipitate both state/elite conflicts and widespread revolt. However, although in some instances war has led to revolution, empirical studies have shown that the relationship between wars and internal political instability in general is weak. To give only the most striking example, in Europe the period from 1670 to 1763 was one of almost constant warfare, from the wars of Louis XIV to the Seven Years War. States used the largest armies seen on the continent to that time. Yet not a single revolution occurred anywhere in Europe. When revolution did come to France in 1789, France had not suffered a military defeat in over twenty-five years and had been at peace for six years following its victory over Britain in the American Revolution. Moreover, twenty of the twenty-six years preceding 1789 were years of peace. Similarly, Germany, Austria, and Russia were free from revolution during their defeats in the Napoleonic wars; revolutionary crises came to Germany and Austria only in 1848, after thirty years of peace. For these two centuries, the broad relationship between defeat in war and revolution is virtually nil.

What then might be the source of the revolutionary conjuncture? I have suggested that the roots of revolutionary crises might lie in the pattern of long waves of population growth and prices.[22] In the sixteenth and seventeenth centuries, when Europe's population was growing, prices rose steadily. As the population increased, high food prices and growing un-employment afflicted the cities. Governments, in order to keep themselves abreast of rising prices, raised taxes and sought to increase control of the countryside. At the same time, ris-ing prices divided the landed elites. Some landlords, dependent on fixed rents, saw their real incomes decline because of rising prices and therefore sought to raise rents and dues; oth-ers, who directly controlled the marketing of products, reaped bonanzas. In short, the steady rise of population and prices produced increasing divisions among the landed elite, attempts by the state to raise taxes and gain greater control of the land, and increased prob-lems of dues and taxes, unemployment, and rising food costs for the populace.

These forces may well have been the major causes behind the conjuncture of state/elite conflicts and popular uprisings that swept across Europe during 1560–1660, with revolution in England and revolts in France, Russia, Austria, and Italy constituting a crisis of the seven-teenth century. When Europe's population ceased growing between 1660 and 1730, food prices stopped rising, and the cycle of political discontent receded. But when population and prices continued their upward march from 1750 to 1850, political instability returned to much of Europe until cheap American and Russian wheat broke the link between population increase and rising prices. If this hypothesis is correct in linking revolutionary conjunctures with problems of population growth, state financial distress, food shortages, and increasing prices, then much of the Third World, particularly Africa, may well experience an extended period of revolution, similar to that of Europe in 1789–1848, in the next few decades.

In the contemporary world, the problems of coping with population change continue to impose strains on governments. However, population growth by itself is not sufficient to topple a regime. Rather, what appears to matter is whether the economy and political sys-tem respond constructively to changes in the size, age, and distribution of population. Where urban populations grow rapidly without a supporting growth of jobs; where ruling a rising population leads to rising state indebtedness; where natural disasters, such as earth-quakes or floods, reveal the incapacity of a corrupt government to assist a struggling popu-lation; in all these cases the stability of government may be threatened.

Moreover, the balances between population and economic and political institutions may be undone in the opposite direction as well. If population decline leads to a shortage of skilled personnel to administer the government, or leaves too few productive workers to pay taxes and accumulate capital to provide employment opportunities for the young, or un-dermines the power and position of formerly dominant groups, then these imbalances can also lead to state crisis and heightened conflicts. In parts of the world most affected by the AIDS epidemic, this dynamic may yet unfold.

In sum, a marked *imbalance* between the demands of a changing population on the econ-omy and the government, and the ability of the government to respond, creates a situation of declining political stability. Whenever such imbalances become widespread, so too does the risk of revolutions.

Finally, a key element in revolutionary conjunctures in the modern world is the willing-ness of international superpowers to support, or resist, revolutionary movements. A permis-sive or supportive world context increases the chance that an unstable situation will blossom into open revolutions. Thus, when the U.S. in 1979, or the U.S.S.R. in 1989, became less will-ing to expend effort to enforce the status quo (as in Nicaragua, Iran, the Philippines, Afghan-istan, and Eastern Europe), a wave of revolutions spread as regimes that were shaky, and depended heavily on foreign support, found themselves cast upon their own frail resources. Despite the trend toward greater globalization, the inclination of Europe and the United States to shore up shaky regimes in Africa and other developing regions has been weak; if past patterns hold, this may lead to yet another wave of revolutions in the coming decades.

CONCLUSION

When the first edition of this text appeared in early 1986, the conclusion argued that the major causes of revolutions—state weakness, conflicts among elites, and problems associated with population growth, lack of employment, and declining welfare—were still evident around the world and that "Revolutions are therefore likely to continue in the near future" (p. 320).

Over the last fifteen years that forecast has been amply fulfilled. In 1986, "people power" revolutions felled dictatorships in the Philippines and in Haiti. In 1989, anti-communist revolts centered on Tiananmen Square shook China, and in 1991, popular and elite revolts brought the collapse of the Soviet Union. In 1989–1991, communist regimes were also overturned throughout eastern Europe from Albania to Romania. In 1987, an "intifada" (uprising) by Palestinians began against Israeli occupation that continues to this day, and in 1994, the apartheid regime in South Africa fell to a combination of protests and reforms. In Latin America, revolutionary guerrilla movements rose and fell in Peru, have drawn worldwide attention to the Chiapas region of Mexico, and occupied large portions of Colombia. In Africa, the dictatorship of Zaire collapsed in the face of regional revolts, and there were assaults on the regimes of Congo, Ivory Coast, Liberia, and Sierra Leone. Elsewhere in the world, a massive pro-democracy uprising occurred in Burma in 1988, and a deadly Islamic revolt began in Algeria in 1992. In 1998, the Indonesian dictatorship was toppled, and in 2000, the Serbian dictatorship followed.

Understanding revolutions—who makes them, why they happen, and what they produce—thus remains as crucial to understanding current events today as it has always been for understanding the history of our world.

REFERENCES

1. Edwards (1927); Pettee (1938); Brinton (1938).
2. Machiavelli (1513), Chapter 8.
3. Davies (1962); Gurr (1970).
4. Smelser (1963); Johnson (1966).
5. Huntington (1968).
6. Tilly (1978).
7. Moore, Jr. (1966).
8. Skocpol (1979).
9. Chorley (1943); Russell (1974).
10. Trimberger (1978).
11. Eisenstadt (1978).
12. Migdal (1974); Paige (1975).

13. Scott (1977), p. 237.
14. Rudé (1964).
15. Gugler (1982); Dix (1983); Farhi (1990).
16. Foran (1993, 1997a, 1997b); Selbin (1993); Emirbayer and Goodwin (1994, 1996); Parsa (2000); Goldstone (2001).
17. This paradox was first observed by de Tocqueville; for a more current discussion, see Goldstone and Tilly (2001).
18. Foran (1997a).
19. Calhoun (1998); Hall (1993).
20. Eisenstadt (1999).
21. Dunn (1989).
22. Goldstone (1991).

PART ONE

THEORIES OF REVOLUTIONS

CHAPTER 1

Classic Approaches

During the nineteenth and early twentieth centuries, scholars seeking to understand revolution concentrated their efforts on the French Revolution of 1789. Attempts to develop general theories of revolution began with the French Revolution as a model, for it was the most dramatic and best-known revolution in European history.

The following selections embody the most influential thinking about revolution to emerge from this period. These classic statements by Marx and Engels, de Tocqueville, and Weber form the starting point for modern studies of revolution.

Manifesto of the Communist Party

KARL MARX AND FREDERICK ENGELS

In the nineteenth century, Karl Marx and Frederick Engels first formulated many of the key issues in the study of revolution. Their *Manifesto of the Communist Party,* published in 1848, has undoubtedly been the most influential essay on revolution ever written. Marx and Engels viewed European history since the Middle Ages as a progression through various modes of production—feudal, capitalist, and in the future, socialist—each more fruitful than the last. They postulated, however, that the transition between these modes had not been—and would not be—peaceful because in each of these modes a particular social class dominated society. This dominant class would have to be dislodged by a revolution before the transition to the next mode of production could be completed. The French Revolution was an example of a revolution waged to dislodge the privileged feudal aristocracy and clear the way for capitalism. However, Marx and Engels argued that the new political freedoms and material benefits following the overthrow of the aristocracy went only to the class of professionals and businessmen—the bourgeoisie—that dominated the capitalist society. The French Revolution was thus essentially a "bourgeois" revolution. A further revolution—in the name of workers—was necessary to extend the benefits of modern industrial technology to all. The major tenets of this view are that revolutions are related to great historical transitions, that revolution is a necessary agent of change, and that revolutions are progressive and beneficial. Also, capitalism, even though it is progressive, benefits only a minority, so socialist revolutions are needed to benefit all society.

These tenets have become articles of faith for many modern revolutionaries. Asking to what extent these conclusions of Marx and Engels are valid poses one of the chief research problems for modern scholars. In the following excerpt from the *Manifesto,* Marx and Engels outline their theory of history, applaud the accomplishments of capitalism, and predict its future demise.

The history of all hitherto existing society is the history of class struggles.

Freeman and slave, patrician and plebeian, lord and serf, guild-master and journeyman, in a word, oppressor and oppressed, stood in constant opposition to one another, carried on an uninterrupted, now hidden, now open fight, a fight that each time ended, either in a revolutionary reconstitution of society at large, or in the common ruin of the contending classes.

In the earlier epochs of history, we find almost everywhere a complicated arrangement of society into various orders, a manifold gradation of social rank. In ancient Rome we have patricians, knights, plebeians, slaves; in the Middle Ages, feudal lords, vassals, guild-masters, journeymen, apprentices, serfs; in almost all of these classes, again, subordinate gradations.

The modern bourgeois society that has sprouted from the ruins of feudal society has not done away with class antagonisms. It has but established new classes, new conditions of oppression, new forms of struggle in place of the old ones.

Our epoch, the epoch of the bourgeoisie, possesses, however, this distinctive feature: it has simplified the class antagonisms. Society as a whole is more and more splitting up into two great hostile camps, into two great classes directly facing each other: Bourgeoisie and Proletariat.

From the serfs of the Middle Ages sprang the chartered burghers of the earliest towns. From these burgesses the first elements of the bourgeoisie were developed.

The discovery of America, the rounding of the Cape, opened up fresh ground for the rising bourgeoisie. The East-Indian and Chinese markets, the colonization of America, trade with the colonies, the increase in the means of exchange and in commodities generally, gave to commerce, to navigation, to industry, an impulse never before known, and thereby, to the revolutionary element in the tottering feudal society, a rapid development.

The feudal system of industry, under which industrial production was monopolized by closed guilds, now no longer sufficed for the growing wants of the new markets. The manufacturing system took its place. The guild-masters were pushed on one side by the manufacturing middle class; division of labor between the different corporate guilds vanished in the face of division of labor in each single workshop.

Meantime the markets kept ever growing, the demand ever rising. Even manufacture no longer sufficed. Thereupon, steam and machinery revolutionized industrial production. The place of manufacture was taken by the giant, Modern Industry, the place of the industrial middle class, by industrial millionaires, the leaders of whole industrial armies, the modern bourgeois.

Modern industry has established the world-market, for which the discovery of America paved the way. This market has given an immense development to commerce, to navigation, to communication by land. This development has, in its turn, reacted on the extension of industry; and in proportion as industry, commerce, navigation, railways extended, in the same

From The Marx-Engels Reader, *edited by Robert C. Tucker. Copyright © 1971 by W. W. Norton & Company.*

proportion the bourgeoisie developed, increased its capital, and pushed into the background every class handed down from the Middle Ages.

We see, therefore, how the modern bourgeoisie is itself the product of a long course of development, of a series of revolutions in the modes of production and of exchange.

Each step in the development of the bourgeoisie was accompanied by a corresponding political advance of that class. An oppressed class under the sway of the feudal nobility, an armed and self-governing association in the medieval commune; here independent urban republic (as in Italy and Germany), there taxable "third estate" of the monarchy (as in France), afterwards, in the period of manufacture proper, serving either the semi-feudal or the absolute monarchy as a counterpoise against the nobility, and, in fact, cornerstone of the great monarchies in general, the bourgeoisie has at last since the establishment of Modern Industry and of the world-market, conquered for itself, in the modern representative State, exclusive political sway. The executive of the modern State is but a committee for managing the common affairs of the whole bourgeoisie.

The bourgeoisie, historically, has played a most revolutionary part.

The bourgeoisie, whenever it has got the upper hand, has put an end to all feudal, patriarchal, idyllic relations. It has pitilessly torn asunder the motley feudal ties that bound man to his "natural superiors," and has left remaining no other nexus between man and man than naked self-interest, than callous "cash payment." It has drowned the most heavenly ecstasies of religious fervor, of chivalrous enthusiasm, of philistine sentimentalism, in the icy water of egotistical calculation. It has resolved personal worth into exchange value, and in place of the numberless indefeasible chartered freedoms, has set up that single, unconscionable freedom—Free Trade. In one word, for exploitation, veiled by religious and political illusions, it has substituted naked, shameless, direct, brutal exploitation.

The bourgeoisie has stripped of its halo every occupation hitherto honored and looked up to with reverent awe. It has converted the physician, the lawyer, the priest, the poet, the man of science, into its paid wage-laborers.

The bourgeoisie has torn away from the family its sentimental veil, and has reduced the family relation to a mere money relation.

The bourgeoisie has disclosed how it came to pass that the brutal display of vigor in the Middle Ages, which Reactionists so much admire, found its fitting complement in the most slothful indolence. It has been the first to show what man's activity can bring about. It has accomplished wonders far surpassing Egyptian pyramids, Roman aqueducts, and Gothic cathedrals; it has conducted expeditions that put in the shade all former Exoduses of nations and crusades.

The bourgeoisie cannot exist without constantly revolutionizing the instruments of production, and thereby the relations of production, and with them the whole reactions of society. Conservation of the old modes of production in unaltered form was, on the contrary, the first condition of existence for all earlier industrial classes. Constant revolutionizing of production, uninterrupted disturbance of all social conditions, everlasting uncertainty and agitation distinguish the bourgeois epoch from all earlier ones. All fixed, fast-frozen relations, with their train of ancient and venerable prejudices and opinions, are swept away, all new-formed ones become antiquated before they can ossify. All that is solid melts into air, all that is holy is profaned, and man is at last compelled to face with sober senses his real conditions of life, and his relations with his kind.

The need of a constantly expanding market for its products chases the bourgeoisie over the whole surface of the globe. It must nestle everywhere, settle everywhere, establish connections everywhere.

The bourgeoisie has through its exploitation of the world-market given a cosmopolitan character to production and consumption in every country. To the great chagrin of Reactionists, it has drawn from under the feet of industry the national ground on which it stood. All old-established national industries have been destroyed or are daily being destroyed. They are dislodged by new industries, whose introduction becomes a life and death question for all civilized nations, by industries that no longer work up indigenous raw material, but raw material drawn from the remotest zones; industries whose products are consumed, not only at home, but in every quarter of the globe. In place of the old wants, satisfied by the productions of the country, we find new wants, requiring for the satisfaction the products of distant lands and climes. In place of the old local and national seclusion and self-sufficiency, we have intercourse in every direction, universal interdependence of nations. And as in material, so also in intellectual production. The intellectual creations of individual nations become common property. National one-sidedness and narrow-mindedness become more and more impossible, and from the numerous national and local literatures, there arises a world literature.

The bourgeoisie, by the rapid improvement of all instruments of production, by the immensely facilitated means of communication, draws all, even the most barbarian nations into civilization. The cheap prices of its commodities are the heavy artillery with which it batters down all Chinese walls, with which it forces the barbarians' intensely obstinate hatred of foreigners to capitulate. It compels all nations, on pain of extinction, to adopt the bourgeois mode of production; it compels them to introduce what it calls civilization into their midst, i.e., to become bourgeois themselves. In one word, it creates a world after its own image.

The bourgeoisie has subjected the country to the rule of the towns. It has created enormous cities, has greatly increased the urban population as compared with the rural, and has thus rescued a considerable part of the population from the idiocy of rural life. Just as it has made the country dependent on the towns, so it has made barbarian and semi-barbarian countries dependent on the civilized ones, nations and peasants on nations of bourgeois, the East on the West.

The bourgeoisie keeps more and more doing away with the scattered state of the population, of the means of production, and of property. It has agglomerated population, centralized means of production, and has concentrated property in a few hands. The necessary consequence of this was political centralization. Independent, or but loosely connected provinces, with separate interests, laws, governments and systems of taxation, became lumped together into one nation, with one government, one code of laws, one national class-interest, one frontier and one customs-tariff.

The bourgeoisie, during its rule of scarce one hundred years, has created more massive and more colossal productive forces than have all proceeding generations together. Subjection of Nature's forces to man, machinery, application of chemistry to industry and agriculture, steam-navigation, railways, electric telegraphs, clearing of whole continents for cultivation, canalization of rivers, whole populations conjured out of the ground—what earlier century had even a presentiment that such productive forces slumbered in the lap of social labor?

We see then: the means of production and of exchange, on whose foundation the bourgeoisie built itself up, were generated in feudal society. At a certain stage in the development of these means of production and of exchange, the conditions under which feudal society produced and exchanged, the feudal organization of agriculture and manufacturing industry, in one word, the feudal relations of property became no longer compatible with the already developed productive forces; they became so many fetters. They had to be burst asunder; they were burst asunder.

Into their place stepped free competition, accompanied by a social and political constitution adapted to it, and by the economical and political sway of the bourgeois class.

A similar movement is going on before our own eyes. Modern bourgeois society, with its relations of production, of exchange and of property, a society that has conjured up such gigantic means of production and of exchange, is like the sorcerer, who is no longer able to control the powers of the nether world whom he has called up by his spells. For many a decade past the history of industry and commerce is but the history of the revolt of modern productive forces against modern conditions of production, against the property relations that are the conditions for the existence of the bourgeoisie and of its rule. It is enough to mention the commercial crises that by their periodical return put on its trial, each time more threateningly, the existence of the entire bourgeois society. In these crises a great part not only of the existing products, but also of the previously created productive forces, are periodically destroyed. In these crises there breaks out an epidemic that, in all earlier epochs, would have seemed an absurdity—the epidemic of over-production. Society suddenly finds itself put back into a state of momentary barbarism; it appears as if a famine, a universal war of devastation had cut off the supply of every means of subsistence; industry and commerce seem to be destroyed; and why? Because there is too much civilization, too much means of subsistence, too much industry, too much commerce. The productive forces at the disposal of society no longer tend to further the development of the conditions of bourgeois property; on the contrary, they have become too powerful for these conditions, by which they are fettered, and so soon as they overcome these fetters, they bring disorder into the whole of bourgeois society, endanger the existence of bourgeois property. The conditions of bourgeois society are too narrow to comprise the wealth created by them. And how does the bourgeoisie get over these crises? On the one hand by enforced destruction of a mass of productive forces; on the other, by the conquest of new markets, and by more thorough exploitation of the old ones. That is to say, by paving the way for more extensive and more destructive crises, and by diminishing the means whereby crises are prevented.

The weapons with which the bourgeoisie felled feudalism to the ground are now turned against the bourgeoisie itself.

But not only has the bourgeoisie forged the weapons that bring death to itself; it has also called into existence the men who are to wield those weapons—the modern working class—the proletarians.

In proportion as the bourgeoisie, i.e., capital, is developed, in the same proportion is the proletariat, the modern working class, developed—a class of laborers, who live only so long as they find work, and who find work only so long as their labor increases capital. These laborers, who must sell themselves piecemeal, are a commodity, like every other article of commerce, and are consequently exposed to all the vicissitudes of competition, to all the fluctuations of the market.

Owing to the extensive use of machinery and to division of labor, the work of the proletarians has lost all individual character, and consequently, all charm for the workman. He becomes an appendage of the machine, and it is only the most simple, most monotonous, and most easily acquired knack, that is required of him. Hence, the cost of production of a work-man is restricted, almost entirely, to the means of subsistence that he requires for his main-tenance, and for the propagation of his race. But the price of a commodity, and therefore also of labor, is equal to its cost of production. In proportion, therefore, as the repulsiveness of the work increases, the wage decreases. Nay more, in proportion as the use of machinery and division of labor increases, in the same proportion the burden of toil also increases, whether by prolongation of the working hours, by increase of the work exacted in a given time or by increased speed of the machinery, etc.

Modern industry has converted the little workshop of the patriarchal master into the great factory of the industrial capitalist. Masses of laborers, crowded into the factory, are or-ganized like soldiers. As privates of the industrial army they are placed under the command of a perfect hierarchy of officers and sergeants. Not only are they slaves of the bourgeois class, and of the bourgeois State; they are daily and hourly enslaved by the machine, by the over-looker, and above all, by the individual bourgeois manufacturer himself. The more openly this despotism proclaims gain to be its end and aim, the more petty, the more hate-ful and the more embittering it is.

The less the skill and exertion of strength implied in manual labor, in other words, the more modern industry becomes developed, the more is the labor of men superseded by that of women. Differences of age and sex have no longer any distinctive social validity for the working class. All are instruments of labor, more or less expensive to use, according to their age and sex.

No sooner is the exploitation of the laborer by the manufacturer, so far, at an end, that he receives his wages in cash, than he is set upon by the other portions of the bourgeoisie, the landlord, the shopkeeper, the pawnbroker, etc.

The lower strata of the middle class—the small tradespeople, shopkeepers, and retired tradesmen generally, the handicraftsmen and peasants—all these sink gradually into the proletariat, partly because their diminutive capital does not suffice for the scale on which Modern Industry is carried on, and is swamped in the competition with the large capitalists, partly because their specialized skill is rendered worthless by new methods of production. Thus the proletariat is recruited from all classes of the population.

The proletariat goes through various stages of development. With its birth begins its struggle with the bourgeoisie. At first the contest is carried on by individual laborers, then by the workpeople of a factory, then by the operatives of one trade, in one locality, against the individual bourgeois who directly exploits them. They direct their attacks not against the bourgeois conditions of production, but against the instruments of production themselves; they destroy imported wares that compete with their labor, they smash to pieces machinery, they set factories ablaze, they seek to restore by force the vanished status of the workman of the Middle Ages.

At this stage the laborers still form an incoherent mass scattered over the whole coun-try, and broken up by the mutual competition. If anywhere they unite to form more com-pact bodies, this is not yet the consequence of their own active union, but of the union of the bourgeoisie, which class, in order to attain its own political end, is compelled to set the whole proletariat in motion, and is moreover yet, for a time, able to do so. At this stage, therefore, the proletarians do not fight their enemies, but the enemies of their enemies, the remnants of absolute monarchy, the landowners, the non-industrial bourgeois, the petty bourgeoisie. Thus the whole historical movement is concentrated in the hands of the bourgeoisie; every victory so obtained is a victory for the bourgeoisie.

But with the development of industry the proletariat not only increases in number; it becomes concentrated in greater masses, its strength grows, and it feels that strength more. The various interests and conditions of life within the ranks of the proletariat are more and more equalized, in proportion as machinery obliterates all distinctions of labor, and nearly everywhere reduces wages to the same low level. The growing competition among the bourgeoisie, and the resulting commercial crises, make the wages of the workers ever more fluctuating. The unceasing improvement of machinery, ever more rapidly developing, makes their livelihood more and more precarious; the collisions between individual workmen and individual bourgeois take more and more the character of collisions between two classes. Thereupon the workers begin to form combinations (Trade Unions) against the bourgeois; they club together in order to keep up the rate of wages; they found permanent associations in order to make provision beforehand for these occasional revolts. Here and there the contest breaks out into riots.

Now and then the workers are victorious, but only for a time. The real fruit of their battles lies, not in the immediate result, but in the ever-expanding union of the workers. This union is helped on by the improved means of communication that are created by modern industry and that place the workers of different localities in contact with one another. It was just this contact that was needed to centralize their numerous local struggles, all of the same character, into one national struggle between the classes. But every class struggle is a political struggle. And that union, to attain which the burghers of the Middle Ages, with their miserable highways, required centuries, the modern proletarians, thanks to railways, achieve in a few years.

This organization of the proletarians into a class, and consequently into a political party, is continually being upset again by the competition between the workers themselves. But it ever rises up again, stronger, firmer, mightier. It compels legislative recognition of particular interests of the workers, by taking advantage of the divisions among the bourgeoisie itself. Thus the ten-hours' bill in England was carried.

Altogether collisions between the classes of the old society further, in many ways, the course of development of the proletariat. The bourgeoisie finds itself involved in a constant battle. At first with the aristocracy; later on, with those portions of the bourgeoisie itself, whose interests have become antagonistic to the progress of industry; at all times, with the bourgeoisie of foreign countries. In all these battles it sees itself compelled to appeal to the proletariat, to ask for its help, and thus, to drag it into the political arena. The bourgeoisie itself, therefore, supplies the proletariat with its own elements of political and general education, in other words, it furnishes the proletariat with weapons for fighting the bourgeoisie.

Further, as we have already seen, entire sections of the ruling classes are, by the advance of industry, precipitated into the proletariat, or are at least threatened in their conditions of existence. These also supply the proletariat with fresh elements of enlightenment and progress.

Finally, in times when the class struggle nears the decisive hour, the process of dissolution going on within the ruling class, in fact within the whole range of society, assumes such a violent, glaring character, that a small section of the ruling class cuts itself adrift, and joins the revolutionary class, the class that holds the future in its hands. Just as, therefore, at an earlier period, a section of the nobility went over to the bourgeoisie, so now a portion of the bourgeoisie goes over to the proletariat, and in particular, a portion of the bourgeois ideologists, who have raised themselves to the level of comprehending theoretically the historical movement as a whole.

Of all the classes that stand face to face with the bourgeoisie today, the proletariat alone is a really revolutionary class. The other classes decay and finally disappear in the face of Modern Industry; the proletariat is its special and essential product.

The lower middle class, the small manufacturer, the shopkeeper, the artisan, the peasant, all these fight against the bourgeoisie, to save from extinction their existence as fractions of the middle class. They are therefore not revolutionary, but conservative. Nay, more, they are reactionary, for they try to roll back the wheel of history. If by chance they are revolutionary, they are so only in view of their impending transfer into the proletariat; they thus defend not their present, but their future interests; they desert their own standpoint to place themselves at that of the proletariat.

The "dangerous class," the social scum, that passively rotting mass thrown off by the lowest layers of old society, may, here and there, be swept into the movement by a proletarian revolution; its conditions of life, however, prepare it far more for the part of a bribed tool of reactionary intrigue.

In the conditions of the proletariat, those of old society at large are already virtually swamped. The proletarian is without property; his relation to his wife and children has no longer anything in common with the bourgeois family-relations; modern industrial labor, modern subjection to capital, the same in England as in France, in America as in Germany, has stripped him of every trace of national character. Law, morality, religion, are to him so many bourgeois prejudices, behind which lurk in ambush just as many bourgeois interests.

All the preceding classes that got the upper hand sought to fortify their already acquired status by subjecting society at large to their conditions of appropriation. The proletarians cannot become masters of the productive forces of society, except by abolishing their own previous mode of appropriation, and thereby also every other previous mode of appropriation. They have nothing of their own to secure and to fortify; their mission is to destroy all previous securities for, and insurances of, individual property.

All previous historical movements were movements of minorities, or in the interests of minorities. The proletarian movement is the self-conscious, independent movement of the immense majority, in the interests of the immense majority. The proletariat, the lowest stratum of our present society, cannot stir, cannot raise itself up, without the whole superincumbent strata of official society being sprung into the air.

Though not in substance, yet in form, the struggle of the proletariat with the bourgeoisie is at first a national struggle. The proletariat of each country must, of course, first of all settle matters with its own bourgeoisie.

In depicting the most general phases of the development of the proletariat, we traced the more or less veiled civil war, raging within existing society, up to the point where that war breaks out into open revolution, and where the violent overthrow of the bourgeoisie lays the foundation for the sway of the proletariat.

Hitherto, every form of society has been based, as we have already seen, on the antagonism of oppressing and oppressed classes. But in order to oppress a class, certain conditions must be assured to it under which it can, at least, continue its slavish existence. The serf, in the period of serfdom, raised himself to membership in the commune, just as the petty bourgeois, under the yoke of feudal absolutism, managed to develop into a bourgeois. The modern laborer, on the contrary, instead of rising with the progress of industry, sinks deeper and deeper below the conditions of existence of his own class. He becomes a pauper, and pauperism develops more rapidly than population and wealth. And here it becomes evident that the bourgeoisie is unfit any longer to be the ruling class in society, and to impose its conditions of existence upon society as an over-riding law. It is unfit to rule because it is incompetent to assure an existence to its slave within his slavery, because it cannot help letting him sink into such a state, that it has to feed him, instead of being fed by him. Society can no longer live under this bourgeoisie, in other words, its existence is no longer compatible with society.

The essential condition for the existence, and for the sway of the bourgeois class, is the formation and augmentation of capital; the condition for capital is wage-labor. Wage-labor rests exclusively on competition between the laborers. The advance of industry, whose involuntary promoter is the bourgeoisie, replaces the isolation of the laborers, due to competition, by the revolutionary combination, due to association. The development of Modern Industry, therefore, cuts from under its feet the very foundation on which the bourgeoisie produces and appropriates products. What the bourgeoisie, therefore, produces, above all, is its own grave-diggers. Its fall and the victory of the proletariat are equally inevitable.

The French Revolution and the Growth of the State
ALEXIS DE TOCQUEVILLE

Alexis de Tocqueville wrote at the same time as Marx and Engels; his book *The Old Regime and the French Revolution* appeared in 1848, the same year as the *Manifesto of the Communist Party*. Yet de Tocqueville saw the French Revolution very differently. He agreed that the Revolution destroyed the power of the old aristocracy and those laws and practices associated with feudal society. But where Marx and Engels saw the defeat of feudalism as a triumph for a new class—the bourgeoisie—that a later socialist revolution would in turn dislodge, de Tocqueville saw the triumph of the centralized state. To de Tocqueville, when the French Revolution destroyed class privileges and set all men equal before the law, it also removed all the obstacles to the authority of the state. Before the Revolution, privileged and powerful groups had existed alongside the state; after the Revolution, the state stood alone, gathering all power to itself. If Marx has inspired a tradition that sees revolution as progressive and beneficial, de Tocqueville inspires caution, noting that revolution often strengthens the power of the state rather than weakening it.

No great historical event is better calculated than the French Revolution to teach political writers and statesmen to be cautious in their speculations. What was its true significance, its real nature, and what were the permanent effects of this strange and terrifying revolution? What exactly did it destroy, and what did it create?

One of the earliest enterprises of the revolutionary movement was a concerted attack on the Church, and among the many passions inflamed by it the first to be kindled and last to be extinguished was of an anti-religious nature. Nevertheless, it is easy enough to see today that the campaign against all forms of religion was merely incidental to the French Revolution, a spectacular but transient phenomenon, a brief reaction to the ideologies, emotions, and events which led up to it—but in no sense basic to its program. The Church was hated not because its priests claimed to regulate the affairs of the other world but because they were landed proprietors, lords of manors, tithe owners, and played a leading part in secular affairs; not because there was no room for the Church in the new world that was in the making, but because it occupied the most powerful, most privileged position in the old order that was now to be swept away.

What I have said about Church authority applies even more strongly to the authority of the central power. Those who saw the Revolution overthrowing all the institutions and customs which had hitherto shored up the social hierarchy and prevented men from running wild were naturally inclined to think that the Revolution spelled the end of all things; not merely of the old order, but of any order in the State, not merely that of any given form of government, but of any government at all—that in fact the nation was heading towards sheer anarchy. Yet, in my opinion, those who held this view were misled by appearances.

Since the object of the Revolution was not merely to change an old form of government but to abolish the entire social structure of pre-revolutionary France, it was obliged to declare war simultaneously on all established powers, to destroy all recognized prerogatives, to make short work of all traditions, and to institute new ways of living, new conventions. Thus one of its first acts was to rid men's minds of all those notions which had ensured their obedience to authority under the old regime. Hence its so markedly anarchic tendencies.

But beneath the seemingly chaotic surface there was developing a vast, highly centralized power which attracted to itself and welded into an organic whole all the elements of authority and influence that hitherto had been dispersed among a crowd of lesser, uncoordinated powers: the three Orders of the State, professional bodies, families, and individuals. Never since the fall of the Roman Empire had the world seen a government so highly centralized. This new power was created by the Revolution, or, rather, grew up almost automatically out of the havoc wrought by it.

Despite its magnitude it was as yet invisible to the eyes of the multitude, but gradually time has made amends and contemporary monarchs, in particular, are fully alive to its significance. They contemplate it with envy and admiration; not only those who owe their present eminence to the Revolution but also those who are least in sympathy with, or frankly hostile to, its achievement. Thus we see all these rulers doing what they can to abolish privileges and remove immunities within their territories. Everywhere they are breaking down class distinctions, leveling out inequalities, replacing members of the aristocracy with trained civil servants, local charters with uniform regulations, and a diversity of powers with a strong, centralized government. They are putting through these revolutionary measures with un-flagging energy, and sometimes even have recourse to the methods and maxims of the Great Revolution when obstacles arise. Thus we often find them championing the poor man's cause against the rich man's, the commoner's against the nobleman's, the peasant's against his lord's. In short, the lesson of the Revolution has not been lost even on those who have most reason to detest it.

Charisma, Bureaucracy, and Revolution
MAX WEBER

Max Weber amplified de Tocqueville's ideas on how revolutions increase state power. The initial impetus to revolution, according to Weber, often comes from a "charismatic" leader who challenges traditional authorities, gathers followers, and leads the overthrow of the old regime. Famous "charismatic" revolutionary leaders include Lenin, Castro, Mao, Zapata, Khomeini, and Mandela. However, Weber points out that the authority of the charismatic leader and his or her follow-ers will last only if it becomes solidified in political institutions. The most effective such institutions are formal bureaucracies, which have generally replaced the tradi-tional rule of hereditary monarchs and nobles. Once in place, bureaucracies have proven more powerful and resistant to change than the traditional regimes that they replaced.

CHARISMATIC AUTHORITY

The term "charisma" will be applied to a certain quality of an individual personality by vir-tue of which he is set apart from ordinary men and treated as endowed with supernatural, superhuman, or at least . . . exceptional powers or qualities. These are such as are not ac-cessible to the ordinary person, but are regarded as of divine origin or as exemplary, and on the basis of them the individual concerned is treated as a leader. In primitive circumstances this peculiar kind of deference is paid to prophets, to people with a reputation for thera-peutic or legal wisdom, to leaders in the hunt, and heroes in war. . . .

Reprinted with the permission of The Free Press, a Division of Simon & Schuster, Inc., from The Theory of Social and Economic Organization *by Max Weber, translated by A. M. Henderson and Talcott Parsons. Edited by Talcott Parsons. Copyright © 1947, copy-right renewed 1975 by Talcott Parsons.*

From a substantive point of view, every charismatic authority would have to subscribe to the proposition "It is written . . . , but I say unto you. . . ." The genuine prophet, like the genuine military leader and every true leader in this sense, preaches, creates, or demands *new* obligations. In the pure type of charisma, these are imposed on the authority of revolution by oracles, or of the leader's own will, and are recognized by the members of the religious, military, or party group, because they come from such a source. . . .

Charismatic authority is thus specifically outside the realm of everyday routine. . . . In this respect, it is sharply opposed both to rational, and particularly bureaucratic, authority, and to traditional authority, whether in its patriarchal, patrimonial, or any other form. Both rational and traditional authority are specifically forms of everyday routine control of action; while the charismatic type is the direct antithesis of this. Bureaucratic authority is specifically rational in the sense of being bound to intellectually analyzable rules; while charismatic authority is specifically irrational in the sense of being foreign to all rules. Traditional authority is bound to the precedents handed down from the past and to this extent is also oriented to rules. Within the sphere of its claims, charismatic authority repudiates the past, and is in this sense a specifically revolutionary force. . . .

THE ROUTINIZATION OF CHARISMA

In its pure form charismatic authority has a character specifically foreign to everyday routine structures. The social relationships directly involved are strictly personal, based on the validity and practice of charismatic personal qualities. If this is not to remain a purely transitory phenomenon, but to take on the character of a permanent relationship forming a stable community . . . or a party organization or any sort of political or hierocratic organization, it is necessary for the character of charismatic authority to become radically changed. Indeed, in its pure form charismatic authority may be said to exist only in the process of originating. It cannot remain stable, but becomes either traditionalized or rationalized, or a combination of both. . . .

These interests generally become conspicuously evident with the disappearance of the personal charismatic leader and with the problem of succession, which inevitably arises. The way in which this problem is met—if it is met at all—is of crucial importance for the character of the subsequent social relationships. . . .

For charisma to be transformed into a permanent routine structure, it is necessary that its anti-economic character should be altered. It must be adapted to some form of fiscal organization to provide for the needs of the group and hence to the economic conditions necessary for raising taxes and contributions. . . . With the process of routinization the charismatic group tends to develop into one of the forms of everyday authority, particularly the patrimonial form in its decentralized variant or the bureaucratic.

THE PERMANENT CHARACTER
OF THE BUREAUCRATIC MACHINE

Once it is fully established, bureaucracy is among those social structures which are the hardest to destroy. Bureaucracy is *the* means of carrying "community action" over into rationally ordered "social action." Therefore, as an instrument for "societalizing" relations of power, bureaucracy has been and is a power instrument of the first order—for the one who controls the bureaucratic apparatus.

Under otherwise equal conditions, a "societal action," which is methodically ordered and led, is superior to every resistance of "mass" or even of "communal action." And where the bureaucratization of administration has been completely carried through, a form of power relation is established that is practically unshatterable.

The individual bureaucrat cannot squirm out of the apparatus in which he is harnessed. In contrast to the honorific or avocational "notable," the professional bureaucrat is chained to his activity by his entire material and ideal existence. In the great majority of cases, he is only a single cog in an ever-moving mechanism which prescribes to him an essentially fixed route of march. The official is trusted with specialized tasks and normally the mechanism cannot be put into motion or arrested by him, but only from the very top. The individual bureaucrat is thus forged to the community of all the functionaries who are integrated into the mechanism. They have a common interest in seeing that the mechanism continues its functions and that the societally exercised authority carries on.

The ruled, for their part, cannot dispense with or replace the bureaucratic apparatus of authority once it exists. For this bureaucracy rests upon expert training, a functional specialization of work, and an attitude set for habitual and virtuoso-like mastery of single yet methodically integrated functions. If the official stops working, or if his work is forcefully interrupted, chaos results, and it is difficult to improvise replacements from among the governed who are fit to master such chaos. This holds for public administration as well as for private economic management. More and more the material fate of the masses depends upon the steady and correct functioning of the increasingly bureaucratic organizations of private capitalism. The idea of eliminating these organizations becomes more and more utopian.

The objective indispensability of the once-existing apparatus, with its peculiar, "impersonal" character, means that the mechanism—in contrast to feudal orders based on personal piety—is easily made to work for anybody who knows how to gain control over it. A rationally ordered system of officials continues to function smoothly after the enemy has occupied the area; he merely needs to change the top officials. This body of officials continues to operate because it is to the vital interest of everyone concerned, including above all the enemy.

During the course of his long years in power, [German prime minister Otto von] Bismarck brought his ministerial colleagues into unconditional bureaucratic dependence by eliminating all independent statesmen. Upon his retirement, he saw to his surprise that they

---

continued to manage their offices unconcerned and undismayed, as if he had not been the master mind and creator of these creatures, but rather as if some single figure had been exchanged for some other figure in the bureaucratic machine. With all the changes of masters in France since the time of the [Napoleonic] Empire, the power machine has remained essentially the same. Such a machine makes "revolution," in the sense of a forceful creation of entirely new formations of authority, technically more and more impossible. . . .

CHAPTER 2

The Debate on Modernization

In the twenty-first century, the French Revolution no longer dominates discussions of revolution. Scholars must also confront the many revolutions of the twentieth century: in Mexico in 1910; in Russia in 1917; in China from 1911 to 1949; in Persia in 1905; in the Ottoman Empire (Turkey) in 1919; and in a host of Third World countries, including Vietnam, Bolivia, and Cuba, in the 1950s and 1960s. As de Tocqueville and Weber suggested, such revolutions usually led to stronger, more centralized, and more bureaucratic states. But the origins of these revolutions rarely fit the pattern that Marx and Engels set forth. Instead of occurring after bourgeois, capitalist revolutions, socialist revolutions have occurred in relatively poor countries that were just beginning the modernization of their economies. Moreover, instead of industrial laborers carrying out socialist revolutions, peasants have often played the major role. Although theorists of revolution continue to value Marx's insight that revolutions arise from the struggle of different groups competing for dominance, it is clear that revolutions can arise in ways Marx did not foresee. Therefore, these revolutions have prompted scholars to reinvestigate the causes of revolution and to seek connections between modernization and revolution.

In the following selections, two prominent scholars discuss the different ways in which revolutions can arise. Their debate suggests that modernization does not necessarily lead to revolution; the key issue is whether modernization leads to a change in the balance of power among those groups in a society that are contending for political power.

Revolution and Political Order

SAMUEL P. HUNTINGTON

Huntington argues that a key aspect of modernization is the demand for increased participation in politics. Where certain groups do not have access to political power, their demands to change and broaden government may lead to revolution. In discussing a wide range of revolutions, including those in France, Russia, China, Mexico, Turkey, Vietnam, and Persia (Iran was called Persia at the time of the fall of the Qajar dynasty in 1925), Huntington identifies different patterns of revolution and examines the roles of moderates, counterrevolutionaries, and radicals.

A revolution is a rapid, fundamental, and violent domestic change in the dominant values and myths of a society, in its political institutions, social structure, leadership, and government activity and policies. Revolutions are thus to be distinguished from insurrections, rebellions, revolts, coups, and wars of independence. A coup d'etat in itself changes only leadership and perhaps policies; a rebellion or insurrection may change policies, leadership, and political institutions, but not social structure and values; a war of independence is a struggle of one community against rule by an alien community and does not necessarily involve changes in the social structure of either community. What is here called simply "revolution" is what others have called great revolutions, grand revolutions, or social revolutions. Notable examples are the French, Chinese, Mexican, Russian, and Cuban revolutions.

Revolutions are rare. Most societies have never experienced revolutions, and most ages until modern times did not know revolutions. More precisely, revolution is characteristic of modernization. Revolution is the ultimate expression of the modernizing outlook, the belief that it is within the power of man to control and to change his environment and that he has not only the ability but the right to do so. For this reason, as Hannah Arendt observes, "violence is no more adequate to describe the phenomenon of revolution than change; only where change occurs in the sense of a new beginning, where violence is used to constitute an altogether different form of government, to bring about the formation of a new body politic . . . can we speak of revolution."[1]

Revolution is thus an aspect of modernization. It is not something which can occur in any type of society at any period in its history. It is not a universal category but rather an historically limited phenomenon. It will not occur in highly traditional societies with very low levels of social and economic complexity. Nor will it occur in highly modern societies. Like other forms of violence and instability, it is most likely to occur in societies which have experienced some social and economic development and where the processes of political modernization and political development have lagged behind the processes of social and economic change.

Political modernization involves the extension of political consciousness to new social groups and the mobilization of these groups into politics. Political development involves the creation of political institutions sufficiently adaptable, complex, autonomous, and coherent to absorb and to order the participation of these new groups and to promote social and economic change in the society. The political essence of revolution is the rapid expansion of political consciousness and the rapid mobilization of new groups into politics at a speed which makes it impossible for existing political institutions to assimilate them. Revolution is the extreme case of the explosion of political participation. Without this explosion there is no revolution. A complete revolution, however, also involves a second phase: the creation and institutionalization of a new political order. The successful revolution combines rapid political mobilization and rapid political institutionalization. Not all revolutions produce a new political order. The measure of how revolutionary a revolution is is the rapidity and the scope of the expansion of political participation. The measure of how successful a revolution is is the authority and stability of the institutions to which it gives birth.

A full-scale revolution thus involves the rapid and violent destruction of existing political institutions, the mobilization of new groups into politics, and the creation of new polit-

---

ical institutions. The sequence and the relations among these three aspects may vary from one revolution to another. Two general patterns can be identified. In the "Western" pattern, the political institutions of the old regime collapse; this is followed by the mobilization of new groups into politics and then by the creation of new political institutions. The "Eastern" revolution, in contrast, begins with the mobilization of new groups into politics and the creation of new political institutions and ends with the violent overthrow of the political institutions of the old order. The French, Russian, Mexican, and, in its first phases, Chinese revolutions approximate the Western model; the latter phases of the Chinese Revolution, the Vietnamese Revolution, and other colonial struggles against imperialist powers approximate the Eastern model.

The first step in a Western revolution is the collapse of the old regime. Consequently, scholarly analysis of the causes of revolution usually focuses on the political, social, and economic conditions which existed under the old regime. Implicitly, such analyses assume that once the authority of the old regime has disintegrated, the revolutionary process is irreversibly underway. In fact, however, the collapse of many old regimes is not followed by full-scale revolution. The events of 1789 in France led to a major social upheaval; those of 1830 and 1848 did not. The fall of the [Chinese] Manchu and [Russian] Romanov dynasties was followed by great revolutions; the fall of the [Austrian] Hapsburg, [German] Hohenzollern, [Turkish] Ottoman, and [Persian] Qajar dynasties was not. The overthrow of traditional dictatorships in Bolivia in 1952 and in Cuba in 1958 set loose major revolutionary forces; the overthrow of traditional monarchies in Egypt in 1952 and in Iraq in 1958 brought new elites to power but did not completely destroy the structure of society. In virtually all these instances, the same social, economic, and political conditions existed under the old regimes whose demise was not followed by revolution as existed under the old regimes whose demise was followed by revolution. Old regimes—traditional monarchies and traditional dictatorships with concentrated but little power—are continually collapsing but only rarely is this collapse followed by a major revolution. The factors giving rise to revolution, consequently, are as likely to be found in the conditions which exist after the collapse of the old regime as in those which exist before its downfall.

In the "Western" revolution very little overt action by rebellious groups is needed to overthrow the old regime. "The revolution," as Pettee says, "does not begin with the attack of a powerful new force upon the state. It begins simply with a sudden recognition by almost all the passive and the active membership that the state no longer exists." The collapse is followed by an absence of authority. "Revolutionists enter the limelight, not like men on horseback, as victorious conspirators appearing in the forum, but like fearful children, exploring an empty house, not sure that it is empty."[2] Whether or not a revolution develops depends upon the number and the character of the groups entering the house. If there is a marked discrepancy in power among the remaining social forces after the old regime disappears, the strongest social force or combination of forces may be able to fill the vacuum and to reestablish authority, with relatively little expansion of political participation. The collapse of every old regime is followed by some rioting, demonstrations, and the projection into the political sphere of previously quiescent or suppressed groups. If a new social force (as in Egypt in 1952) or combination of social forces (as in Germany in 1918–19) can quickly secure control of the state machinery and particularly the instruments of coercion left behind by the old regime, it may well be able to suppress the more revolutionary elements intent on mobilizing new forces into politics (the Moslem Brotherhood, the Spartacists) and thus forestall the emergence of a truly revolutionary situation. The crucial factor is the concentration or dispersion of power which follows the collapse of the old regime. The less traditional the society in which the old regime has collapsed and the more groups which are available and able and inclined to participate in politics, the more likely is revolution to take place.

If no group is ready and able to establish effective rule following the collapse of the old regime, many cliques and social forces struggle for power. This struggle gives rise to the competitive mobilization of new groups into politics and makes the revolution revolutionary. Each group of political leaders attempts to establish its authority and in the process either develops a broader base of popular support than its competitors or falls victim to them.

Following the collapse of the old regime, three social types play major roles in the process of political mobilization. Initially, as Brinton and others have pointed out, the moderates (Kerensky in Russia, Madero in Mexico, Sun Yat-sen in China) tend to assume authority. Typically, they attempt to establish some sort of liberal, democratic, constitutional state. Typically, also, they describe this state as the restoration of an earlier constitutional order: Madero wanted to restore the constitution of 1856; the liberal Young Turks the constitution of 1876; and even Castro in his initial moderate phase held that his goal was the restoration of the constitution of 1940. In rare cases, these leaders may adapt to the subsequent intensification of the revolutionary process: Castro was the Kerensky and the Lenin of the Cuban Revolution. More frequently, however, the moderates remain moderate and are swept from power. Their failure stems precisely from their inability to deal with the problem of political mobilization. On the one hand, they lack the drive and the ruthlessness to stop the mobilization of new groups into politics; on the other, they lack the radicalism to lead it. The first alternative requires the concentration of power, the second its expansion. Unable and unwilling to perform either function, the liberals are brushed away either by counterrevolutionaries who perform the first or by more extreme revolutionaries who perform the second.

In virtually all revolutionary situations, counterrevolutionaries, often with foreign assistance, attempt to stop the expansion of political participation and to reestablish a political order in which there is little but concentrated power. Kornilov in Russia, Yuan Shih-kai in China, Huerta in Mexico, and, in a sense, Reza Shah in Persia and Mustafa Kemal in Turkey all played these roles in the aftermath of the downfall of the Porfirian regime and of the Romanov, Ch'ing, Qajar, and Ottoman dynasties. As these examples suggest, the counterrevolutionaries are almost invariably military men. Force is a source of power, but it can have longer range effectiveness only when it is linked to a principle of legitimacy. Huerta and Kornilov had nothing but force and failed in the face of the radicalization of the revolution and the mobilization of more social groups into politics. Yuan Shih-kai and Reza Shah both attempted to establish new, more vigorous traditional systems of rule on the ruins of the previous dynasty.

That Yuan Shih-kai failed to establish a new dynasty while Reza Shah Pahlevi succeeded is due primarily to the fact that political mobilization had gone much further in China than it had in Persia. The middle-class in the Chinese cities was sufficiently well developed to have supported a nationalist movement since the 1890s. Students and intellectuals played a crucial role in Chinese politics while they were almost absent from the Persian scene. The lower level of social mobilization in Persia made it possible to give new vigor to traditional forms of rule.

The radical revolutionaries are the third major political group in a revolutionary situation. For ideological and tactical reasons, their goal is to expand political participation, to bring new masses into politics, and thereby to increase their own power. With the breakdown of the established institutions and procedures for co-opting groups into power and socializing them into the political order, the extremists have a natural advantage over their rivals. They are more willing to mobilize more groups into politics. Hence the revolution becomes more radical as larger and larger masses of the population are brought into the political scales. Since in most modernizing countries the peasants are the largest social force, the most revolutionary leaders are those who mobilize and organize the peasants for political action. In some instances, the appeals to the peasants and other lower class groups may be social and economic; in most instances, however, these will be supplemented by nationalist appeals. This process leads to the redefinition of the political community and creates the foundations for a new political order.

In Western revolutions the symbolic or actual fall of the old regime can be given a fairly precise date: July 14, 1789; October 10, 1911; May 25, 1911; March 15, 1917. These dates mark the beginning of the revolutionary process and the mobilization of new groups into politics as the competition among the new elites struggling for power leads them to appeal to broader and broader masses of the people. Out of the competition one group eventually establishes its dominance and reestablishes order either through force or the development of new political institutions. In Eastern revolutions, in contrast, the old regime is modern, it has more power and legitimacy, and hence it does not simply collapse and leave a vacuum of authority. Instead it must be overthrown. The distinguishing characteristic of the Western revolution is the period of anarchy or statelessness after the fall of the old regime while moderates, counterrevolutionaries, and radicals are struggling for power. The distinguishing characteristic of the Eastern revolution is a prolonged period of "dual power" in which the revolutionaries are expanding political participation and the scope and authority of their institutions of rule at the same time that the government is, in other geographical areas and at other times, continuing to exercise its rule. In the Western revolution the principal struggles are between revolutionary groups; in the Eastern revolution they are between one revolutionary group and the established order.

In the Western revolution the revolutionaries come to power in the capital first and then gradually expand their control over the countryside. In the Eastern revolution they withdraw from central, urban areas of the country, establish a base area of control in a remote section, struggle to win the support of the peasants through terror and propaganda, slowly expand the scope of their authority, and gradually escalate the level of their military operations from individual terroristic attacks to guerrilla warfare to mobile warfare and regular warfare. Eventually they are able to defeat the government troops in battle. The last phase of the revolutionary struggle is the occupation of the capital.

In a Western revolution the capture of the central institutions and symbols of power is usually very rapid. In January 1917 the Bolsheviks were a small, illegal, conspiratorial group, most of whose leaders were either in Siberia or in exile. Less than a year later they were the principal, although far from undisputed, political rulers of Russia. "You know," Lenin observed to Trotsky, "from persecution and a life underground, to come so suddenly into power. . . . *Es schwindelt!*"[3] The Chinese Communist leaders, in contrast, experienced no such exhilarating and dramatic change in circumstances. Instead they had to fight their way gradually and slowly to power over a 22-year period from their retreat into the countryside in 1927, through the fearsome battles of Kiangsi, the exhaustion of the Long March, the struggles against the Japanese, the civil war with the Kuomintang, until finally they made their triumphal entry into Peking. There was nothing "dizzying" about this process. During most of these years the Communist Party exercised effective political authority over substantial amounts of territory and numbers of people. It was a government attempting to expand its authority at the expense of another government rather than a band of conspirators attempting to overthrow a government. The acquisition of national power for the Bolsheviks was a dramatic change; for the Chinese Communists it was simply the culmination of a long, drawn-out process.

One major factor responsible for the differing patterns of the Western and Eastern revolutions is the nature of the prerevolutionary regime. The Western revolution is usually directed against a highly traditional regime headed by an absolute monarch or dominated by a land-owning aristocracy. The revolution typically occurs when this regime comes into severe financial straits, when it fails to assimilate the intelligentsia and other urban elite elements, and when the ruling class from which its leaders are drawn has lost its moral self-confidence and will to rule. The Western revolution, in a sense, telescopes the initial "urban breakthrough" of the middle class and the "green uprising" of the peasantry into a single convulsive, revolutionary process. Eastern revolutions, in contrast, are directed against at least partially modernized regimes. These may be indigenous governments that have absorbed some modern and vigorous middle-class elements and that are led by new men with the ruthlessness, if not the political skill, to hang on to power, or they may be colonial regimes in which the wealth and power of a metropolitan country gives the local government a seemingly overwhelming superiority in all the conventional manifestations of political authority and military force. In such circumstances no quick victory is possible and the urban revolutionaries have to fight their way to power through a prolonged rural insurrectionary process. Western revolutions are thus precipitated by weak traditional regimes; Eastern revolutions by narrow modernizing ones.

In the Western revolution the principal struggle is usually between the moderates and the radicals; in the Eastern revolution it is between the revolutionaries and the government. In the Western revolution the moderates hold power briefly and insecurely between the fall of the old regime and the expansion of participation and conquest of power by the radicals. In the Eastern pattern, the moderates are much weaker; they do not occupy positions of authority; and as the revolution gets under way, they are crushed by the government or the revolutionaries or they are forced by the polarization process to join one side or the other. In the Western revolution, terror occurs in the latter phases of the revolution and is employed by the radicals after they come to power primarily against the moderates and other revolutionary groups with whom they have struggled. In the Eastern revolution, in contrast, terror marks the first phase of the revolutionary struggle. It is used by the revolutionaries when they are weak and far removed from power to persuade or to coerce support from peasants and to intimidate the lower reaches of officialdom. In the Eastern pattern, the stronger the revolutionary movement becomes the less it tends to rely on terrorism. In the Western pattern the loss of the will and the ability to rule by the old elite is the first phase in the revolution; in the Eastern model it is the last phase and is a product of the revolutionary war waged by the counterelite against the regime. Emigration, consequently, reaches its peak at the beginning of the revolutionary struggle in the Western model but at the end of the struggle in the Eastern pattern.

INSTITUTIONAL AND SOCIAL CIRCUMSTANCES OF REVOLUTION

Revolution, as we have said, is the broad, rapid, and violent expansion of political participation outside the existing structure of political institutions. Its causes thus lie in the interaction between political institutions and social forces. Presumably revolutions occur when there is the coincidence of certain conditions in political institutions and certain circumstances among social forces. In these terms, the two prerequisites for revolution are, first, political institutions incapable of providing channels for the participation of new social forces in politics and of new elites in government, and, secondly, the desire of social forces, currently excluded from politics, to participate therein, this desire normally arising from the group's feeling that it needs certain symbolic or material gains which it can achieve only by pressing its demands in the political sphere. Ascending or aspiring groups and rigid or inflexible institutions are the stuff of which revolutions are made.

The many recent efforts to identify the causes of revolution have given primary emphasis to its social and psychological roots. They have thus tended to overlook the political and institutional factors which affect the probability of revolution. Revolutions are unlikely in political systems which have the capacity to expand their power and to broaden participation within the system. It is precisely this fact that makes revolutions unlikely in highly institutionalized modern political systems—constitutional or communist—which are what they are simply because they have developed the procedures for assimilating new social groups and elites desiring to participate in politics. The great revolutions of history have taken place either in highly centralized traditional monarchies (France, China, Russia), or in narrowly based military dictatorships (Mexico, Bolivia, Guatemala, Cuba), or in colonial regimes (Vietnam, Algeria). All these political systems demonstrated little if any capacity to expand their power and to provide channels for the participation of new groups in politics.

Perhaps the most important and obvious but also most neglected fact about successful great revolutions is that they do not occur in democratic political systems. This is not to argue that formally democratic governments are immune to revolution. This is surely not the case, and a narrowly based, oligarchical democracy may be as incapable of providing for expanded political participation as narrowly based oligarchical dictatorship. Nonetheless, the absence of successful revolutions in democratic countries remains a striking fact, and suggests that, on the average, democracies have more capacity for absorbing new groups into their political systems than do political systems where power is equally small but more concentrated. The absence of successful revolutions against communist dictatorships suggests that the crucial distinction between them and the more traditional autocracies may be precisely this capacity to absorb new social groups.

Revolution requires not only political institutions which resist the expansion of participation but also social groups which demand that expansion. In theory, every social class which has not been incorporated into the political system is potentially revolutionary. Virtually every group does go through a phase, brief or prolonged, when its revolutionary propensity is high. At some point, the group begins to develop aspirations which lead it to make symbolic or material demands on the political system. To achieve its goals, the group's leaders soon realize that they must find avenues of access to the political leaders and means of participation in the political system. If these do not exist and are not forthcoming, the group and its leaders become frustrated and alienated. Conceivably this condition can exist for an indefinite period of time; or the original needs which led the group to seek access to the system may disappear; or the group may attempt to enforce its demands on the system through violence, force, or other means illegitimate to the system. In the latter instance, either the system adapts itself to accord some legitimacy to these means and thus to accept the necessity of meeting the demands which they were used to support, or the political elite attempts to suppress the group and to end the use of these methods. No inherent reason exists why such action should not be successful, provided the groups within the political system are sufficiently strong and united in their opposition to admitting the aspiring group to political participation.

Frustration of its demands and denial of the opportunity to participate in the political system may make a group revolutionary. But it takes more than one revolutionary group to make a revolution. A revolution necessarily involves the alienation of many groups from the existing order. It is the product of "multiple dysfunction" in society. One social group can be responsible for a coup, a riot, or a revolt, but only a combination of groups can produce a revolution. Conceivably, this combination might take the form of any number of possible group coalitions. In actuality, however, the revolutionary alliance must include some urban and some rural groups. The opposition of urban groups to the government can produce the continued instability characteristic of a praetorian state. But only the combination of urban opposition with rural opposition can produce a revolution. In 1789, Palmer observes, "Peasant and bourgeois were at war with the same enemy, and this is what made possible the French Revolution."[4] In a broader sense, this is what makes possible every revolution. To be more precise, the probability of revolution in a modernizing country depends upon: (a) the extent to which the urban middle class — intellectuals, professionals, bourgeoisie — are alienated from the existing order; (b) the extent to which the peasants are alienated from the existing order; and (c) the extent to which urban middle class and peasants join together not only in fighting against "the same enemy" but also in fighting for the same cause. This cause is usually nationalism.

Revolutions are thus unlikely to occur if the period of the frustration of the urban middle class does not coincide with that of the peasantry. Conceivably, one group might be highly alienated from the political system at one time and the other group at another time; in such circumstances revolution is improbable. Hence a slower general process of social change in a society is likely to reduce the possibility that these two groups will be simultaneously alienated from the existing system. To the extent that social-economic modernization has become more rapid over time, consequently, the probability of revolution has increased. For a major revolution to occur, however, not only must the urban middle class and the peasantry be alienated from the existing order, but they must also have the capacity and the incentive to act along parallel, if not cooperative, lines. If the proper stimulus to joint action is missing, then again revolution may be avoided.

REFERENCES

1. Arendt (1963), p. 28.
2. Pettee (1938), pp. 100–101.
3. Trotsky (1930), p. 337, quoted in Fainsod (1953), p. 84.
4. Palmer (1959–1964), vol. 1, p. 484.

Does Modernization Breed Revolution?

CHARLES TILLY

In this essay Tilly offers a critical appraisal of Huntington's views. Tilly argues that Huntington's theory of revolution is "needlessly weak" because of ambiguities and contradictions. Tilly notes that the terms *modernization* and *instability* require more precise definition than Huntington offers. How would we know modernization when we see it? How would we go about estimating the probabilities of revolution within the next few years if we had been in France in 1788 (or, for that matter, in Iran in 1978)? Focusing on modernization, Tilly claims, is more an orientation than a predictive theory.

Tilly suggests that when we study a society, we ask the following questions: What groups are contending for power? What claims are they making on the central government? What ability do contending groups and the government have to mobilize resources—money, human resources, weapons, information, and leadership—in order to enforce their claims? Revolution is likely only when powerful groups press competing claims on the government and when the government lacks the resources either to satisfy the claims of contending groups or to defeat them.

Therefore, Tilly's theory is one of "collective mobilization." It emphasizes the mobilization of resources by contending groups and the conflict of such groups with the state.

I want to ask whether modernization breeds revolution. That first formulation of the question is compact, but ambiguous. We shall, unfortunately, have to put a large part of our effort into the preliminary task of reducing the ambiguities. "Modernization" is a vague, tendentious concept. "Revolution" is a controversial one as well.

Instead of trying to pace off modernization precisely, I shall ordinarily substitute for it somewhat better defined processes, such as industrialization or demographic expansion. Instead of trying to grasp the essential genius of revolution, I shall offer a rather arbitrary set of definitions which appear to me to have considerable theoretical utility. I shall compensate

From *Comparative Politics, vol. 5, pp. 425–47 (1973). Copyright © The City University of New York.*

for my arbitrariness by discussing violence, instability, and political conflict more extensively than a strict concentration on revolution would justify.

HUNTINGTON'S SYNTHESIS

One of the most sophisticated recent syntheses of the standard views concerning all these matters comes from Samuel Huntington. In his *Political Order in Changing Societies,* Huntington argues that the widespread domestic violence and instability of the 1950s and 1960s in many parts of the world "was in large part the product of rapid social change and the rapid mobilization of new groups into politics, coupled with the slow development of political institutions."[1]

Huntington applies this lead-lag model to Western revolutions, treating them as extreme cases of the conflicts which emerge when political institutionalization proceeds too slowly for the pace of large-scale social change (which Huntington treats as more or less identical with "modernization") and of mobilization. Moreover, John Gillis has recently argued that the model applies specifically to the European modernizing revolutions of the eighteenth and nineteenth centuries.[2] It is therefore legitimate to ask how strong a grip on the Western experience with revolutions and violent conflict Huntington's analysis gives us. My answer is that the grip is needlessly weak—weak, because the scheme founders in tautologies, contradictions, omissions, and failures to examine the evidence seriously. Needlessly, because several of the main arguments concerning mobilization, political participation, and conflict improve vastly on the usual social-psychological tracing of "violence" or "protest" back to "strain" or "discontent."

Although it would be worth trying, this article will not attempt to wrench Huntington's theory into shape. I shall dwell on it in other ways, for other reasons, because in one manner or another it sums up most of the conventional wisdom connecting revolution to large-scale structural change; because Huntington places an exceptional range of contemporary and historical material within its framework; because the variables within it appear to be of the right kind; and because it is sturdy enough to exempt me from the accusation of having erected, and then burned, a straw man as I build up an alternative line of argument.

Huntington offers several criteria for the institutionalization of the existing political organization: adaptability, complexity, autonomy, coherence (with the latter essentially meaning consensus among the active participants in the political system). This sort of definition-making increases the risk that Huntington's arguments will become tautological. To the extent that one judges adaptability, complexity, autonomy, and coherence on the basis of the absence of containment of domestic violence and instability, the circle of truth by definition will close.

Nevertheless, Huntington's balanced-development theory is appealing in its combination of three factors—rapid social change, mobilization, and political institutionalization— which other authors have employed separately in one-factor explanations of stability and instability. It does, furthermore, provide a plausible explanation of the twentieth century concentration of revolution, governmental instability, and collective violence in the poorer (but not the poorest) countries of the world; the more plausible because it appears to dispose of the anomaly that by many standards the relatively peaceful richer countries are also the faster changing. Huntington's stress on the importance of group claims on the political system by mobilizing segments of the population is a distinct improvement over the more usual model of accumulating individual grievances. Indeed, the most attractive general feature of Huntington's scheme is its deliberate flight from psychologism, from the assumption that the central things to be explained by a theory of revolution are why, when, and how large numbers of individual men and women become discontented.

HUNTINGTON ON REVOLUTION

Huntington restricts the term *revolution* to the deep and rapid transformations of whole societies, which others have called Great Revolutions; the French, Chinese, Mexican, Russian, and Cuban revolutions epitomize what he has in mind. Nevertheless, Huntington asserts a fundamental continuity between revolution and lesser forms of conflict:

> Revolution is thus an aspect of modernization. It is not something which can occur in any type of society at any period in its history. It is not a universal category but rather an historically limited phenomenon. It will not occur in highly traditional societies with very low levels of social and economic complexity. Nor will it occur in highly modern societies. Like other forms of violence and instability, it is most likely to occur in societies which have experienced some social and economic development and where the processes of political modernization and political development have lagged behind the processes of social and economic change.[3]

Thus the imbalances which account for other forms of "disorder" also account for revolution: "The political essence of revolution is the rapid expansion of political consciousness and the rapid mobilization of new groups into politics at a speed which makes it impossible for existing political institutions to assimilate them. Revolution is the extreme case of the explosion of political participation."[4]

Huntington then distinguishes between an Eastern and a Western pattern of revolution. In the *Eastern,* new groups mobilize into politics, they fashion new political institutions, and they overthrow the old order; anticolonial revolutions are the type case. In the *Western,* the old political institutions disintegrate and only then do new groups mobilize into politics, create new political institutions, and come to power. The Russian Revolution is typical. The "decay" of established institutions plays a large part in the Western pattern, according to Huntington, and a small part in the Eastern. As a result, the sequences are rather different. Nevertheless, in both cases the immediate cause of revolution is supposed to be the discrepancy between the performance of the regime and the demands being made upon it. In both cases that discrepancy is supposed to increase as a consequence of the mobilization of new groups into politics, which in turn occurs as a more or less direct effect of rapid social and economic change.

The danger of circular argument is just as apparent here as before. In his detailed argumentation, Huntington does not really escape the fateful circularity of judging the extent of the discrepancy from the character of the revolution which presumably resulted from the discrepancy. He tells us, for example, that:

> The great revolutions of history have taken place either in highly centralized traditional monarchies (France, China, Russia), or in narrowly based military dictatorships (Mexico, Bolivia, Guatemala, Cuba), or in colonial regimes (Vietnam, Algeria). All these political systems demonstrated little if any capacity to expand their power and to provide channels for the participation of new groups in politics.[5]

Suppose we suppress the urge to blurt out questions about England in the 1640s or the United States in the 1860s and stifle suspicions that the implicit standard for great revolutions at work in this passage simply restricts them logically to centralized, authoritarian regimes. We still must wonder how we could have known before the fact of revolution that the expansive capacity of these governments was inferior to that of the many other monarchies, military dictatorships, and colonial regimes which did not experience revolutions.

Huntington does not answer. In its present form his scheme does not, it appears, give us any solid guidance in the anticipation or production of revolutions. Not even in the weak sense of projecting ourselves back into the France of 1788 and saying how we would have gone about estimating the probabilities of revolution within the next few years. That is true of the whole argument, and not just of the treatment of revolution. Even in principle, the scheme is not really a predictive one. It is an orientation, a proposal to weight several clusters of variables differently from the way they have been estimated in the past, and a presentation of an exceptionally wide range of observations in the light of the orientation and the weighting.

ALTERNATIVES

How else could we proceed? We should hold onto several of Huntington's perceptions: (a) that revolutions and collective violence tend to flow directly out of a population's central political processes, instead of expressing diffuse strains and discontents within the population; (b) that the specific claims and counterclaims being made on the existing government by various mobilized groups are more important than the general satisfaction or discontent of those groups, and that claims for established places within the structure of power are crucial; (c) that large-scale structural change transforms the identities and structures of the potential aspirants for power within the population, affects their opportunities for mobilization, governs the resources available to the government, and through it to the principal holders of power. Accepting those insights will encourage us to concentrate our analysis on processes of mobilization, on structures of power, and on the changing demands linking one to the other.

We have to go further. By contrast with Huntington's global strategy, we must clearly distinguish among different forms of conflict before seeking to identify their connections; we must disaggregate revolution into its components instead of treating it as a unitary phenomenon; we must investigate the precise ways in which urbanization or political centralization affects the mobilization and demobilization of different segments of the population; and we must specify and trace the relations of each major segment to the changing structure of power.

A MODEL OF POLITICAL CONFLICT

First, a simple model of political action. Let us distinguish three kinds of social unit within any specified population. A *government* is an organization which controls the principal concentrated means of coercion within the population; a *contender for power* is a group within the population which at least once during some standard period applies resources to influence that government; and a *polity* is the set of contenders which routinely and successfully lays claims on that government. (We may call these individual contenders *members* of the polity, while *challenger* is a good name for a contender laying claims in an irregular or unsuccessful fashion.) Almost any population beyond a very small scale will include more than one contender. Almost any large population will include more than one government, hence more than one polity. But many theoretically possible contenders will not contend during any particular period; some will never contend. A group gains the capacity to contend by mobilizing; by acquiring collective control over resources—land, labor, information, arms, money, and so on—which can be applied to influence the government; it loses that capacity by demobilizing—losing collective control over resources.

Every polity, then, collectively develops tests of membership. The tests always include the capacity to bring considerable numbers of men into action; they may also include the possession of wealth, certified birth, religious stigmata, and many other characteristics. Challengers acquire membership in the polity by meeting the tests, despite the fact that existing members characteristically resist new admissions and employ the government's resources to make admissions more difficult. The members also test each other more or less continuously; a member failing the tests tends to lose membership in the polity. Each change in membership moves the tests in a direction harmonious with the characteristics and capacities of the set of members emerging from the change. The members of the polity come to treat the prevailing criteria of membership as having a special moral virtue. Challengers denied admission tend to define themselves as being deprived rights due them on general grounds. Members losing position tend, in contrast, to accent tradition, usage, and particular agreements in support of their claims to threatened privileges and resources. Thus contenders both entering and leaving the polity have a special propensity to articulate strongly moral definitions of their situations.

The scheme permits us to specify the close relationship between collective violence and the central political process: (a) political life consists largely of making collective claims for resources and privileges controlled by governments; (b) collective violence is largely a byproduct of situations in which one contender openly lays such claims and other contenders (or, especially, the government) resist these claims; (c) such situations occur with particular frequency when groups are acquiring or losing membership—that is, partly because testing tends to take that form, partly because the moral orientations of the groups whose memberships are disputed encourage the individuals within them to take exceptional risks of damage or injury, partly because the activation of the coercive forces of the government increase the likelihood of damage or injury to other participants; (d) hence collective violence tends to cluster around major or multiple entries and exits; (e) governments themselves act to maintain priority over substantial concentrations of coercive resources, so that a contender accumulating such resources outside the control of the government is likely to find itself in acute conflict with the agents of the government.

REVOLUTIONS

We now have the means of moving on to revolution. The multiplication of polities is the key. A revolution begins when a government previously under the control of a single, sovereign polity becomes the object of effective, competing, mutually exclusive claims from two or more separate polities. A revolution ends when a single polity—by no means necessarily the same one—regains control over the government. This multiple sovereignty can result from the attempt of one polity to subordinate another heretofore independent polity; from the assertion of sovereignty by a previously subordinate polity; from the formation of a bloc of challengers which seizes control of some portion of the government apparatus; from the fragmentation of an existing polity into blocs, each of which controls some part of the government. Many observers would prefer to restrict the label "revolution" to the action by challengers; many others would prefer to call each of these a different major type of revolution: civil war, national revolution, and so on. I begin with an exceptionally broad definition to call attention to the common properties of the various paths through multiple sovereignty.

What observable political conditions, then, ought to prevail before a revolution begins? Three conditions appear to be necessary, and a fourth strongly facilitating. The three apparently necessary conditions are:

1. The appearance of contenders or coalitions of contenders, advancing exclusively alternative claims to the control over the government currently exerted by the members of the polity;
2. commitment to those claims by a significant segment of the subject population;
3. unwillingness or incapacity of the agents of the government to suppress the alternative coalition or the commitment to its claims.

The strongly facilitating condition is:

4. formation of coalitions between members of the polity and the contenders making the alternative claims.

Let me confess at once that the list contains little news not already borne by the definition of revolution as a state of multiple sovereignty. The purpose of the list is simply to focus the explanation of revolution on the structure of power, and away from the general level of strain, discontent, disequilibrium, or mobilization. At first approach, the argument therefore resembles Huntington's; both of them attach great importance to encounters between existing political arrangements and specific mobilized groups making new and powerful demands on the government. This analysis veers away from Huntington's, especially in denying the significance of a discrepancy between the overall rates of mobilization and institutionalization, in attaching great importance to conflicts over claims, duties, privileges, and conceptions of justice embedded in particular contenders for power, and in drawing attention to the important possibility that the crucial contenders will be disaffected members of a polity rather than newcomers to power.

The explanation of revolution, within this formulation, becomes the identification of the probable causes for the three necessary conditions and the fourth facilitating condition: the appearance of a bloc advancing exclusive alternative claims, commitment to those claims, failure of repression and formation of coalitions between the alternative bloc and members of the polity. An alternative bloc can come into being via three different routes: (a) the mobilization of a new contender outside the polity; (b) the turning away of an existing challenger from acceptance of the polity's current operating rules; (c) the turning away of an existing member from its established place in the polity. In order to gauge the probabilities of employment of any of the routes, we would have to know a good deal about the operating rules of the polities involved. But several general conditions very likely increase those probabilities: contraction of the resources available to the government for the meeting of its commitments, a shift in the direction of structural change within the base population such that not just new groups but new *kinds* of groups are coming into being, disappearance of the resources which make possible the membership in the polity, and the continuing collective life of some contender.

The expansion of commitment to the claims of the alternative bloc occurs both through their acceptance by groups and individuals not belonging to the bloc and through the further mobilization of the bloc itself. The two undoubtedly reinforce each other. Acceptance of the alternative claims is likely to generalize when: the government fails to meet its established obligations; it greatly increases its demands on the subject population; the alternative claims are cast within the moral framework already employed by many members of the population; there is a strong alliance between the existing government and a well-defined enemy of an important segment of the population; and the coercive resources of the alternative bloc increase.

The Marxist account of the conditions for radicalization of the proletariat and the peasantry remains the most powerful general analysis of the process, expanding commitment to a revolutionary bloc. Where it falls down is in not providing for contenders (communities, ethnic minorities, religious groups, and so on) which are not class-based, and in obscuring the revolutionary importance of defensive reactions by segments of the population whose established positions are threatened. Eric Wolf's superb study of twentieth-century peasant wars makes apparent the revolutionary potential of such defensive responses to land enclosure, expansion of the market, and the encroachment of capitalism. [See the essay by Wolf in this volume.—Ed.]

The agents of the government are likely to become unwilling or unable to suppress the alternative bloc and the commitment to its claims when their coercive resources contract, their inefficiency increases, and inhibitions to their use arise. Defeat in war is a quintessential case, for casualties, defections, and military demobilization all tend to decrease the government's coercive capacity; the destruction of property, disruption of routines, and displacement of population in defeat are likely to decrease the efficiency of the established coercive means; and the presence of a conqueror places constraints on the government's use of coercion. (The routine of modern military occupation, however, tends to substitute the coercive capacity of the victors for that of the vanquished.) The end of any war, won or lost, tends to restore men with newly acquired military skill to most of the contenders in the political system. Where military demobilization proceeds rapidly, it is likely to shift the balance of coercive resources away from the government, and may shift it toward an alternative bloc. Even without war, the increase in the coercive resources of the alternative bloc (which can occur through theft, purchase, training, the imposition of military discipline, and the lending of support by outsiders) is equivalent to the contraction of the government's own coercive resources. The efficiency of governmental coercion is likely to decline, at least in the short run, when the character, organization, and daily routines of the population to be controlled change rapidly; this appears to be one of the most direct effects of large-scale structural change on the likelihood of revolution. Inhibitions to the use of coercion are likely to increase when the coercive forces themselves are drawn from (or otherwise attached to) the populations to be controlled, when new members of the polity act against the coercive means that were employed to block their acquisition of membership, and effective coalitions between members of the polity and revolutionary challengers exist.

The final condition for revolution—this one strongly facilitating rather than necessary—is the formation of just such coalitions between polity members and revolutionary challengers. Modern European history, for example, provides many examples of temporary coalitions between professionals, intellectuals, or other fragments of the bourgeoisie well established within the polity and segments of the working class excluded from power. The revolutions of 1830 and 1848 display this pattern with particular clarity. The payoff to the challengers consists of a hedge against repression, some protection against the devaluation of their resources, and perhaps the transfer of information and expertise from the member. The payoff to the member consists of an expansion of the resources available for application to the government and to other members of the polity—not least the ability to mount a credible threat of mass action. This sort of coalition-formation is likely to occur, on the one hand, when a challenger rapidly increases the store of resources under its control and, on the other, when a member loses its coalition partners within the polity, or the polity is more or less evenly divided among two or more coalitions, or an established member is risking loss of membership in the polity through failure to meet the tests of other members.

THE HISTORY OF REVOLUTION IN THE WEST

In the West of the past five centuries, perhaps the largest single factor in the promotion of revolutions and collective violence has been the great concentration of power in national states. (I concede that the rise of the national state depended to such a large degree on the growth of production, the expansion of large-scale marketing, the strengthening of the bourgeoisie, and the proliferation of bureaucracy that such a statement commits a dramatic oversimplification.) This factor shows up most clearly in the frequency of tax rebellions in Western countries over those centuries, and in the prominence of grievances concerning taxation in revolutions, such as those of the 1640s or the 1840s. The frequency of violent resistance to military conscription points in the same direction.

States are warmakers, and wars are state-makers. At least in modern Europe, the major increases in the scope and strength of national states (as indicated by national budgets, national debts, powers of intervention, and sizes of staffs) have, on the whole, occurred as a direct result of war-making or preparation for war. What is more, the armed forces have historically played a large part in subordinating other authorities and the general population to the national state. They backed up the collection of taxes, put down tax rebellions, seized and disposed of the enemies of the crown, literally enforced national policy. The relationship was neatly reciprocal: war provided the incentive, the occasion, and the rationalization for strengthening the state, while war-makers assured the docility of the general population and the yielding of the resources necessary to carry out the task. The fairly recent division of labor between specialized police forces for domestic control and military forces for the remaining tasks has not fundamentally changed the relationship.

The connection matters here because a series of important relationships between war and revolution also exists. It is not just that they overlap to some extent. In some circumstances, war promotes revolution. That assertion is true in several different ways: the extraction of resources for the prosecution of war has repeatedly aroused revolutionary resistance; the defeat of states in war has often made them vulnerable to attacks from their domestic enemies; the complicity of some portion of the armed forces with the revolutionary bloc has been absolutely essential to the success of the modern revolution, and the most frequent variety of revolution—the coup—has depended mainly on the alignments of armed forces; the waning phases of major movements of conquest (the weakening of the Napoleonic regimes outside of France, the Nazi regimes outside of Germany, and the Japanese regimes outside of Japan being prime examples) are strikingly propitious for revolution; and the periods of readjustment immediately following large international conflicts also seem favorable to revolution, often with the collusion of major parties to the conflict. All of this suggests a strong connection between realignments in the international system and conflicts within individual countries, a connection mediated by the repressive policies and capacities of the governments involved.

Those who find at least some of the preceding analysis useful and plausible will do well to reflect on the sorts of variables that have been in play. Despite the many recent attempts to psychologize the study of revolution by introducing ideas of anxiety, alienation, rising expectations, and the like, and to sociologize it by employing notions of disequilibrium, role conflict, structural strain, and so on, the factors which hold up under close scrutiny are, on the whole, political ones. The structure of power, alternative conceptions of justice, the organization of coercion, the conduct of war, the formation of coalitions, the legitimacy of the state—these traditional concerns of political thought provide the main guides to the explanation of revolution. Population growth, industrialization, urbanization, and other large-scale structural changes do, to be sure, affect the probabilities of revolution. But they do so indirectly, by shaping the potential contenders for power, transforming the techniques of government control, and shifting the resources available to contenders and governments. There is no reliable and regular sense in which modernization breeds revolutions.

REFERENCES

1. Huntington (1968), p. 4.
2. Gillis (1970), pp. 344–70.
3. Huntington (1968), p. 265.
4. Ibid., p. 266.
5. Ibid., p. 275.

CHAPTER 3

The Origins of Revolutions

The classical and modernization debates on revolutions make it clear that revolutions are too complex to be captured by a simple, one-cause formula, such as "class struggle" or "modernization." Therefore, current theories of revolution examine multiple causes of the development of revolutions. In discussing these causes, Eric R. Wolf shows that a number of different social processes contribute to the mobilization of peasants into revolutionary movements. Theda Skocpol and Ellen Kay Trimberger examine several different relationships among the state, elites, and popular groups, and show how these relationships have been important in the development of great revolutions. Jack A. Goldstone demonstrates that multiple vulnerabilities lie behind the revolutionary overthrow of modern dictatorships. Eric Selbin examines the critical role played by rebel leaders and their ideology in shaping revolutionary strategy and goals. In each essay, although the precise causes differ for different revolutions, the authors agree on a fundamental principle: Explaining revolutions depends on understanding how multiple causes combine to create a situation in which states are weakened and in which elites and popular groups have both the capacity and the motivation to revolt.

Peasants and Revolutions

ERIC R. WOLF

In this essay, Wolf notes that peasant rebellions are generally defensive. The participants wish to protect traditional lifestyles against mounting strains. Wolf identifies three sources of such strains: (1) population growth, (2) commercialization and the growth of markets, and (3) dislocation among the local elites that traditionally mediate peasants' interactions with government authorities and the outside world.

However, mobilizing the peasantry for revolution is no easy task. Wolf argues that peasants are able to translate their resistance to such pressures into active rebellion only if they have "tactical freedom" to act. Such freedom may be available to peasants who possess their own resources—that is, a land-owning middle peasantry; to peasants who live in areas far from the strongholds of central authority, especially in defensible mountainous regions; and to peasants who live in self-administering communal villages not under the direct supervision of landlords. Each kind of peasantry forms a potential enclave of rebellion in times of mounting pressures on peasants' traditional ways of life.

Still, peasant rebellions have become revolutions only when combined with the actions of dissident elites. Wolf describes the problematic nature of this connection and its role in building revolutions.

Six major social and political upheavals, fought with peasant support, have shaken the world of the twentieth century: the Mexican Revolution of 1910; the Russian Revolutions of 1905 and 1917; the Chinese Revolution, which metamorphosed through various phases from 1921 on; the Vietnamese Revolution, which had its roots in World War II; the Algerian Revolution of 1954; and the Cuban Revolution of 1958–59. All of these were to some extent based on the participation of rural populations. It is to the analysis of this participation that the present paper directs its attention.

Romantics to the contrary, it is not easy for a peasantry to engage in sustained rebellion. Peasants are especially handicapped in passing from passive recognition of wrongs to political participation as a means for setting them right. First, a peasant's work is most often done alone, on his own land, rather than in conjunction with his fellows. Moreover, all peasants are to some extent competitors for available resources within the community, as well as for sources of credit from without. Second, the tyranny of work weighs heavily upon peasants—their life is geared to an annual routine and to planning for the year to come. Momentary alterations of routine threaten their ability to take up the routine again later. Third, control of land enables him, more often than not, to retreat into subsistence production, should adverse conditions affect his market crop. Fourth, ties of extended kinship and mutual aid within the community may cushion the shocks of dislocation. Fifth, peasants' interests—especially among poor peasants—often crosscut class alignments. Rich and poor peasants may be kinfolk, or a peasant may be at one and the same time owner, renter, sharecropper, laborer for his neighbors, and seasonal hand on a nearby plantation. Each different involvement aligns him differently with his fellows and with the outside world. Finally, past exclusion of the peasant from participation in decision-making beyond the bamboo hedge of his village deprives him all too often of the knowledge needed to articulate his interests with appropriate forms of action. Hence peasants are often merely passive spectators of political struggles, or they long for the sudden advent of a millennium, without specifying, for themselves and their neighbors, the many rungs on the staircase to heaven.

If it is true that peasants are slow to rise, then peasant participation in the great rebellions of the twentieth century must obey some special factors that exacerbate the peasant condition. We will not understand that condition unless we keep constantly in mind that it has suffered greatly under the impact of three great crises: the demographic crisis, the ecological crisis, and the crisis in power and authority. The demographic crisis is most easily depicted in bare figures, though its root causes remain ill understood. Yet the bare numbers suffice to indicate the seriousness of the demographic problem. Mexico had a population of 5.8 million at the beginning of the nineteenth century; in 1910—at the outbreak of the revolution—it

Demographic

had 16.5 million. European Russia had a population of 20 million in 1725; at the turn of the twentieth century it had 87 million. China numbered 265 million in 1775, 430 million in 1850, and close to 600 million at the time of the revolution. Vietnam is estimated to have sustained a population of between 6 and 14 million in 1820; it had 30.5 million inhabitants in 1962. The indigenous population of Algeria numbered 10.5 million in 1963, representing a fourfold increase since the beginnings of French occupation in the first part of the nineteenth century. Cuba had 550,000 inhabitants in 1800; by 1953 it had 5.8 million. Population increases alone and by themselves would have placed a serious strain on inherited cultural arrangements.

The ecological crisis is in part related to the sheer increase in numbers; yet it is also an important measure independent of it. Population increases of the magnitude just mentioned coincided with a period of history in which land and other resources were increasingly converted into commodities to be bought and sold. As commodities, they were subjected to the demands of a market that bore only a very indirect relation to the needs of the rural populations subject to it. Where in the past market behavior had been largely subsidiary to the problems of subsistence, now existence and its problems became subsidiary to the market. The alienation of peasant resources proceeded directly through outright seizure or through coercive purchase, as in Mexico, Algeria, and Cuba, or it took the form—especially in China and Vietnam—of stepped-up rents, which resulted in the transfer of resources from those unable to keep up to those able to pay. In addition, the peasant economy was burdened by the pressure of taxation, by demands for redemption payments, and by an increased need for industrially produced commodities on the part of the peasantry itself. All together, these various pressures disrupted the precarious ecological balance of peasant society. Where the peasant had required a certain combination of resources to effect an adequate living, the pressures on these resources broke that ecological nexus. This is perhaps best seen in Russia, where successive land reforms threatened continued peasant access to pasture, forest, and plowland. Yet it is equally evident in cases where commercialization threatened peasant access to communal lands (Mexico, Algeria, Vietnam), to unclaimed land (Mexico, Cuba), to public granaries (Algeria, China), or threatened the balance between pastoral and settled populations (Algeria). At the same time that commercialization disrupted rural life, it also created new and unsettled ecological niches in industry. Disruptive change in the rural area went hand in hand with the opening up of incipient but uncertain opportunities for numerous peasants. Many of these retained formal ties with their home villages (Russia, China, Algeria); others migrated between country and industry in continuous turnover (especially Vietnam). Increased instability in the rural areas was thus accompanied by a still unstable commitment to industrial work.

Finally, both the demographic and the ecological crises converged in the crisis of authority. The development of the market produced a rapid circulation of the elite. The manipulators of the new "free floating resources"—labor bosses, merchants, industrial entrepreneurs—challenged the inherited power of the controllers of fixed social resources—the tribal chief, the mandarin, the landed nobleman. Undisputed and stable claims thus yielded to unstable and disputed claims. This rivalry between primarily economic powerholders contained its own rules: the economic entrepreneur did not concern himself with the social cost of his activities; the traditional powerholder was often too limited in his power to offer assistance or was subject to cooptation by his successful rivals. The advent of the market thus produced not merely a crisis in peasant ecology; it deranged the numerous middle-level ties between center and hinterland, urban and rural sectors. Commercialization disrupted the hinterland; at the very same time it also lessened the ability of powerholders to perceive and predict changes in the rural area. The result was an ever widening gap between the rulers and the ruled. That such a course is not inevitable is perhaps demonstrated by Barrington Moore,[1] who shows how traditional feudal forms were utilized in both Germany and Japan to prevent the formation of such a gap in power and communication during the crucial period of transition to a commercial and industrial order. Where this was not accomplished—precisely where an administrative, militarized feudalism was absent—the continued widening of the power gap invited the formation of a counterelite that could challenge both a disruptive leadership based on the operation of the market and the impotent heirs of traditional power, while forging a new consensus through communication with the peasantry. Such a counterelite is most frequently made up of members of provincial elites, relegated to the margins of commercial mobilization and political office; of officials or professionals who stand midway between the rural area and the center, and are caught in the contradictions between the two; and of intellectuals who have access to a system of symbols which can guide the interaction between leadership and rural area.

Sustained mobilization of the peasantry is, however, no easy task. Such an effort will not find its allies in a rural mass that is completely subject to the imperious demands of necessity. Peasants cannot rebel successfully in a situation of complete impotence; the powerless are easy victims. Therefore only a peasantry in possession of some tactical control over its own resources can provide a secure basis for ongoing political leverage. Power, as Richard Adams has said, refers ultimately

> to an actual physical control that one party may have with respect to another. The reason that most relationships are not reduced to physical struggles is that parties to them can make rational decisions based on their estimates of tactical power and other factors. Power is usually exercised, therefore, through the common recognition by two parties of the tactical control each has, and through rational decision by one to do what the other wants. Each estimates his own tactical control, compares it to the other, and decides he may or may not be superior.[2]

The poor peasant or the landless laborer who depends on a landlord for the largest part of his livelihood (or the totality of it) has no tactical power; he is completely within the power domain of his employer, without sufficient resources of his own to serve him as resources in the power struggle. Poor peasants and landless laborers, therefore, are unlikely to pursue the course of rebellion, *unless* they are able to rely on some external power to challenge the power that constrains them. Such external power is represented in the Mexican case by the action of the Constitutionalist Army in Yucatán, which liberated the peons from debt bondage "from above"; by the collapse of the Russian Army in 1917 and the reflux of the peasant soldiery, arms in hand, into the villages; by the creation of the Chinese Red Army as an instrument designed to break up landlord power in the villages. Where such external power is present, the poor peasant and landless laborer have latitude of movement; where it is absent, they are under almost complete constraint. The rich peasant, in turn, is unlikely to embark on the course of rebellion. As employer of the labor of others, as moneylender, as notable coopted by the state machine, he exercises local power in alliance with external power holders. His power domain within the village is derivative; it depends on the maintenance of the domains of power holders outside the village. Only when an external force, such as the Chinese Red Army, proves capable of destroying these other superior power domains, will the rich peasant lend his support to an uprising.

There are only two components of the peasantry that possess sufficient internal leverage to enter sustained rebellion. These are (1) a landowning "middle peasantry" or (2) a peasantry located in a peripheral area outside the domains of landlord control. Middle peasantry refers to a peasant population that has secure access to land of its own and cultivates it with family labor. Where these middle peasant holdings lie within the power domain of a superior, possession of their own resources provides middle peasants with the minimal tactical freedom required to challenge their overlords. The same, however, holds for a peasantry, poor or middle, whose settlements are only under marginal control from the outside. Here land holdings may be insufficient for the support of the peasant household; but subsidiary activities such as casual labor, smuggling, livestock raising—not under the direct constraint of an external power domain—supplement land in sufficient quantity to grant the peasantry some latitude of movement. We mark the existence of such a tactically mobile peasantry in the villages of Morelos in Mexico, in the communes of the Central Agricultural Region of Russia, in the northern bastion established by the Chinese Communists after the Long March, as a basis for rebellion in Vietnam, among the fellahin in Algeria, and among the squatters of Oriente Province in Cuba.

Yet this recruitment of a "tactically mobile peasantry" among the middle peasants and the "free" peasants of peripheral areas poses a curious paradox. This is also the peasantry in whom anthropologists and rural sociologists have tended to see the main bearers of peasant tradition. If our account is correct, then (strange to say) it is precisely this culturally conservative stratum that is the most instrumental in dynamiting the peasant social order. This paradox dissolves, however, when we consider that it is also the middle peasant who is relatively the most vulnerable to economic changes wrought by commercialism, while his social relations remain encased within the traditional design. He is in a balancing act in which his balance is continuously threatened by population growth, the encroachment of rival landlords, the loss of rights to grazing, forest, and water, failing prices and unfavorable conditions of the market, and interest payments and foreclosures. Moreover, it is precisely this stratum that depends most on traditional social relations of kin and mutual aid between neighbors; middle peasants suffer most when these relations are abrogated, just as they are least able to withstand the depredations of tax collectors or landlords.

Finally—and this is again paradoxical—middle peasants are also the most exposed to influences from the developing proletariat. The poor peasant or landless laborer, in going to the city or the factory, also usually cuts his tie with the land. The middle peasant, however, stays on the land and sends his children to work in town; he is caught in a situation in which one part of the family retains a footing in agriculture, while the other undergoes "the training of the cities." This also makes the middle peasant a transmitter of urban unrest and political ideas. The point bears elaboration: it is probably not so much the growth of an industrial proletariat as such that produces revolutionary activity, as it is the development of an industrial work force still closely geared to life in the villages.

Thus, it is the very attempt of the middle and free peasant to remain traditional that makes him revolutionary.

If we now follow out the hypothesis that it is middle peasants and poor but "free" peasants—not constrained by any power domain—that constitute the pivotal groupings for peasant uprisings, then it follows that any factor that serves to increase the latitude granted by that tactical mobility reinforces their revolutionary potential. One of these factors is peripheral location of the peasantry with regard to the center of state control. In fact, frontier areas quite often show a tendency to rebel against the central authorities, regardless of whether they are inhabited by peasants or not. South China has constituted a hearth of rebellion within the Chinese state, partly because it was first a frontier area in the southward march of the Han people, and later because it provided the main zone of contact between Western and Chinese civilization. The Mexican North has similarly been a zone of dissidence from the center in Mexico City, partly because its economy was based on mining and cattle raising rather than maize agriculture, and partly because it was open to influences from the United States to the north. In South China it was the dissident gentry with a peasant following that frequently made trouble for the center; in the Mexican North it was the provincial businessmen, ranchers, and cowboys. Yet when a poor peasantry is located in such a peripheral area beyond the normal control of the central power, the tactical mobility of such a peasantry is "doubled" by its location. This has been the case with Morelos in Mexico, Nghe An Province in Vietnam, Kabylia in Algeria, and Oriente in Cuba. The tactical effectiveness of such areas is "tripled" if they also contain defensible mountainous redoubts—this has been true of Morelos, Kabylia, and Oriente. The effect is "quadrupled" where the population of these redoubts differs ethnically or linguistically from the surrounding population. Thus we find that the villagers of Morelos were Nahuatl speakers; the inhabitants of Kabylia, Berber speakers. Oriente Province showed no linguistic differences from the Spanish spoken in Cuba, but it did contain a significant Afro-Cuban element. Ethnic distinctions enhance the solidarity of the rebels; possession of a special linguistic code provides an autonomous system of communication.

It is important, however, to recognize that separation from the state or the surrounding populace need not be only physical or cultural. The Russian and the Mexican cases both demonstrate that it is possible to develop a solid enclave population of peasantry through state reliance on a combination of communal autonomy with the provision of community services to the state. The organization of the peasantry into self-administering communes with stipulated responsibilities to state and landlords created, in both cases, veritable fortresses of peasant tradition within the body of the country itself. Held fast by the surrounding structure, they acted as sizzling pressure cookers of unrest which, at the moment of explosion, vented their force outward to secure more living space for their customary corporate way of life. Thus we can add a further multiplier effect to the others just cited. The presence of any one of these will raise the peasant potential for rebellion.

But what of the transition from peasant rebellion to revolution, from a movement aimed at the redress of wrongs to the attempted overthrow of society itself? Marxists in general have long argued that peasants without outside leadership cannot make a revolution; our case material would bear them out. Where the peasantry has successfully rebelled against the established order—under its own banner and with its own leaders—it was sometimes able to reshape the social structure of the countryside closer to its heart's desires; however, it did not lay hold of the state, of the cities that house the centers of control, of the strategic nonagricultural resources of the society. Zapata stayed in his Morelos; the "fold migration" of Pancho Villa simply receded after the defeat at Torreon; the Ukrainian rebel Nestor Makhno stopped short of the cities; the Russian peasants of the Central Agricultural Region simply burrowed more deeply into their local communes. Thus a peasant rebellion that takes place in a complex society already caught up in commercialization and industrialization tends to be self-limiting and hence anachronistic.

The peasant utopia is the free village, untrammeled by tax collectors, labor recruiters, large landowners, or officials. Ruled over, but never ruling, peasants also lack any acquaintance with the operation of the state as a complex machinery; rather, they experience it only as a "cold monster." Willing to defend the peasants if it proved to be in their own interest, the traditional local power holders provided a weak, unreliable shield against the hostile force of the state. Thus, for the present, the state is a negative quality, an evil, to be replaced in short shrift by their own "homemade" social order. That order, they believe, can run without the state; hence peasants in rebellion are natural anarchists.

Often this political perspective is reinforced still further by a wider ideological vision. The peasant experience tends to be dualistic, in that he is caught between his understanding of how the world ought to be properly ordered and the realities of a mundane existence, beset by disorder. Against this disorder, the peasant has always set his dreams of deliverance— the vision of a *mahdi* who would deliver the world from tyranny, of a Son of Heaven who would truly embody the mandate of Heaven, of a "white tsar" as against the "black tsar" of the disordered present. Under conditions of modern dislocation, the disordered present is all too frequently experienced as world order reversed, and hence evil. The dualism of the past easily fuses with the dualism of the present. The true order is yet to come, either through miraculous intervention, rebellion, or both. Peasant anarchism and an apocalyptic vision of the world together provide the ideological fuel that drives the rebellious peasantry.

Thus, the processes of rebellion and of revolution involve not merely organizational changes, but also changes in the perception and understanding of the world one inhabits. The Mexican Revolution was preceded by the wide spread of anarchist ideals. The Algerian Revolution was preceded by the Badissa, a reformist Islamic movement. The Chinese Revolution of 1911 was preceded by the Taiping, Nien, and Boxer rebellions, and the mushroomings of heterodox secret societies. The Russian Revolution was prepared by the secession of the Old Believers and the spread of a millenarian ideology among the peasantry. The Vietnamese Revolution followed after the growth of novel sects like the Cao Dai and the Hoa Hao. Such ideological movements provide the opportunity to imagine alternatives to present conditions, to experiment mentally with alternative forms of organization, and to ready the population for the acceptance of changes to come. They are the mental rehearsals of revolutionary transformations.

Given these volatile cultural and ideological characteristics of peasant societies and the triple crisis impacting the peasant order in the modern age, what other social groupings and processes intercede to give certain twentieth-century peasant rebellions their revolutionary character? The pressures that affect the peasantry affect in other ways the middlemen who stand guard over the relays of communication and power between the developed sector and the hinterland. These middlemen are not homogeneous; they are not in any way like a European middle class. They include economic brokers, members of the lower orders of bureaucracy, and teachers. They also include the middlemen of the past social order, now shattered by the interrelated crises of overpopulation, ecological imbalance, and eroded authority. These are the landlords clinging to a decaying grandeur; the notables whose words were once decisive in the deliberations of the village assemblies; the literati learned in the canons of an outworn wisdom. But rarely do such men make good revolutionaries themselves. Their sons, however, characteristically caught between the decadent style of their fathers and the new and raucous style of their competitors in the business of social brokerage, can envision a future purged of the contradictions of the present. Such middlemen—old and new—are the social agents of articulation; but they are also society's victims. They occupy the social positions of greatest strain. Middlemen and middle peasants together constitute the population from which the revolution recruits its army. The middle peasants furnish the first infantry battalions; the middlemen, the first officers of line and staff. But not all peasants or all brokers participate in the revolutionary process. Rather, the political process leading to revolution is a process of social selection—different political groups compete with each other in articulating their interests into viable coalitions. Recent revolutions exhibit a patterned sequence of such attempts. First, the middle layers produce a set of political leaders who agitate for ameliorative reforms. Next follows a phase of coalition-building in which various political groups compete in making contacts with urban artisans and wage workers. The urban artisans produce "petty bourgeois anarchist" demands; the workers initiate trade-union demands. Then follows the third and most problematic phase, the social selection of some group or groups of cadre capable of linking up with the potential peasant rebels. I know of no twentieth-century revolution in which such a coalition was achieved without revolutionary warfare.

Revolutionary warfare is the strongest catalyst in effecting the link between cadre and rebels. In peaceful times, revolutionary leaders may scour the countryside in attempts to "go to the people," in the words of the pre-1905 Russian Narodniki. Yet, all too frequently they do so as outsiders, as people city-bred and city-trained, drawing their behavior patterns and cultural idioms from the dominant sector and the enclave society. They must first unlearn these patterns, if they are to enter into successful contact with the peasant rebels. Any anthropologist who has worked with peasants will appreciate the unreality suggested by the picture of the dedicated commissar, newly descended upon the peasant village, busily molding the minds of five hundred, a thousand, or two thousand peasants. This is not to say that the revolutionary leaders do not build and extend mechanisms of control wherever and whenever they can—but this building and extension of control must involve a complex dialogue with the villagers in which the outsider learns as much, if not more, about local organization and criteria of relevance than the local inhabitants. Guerrilla warfare both speeds and deepens this learning as cadre and peasant activists synchronize their behavior and translate from one cultural idiom to the other.

This phase is clearly the most problematical. First, mutual learning and consequent synchronization may fail. Second, the cadre may not be able to effect the transition from urban-based political activity to revolutionary warfare in the hinterland. Third, even if successful, the rebels among the peasantry rarely exceed ten percent of the peasant population. Hence the movement must gain tacit as well as overt support of the peasantry. To this end, the revolutionaries must construct, in the backward sector, a network of institutions (an "infrastructure" or "parallel hierarchy"), or at least inhibit the capacity of the government to exercise or extend its own power in the hinterland.

Such a new infrastructure cannot be built from whole cloth; it can only be the outcome of a complex interaction between leaders and followers. More often than not, the resultant form of organization is based on already existing peasant patterns and experience. Behind the new revolutionary organization of Mexican villages lies an age-old experience with communal land tenures; behind the sudden rise of the Russian soviets lies the experience of the traditional Russian village community of the *mir*. Behind the new organization of the population of Chinese villages, we discern quite traditional patterns of village associations, as well as the organizational experience gained by peasant rebels in such uprisings as the Taiping and the Nien. Even behind the organization of the Chinese Communist Party lie such traditional patterns of secret society as the Ko Lao Hui. This is not to say that no new patterns are introduced into the villages. Frequently, it is warfare itself—and the break it represents with the past—that allows the rural population to accept innovations under their *own* auspices, innovations they would have resisted if imposed by the agents of the dominant sector.

Such a self-made social structure speeds learning. By removing the constraints of the inherited order, it releases the manifold contradictions hitherto held in check—the opposition of old and young, men and women, rich and poor—and directs the energies thus freed into new organizational channels. It is this, above all, that makes revolution irreversible. It also speeds the rise of leaders from the peasantry itself, providing new channels of mobility not contained in the old system, and intensifying the fusion between peasantry and leadership which sparked the revolutionary effort.

REFERENCES

1. Moore, Jr. (1966).
2. Adams (1966), pp. 3—4.

Revolutions: A Structural Analysis
THEDA SKOCPOL AND ELLEN KAY TRIMBERGER

Building on the work of Karl Marx, Skocpol and Trimberger argue for a "structural" approach to revolutions that examines multiple relationships among important political actors. Beginning with a concern for the power of the state, they focus on several key relationships that may reinforce or undermine state power—relationships between states and elite groups, between peasants and landlords, and between states competing in the international arena. Skocpol and Trimberger thus find the causes of revolutions in the very structure of certain states and societies.

MARX ON REVOLUTION: A CRITIQUE

Karl Marx's theory of revolution was elegant, powerful, and politically relevant because it linked the causes and consequences of revolutions directly to the historical emergence and transcendence of capitalism. Nevertheless, events and scholarship since Marx's time show that there is a need for revised ways of understanding revolutions in relation to the world-historical development of capitalism.

Before we launch into critical discussion, let us briefly underline some aspects of Marx's approach to revolutions that are still compelling and which we want to recapitulate in our own approach. First, unlike many contemporary academic and social scientists, Marx did not try to create a general theory of revolution relevant to all kinds of societies at all times. Instead, he regarded revolutions as specific to certain historical circumstances and to certain types of societies.

Second, Marx developed a social-structural theory of revolutions which argued that organized and conscious movements for revolutionary change succeed only where and when there is an objectively revolutionary situation, due to contradictions in the larger societal structure and historical situation: thus Marx's oft-quoted saying that men make their own history, but not in circumstances of their own choosing and not just as they please.

Third, Marx made class domination central to his conception of social order, and class conflict a defining feature of revolution, and we retain such concerns.

Taking off from these continuities with Marx's approach to revolutions, we can now identify various points at which Marx's original theory of revolutions stands in need of revision when juxtaposed to historical revolutions as we understand them. We shall discuss in turn issues about causes, processes, and outcomes of revolutions.

CAUSES

Marx held that a revolutionary situation occurs when an existing mode of production reaches the limits of its contradictions. The decisive contradictions are *economic* contradictions that develop between the social forces and the social relations of production. In turn, intensifying class conflict is generated between the existing dominant class and the rising, revolutionary class. Thus Marx theorized that revolutionary contradictions are internally generated within a society. What is more, his perspective strongly suggested that revolutions should occur first in the most economically advanced social formations of a given mode of production.

Actual historical revolutions, though, have not conformed to Marx's theoretical expectations. From the French Revolution on, they have occurred in predominantly agrarian countries where capitalist relations of production were only barely or moderately developed. In every instance, political-military pressures from more economically advanced countries abroad have been crucial in contributing to the outbreak of revolution. Marx be-

From "Revolutions and the World-Historical Development of Capitalism" by Theda Skocpol and Ellen Kay Trimberger. Reproduced with permission of the authors from the Berkeley Journal of Sociology, vol. 22, pp. 101–113. Copyright © 1978 by Berkeley Journal of Sociology.

gan an analysis of uneven world capitalist development, but he did not link this directly to the cause of revolutions. Nor do we agree that the objective conditions within the old regimes that explain the emergence of revolutionary situations have been primarily economic. Rather, they have been *political* contradictions centered in the structure and situation of states caught in cross-pressures between, on the one hand, military competitors on the international scene and, on the other hand, the constraints of the existing domestic economy and (in some cases) resistance by internal politically powerful class forces to efforts by the state to mobilize resources to meet international competition. To mention some examples: the Japanese Meiji Restoration (a bureaucratic revolution from above) occurred because the Tokugawa state (which was already highly bureaucratic) came under severe and novel pressures from imperialist capitalist Western powers; the French and Chinese Revolutions broke out because the Bourbon and Manchu regimes were caught in contradictions between pressures from economically more developed foreign states and resistance from dominant class forces at home; and the Russian Revolution broke out because the Tsarist bureaucracy and military dissolved under the impact of World War I upon economically backward Russia. Thus, it is conflict between nation-states in the context of uneven development of world capitalism that is central to the genesis of revolutions.

Processes

Marx theorized that, given a revolutionary situation, revolutions are fundamentally accomplished through class struggles led by that class which emerges within the womb of the old mode of production and becomes central to the new, post-revolutionary mode of production. Historically, only two classes play this leading revolutionary role. In bourgeois revolutions, a capitalist class that has grown up within feudalism plays the leading role. In socialist revolutions in advanced capitalist societies, the proletariat plays the leading role.

On the basis of the historical record, a reservation must be made on which classes actually are central to revolutions. In our view, revolutionary leadership has never come from those who controlled the means of production. Hence, we find no instance of a class-conscious capitalist bourgeoisie playing the leading political role in a revolution (though of course some revolutions have contributed in their outcomes to the further or future growth of capitalism and bourgeois class dominance). Moreover, because social revolutions from below have occurred in agrarian states situated in more or less disadvantaged positions within developing world capitalism, their successful occurrence has not been determined by the struggle of proletarians against capitalists, but rather by the class struggles of *peasants* against dominant landed classes and/or colonial or neo-colonial regimes.

Outcomes

Finally, we arrive at the issue of what revolutions immediately accomplish, once they have successfully occurred. Marx held that revolutions mark the transition from one mode of production to another, that they so transform class relations as to create conditions newly appropriate for further economic development. Transformations of ideology and the state also occur, but these were seen by Marx as parallel to and reinforcing the fundamental changes in class relations.

Yet, historically, revolutions have changed *state structures* as much as, or more than, they have changed class relations of production and surplus appropriation. In all of the cases of revolution from above and below that we studied, state structures became much more centralized and bureaucratic. Moreover, Third World revolutions since World War II have broken or weakened the bonds of colonial and neocolonial dependency above all by creating truly sovereign and, in some cases, mass-mobilizing national governments.[1] Equally important, the effects that revolutions have had upon the subsequent economic development of the nations they have transformed have been traceable not only to the changes in class structures but also to the *changes in state structures and functions* that the revolutions accomplished. As Immanuel Wallerstein has very aptly argued, "development [i.e., national economic development] does require a 'breakthrough.' But it is a political breakthrough that in turn makes possible the far more gradual economic process."[2]

SOCIAL STRUCTURE AND REVOLUTION

If Marx's original, elegant theory is no longer entirely adequate, then how can we make sense in new ways of revolutions in relation to the development of capitalism? Obviously, we are not going to be able to provide complete answers here. But we can propose three analytic principles that we have found especially useful in our own efforts to explain revolutions from above and below in agrarian states situated within developing world capitalism. These are: (1) a non-reductionist conception of states; (2) social-structural analyses of the situation of the peasantry within the old and new regimes; and (3) a focus on international military competition among states within the historically developing world capitalist economy. Let us elaborate each point in turn.

The State and Political Crises

We believe that states should be viewed theoretically as conditioned by, but not entirely reducible to, economic and/or class interests. States are not mere instruments of dominant class forces. Rather, states are fundamentally administrative and military organizations that extract resources from society and deploy them to maintain order at home and to compete against other states abroad. Consequently, while it is always true that states are greatly constrained by economic conditions and partly shaped and influenced by class forces, nevertheless, state structures and activities also have an underlying integrity and a logic of their own. These are keyed to the dynamics of international military rivalries and to the geo-political as well as world-economic circumstances in which given states find themselves.

This conception of states helps to make sense of certain of the facts about the causes of revolutions that seemed so jarring when placed in juxtaposition with Marx's original notions. For if states are coercive organizations not reducible to class structures, then it makes sense that processes that serve to undermine state strength should be crucial in bringing about revolutions.

In all of the five countries that we have studied most intensively—France, Russia, China, Japan and Turkey—there were, prior to the revolutions, relatively centralized and partially bureaucratic monarchical states, none of which had been incorporated into a colonial empire. As they came under pressure in a capitalist world, these states tried to mobilize national resources to stave off foreign domination—something that occurred through revolution from above in Japan and Turkey, whereas the old regimes broke down completely in France, Russia, and China, clearing the way for revolutions from below. Thus, Trimberger has demonstrated how in Japan military bureaucrats undertook a revolution from above without mass participation, which destroyed the traditional aristocracy, and established a modern state that fostered capitalist development. With more difficulty and less success, a similar process took place in Turkey. But in Bourbon France and Imperial China, as Skocpol has shown, politically powerful landed classes were able to resist state bureaucrats, undermining their attempts at modernizing reforms and causing the disintegration of centralized repressive controls over the lower classes. In Russia, the landed nobility was much less politically powerful vis-à-vis reforming state authorities, but the agrarian class structure nevertheless limited Russia's ability to prepare for the exigencies of modern warfare, so that the Tsarist state was overwhelmed and destroyed in World War I. The theoretically relevant point that applies to all of these cases regardless of the various patterns is that if one treats states theoretically as potentially autonomous vis-à-vis the existing dominant class, then one can explore the dynamic *interactions* between the state organizations and dominant class interests. In situations of intense foreign political and military pressure, these interactions can lead either to military bureaucrats' action against dominant class interests or to dominant classes acting in ways that undermine the state. Thus, our theoretical approach to the state helps make sense of the specifically political crises that launch revolutions.

This conception of the state also helps to render understandable those aspects of the processes and outcomes of revolutions that Marx's class conflict theory of revolutions seems to downplay or ignore. Revolutions are not consolidated until new or transformed state administrative and coercive organizations are securely established in the place of the old regime. Consequently, it makes sense that political leaderships—parties or bureaucratic/military cliques—that act to consolidate revolutionized state organizations should play a central role in revolutionary processes. And if states are extractive organizations that can deploy resources to some extent independently of existing class interests, then it makes sense that revolutions create the *potentials* for breakthroughs in national economic development in large part by giving rise to more powerful, centralized, and autonomous state organizations. This was true for all of the revolutions from above and below that we studied, although the potential for state-guided or initiated national economic development was more thoroughly realized in Japan, Russia, and China than it was in France and Turkey. Thus, the actual realization of the revolution-created potential depends upon the international and world-historical economic constraints and opportunities that are specific to each case after the revolution.

THE SITUATION OF THE PEASANTRY

In addition to looking at states as relatively autonomous and in dynamic interrelation with dominant classes, one should pay careful attention to the situation of the peasantry in relation to the state and dominant class. Historically, mass-based social revolutions from below have successfully occurred only if the breakdown of old-regime state organizations has happened where peasants, as the majority, producing class, possess (or obtain) sufficient local economic and political autonomy to revolt against landlords. Such revolts occurred success-fully in the French, Russian, and Chinese Revolutions alike. By contrast, the German Revo-lution of 1848–50 failed largely because conditions conducive to peasant rebellion were ab-sent east of the Elbe. And it was certainly an important condition for revolutions *from above* in Japan and Turkey that peasants in those countries remained immured within traditional structures not conducive to widespread revolts against landlords.

THE INTERNATIONAL STATE SYSTEM

Finally we arrive at an analytic emphasis that can help make sense of the entire context within which the causes and outcomes of revolutions have been shaped and their consequences de-termined. This point has two parts: (a) capitalism should be conceived not only as a mode of production based upon a relationship between wage labor and accumulating capital, but also as a world economy with various zones that are interdependent and unequal; and (b) capi-talism from its inception has developed within, around, and through a framework of "mul-tiple political sovereignties"—that is, the system of states that originally emerged from Eu-ropean feudalism and then expanded to cover the entire globe as a system of nations.

The analysis of capitalism as a competitive world system helps us to understand why there has been continual disillusionment when revolutionary outcomes have failed to mesh with ideological claims. Although there have been important variations in the state struc-tures that have emerged from revolutions, all revolutions during the evolution of world cap-italism have given rise to more bureaucratized and centralized states. We do not completely reject analyses that trace post-revolutionary bureaucratization to influences of the old re-gime or revolutionary parties. But our analysis does shift the emphasis to the necessity faced by the revolutionized regimes of coping with international pressures comparable to those that helped create the revolutionary crises in the first place. It is not just revolutions from above, but all revolutions that have become "bureaucratic revolutions" in the specific sense of creating larger, more centralized, and more autonomous state organizations than existed under the old regimes. Revolutionary leaders have sought to enhance national standing and have seen the state apparatus as the most important tool to achieve this, especially where the state could be used to guide or undertake national industrialization. International pressures have been more effective in determining the outcomes of revolutions than internal pressures for equality, participation, and decentralization. Even in China, where organized interests have fought for more equality and participation, China's vulnerable international situation has always encouraged centralization and bureaucracy.

How are we, finally, to reason about the consequences of revolutions for the develop-ment of capitalism and its eventual transformation into socialism? For Marx, this problem could be straightforwardly handled: some revolutions (i.e., bourgeois revolutions) estab-lished capitalism, while others (i.e., socialist revolutions) abolished capitalism and created the conditions for the rapid emergence of communism.

But actual revolutions have not readily conformed to the types and sequences originally projected by Marx or his successors. Certainly no country has had two successive revolu-tions, one bourgeois and the other socialist, and even revolutions that bear certain superficial resemblances to the "bourgeois" and "socialist" types do not really fit. Revolutions from above and below that have furthered bourgeois-capitalist development have not been "made by" class conscious bourgeoisie. As for "socialist revolutions," there have been revolutions made in part through class revolts from below that have culminated in the abolition of private property and the bourgeois class; yet these have occurred in "backward" agrarian countries, and not solely or primarily through proletarian class action. The outcomes of these revolutions can be described as "state socialist" in the sense that party-states have taken direct control of national economies. Yet these regimes act, so to speak, in the place of the bourgeoisie to promote national industrialization and do not conform to (or converge upon) Marx's original vision of socialism or communism.

From the perspective that capitalism is transnational in scope, we see why Marx's original typology of revolutions cannot hold. Since revolutions have occurred only in specific countries within the capitalist world economy and the international state system, and at particular times in their world-historical development, it follows that no single revolution could possibly either fully establish capitalism or entirely overcome capitalism and establish socialism.

Still, some revolutions have done better than others, and different international circumstances provide only part of the reasons. The specific societal configurations of state, economic, and class forces make a great difference in structuring the type of revolutionary outbreak and its consequences for both national and world-capitalist development.

REFERENCES

1. Dunn (1989).
2. Wallerstein (1971), p. 364.

Revolutions in Modern Dictatorships

JACK A. GOLDSTONE

Great revolutions have transformed the distant past, but they have also shaken the past hundred years. Not just kings and emperors, but modern dictators such as Porfirio Díaz in Mexico, Fulgencio Batista in Cuba, Anastasio Somoza Debayle in Nicaragua, the Shah of Iran, and Ferdinand Marcos in the Philippines were overthrown by revolutionary movements. Theories of revolution must try to explain how these events arose, and how they differed from revolutions in traditional monarchies and empires.

The classic revolutions of France in 1789, Russia in 1917, and China in 1911–1949 were revolutions against traditional monarchies or imperial states. These were premodern states dominated by traditional elites, and their revolutions drew heavily on revolts by rural peasants. However, the twentieth century has seen a different kind of revolution—revolutions

---

From Superpowers and Revolutions, *edited by Jonathon Adelman, pp. 38–48. Copyright © 1986 by Praeger Publishers, an imprint of Greenwood Publishing Group, Inc.*

against modern dictatorships. In Mexico in 1911, in Cuba in 1959, in Nicaragua and Iran in 1979, and in the Philippines in 1986, dictators who ruled semimodern states, led by modernized bureaucracies and armies instead of traditional landed elites, were overthrown. Although peasants played a significant role in several of these revolutions, a greater role was played by urban groups—both workers and modern professionals.[1] Indeed, in Iran and the Philippines, urban groups were solely responsible for the revolutions. These new kinds of revolutions call for new explanations: What were the vulnerabilities of these states that led to the overthrow of seemingly all-powerful dictators?

Revolutions occurred in traditional monarchies and imperial states, such as France, Russia, and China, when those states faced either overwhelming foreign pressures, as Russia did in World War I, or moderate foreign pressures combined with paralyzing opposition to needed economic and administrative change from traditional elites. Failure to cope with war or paralysis due to the opposition of traditional elites opened the way for popular revolts that undermined the old regime. Modernizing elites drawn from urban professional and middle-class groups completed the dismantling of old regime institutions and sought to restructure state and society on a more modern basis.

Foreign pressures, conflict with elites, and popular revolts have all combined in bringing about recent revolutions, and we shall return to many of these themes. However, one key lesson of comparative studies is that the vulnerability of states to revolutions differs among states with different institutions. Thus we need to consider how contemporary states differ from traditional monarchies and imperial states, and why modern dictatorships have been vulnerable to revolution.

Contemporary states generally have governments in which the chief executive's and other officials' rule are based on some form of constitutional and parliamentary political arrangements rather than simply hereditary authority, and in which traditional landed elites have no institutionalized roles in administration. Instead, the chief executive's role is organized through political party mechanisms and sanctioned through a combination of electoral, bureaucratic, and military rule.

Some contemporary states seem to show such modern party-based governments, but in fact these governments are so strongly manipulated by a single, powerful individual that they are, in practice, dictatorships. Among such states, the United States has often sought regional allies based on personal relationships with strong leaders, such as the Somozas in Nicaragua or the Shah in Iran. However, these states have characteristics that make them vulnerable to revolution. To understand the processes that can lead such states to revolution, we need to examine the structure and the weaknesses of these states.

THE NEOPATRIMONIAL STATE
AND ITS VULNERABILITIES

S. N. Eisenstadt (1978) has described as "neopatrimonial" those partially modernized states in which there appears to be modern bureaucratic and party-based government, but in fact a single powerful person rules society through an extensive system of personal patronage, rather than obedience to impersonal laws. Such states may have democratic trappings, including parliaments and political parties, constitutions and elections. However, it is recognized by all that the decisions of the chief of state are quite secure, as the patronage system, plus coercion where necessary, secures the compliance of the legislature and the political parties, the favorable interpretation of the constitution, and electoral victories. Examples include Mexico under Porfirio Díaz, Nicaragua under the Somozas, the Philippines under Ferdinand Marcos, and Iran under the Shah.

In such states, the masses are generally depoliticized. They may participate in periodic elections under the eye of local state servants; however, their interest in the economy and the polity is largely defensive. Their goal is merely to preserve their livelihood, with as little contact with the state authorities as possible. Whether in urban or rural settings, a secure if modest income and traditional habitations and culture are their requisites.

The elites in such states, by contrast, are highly politicized. The chief executive therefore is in a situation where he or she must broker among highly active elite segments. These commonly include traditional oligarchs, new professionals, and military/bureaucratic elites. Traditional oligarchs are generally strong supporters of the state; they usually depend on ownership of land, and while they have traditionally enjoyed the support of the state, they have also controlled their own networks of patronage and coercion. New professionals are the products of the introduction of modern systems of education, law, medicine, and communication. Engineers, journalists, lawyers, doctors, teachers, and business people, they are characteristically rooted in urban settings, and have strong contacts with international business and culture. If one adds skilled workers to these groups, they constitute the bulk of the urban middle classes.

The military/bureaucratic elites comprise the arms of the state. However, they are a force unto themselves with their own interests. They may support the old oligarchs, the new professionals, or the chief executive in the event of policy or financial conflicts. Or they may be rendered impotent by internal splits and corruption. Their loyalty to the chief executive varies, for that loyalty too depends on the workings of the patronage system. In short, neopatrimonial states rely on the support of a diverse assemblage of elites, themselves often divided, to maintain authority over a largely depoliticized population.

This kind of state has varied vulnerabilities. First, since it relies chiefly on elite support, rather than on mass support, alienation of too many segments of the elite can be fatal. Second, since the elites themselves are divided, the chief executive must perform a complex balancing act to preserve the alliance of diverse elites while fending off their intra-elite conflicts. Third, since the population is depoliticized, the state can be threatened by mass-mobilizing movements that place new forces in the political arena. Thus, the defection of elites, plus the willingness of elites to mobilize masses against the state, can leave the chief executive with few defenses other than sheer armed force, whose loyalty itself is never assured.

How does the chief executive maintain authority, indeed an authority that seems near absolute, in such precarious conditions? The typical strategy is a mix of divide and conquer, carrot and stick, and indispensability approaches.

In neopatrimonial states, the chief executive generally faces elites with divided goals. Rather than attempt to unify them, the executive generally chooses to reinforce their divisions. The armed forces, political parties, urban professionals, landed oligarchs, and state bureaucrats are each encouraged to form direct, competing links to the chief executive's patronage network. The armed forces, political party leaders, and state officials may be encouraged to share in corruption or in secret deals and partnerships in order to isolate them from other groups. As a result, different elite segments find themselves in competition for the ear of, and the official power and financial advantages conferred by, the chief executive.

The chief executive then becomes the crucial broker of power in the society, its sole political "center." The divisions among the elites make reliance on the chief executive essential for political coordination and conflict management.

Of course, the ability of the executive to manage such conflict and provide central coordination depends on the ability to dispense resources valued by the elite, chiefly money and political power. Thus chief executives seek to implement policies for rapid economic growth, or for massive infusions of foreign aid. Such growth enriches the executive, of course, but it also provides the essential fuel to power political machinery.

Contemporary neopatrimonial states usually seek to turn economic growth to modernization of the armed forces, growth of enterprises requiring professional and skilled workers, and growth of the state bureaucracy. This gives the executive the ability to dispense the carrots of military and bureaucratic posts, and economic contracts that will profit the elite. In addition, securing the loyalty of the landed elite generally requires that land reforms be kept moderate. Depoliticization of the masses is also served by economic growth sufficient to allow growing populations to sustain themselves at traditionally accustomed levels of food, clothing, and shelter.

Policies for promotion of economic growth are coupled with the stick—the threat of loss of wealth, position, liberty, or life for opposing the chief executive. Potential opposition leaders are often jailed or exiled, political freedoms (including freedom of speech) are limited, and even loyal aides whose accomplishments or influence threaten to make them alternative leaders may be promptly disposed of.

In addition to these strategies, the chief executive seeks to increase his or her "indispensability" by monopolizing key contact points in the society. The chief executive may be the only contact between the military and the civilian elites. The executive (and his or her close associates) may monopolize contact with foreign nations, seeking to become the indispensable conduit for foreign aid and investment. The chief executive generally seeks to avoid appointing, or even favoring, possible successors. Thus, the executive seeks to reinforce the fear that, if he or she is lost, political coordination, conflict management, and the flow of foreign resources will fail, leading to chaos.

These are potent strategies. Provided that economic growth provides resources, a politically adept chief executive, by skillful manipulation of elite aspirations and rewards, forging of strong ties to foreign powers, and limited coercion, can achieve and maintain a substantial concentration of power. The Shah of Iran, the Somozas in Nicaragua, the Diem regime in South Vietnam, Díaz in Mexico, Marcos in the Philippines, Batista in Cuba, Chiang Kai-shek in China, Mobutu in Zaire, and Suharto in Indonesia are examples of chief executives who typified this pattern.

PRESSURES AND PROBLEMS
IN NEOPATRIMONIAL STATES

Despite the initial considerable success of most neopatrimonial executives, their vulnerabilities do not disappear; indeed, they may increase over time.

First, as economic growth continues, the ability of the executive to broker the conflicting demands of the elites becomes more difficult. As foreign investment grows, domestic urban and professional elites may seek greater domestic control of the economy. Nationalism then becomes a potent ideology among a segment of the elites. The executive must thus balance increased reliance on foreign aid and foreign investment, which increases the resources that the executive controls but requires satisfaction of foreign investors and states, against satisfying the demands of domestic professional and economic elites for national self-determination.

Second, as urbanization and industry grow, the urban and professional elite and skilled workers may seek a domestic economy more geared to satisfaction of domestic consumption than to export growth and luxury imports. Yet establishing light industry and a domestic consumer market requires improving the education and economic status of the populace, including the peasantry. This goal can come into conflict with the desires of the landed oligarchy to maintain their control of land and the rural labor force.

Third, as the state bureaucracy expands, it eventually comes into conflict with traditional organizations, including guilds, local village councils, and religious organizations. Where the state is successful in absorbing or circumventing the influence of these bodies, state power may increase. Yet this is difficult where the autonomy of these organizations is well established, and the traditional organizations control considerable resources and cultural authority. Conflicts between state and church may arise over secularization of economic life, over control of popular education and local justice, over disposal of church resources, and over cultural and ideological hegemony. Any of these conflicts can spur religious elites to seek alliances with other elite segments against the state, or to support popular mobilization against the state, as happened in Iran.

Fourth, the temptation to monopolize resources may become a self-defeating one. If the chief executive concentrates power and the proceeds of corruption too closely in the hands of family and cronies, the flow of carrots to diverse elite segments diminishes. Where elites find themselves excluded from their traditional, albeit limited, share in government and wealth, dependency on the chief executive quickly turns to animosity. Overuse of the stick and restriction of carrots is one of the most common errors of neopatrimonial executives over the course of their rule.

Fifth, a temptation to rely too heavily on foreign support may become fatal. Foreign support, whether in terms of financial aid through grants and foreign investment, or military aid, is highly attractive to neopatrimonial executives. It is a source of economic and political resources and, most importantly, a source over which the chief executive can establish exclusive control. As it becomes more difficult to satisfy conflicting demands and aspirations, and since there is no mass popular base to counterbalance the elites, there is a temptation to rely increasingly on foreign support. Yet this can further alienate the elites by frustrating their nationalist ambitions, and leaves the executive in a highly extended and vulnerable position if foreign support should fall.

Finally, the economic growth that fuels the patronage machine may falter. Growth may also fail to trickle down to the masses, or population increase may outrun economic growth, resulting in growing inequality and failure to meet traditional popular aspirations for diet, habitation, and family life.

If several of these problems develop at the same time, this combination of pressures can cause a patrimonial regime to unravel with astonishing rapidity. Economic setbacks and overuse of coercion may begin a trend of elite defection and attempts at mobilizing the masses against the state. Overdependence on foreign support may leave the chief executive isolated and vulnerable to nationalist movements. Finally, if elites overcome their divisions to unite against the executive, and if the loyalty of the army should falter or be pressed by widespread popular mobilization against the regime in urban or rural revolts, revolution becomes nearly inevitable. This course of events unfolded in the Mexican, Cuban, Nicaraguan, Philippine, and Iranian revolutions.

The very indispensability of the chief executive works against a smooth transfer of power to another leader, and against maintenance of existing institutions. These are too deeply identified with the chief executive's system of personal rule to survive his or her fall from power. For example, the solution of "Somozism without Somoza" in Nicaragua, or of a new minister (Bahktiar) at the head of the Shah's state in Iran, had little appeal to elites seeking to establish their autonomy, reverse their exclusion from control of the state, and satisfy the aspirations of their now-mobilized popular supporters. Once the chief executive has lost elite support, and the masses are mobilized against him or her, the result is almost certain to be transformation of state institutions and unpredictable turns in policy and economic organization as elite segments vie for state control, court popular support, and seek to reconstruct state institutions.

THE ROLE OF INTERNATIONAL SUPERPOWERS IN MODERN REVOLUTIONS

International pressures have always been an important factor in the development of revolutionary crises. Such pressures have become even more important in the contemporary world, as international superpowers—the United States and the Soviet Union—have sought to support or undermine regimes in developing states in pursuit of geopolitical strategy. Yet U.S. efforts to support regional allies in Vietnam, Nicaragua, Iran, and the Philippines have been overturned by revolutions. In light of U.S. support for these fallen regimes, we need to ask: How did U.S. policy exacerbate the vulnerability of neopatrimonial states? And what effect did U.S. actions have once a revolution had begun?

U.S. policy eventually weakened neopatrimonial regimes in three ways. First, overdependence on the United States was encouraged. A massive flow of foreign and military aid often precluded the need for a foreign executive to build a domestic base. Instead, the resource flow encouraged the executive to continue to play the game of selectively dispensing or withholding patronage resources.

Second, overidentification of the chief executive with U.S. aid irritated elites and provoked nationalist opposition to the regime. In the eyes of many elites and popular groups, opposition to the chief executive became synonymous with opposition to the United States and with asserting national self-determination.

Third, while the United States sought to increase the dependence of the chief executive on U.S. aid, it also sought to impose domestic policies that weakened the executive—limits on coercion, greater political expression for professional elites and skilled workers, meaningful elections, and restrictions on corruption. All of these are desirable steps in the democratization of regimes; however, these steps also undermine the power of dictatorship. U.S. policy thus sought inherently contradictory objectives; choosing neopatrimonial rulers as allies and seeking to support their regimes meant that the overriding goal of U.S. foreign policy—encouraging democratization—was incompatible with keeping these geopolitical allies, for democratization would undermine the rulers that the United States claimed to support.

U.S. policy thus swung back and forth between its contradictory goals. Initially, the United States would support the neopatrimonial rulers with arms and money, while giving only lip service to the goals of greater human rights, political freedom, and democratization in these states. Later, when the ruler's abuses of power became too visible, the United States would demand that neopatrimonial rulers take action to pursue democratization. These policy swings precipitated disasters by putting neopatrimonial rulers in an impossible position—if they enacted liberalizing reforms, they undermined the basis of their rule; if they did not enact such reforms, they lost the U.S. aid essential to maintaining the patronage that supported their rule.

Moreover, such policy swings not only guaranteed that the neopatrimonial rulers would falter, but they also reduced the credibility and influence of the United States with opponents and likely successors of the regime. In times when the United States seemed satisfied with lip service regarding protection of human rights and democratization, the United States came to be viewed by domestic elites and popular groups as an insincere and untrustworthy advocate of popular rights and national self-determination. Thus, in the event that the executive faltered, successor elites were unlikely to view the United States favorably, either as a mediator for succession or as a continuing ally.

Exactly this course was followed in Iran and Nicaragua in the late 1970s. After decades of almost unconditional support of the Shah and the Somoza family, during which time the privileges of domestic elites were gradually curtailed and the chief executive was aggrandized through manipulation of growing foreign investment and aid, the United States began to insist on a human rights policy that undermined the neopatrimonial patterns of rule. The result was greater room to maneuver for the domestic opposition to the Shah in Iran, and to Somoza in Nicaragua. Yet the Shah and Somoza sought to enact only limited reforms, to change as little as possible while still satisfying the United States. Continued support for the Shah and for Somoza thus brought policy debacles: The domestic elites perceived the United States as hypocritically supporting reforms that changed little, and maintaining support for a repressive regime; yet the atmosphere of reform and U.S. pressure hindered the chief executives while emboldening the oppositions in their quest for change. The increased vigor of the oppositions, and the ambiguous, shifting support for the rulers, initiated an escalation of opposition that culminated in 1979 in revolutions in both Iran and Nicaragua. Both revolutions brought to power elites who were hostile to the United States and who sought to realign the foreign policy of what had been a steadfast ally. Even in the Philippines, where a similar pattern of support for Marcos' neopatrimonial regime had been changed more dramatically (although at the last moment), to support for the democratic opposition, the credibility of the United States had been so damaged by its former support for Marcos that nationalist and anti-United States feelings remained strong. As a result, the United States lost the use of major military installations in the Philippines, and is still viewed with suspicion by the shifting set of elites who have replaced the Marcos regime.

CONCLUSION

Modern personalist dictatorships, which are structured as neopatrimonial regimes, can appear very strong in the short term. When they can keep elites divided, use patronage to keep key elites and the military loyal, and keep the population depoliticized, neopatrimonial rulers can maintain their regimes for decades. But they are vulnerable on several points. First, the regime has a precarious dominance over diverse elites; elite loyalty can quickly be withdrawn if the regime fails to provide the rewards the elites have come to expect. Second, lacking its own mass base, the regime is highly vulnerable to mass mobilization by domestic elites in opposition to the regime. Moreover, many trends in early economic development—growing inequality; failure of popular income to provide traditional levels of food, habitation, and family lifestyles; the growth of urban professional and skilled workers; dependence on exports subject to cycles of boom and bust; international debt; and inflation—are precisely those that encourage mass mobilization. Third, superpower influence can be beneficial in limited amounts, but also can be pernicious and threatening to national self-determination in large amounts. Indeed, superpower influence can be fatal to neopatrimonial regimes when superpower policy swings between contradictory goals, undermining the basis for such regimes.

All of these vulnerabilities can rapidly appear once a neopatrimonial regime starts to lose its control of economic resources or foreign support. Thus, the same dictatorships that appeared so strong can quickly become the sites of modern revolutions.

REFERENCE

1.   The special characteristics of revolutions in modern dictatorships have been pointed out by Dix (1983), Farhi (1990), Gugler (1982), Liu (1988), and Shugart (1989).

Agency and Culture in Revolutions
ERIC SELBIN

In the 1970s and 1980s, scholars studying revolutions focused their attention on long-term characteristics of states and societies that heighten their risk of revolution. These might include the presence of elites who have leverage against the state, or a state having military and financial resources that are weaker than those of its main foreign opponents. However, in focusing on these "macro" or large-scale structural causes, scholars seemed to lose an appreciation for the critical role of ideas, and the decisions of key individuals, as elements that make revolutions happen. In this essay, Selbin aims to redress that imbalance by emphasizing the pivotal role of individual actors ("agency") and ideas ("culture") in the development of revolutionary struggles.

In 1958, at a critical juncture in the struggle of the Cuban revolutionaries for political power, Fidel Castro made a consequential decision. In one of the most important military and psychological campaigns of the revolution, Castro paired his most charismatic lieutenants and sent Ché Guevara and Camilo Cienfuegos out to replicate the famous "incendiary" march of the Cuban War of Independence when national heroes Antonio Maceo and General Máximo Gómez lit up the sugar cane fields. This exploit was hugely successful, consciously evoking the link with Cuba's struggle for independence from Spain and capturing the popular imagination. Moreover, the ability of Guevara and Cienfuegos to rally the population to the revolutionary cause, along with their military skill, became important elements in Cuban revolutionary mythology as well as a component in the enshrinement of both Guevara and Cienfuegos as national heroes.

Symbolic politics, collective memory, and the social context of politics—all profoundly voluntaristic constructions—are central to understanding and exploring revolutionary processes. What I want to propose here is that ideas and actors, not structures and some broad sweep of history, are the primary forces in revolutionary processes. Revolutions are human creations—with all the messiness inherent in such a claim—rather than inevitable natural processes. The focus, therefore, needs to be on people, not structures; choices, not determinism; and the transformation of society, not simply transitions.

Forrest Colburn and I have called for the return of people and their ideas to a place of prominence in understanding and exploring revolutionary processes.[1] Some of the leading young figures in the field, such as John Foran, Jack Goldstone, Jeff Goodwin, and Timothy Wickham-Crowley, have cast their nets somewhat wider, calling for increased attention to the role of culture as at least a variable in the mix of factors. All of us have sought to varying degrees to wrestle with the paradox of agents and structures and their role and utility in theorizing about revolutions.

Since 1979 theorizing has been dominated by Theda Skocpol's brilliant, paradigmatic statement in *States and Social Revolutions*. Her memorable invocation of Wendell Phillips's declaration that "revolutions are not made; they come" stands as the *sine qua non* structuralist position. A structuralist perspective, according to Skocpol, stresses "objective relationships and conflicts among variously situated groups and nations, rather than the interests, outlooks, or ideologies of particular actors in revolution."[2] People's responses to structural conditions are construed as irrelevant and those who make the revolution are conspicuous by their absence. The failure to include the efforts and intentions of people assumes that structural conditions dictate absolutely what people can do.

The younger scholars of revolution mentioned above have moved beyond such smothering structuralism. Meaningful places for agents and the impact of culture have crept into the discussion and been treated by and large as having a legitimate place at the table, although the place traditionally reserved for children—seen and not heard unless politely asking for someone to pass the platter. Most of these scholars remain profoundly in the thrall of structuralist perspectives; the small place made for agents and culture needs to be expanded.

I believe that it is possible to construct sophisticated and substantively grounded theories that recognize the power and importance of people *and* structures; the utility gained by

---

holding these analytically distinct pales next to the violence done to reality. The cases with which I am most familiar, the modern Latin American revolutions, have been typified by profoundly multi-class alliances and high degrees of voluntarism: the conscious choices and intentional actions of people have played clearly critical roles throughout the revolutionary processes. The structuralist tendency to omit people and their choices serves us poorly in our efforts to be theoretically sophisticated and substantively grounded.

THE BRIEF FOR AGENCY AND CULTURE

The legacy of revolutionary activity in Latin America and the Caribbean is most commonly symbolized by places, dates, and, above all, by heroes: Túpac Amaru, Toussaint L'Ouverture, Jóse Martí, Zapata, Mariátegui, Sandino, Farabundo Martí, Prestes, and "Ché." From the first defiance against the Spanish conquerors, subsequent generations of revolutionaries have sought to enable and ennoble their efforts by invoking these figures and the ideals that they and their struggles purportedly represent; conversely, populations have sought to identify and understand their struggles through the mythos generated around these figures. The cult of the heroic revolutionary has produced in many places a popular political culture of resistance, rebellion, and revolution.

The proposition here is that a crucial component of the revolutionary potential in any population is an understanding of the population's perception of the options that are available and seem plausible to them; these options constitute "repertoires of collective action" and/or a "tool-kit" of symbols, stories, rituals and world-views, which provide actors with resources necessary for constructing strategies of action for dealing with their society. In societies where revolution is considered a viable response to oppression—due to a long-standing history of rebellious activities being celebrated in folk culture or to revolutionary leaders having created, restored, or magnified such traditions in the local culture or some combination of these—revolutionary activities are more likely to be undertaken, more likely to receive broad popular support, and more likely to conclude successfully when such traditions are invoked.

In what follows, I shall undertake to make a case that it is imperative that agents and the world they manufacture, the culture they create, be included in any serious analysis of revolution.

AGENCY: IDEAS, IDEALS, AND LEARNING

People's thoughts and actions—even if haphazard or spontaneous—are the mediating link between structural conditions and social outcomes. Structural conditions, moreover, do not unconditionally dictate what people do; instead, they place certain limits on people's actions or demarcate a certain range of possibilities. Within the revolutionary process, there is more than one path and more than one potential outcome. Structural conditions may define the possibilities for revolutionary insurrections or the options available after political power has been seized, but they do not explain how specific groups or individuals act, what options they pursue, or what possibilities they may realize. The question is where and how people enter the revolutionary process.

There are two places in which the critical role of individuals is discernible in the revolutionary process. Leaders play a unique role in social revolutions, organizing the population, and, perhaps most importantly, articulating the vision—the ideas and ideals—around which they rally. The population, in turn, responds to these entreaties or not; if they do, it is they who determine how far and how fast the process unfolds and often shape the efforts of the leaders to their reality. We need fundamentally to refocus the discussion of profound change or transformation on the power and possibility of individuals to control their destiny.

Social revolutionary leaders invoke, manipulate, and build on timeless conceptions to arouse and mobilize the population. The ideals of justice, liberty, equality, democracy, opportunity, and freedom (from fear, from hunger, from disease; of assembly, of speech, of religion) remain powerful and compelling in a world where many people's daily lives reflect none of these. Aware of the dangers, some people nonetheless chose to struggle to transform their world. Revolutionary ideals become the talisman or the touchstone which carries the revolutionaries and the population through the arduous struggle.

Idea streams—transmitted via people—are powerful and pervasive and travel across time and space. People learn, taking into account past experiences and factoring in new information. While it would be disingenuous to suggest that social revolutions somehow constitute an unbroken process, it is evident that modern revolutionaries have to some degree imitated the "classic" revolutions of France, Russia, Mexico, and China. There are also strong historical and contemporary connections among the modern revolutions. Both types of connections are discernible in the modern Latin American revolutions.

The Cuban revolutionaries drew on a wide array of sources, including Cuba's earlier struggle for independence, the Mexican Revolution, the revolt of Sandino in Nicaragua, the incomplete revolution in Bolivia, even the destruction of democracy in Spain (1936–39) and Guatemala (1954).

The Nicaraguan revolutionaries were inspired and influenced by the Mexican Revolution, past revolts in Nicaragua, and the Cubans. And connections were not solely limited to the continent. Iran's leftist guerrilla movements, inspired in part by the Cuban Revolution and the writings of Ché Guevara, played a decisive role in the 1979 victory of the Iranian Revolution. In the spring and summer of 1979 one of the most popular items in Teheran were Ché T-shirts. The connections are across time and within time, across cultural boundaries and within them.

CULTURE: STORIES OF RESISTANCE AND REBELLION

Traditionally, history has been constructed from above, composed by the victorious, orchestrated by the powerful, played for the population. There is another history, rooted in people's perception of how the world around them has and continues to unfold and their place in that process. This is a history informed by people's ideology and which reflects the context—material as well as ideological—of people's everyday lives, a history revealed and articulated by the various instruments of popular political culture.

The supposition here is that this history is accessible to us in people's narratives of their lives and the popular political culture of their society, and that these create the possibility—or lack thereof—for fundamental change. The proposition is that through in-depth interviewing and the collection of instruments of popular culture—folk tales, songs, plays, etc.—it may be possible to ascertain the extent to which high-profile collective action, specifically rebellion or revolution, is possible, perhaps even probable in any given society.

It seems simultaneously risky and trite to invoke culture. Risky thanks to the rather sordid legacy of "cultural explanations" which once and, on occasion, continue to besmirch the social sciences: stolid Brits, hot-blooded Latins, obedient and efficient Germans, indolent Italians, breezy "Americans," mysterious Asians, and so on. Such gross and racist generalizations did little to advance either social science or humanity. Trite because any number of scholars have directly or indirectly recognized the importance and utility of culture in the study of a wide array of issues, including those that fall within the social sciences. There are sightings aplenty among students of revolution and popular collective action.

Nonetheless, "culture" poses a problem, not least with the word itself, a wildly imprecise term that in its promiscuity veers dangerously close to losing any utility at all. In an effort to surmount such problems, I start with a fairly traditional notion of culture and seek to expand it by invoking the power and depth of collective memory and the potency and prominence of symbols. These are drawn together by the now familiar demand that a focus on individuals is critical in our efforts to understand revolutionary processes.

How much did the Cuban revolutionaries' ability to invoke José Martí and his vision figure in their success? Did the Bolivians' unwillingness to evoke a revolutionary or even rebellious tradition serve to derail the revolutionary process? There seems little question that in Nicaragua the revolutionaries' use of the figure and persona of Sandino was central to their success. Might a similar culture of resistance and rebellion have made a difference for the Grenadians? How were/are the efforts of Salvadoran, Peruvian, and, most recently, Mexican revolutionaries affected by their ability to invoke, evoke, and manipulate the legacies of Farabundo Martí, Mariátegui and Amaru, and Zapata, respectively?

Culture alone is not enough. The ability of revolutionaries, specifically revolutionary leaders, to conjure a context in which such traditions play out—are summoned, manipulated, rewritten—is often significant. Yet the population is not passive, waiting to be acted upon. While the revolutionaries may provide an impetus and may present the population with a vocabulary or intellectual framework that helps organize and channel their visions, revolutionary leaders can go no farther than the population is prepared for them to go. People have their context, independent of the desires of the revolutionaries.

The means by which we can gain access to such stories is primarily through narrative. There is, apparently, an old Andean tradition, specifically female, which conceives of history as a woven cloth; it consists in recognizing the warp and weft, the texture, the forms of relationships, in knowing the back from the front, the value and significance of the detailed pattern, and so on. In other words, we are trying to read in the book of life that which has never been recorded in written form; we are attempting to capture the image brought to mind and revealed in the moment of the interview before it is lost again to silence.[3]

The scattered shards and remnants are out there for us to gather.

Finding a balance between the important and powerful information that a cultural perspective can provide us with and the powerful and compelling picture provided us by structural perspectives seems crucial. Those of us labeled as advocates of a more culturally oriented position have an obligation to match the rigorous and sophisticated methods of our more structuralist colleagues; they might do well to recognize that in their concern with independent and dependent variables they too often omit critical elements of the story. A surprising number of people under an array of circumstances have left the private space of their homes and fought in public space for public goods in pursuit of private desires. How and why they cross that threshold from the inside to the outside in an effort to transform their world remains the central puzzle for us all.

THE MARRIAGE OF AGENCY AND CULTURE:
THE SOCIAL CONTEXT OF POLITICS

John Foran has asked what the precise mechanisms of cultural influence on revolutionary processes are and how we might marry increased roles for agency and culture with previous insights on structure and political economy. His answers involve "the concept of 'political cultures of resistance and opposition' . . . and how these interact with the social forces that make revolutions."[4] I concur with Foran's prescription.

Students of revolution need to take seriously the notion that theories of revolution are rooted in and driven by a focus on individuals and the culture that they create and transmit. This occurs through the mechanisms of collective memory, symbolic politics, and the social context of politics they create. While any good theory must blend elements of agents and structures, the contention here is that without people articulating compelling stories with engaging and empowering plots, revolutions will not come.

Culture denotes "a system of shared meanings, attitudes, and values and the symbolic forms (performances, artifacts) in which they are expressed or embodied"; in this sense, "culture . . . is part of a total way of life but not identical with it,"[5] a place where simultaneously life is justified and explained and where the possibility of changing that life is raised. The capacity of people to create, enshrine, manipulate, and discard symbols is central to the conception of culture. Those symbols which can integrate the past, present, and future into a coherent view of the world, into one usable myth with near universal overtones, are of particular importance and power. Those in power endeavor to invoke/create symbols which will maintain their status; those arrayed against them seek to use symbols—sometimes the very same symbols—to overturn them. Thus popular culture, beliefs and practices held by a wide array of those in any given society, becomes a battleground.

Contention and confrontation over these symbols are intense and the ramifications and implications profound. The material and ideological conditions of people's everyday lives lead inexorably to issues of power and choice and their attendant interplay. Political culture, at least in theory, should offer us access to that world.

COLLECTIVE MEMORY AND SYMBOLIC POLITICS

Remembering serves a multitude of functions; primarily it places the past in the service of the present; as the maxim has it, those who control the past control the present. The implication is clear: there is a societal memory which is up for grabs, a battlefield where various groups struggle to protect and extend their interpretations of a society's past.

Most resistance movements conceive of and understand their struggles as continuing some long process of struggle that many societies hold in their collective memory. Such collective memory is usually long on the grand and glorious but often features the implicit and the informal as well; this shared memory includes the origins, purpose, development, and group life. Similar to ideology, collective memory gives shape to people's lives, providing not only a base from which individuals can look back and explain their experiences and actions, but also a platform on which to build and guide the future. Revolutionaries, historically, have recognized the need to tap into and build on popular expressions of this collective memory.

How do societies remember? "What are 'the channels and repositories of memory'?" Collective memory, Jelin suggests, "is the part of history that can be integrated into a current value system; the rest is ignored, forgotten, although at times it may be reclaimed and remembered."[6] Jelin's analysis is compelling but incomplete; reclamation and remembering do not occur "at times." People's history, captured in their memories, runs constantly in the background, always available.

As a result, the past is continually rewritten, often to fit the exigencies of the present. This is especially the case when current reality makes people think about their role in shaping that process. This process may not be entirely intentional, since the past is not conveniently organized like a filing cabinet or library. Intentionality is evident, however, in the degree to which people use memory to explain themselves, justify themselves, and to give legitimacy to the current order, or to contest it. The result is that "the historical present is constructed by subjects in dispute about the meaning of history and the contents of tradition and values," a dispute that centers largely on individual and collective memories.[7]

And when those individual memories are shared, perhaps quietly in the evenings, perhaps more openly in songs or skits, together those individual memories form a collective memory, a shared history. This history is "a reservoir where glimpses of freedom, and the remembrance of atrocities and triumphs are all preserved."[8] Such a "reservoir" need not be reclaimed and remembered; it is, rather, in use or on tap, waiting to be drawn upon. These reservoirs are not the province of any one individual; rather, human repositories contribute to a collective maintenance of knowledge.

The importance of symbolic politics has been ignored for too long in the study of revolution; revolutionary thinkers have all discussed at length the complex but critical process whereby the revolutionaries must gain the support of the people, that is, to win their hearts and minds. In 1995 Alison Brysk provided a wonderful and compelling reintroduction to the power and persuasiveness of symbolic politics. Noting that dominant "models of collective action slight this ancient, universal source of social change," she invoked "a renewed consideration of the subjective influences of ideas, learning, and information as sources of political change." Perhaps most importantly for our purposes, Brysk claims that "symbolically mobilized political actors can create new political opportunities by revealing, challenging, and changing narratives about interests and identities."[9] In those societies where resistance, rebellion, and revolution are part of the popular political culture, revolutionary activities are more likely to be undertaken.

CONCLUSIONS

The historical world, that is, the world's past as we understand it, is fundamentally the world of human action. Structures have their place. Few subscribe wholeheartedly to one extreme or the other anymore in the debate over the relative weight and dialectical relationship between individual and collective will as opposed to historical circumstances in determining the outcome of a given event or process. Structuralism and agency may each, in particular circumstances, be significant; the scope for human action depends on historically specific conditions. People's actions clearly confront certain limits that structures engender; often structures demarcate a certain range of possibilities. But structures do not unconditionally dictate what people do. The interplay of circumstance and action—neither of which can exist without the other—creates human history; options are considered, choices are made, paths are pursued. Meaningful explorations and satisfactory answers lie with those theories which can take agents and structures, both with meaningful roles, into account.

Assessing the degree to which traditions of revolutionary activity and struggle broaden the array of possibilities that oppressed citizens view as accessible to them is a larger project which remains to be undertaken. The focus needs to be on what options populations consider available to them when they seek redress of their grievances and to what extent popular political culture and its instruments serve to keep alive and glorify people and processes which can serve as latent forms of empowerment, memories waiting to be animated either by popular leaders or by the population themselves. Such a project would endeavor to map out the ways in which the populations of a variety of countries have told and retold their history with specific reference to rebellion and revolution and the impact these acts have had on the possibilities for and occurrence of such phenomena in the respective countries.

Foran has argued that it is critical to better integrate "understandings of how culture . . . becomes effective in the causation, course, and outcomes of social revolutions . . . [and] the whole issue of agency[:] . . . who makes revolutions and why." The key here is accepting the mutually reinforcing arguments of Goldstone and Tilly with regard to analyzing revolution: the former has argued that "analyzing revolutions does not depend on identifying a particular fixed characteristic set of causes—there is none. Instead, analyzing revolutions depends on understanding the process of revolution and being able to track its trajectory in diverse cases"; the latter has maintained that we must "break revolutions into components . . . which [are] theoretically coherent, then construct separate theories of those components."[10] People are part of that trajectory; culture is a key component.

The contention here is that structural theories alone will never allow us to ascertain whether a social revolution occurred in any particular instance. It is time to turn around Phillips's statement: revolutions do not come; they are made.

REFERENCES

1. Colburn (1994); Selbin (1993).
2. Skocpol (1979), p. 291.
3. Rivera Cusicanqui (1990), p. 180.
4. Foran (1997a), p. 207.
5. Burke (1978), p. 1.
6. Jelin (1994), p. 50.
7. Ibid., p. 50.
8. Watson (1993), p. 15.
9. Brysk (1995).
10. Foran (1995), p. 133; Goldstone (1995), pp. 45–46; Tilly (1994), p. 802.

CHAPTER 4

The Outcomes of Revolutions

Revolutions have numerous accomplishments to their credit. They have redistributed land, done away with tyrannical dictators and oppressive systems of land tenure, and eliminated the hereditary privileges of traditional aristocracies. They have brought increases in literacy, better education and health care, greater pride in national strength, and independence to hundreds of millions. Yet revolutions have generally failed to deliver on their chief promises: greater freedom, material well-being, and equality for all. In many countries, revolutions have led to more powerful and authoritarian regimes than the ones they replaced. And peasants' initial gains have often been weakened through policies of industrialization (in both capitalist and socialist countries) that diverted resources from the peasantry to urban centers. The implementation of these policies maintained or increased inequality while the lot of peasants stagnated or even deteriorated with population increase.

Furthermore, we must always ask the question: Have the accomplishments been worth the price? Civil and international wars and severe economic dislocations often accompany revolutionary transformations. Experts estimate that over 100,000 people died in the civil wars of the English Revolution, that 1.3 million of a total French population of 26 million died in 1789–1815 in the civil and Napoleonic wars, that over 2 million of a population of 16–17 million died in the course of the Mexican Revolution, and that in the civil wars and the initial steps to collectivize agriculture in Russia and China, war and dislocations in agriculture led to tens of millions of deaths. The recent Nicaraguan Revolution caused some 50,000 deaths in a population of 2.5 million, and the casualties of Iran's war with Iraq, which followed Iran's revolution, were in the hundreds of thousands.

The following essays present a variety of evidence to examine these difficult issues. Though they differ in approach, all these analyses share two conclusions. First, revolutions do not create a "clean slate." The conditions and habits of people under the old regime very much affect the outcomes of revolutions. Second, these outcomes reveal zigs and zags in state policies and their results so that these outcomes are never quite what the revolution's leaders or supporters first expected.

Revolution and the Rebirth of Inequality:
Stratification in Postrevolutionary Society

JONATHAN KELLEY AND HERBERT S. KLEIN

Revolutions generally seek to bring greater justice and equality to societies. Therefore, they aim to change the magnitude of the differences in wealth, income, and status among individuals (inequality), and the system by which rewards and status are
assigned by society (stratification). In this chapter, Jonathan Kelley and Herbert S.
Klein describe why, despite the efforts of revolutionaries, inequality and stratification systems are likely to reemerge in any postrevolutionary society. Kelley and
Klein note that in the short run, revolutions generally reduce inequality. But in the
long run, inequality is likely to reemerge. Revolutions may destroy hereditary titles
and privileges and break up large landholdings. They may even do away with private
property entirely. Yet revolutions also provide new opportunities in administration and management and, where private property is maintained, in small business
and services. In these pursuits, those possessing education and skills—that is, human capital—have an advantage. That advantage generally translates into higher
position and higher income. In addition, industrialization places an even greater
premium on academic, technical, and managerial skills. To the extent that postrevolutionary regimes aggressively pursue industrialization, inequalities of opportunity and reward are likely to increase rapidly.

In addition, individuals with advanced education, official position, and income
are often able to pass some of these advantages on to their children. Thus, a new
hereditary system of inequality will tend to emerge.

> Humanity left to its own does not necessarily re-establish capitalism, but it does
> re-establish inequality. The forces tending toward the creation of new classes
> are powerful.
>
> —*Mao Zedong, 1965*

Probably the most shattering and dramatic transformation of human society is the violent
overthrow of traditional elites by a revolution of the oppressed masses. Most such revolutions
have occurred in the mainly rural, peasant-dominated societies in which the majority of humanity has lived. Local landlords have been dispossessed and chiefs deposed ever since exploitative governments arose in advanced agrarian societies. Large-scale peasant revolutions
appear throughout history but particularly in the modern period (e.g., in the Peloponnese
in 227 B.C., England in 1381, France in 1789, Mexico in 1910, Russia in 1917, China beginning in 1921, Bolivia in 1952, and Cuba in 1958). For the old elite, the consequences of a

From American Journal of Sociology, *vol. 83, no. 1, pp. 78—90 (July 1977). Copyright © 1976 by the University of Chicago
Press.*

successful revolution are clear. But for the mass of ordinary people, they are not. Revolutions generally promise peasants justice and at least some relief from rent, taxes, usury, and traditional restrictions on their movement. They surely benefit from that relief and, at least in the short run, from the more open and equalitarian society that results. But whether some benefit more than others and why is unclear. The long-term effects are even less clear. Does equality endure, or does inequality reemerge, perhaps in new and more virulent forms? Does social mobility grow or decline? Who benefits from the forces unleashed by revolution and how? In this paper we propose a theory about the effects of revolution on inequality. We show that, in the short run, a revolution can be expected to reduce economic inequality and status inheritance, as anticipated, but also to benefit its well-to-do supporters more than its poorer ones and to make human capital more important for all. In the long run, peasants will still be better off, but stratification reemerges. Economic inequality and status inheritance grow steadily, in some circumstances eventually exceeding their prerevolutionary levels.

SCOPE

Our theory deals with the predominantly rural, premodern, peasant-dominated societies in which most revolutions have occurred. We claim that it applies to any revolution meeting the following conditions: (1) a politically and economically dominant traditional elite has previously been able to expropriate a large fraction of the surplus produced by peasants (e.g., by control over land, forced labor, discriminatory taxation, usury, or through monopoly privileges in agriculture, trade, or government), and (2) the revolution has liberated peasants from the traditional exploitation (e.g., by redistributing land, allowing freer access to opportunities in farming and business, expropriating or destroying accumulated capital). We call this combination of events a radical revolution, and we limit consideration of short-term effects to revolutions of this kind.

The predictions about long-term effect (Hypotheses 4 through 8 below) are more general; they apply not only to radical revolutions but also to any social changes which reduce exploitation or increase economic opportunities. Such changes include economic "revolutions" which liberate people from stifling restrictions or increase their productivity by technical means: specifically, the early phases of the Industrial Revolution, the Green Revolution in agriculture, the introduction of cash crops or a market economy in nonmarket societies, and the like. They also include political changes which have increased opportunities for blacks and women in the United States, untouchables in India, the Ainu in Japan, and other minorities.

We deal with the apolitical mass of the rural and small-town population, deliberately excluding the revolution's political and military leaders, the revolutionary intelligentsia, and other revolutionary elites. Nonetheless, their ideology and the policies of the government they establish are extremely important. The peasants' goals will generally be what they regard as simple justice—personal (or communal) control over their land, minimal taxation, and the right to sell their produce on the open market. That leads to a predominantly market economy with peasants (or peasant communities) functioning essentially as small capitalist entrepreneurs accumulating income and property. In that case our model applies with full force. But the revolutionary elite may oppose the return to a classical peasant economy, instead pursuing more radical and collectivist goals. If successful this will mean the end of a conventional peasantry and the rise of a rural working class, usually employed in state-owned communal farms. Our model still applies in this case, but the changes will be slower and somewhat attenuated, in ways we specify.

SHORT-TERM EFFECTS

INEQUALITY

We are dealing with radical revolutions which, by definition, at least partly free peasants from their traditional exploitation and thereby improve their economic position at the expense of the traditional elite. Transferring resources from the rich to the poor clearly reduces inequality (as we define it) in the society as a whole, which is of course typically one of the revolution's main goals. In practice, the redistribution is often extensive. Radical revolutions often redistribute land, the fundamental fixed asset in peasant societies, and hence redistribute income. They usually redistribute liquid capital as well, expropriating or destroying rents, savings, debts, pensions, and monopolies; such redistribution reduces inequality, especially in the rare cases where the expropriation is partly inadvertent. Property is abandoned during the crisis, and the collapse of the old government often leads to dramatic inflation which destroys the value of savings, salaries, and rents; these are more damaging to the old rich. Taxes and rents which fall most heavily on the poor are often reduced or eliminated. In precapitalist societies, labor taxes extracted by the state or by landlords are often the main form of exploitation, and abolishing them increases the time peasants have to work for their own benefit, leading to further equalization. In modern times, revolutionary governments usually establish new health, education, and welfare programs which result in major transfers of resources to the poor and further reduce inequality.

Human Capital   In the short run, we predict that radical revolutions will make human capital more valuable. In practice the range of opportunities for utilizing education, knowledge, technical skills, and other forms of human capital increases greatly. (1) Especially in previously isolated and traditional rural areas, rapid changes in marketing and the expansion of the money economy upset traditional economic arrangements and reward the adaptability, rationality, and cosmopolitan orientations that education provides. Literacy and elementary bookkeeping skills are valuable even in very primitive economies. (2) New political and economic power creates new opportunities for cultural brokers and go-betweens (politicians, lawyers, expediters, etc.) to mediate between peasant communities and nonpeasant society. To do so requires knowledge, contacts, and linguistic and political skills. Modern revolutions generally create numerous new positions in schools, health and welfare agencies, the government bureaucracy, and nationalized industry. Economic growth, a goal of almost all modern revolutions, expands the market economy and increases employment in professional, managerial, and clerical jobs and in transportation; and success in these requires educational, technical, and linguistic skills. (3) Educational credentials may become more important quite apart from any real connection with performance, since requiring fixed levels of education is an effective and convenient way of restricting access to jobs, especially in the expanding bureaucracies. (4) In societies in which there are several languages (or the educated classes speak a different dialect), skills in the dominant language often become more valuable after the revolution. They give access to new opportunities in education and commerce and are useful in dealings with the bureaucracy. With increasing contact between urban and rural areas and the atrophy of the old landlords' role as intermediary, facility in the national language helps in dealing with the police, bureaucracy, merchants, and employers.

These new opportunities will, we predict, make education, technical and linguistic skills, and other forms of human capital more valuable, giving a larger return in occupational status and income. Some will be able to take direct advantage of their skills by self-employment, taking up more attractive and profitable opportunities than were available before the revolution. To match these new opportunities in self-employment, employers will have to offer more to attract skilled employees. Also the growth in the number of jobs requiring education and linguistic skills increases the demand for skilled personnel, and, since the supply can increase only slowly, skilled workers will use their improved bargaining position to extract better wages.

Who Benefits? Radical revolutions benefit most of their supporters, since their surplus is no longer expropriated by the old elite. But we predict that revolutions do not benefit the poorest as much as those who already possessed human or physical capital. Those with human capital, already better off before the revolution, have a great advantage in the new bureaucratic, commercial, and political jobs (e.g., in the Soviet Union), and in commercial agriculture. In addition, there are typically substantial differences in the amount and value of land peasants worked before the revolution, and they are often able to maintain or strengthen their customary rights afterward (e.g., in Bolivia); then with their surplus no longer expropriated, well-to-do peasants benefit more from their advantages.

STATUS INHERITANCE

Because a radical revolution leads to the redistribution of wealth, we predict that it leads to less inheritance of status—that is, more pure social mobility—for those who came of age just after the revolution. Since many prerevolutionary elite parents lose their wealth, they have less of an advantage to pass on to their children, whereas some poor parents gain new resources and have more to give theirs. So on the average there is less variation in the wealth that parents can pass on to their children and hence less status inheritance.

But status inheritance does not disappear. Some economic inequalities are likely to remain after even the most dedicated and efficient attempts at redistribution. Human capital remains; education, literacy, technical and linguistic skills, and the like retain or even increase their value and cannot be redistributed. The old elite and others who were better off before the revolution have more of these resources and are able to pass some of their skills on to their children. So an effective means of transmitting status from one generation to the next remains; in the short run, a revolution will reduce status inheritance but not eliminate it.

SUMMARY

Hypothesis 1 In the short run, a radical revolution produces a more equal distribution of physical capital and, for those coming of age just afterward, less status inheritance.

Hypothesis 2   In the short run, a radical revolution causes a shift in the basis of stratification, making human capital (education, knowledge, technical or linguistic skills, etc.) a more valuable source of occupational status and income.

Hypothesis 3   A revolution does not immediately benefit the poorest of its supporters as much as it benefits those who possess human capital or have been able to retain physical capital.

LONG-TERM EFFECTS

STRATIFICATION AMONG PEASANTS

A radical revolution allows peasants to obtain a higher return on their physical capital since, by definition, it reduces exploitation. (1) By reducing rents or taxes on land, it allows peasants to retain more of what they produce. The destruction of forced labor obligations—the crucial tax in many agrarian societies—allows peasants more time to work their land for their own benefit (e.g., an additional one to three days per week in medieval Europe and three or more days in twentieth-century Bolivia). (2) Revolution is likely to reduce the costs peasants pay for goods and services by destroying traditional monopolies on trade, credit, and justice. Monopolies allowed traditional elites to charge exorbitant prices; even where the revolutionary government makes no deliberate attempt to reduce prices, competition is likely to drive them down. (3) Prior to the revolution, peasants' opportunities are often restricted to the least profitable sector of the rural economy. However, the destruction of serfdom, forced labor, and other laws tying peasants to the land opens up new opportunities. They can sell their own produce and take up wage-paying jobs in addition to agriculture, which in some cases increases their income dramatically. Some become traders and merchant middlemen, replacing the old elite's commercial monopolies. (4) Economic change may have the same effects, with or without revolution. The introduction of new cash crops or new agricultural techniques, the opening of new markets, and the like all provide new and often profitable opportunities. Ending economic discrimination against blacks, untouchables, the Ainu, etc. opens up opportunities for them.

These new opportunities will, we predict, lead eventually to greater economic inequality among peasant proprietors and the mass of the previously exploited population. Even in prerevolutionary times, peasants differ in their physical capital (e.g., size and quality of usufruct landholdings), in human capital (e.g., agricultural or linguistic skills, education, experience with the outside world), and in ability, motivation, luck, and the like. By expropriating the surplus and restricting opportunities to use capital effectively, the old system prevented fortunate peasants from getting the full benefit of their advantages and so restrained the growth of inequality. Revolution removes the restraints, allowing them to take full advantage of their resources. In the long run, that creates steadily growing inequality among peasants and other previously exploited groups. This leads to what might be called the kulak stage—the rise of a newly enriched sector of the peasant population and the emergence of an essentially capitalist rural stratification system. Since fortunate peasants have increasingly large advantages to pass on to their children, we predict that revolution will in the long run lead also to steadily increasing status inheritance among them. The same reasoning applies to those economic revolutions and social changes that reduce exploitation, and in fact there is evidence that they increase both inequality (e.g., in agriculture following the Green Revolution) and status inheritance (e.g., among American blacks in the past decade).

Human Capital   In the long run, a radical revolution leads to greater inequality in human capital among the peasantry and previously exploited masses. (1) Revolution provides additional reasons for acquiring human capital. Education, linguistic skills, and other forms of human capital are always valuable, and if anything, revolution makes them more so. Peasants can expect greater benefits from education after the revolution, since they have new opportunities to use it and can keep more of what they earn. Investing in education therefore becomes more attractive on straightforward economic grounds. Economic revolutions often have the same effect. (2) Modern revolutions supply the means. Whether from conviction or because of peasants' new political power, revolutionary governments generally expand the school system, making education available where it was not before. (3) Educational inequality increases because some children benefit more than others. Able and motivated children have an advantage, as do children from privileged families. Throughout the world, well-educated, high-status families are much more successful in getting their children educated (e.g., in tribal societies, in socialist societies, and in industrial societies); they provide encouragement and role models, teach linguistic and academic skills, force their children to work harder, and the like. Schooling is usually expensive, both in direct costs (fees, supplies, clothing, etc.) and indirect costs (income the student could otherwise have earned); prosperous families can better afford these costs.

   This growing inequality in human capital will, we predict, in the long run lead to greater economic inequality and more status inheritance among peasants. Since education and other forms of human capital are quite valuable, greater inequality in human capital leads to greater inequality in income and wealth. That, we have argued, leads to greater status inheritance. Educational changes also increase status inheritance directly. As educational inequality grows among parents—that is, as the gap between well- and poorly-educated parents increases—it becomes more of an advantage to be born into a well-educated family.

Government Intervention   A revolutionary government can try to restrain these forces by limiting the private accumulation and inheritance of capital. Populist and middle-class revolutionary parties are unlikely to have either the ideological justification or the dedicated cadre with which to do so, although many socialist and communist governments make the attempt. But it is unlikely to succeed. Expropriating large landowners, large capitalists, and foreign investments and thereby securing the "commanding heights" of the economy will not be enough, since accumulation by the mass of upper peasants and the educated middle class leads, we have argued, to inequality. To restrain these groups, private capital will have to be abolished throughout the economy. In practice this is usually accomplished by socializing the industrial economy and collectivizing the land and sometimes by the physical extinction of the kulaks. Many people have something to lose from such actions, and they are not without recourse. Small businessmen have money and can threaten to withdraw valuable services; the upper levels of the peasantry know they have much to lose; the educated middle class and party workers newly ensconced in the bureaucracy will want to secure their advantage by accumulating wealth. To fully overcome the opposition of these groups requires from the party's cadres a level of commitment, dedication, and resistance to temptation that is difficult to maintain over the years; it also requires an extensive and efficient bureaucratic apparatus which can extend its control to the very grass roots, an apparatus few societies have ever possessed. China's cultural revolution may have been in part an attempt to overcome this kind of opposition and prevent the reemergence of inequality. Even in China, however, the costs were great, opposition was strong, and success uncertain; other examples are not easy to find.

But the abolition of private capital is not in itself enough to prevent the long-term growth of inequality, since much (indeed most) inequality arises from differences in education, skills, language, and other forms of human capital which are almost immune to redistribution. Human capital is crucial; to run even a moderately complex society requires an educated elite—business, industry, and government require a variety of administrative and technical skills, and even farming and small trading are greatly facilitated by literacy, bookkeeping, and specialized technical skills. Although it is sometimes claimed that schools impart few skills of any genuine importance but merely screen or certify or are otherwise dispensable, that claim is inconsistent with detailed evidence for modern industrial societies and with the clear importance of education in societies with very different economic and institutional structures. Ignoring these skills in favor of political or equity considerations is exceedingly costly; to date only China has systematically and persistently attempted it after the revolutionary government was firmly established and the threat of counterrevolution past. Nor can governments effectively prevent human capital from being passed from one generation to the next without draconian changes in the family. The knowledge, values, culture, and language skills acquired in elite homes give children an enormous and enduring advantage in socialist as well as capitalist societies; discriminatory admissions policies for higher education and government can reduce the advantage somewhat but not eliminate it, save at enormous cost. Thus a revolution able to abolish private property will slow the long-term growth of inequality and status inheritance but will not prevent it.

Stratification in the Society as a Whole

In the long run, a radical revolution will, we have argued, create more inequality and status inheritance among peasants and the previously exploited rural masses. But its effects on the society as a whole are less clear. We will argue that inequality and status inheritance first decrease and then remain low for a period; in most circumstances they then increase steadily and, in some circumstances, eventually exceed their prerevolutionary levels.

Economic development increases inequality. Even if everyone retains the same relative position, development increases the absolute size of the gap between rich and poor and therefore increases inequality. If, for example, the introduction of new cash crops doubles everyone's income, it also doubles the gap between poor peasants and rich merchants, so the peasant has twice the obstacle to overcome if he is to live as well as a merchant, and a peasant's son has twice the handicap to overcome if he is to catch up with a merchant's son. In addition, anyone with physical capital, human capital, or other advantages will be better able to take advantage of new opportunities opened up by economic development and that increases inequality by any definition.

The benefits that revolution provides for peasants and the exploited rural masses will at first decrease inequality in the society as a whole. Peasants' income, wealth, and human capital almost always begin well below the average for the whole society, while the commercial and administrative sectors in rural towns and most urban groups are markedly better off initially. The revolution reduces exploitation, improving the economic position of all peasants. That reduces inequality. Most peasants go no further. But those with physical or human capital or other resources will continue to improve their position, especially if the revolution is one which produces economic development. As they surpass the average income level in increasing numbers, inequality first stabilizes and then (depending on how many surpass it and by how much) may increase. So there is a standard sequence following the revolution. Inequality first declines and then stabilizes. If peasants continue to improve their economic position, the decline lasts longer, but eventually inequality begins to increase again and eventually may exceed its prerevolutionary level.

How far along this sequence a society proceeds depends not only on what happens to the peasants but also on how high the average income is to begin with and how it changes subsequently. Most prerevolutionary peasant societies are very poor, with a small surplus extracted by a tiny elite. The average is low and, other things being equal, that makes it easier to surpass, and the society will then go through the sequence quickly, often reaching the stage where inequality increases. In richer societies (e.g., Eastern Europe following the communist revolutions), peasants have further to go, and the society passes along the sequence more slowly. The average also depends on what happens to the urban population and the postrevolutionary elite, but that reflects the power and ideology of the revolutionary leadership, the society's economic and administrative capacity, international political and economic restraints, and a variety of other factors beyond the scope of our theory.

There may be further redistribution after the revolution; this too affects inequality. Particularly where there is no sustained economic growth, gains by rich peasants are someone else's losses. If they gain entirely at the expense of the elite, there will be more equality. But in practice, their gains will most probably be at the cost of poor peasants and lower and middle classes in the towns. As rich peasants take over marketing, credit, and middleman functions, they displace middle- and lower-class urbanites, and liberated peasants compete for desirable urban jobs. Successful peasants will produce cash crops more efficiently, undercutting poor peasants' market positions and driving them off the land. When rich peasants begin to pass the mean, inequality will eventually increase as long as their gains are mainly at the expense of groups below the average.

A revolution's effects on inequality in the society as a whole thus depend crucially on the speed of economic development, the economic position of urban groups and the postrevolutionary elite, and government policies toward accumulation. We predict that inequality will increase most dramatically if the revolution generates economic development (which directly increases inequality) and if the entire society was poor to begin with (since rich peasants exceed the mean sooner). Since modern revolutions in poor societies (e.g., Mexico in 1910, Bolivia in 1952) almost always promote economic development, we predict that they will eventually create more inequality than existed before the revolution unless governments make strenuous efforts to prevent it. The scattered evidence now available suggests that inequality does increase. Economic revolutions—the decay of feudalism, the early stages of industrial revolution, the introduction of cash crops and a money economy in premarket Asian and African society, the Green Revolution in agriculture, etc.—lead to economic development. We predict that therefore they will cause inequality in the long run; the evidence indicates that they do. In contrast, we predict that classical peasant revolutions in traditional

societies in which urban areas remain richer than the countryside and no economic development results will reduce inequality (e.g., Punjab in the late nineteenth century). Changes in
status inheritance in the society as a whole will, we predict, parallel changes in inequality for
the reasons set out earlier.

SUMMARY

Hypothesis 4   In the long run, peasants are better off after a radical revolution.
Hypothesis 5   By allowing peasants to utilize their resources more fully, radical revolutions set loose forces which tend in the long run to produce steadily increasing economic inequality among them.
Hypothesis 6   In the long run, radical revolutions produce increasing educational inequality among peasants.
Hypothesis 7   Among peasants, radical revolutions create forces which tend in the long
run to produce more status inheritance through both economic advantage and education.
Hypothesis 8   In the society as a whole, inequality and status inheritance following a radical revolution will first decrease, then stabilize, then (a) remain low if nonpeasants remain
well off and there is no economic development in the countryside but (b) steadily increase
and perhaps in time exceed prerevolutionary levels in poor societies in which there is substantial economic development.

Hypotheses 4–8 apply not only to radical revolutions but also to any social changes
which reduce exploitation or increase economic opportunities, with the poor and exploited
taking the role of peasants.

Gender and Revolutions

VALENTINE M. MOGHADAM

In recent years, analysts have paid much more attention to the role of gender issues
in revolutions. Revolutions seek to change the political order, and often also seek
to change the structures of economic and social inequality. However, revolutions
vary greatly in how they approach *gender* inequality. Some revolutions have appealed to very traditional ideals of elevated men and subordinated women as part
of their effort to gain support; other revolutions have sought to restructure gender
relations as well as other aspects of society. This variation holds true despite the fact
that women have played a considerable role in almost every revolutionary conflict,
even those adopting traditional family ideals. In this essay, Moghadam charts these
differences from the French Revolution of 1789 to the Iranian Revolution of 1979.

The scholarship on revolution is prodigious and rich, but it is deficient in incorporating gender into the analysis. The study of revolution has not yet considered systematically the promi-

nent position assumed by gender issues in the discourse of revolutionaries and the laws of revolutionary states. In the sociology of revolution, gender, unlike class or the state or the world-system, is not seen as a constitutive category.

In contrast, feminist scholarship has been attentive to the theme of women and revolution. Feminists have produced prolific research into the role and position of women in revolutionary France, Russia, China, Vietnam, Cuba, Algeria, Nicaragua, Iran, and elsewhere.[1] This body of literature strongly suggests that gender relations constitute an important part of the culture, ideology, and politics of revolutionary societies. Some scholars of the French Revolution have examined how gender was constructed in the political discourse and discovered the legal disempowerment and exclusion of women based on the "natural fact" of sexual difference. Siân Reynolds makes the interesting point that the participation of women as mothers and food distributors has a profoundly legitimizing effect on a revolution—at least in its early stages.[2] Mary Ann Tétreault observes that all twentieth-century revolutionaries retain or recreate private space and family forms.[3] Hanna Papanek maintains that the construction of the "ideal society" entails a notion of the "ideal woman."[4] In a previous essay I have classified revolutions in terms of gender outcomes: one group of revolutions is modernizing and egalitarian, with women's emancipation an explicit goal; another group is patriarchal, tying women to the family and stressing gender differences rather than equality.[5] Certainly revolutionary states expend considerable effort legislating the social positions of women, revising family law, and defining the prerogatives of men.

In this chapter I hope to show not only that women—like men—have been active participants in revolutionary movements, but also that revolutions have a gender dimension that must be taken into account in analyses of their causes, courses, and outcomes. Gender is an integral part of the social structure, a basic element of production and reproduction, and a central feature of concepts of the ideal society and of national identity. For these reasons, gender affects and is affected by revolutionary processes in profound ways, as the empirical sections in this chapter will show. I shall further try to show that since the French Revolution, and especially during the twentieth century, revolutions have evinced either patriarchal or emancipatory agendas for women. Outcomes for women seem to be determined by the explicit ideology, goals, and social program of the revolution, by the nature of pre-existing gender relations, and by the scope of women's involvement in the revolutionary movement.

EN-GENDERING REVOLUTION

What do revolutions have in common? In all revolutions, the explicit goal is thorough upheaval of the previous system and its replacement by a new system. In general, revolutionaries have some idea, if not a detailed program or blueprint, of what they mean the new society to look like. The basic premise is that it should look as different as possible, in all aspects—economic, political, and cultural—from the previous system. Gender-specific outcomes are very much influenced by this aspect of revolutions. Almost always, the family is redefined, usually in the new government's body of laws. Women experience the effects of revolutionary upheavals differentially by class (and in some societies, by race or ethnicity). However, laws on women and the family, especially those pertaining directly to reproductive issues or legal status, may affect all women in similar ways.

Changes in gender relations are especially obvious in revolutionary *outcomes*, most dramatically in such twentieth-century revolutions as Russia, China, and Iran (albeit in very different ways). There is less evidence thus far to support a role for gender in *causality*. In the case of the Iranian Revolution, however, it is plausible to hypothesize that gender intersected with class to constitute a causal factor in the revolt against the Shah and the turn to Islamization, at least for a section of the revolutionary coalition. That is, the growing visibility of middle-class women and the "Westernization" of bourgeois women offended the men of the lower middle class who sought to recuperate traditional gender roles as part of their revolutionary goals. For all revolutions it is possible to posit that gender ideology profoundly *shapes* all manner of actions and decisions, from macro to micro, from patterns of revolutionary mobilization, state-building, and the establishment of constitutions, laws, and policies, to household dynamics and relations within families.

REVOLUTIONS AND WOMEN'S INTERESTS

Do revolutions have the same gender outcomes for all women? Molyneux has distinguished women's interests, practical gender interests, and strategic gender interests. "Women's interests" are specific to particular class, ethnic, or age groups within a given society. Women's interests are revealed by specifying "how the various categories of women might be affected differently and act differently on account of the particularities of their social positioning and their chosen identities." In contrast, strategic gender interests "are derived . . . deductively. . . from an analysis of women's subordination and from the formulation of an alternative, more satisfactory set of arrangements."[6] Thus, strategic gender interests often take the form of broad reforms which question the structural basis of gender inequality: suffrage, legal reform of family law, freedom of choice over childbearing, abolition of the sexual division of labor. Practical gender interests are inductive and usually formulated by women (or men) in concrete positions within the gendered division of labor. Practical gender interests do not challenge the division of labor itself or gender inequality more broadly, but focus on women's basic needs and their access to resources and welfare. Molyneux's threefold distinction of women's interests, practical gender interests, and strategic gender interests correctly emphasizes the gender dimension of revolutions, with attention to the differential impact of revolution and social transformation on women of different social classes, and with an understanding that different types of revolutions and revolutionary state policies will have different outcomes for women. In her analysis of Nicaragua, Molyneux has explored the effects of economic resources, conflict, and religious pressures on women and gender, pointing out that the Nicaraguan Revolution's legal reforms, redistributive policies, and political mobilization positively affected women's practical needs and strategic gender interests "even though fundamental structures of gender inequality were not dismantled."[7]

On the other hand, many feminists have noted that revolutionary movements subordinate women's interests and gender interests to "broader" or "basic" goals of emancipation. For this reason, there has been a veritable indictment of all revolutions and liberation movements as essentially inimical to women's interests. Maria Mies, for example, has pointed to a dramatic shift in nationalist imagery in postrevolutionary states:

> In this phase, the female image of the nation, found on the revolutionary posters mentioned above, is replaced by the images of the founding-fathers: Marx, Engels, Lenin, Stalin, Mao, Ho Chi Minh, Castro, Mugabe, to name only a few. Typically, among this gallery of socialist patriarchs, there are no women.[8]

It cannot be denied, however, that some revolutionary experiences have been profoundly liberating for women as women, especially in those cases where patriarchal gender roles are challenged, and where new legislation is enacted towards greater equality and autonomy for women. For example, Molyneux and Norma Chinchilla are very positive in their assessments of Nicaragua.[9] According to Linda Lobao, of the five Latin American guerrilla movements she discusses, the issue of women's rights was recognized as significant for the movements' present and future success in Nicaragua and El Salvador.[10] Chinese communism brought about a genuinely revolutionary change in women's legal status and social positions, especially in the urban areas. Stephanie Urdang writes, correctly, in my view:

> In Mozambique and other postrevolutionary societies, there are real gains that have been made by women. To ignore these and the kind of support — economic and political — that women get from their governments and political party is to ignore some real, tangible advances.[11]

REVOLUTIONS AND GENDERED OUTCOMES: A TYPOLOGY AND FRAMEWORK

I distinguish two types of revolutions: (1) the "woman-in-the-family" or patriarchal model of revolution, and (2) the "women's emancipation" or modernizing model. These conform to events in revolutionary France and revolutionary Russia, respectively, which also happen to be the reference points for most twentieth-century revolutions (see Table 1).

Combining my terminology with that of Molyneux, I would propose that the women's emancipation model of revolution serves (at least some) strategic gender interests, especially through its explicit espousal of gender equality and the full integration of women in public life; addresses practical gender interests to the extent that resources allow it to; and is in the interests of most strata of the female population — although some groups of women may oppose it due to class and ideological differences. By contrast, the woman-in-the-family model of revolution, by virtue of its insistence on gender differences and female domesticity, is inimical to the strategic gender interests of women, though it may address some practical gender needs and the specific interests of some groups of women.

In the sections that follow, I present my two types of revolutions. Elaboration of each will be supplemented by examples from twentieth-century revolutions. Whether the cases are examples of patriarchal or modernizing revolutions, they highlight the centrality of gender

Table 1   Revolutions by Gender Outcomes: A Typology

TYPE OF REVOLUTION	BOURGEOIS REVOLUTIONS	SOCIALIST REVOLUTIONS AND THIRD WORLD POPULIST REVOLUTIONS
Women's emancipation a major goal or outcome	Kemalism in Turkey	France (1848) Russia (1917) China Cuba Vietnam Democratic Yemen Eritrea Afghanistan Nicaragua El Salvador
Family attachment of women a major goal or outcome (patriarchal)	French Revolution Perestroika in the Soviet Union 1989 revolutions of Eastern Europe	Mexico Algeria Iran

issues in the revolutionary process. What follows are ideal types, but they represent fairly faithfully the kinds of revolutions that have occurred and their gender dynamics.

THE WOMAN-IN-THE-FAMILY MODEL OF REVOLUTION

This type of revolution excludes or marginalizes women from definitions and constructions of independence, liberation, and liberty. It frequently constructs an ideological linkage between patriarchal values, nationalism, and the religious order. It assigns women the role of wife and mother, and associates women not only with family but also with tradition, culture, and religion. Although family issues and especially improvement of the quality of life of families among the popular classes may be among the goals of modernizing revolutions, here the family is exalted and women's role within it made paramount. The historical precursor of the patriarchal model was the French Revolution, which, despite its many progressive features, had an extremely conservative outcome for women.

With the collapse of the authority of the church and the old regime, the French revolutionaries sought a new moral basis for family life. They made divorce possible, accorded full legal status to illegitimate children, and abolished primogeniture. (Napoleon later reversed the most democratic provisions of the laws on family life, restoring patriarchal authority.) But there was another trend at work during the revolution. At the height of the French Revolution virtue was the central ingredient of a new political culture. To the revolutionaries, virtue was virile. At the same time, the cult of virtue produced a revalorization of family life. Banners and slogans proclaimed: "Citizenesses! Give the Fatherland Children!" and

"Now is the time to make a baby." Mothers had a certain legitimacy which unmarried *citoyennes* did not. Robespierre's Reign of Virtue involved an ideal of women as passive nurturers. Women should bear children for the revolution and sacrifice them for France. He abhorred the active women in the revolutionary club, describing them as "unnatural" and "sterile as vice."

On the grounds that women's active participation in politics would lead to "the kinds of disruption and disorder that hysteria can produce," the Convention outlawed all women's clubs at the end of October 1793. The Jacobin Chaumette said, "The sans-culottes had a right to expect his wife to run the home while he attended public meetings: hers was the care of the family, this was the full extent of her civic duties."[12] And what was to be the place of women in the new society of revolutionary France? According to the Jacobin deputy Andri Amar:

> Morality and nature itself have assigned her functions to her: to begin the education of men, to prepare the minds and hearts of children for the exercise of public virtues, to direct them early in life towards the good, to elevate their souls, to educate them in the cult of liberty—such are their functions after household cares. . . . When they have carried out these duties they will have deserved well of the fatherland.[13]

The exclusion of women from the construction of the republic, their relegation to the sphere of the family, and their education in Catholic schools (until the 1850s) made them especially vulnerable in the anti-clerical politics of the Second and Third Republics. Not until after World War II did women in France obtain the right to vote. Harriet Applewhite and Darline Levy write:

> In the most general terms, for men, the revolutionary period established the principle of democratic citizenship, constitutionally guaranteed rights, and collective empowerment through participation in new political, economic, and social institutions. For women, revolutionary outcomes were far more complex and confused. . . . The age of democratic revolution nowhere produced political democracy that included women as citizens; nowhere did women achieve political and civil rights that middle-class white male proprietors had established for themselves. . . . In the aftermath of revolution or civil unrest in the political cultures treated here, women were excluded from modern political institutions like labor organizations, political parties, militias, and legislatures.[14]

In twentieth-century revolutions that had similarly patriarchal outcomes for women—notably Mexico, Algeria, and Iran—women were relegated to the private sphere despite the crucial roles they had played in the revolutionary movements. In these three cases, men took over the reins of power, assigned to women responsibility for family, religion, and tradition, and enacted legislation to codify patriarchal gender relations, including second-class citizenship for women. Similarly, in the 1989–1991 revolutions of East Central Europe and in the former Soviet Union the new revolutionaries resurrected patriarchal discourses on women and the family, launched an attack on reproductive rights, and proceeded to establish what East European feminists called "democratization with a male face" and "male democracies."

THE ALGERIAN CASE

The French took over Algeria in June 1830. Unlike colonial policy in Morocco after 1912 and Tunisia after 1882, an attempt was made in Algeria to dismantle Islam, its economic infra-structure, and its cultural network of lodges and schools. By the turn of the century, there were upwards of a million French-speaking settlers (*petits colons*) in Algeria. European competition ruined most of the old artisan class by 1930. Fierce economic competition, cultural disrespect, and residential segregation characterized the Algerian situation.

In this context, many Algerians regarded Islam and Muslim family law as sanctuaries from French cultural imperialism. To many Algerian men the unveiled woman represented a capitulation to the European and his culture; she was a person who had opened herself up to the prurient stares of the foreigners, a person more vulnerable to rape. The popular re-action to the *mission civilisatrice* was a return to the land and to religion, the foundations of the old community. Islam was reinforced, the patriarchal family became increasingly important, and the protection and seclusion of women were seen by Algerians as imperative to their identity and integrity.

When the revolutionary *Front de Libération Nationale* (FLN) was formed there was no provision for women to enjoy any political or military responsibilities. Nonetheless, mili-tary exigencies soon forced the officers of the *Armée de Libération Nationale* (ALN) to use some women combatants. Upwards of 10,000 women participated in the Algerian Revolution. The overwhelming majority of those who served in the war were nurses, cooks, and laun-dresses. But many women played an indispensable role as couriers, and because the French rarely searched them, women were often used for carrying bombs. Among the heroines of the Algerian Revolution were Djamila Boujhired (the first woman sentenced to death), 20-year-old Hassiba Ben Bouali, killed in the casbah, and Djennet Hamidou, who was shot and killed as she tried to escape arrest. Yamina Abed, who was wounded in battle, suffered amputation of both legs. These Algerian women, like the women of Vietnam after them, became the stuff of legends.

After independence, the September 1962 Constitution guaranteed equality between the sexes and granted women the right to vote. It also made Islam the official state religion. Ten women were elected deputies of the new National Assembly, and one of them, Fatima Khe-misti, drafted the only significant legislation to affect the status of women passed by the Na-tional Assembly after independence. In this optimistic time, when heroines of the revolution were being hailed throughout the country, the *Union Nationale des Femmes Algériennes* (UNFA) was formed. The heroic Algerian woman fighter was an inspiration to the 1960s and 1970s generation of Algerians, particularly Algerian university women.

But another, more patriarchal, tendency was at work during and after the Algerian Revo-lution. One expression of this was pressure on women fighters during the liberation struggle to get married and thus prevent spurious talk about their behavior. Moreover, despite the incredible sacrifices of Algerian women, the Algerian Revolution has tended be cast in terms of male exploits, while the heroic female feats have not received as much attention.

In the 1960s, Algerian marriage rates soared. In 1967 some 10 percent of Algerian girls were married at 15 years of age; at 20 years of age, 73 percent of the women were married. The crude fertility rate was 6.5 per woman. The government's policy on demographic growth was predicated on the assumption that a large population is necessary for national power. It was, therefore, opposed to all forms of birth control unless the mother had already produced at least four children. By the end of 1979, 97.5 percent of Algerian women were without paid work. (Some 45 percent of Algerian men were unemployed or underemployed.) The UNFA had become the women's auxiliary of the FLN, devoid of feminist objectives.

The Algerian Revolution has frequently been identified as one of the clearest cases of postrevolutionary marginalization of women—notwithstanding their critical roles during the liberation struggle. As such, it conforms to the woman-in-the-family model of revolution.

THE IRANIAN CASE

The Iranian Revolution against the Shah, which unfolded between early 1967 and February 1979, was joined by countless women. Like other social groups, their reasons for opposing the Shah were varied: economic deprivation, political repression, identification with Islamism, aspirations for a socialist future. The large street demonstrations included huge contingents of women wearing the veil as a symbol of opposition to bourgeois or Westernized Pahlavi decadence. Many women who wore the veil as a protest symbol did not expect *hijah* (veiling) to become mandatory. Thus when the first calls were made in February 1979 to enforce *hijah* and when Ayatollah Khomeini was quoted as saying that he preferred to see women in modest Islamic dress, many women were alarmed. Spirited protests and sit-ins were led by middle-class leftist and liberal women, most of them members of political organizations or recently formed women's organizations. Limited support for the women's protests came from the main political groups. As a result of the women's protests, the ruling on *hijah* was rescinded—but only temporarily. With the defeat of the left and liberals in 1980 and their elimination from the political terrain in 1981, the Islamic state was able to make veiling compulsory, and to enforce it strictly. Iranian women were deeply divided over the revolution, and the Islamization of Iran had its many female adherents, drawn mainly from the lower middle class, which was also the class base of new Islamist leadership.

The idea that women had "lost honor" during the Pahlavi era was a widespread one. Such attitudes were behind the early legislation pertaining to women enacted to alter gender relations and make them as different as possible from gender norms in the West. In particular, the Islamic Republic emphasized the distinctiveness of male and female roles, a preference for the privatization of female roles (although public activity by women was never barred and they retained the vote), the desirability of sex segregation in public places, and the necessity of modesty in dress and demeanor. In the Islamic Republic, "the family is the basic unit of the society and plays a crucial role in prosperity, public morals and education of new generations, as well as social integration and social stability."[15] That it devolves upon women to maintain family and social cohesion and the integrity of the Islamic revolution through veiling and proper comportment is the distinctive Iranian contribution to the patriarchal model of revolution.

THE WOMEN'S EMANCIPATION MODEL
OF REVOLUTION

The women's emancipation model holds that the emancipation of women is an essential part of the revolution or project of social transformation. It constructs Woman as part of the productive forces and citizenry, to be mobilized for economic and political purposes; she is to be liberated from patriarchal controls expressly for that purpose. Here the discourse is more strongly that of sexual equality rather than difference. The first example historically of such a revolution is the Bolshevik Revolution in Russia, which, especially with respect to its early years, remains the avant-garde revolution *par excellence,* more audacious in its approach to gender than any revolution before or since.

World War I brought more Russian women into factory production, leading the Bolsheviks to recognize them as a potential social and political force. The Bolsheviks also had supporters among laundresses, domestic servants, restaurant and textile workers, and soldiers' wives. They launched *Rabotnitsa,* a paper for women workers, and encouraged women to join factory committees and unions. The success of *Rabotnitsa* resulted in the Petrograd Conference of Working Women in November 1917 and the formation of the *Zhenotdel,* or women's department, within the party in 1919.

Under Alexandra Kollantai, People's Commissar for Social Welfare, labor legislation was passed which gave women an eight-hour day, social insurance, pregnancy leave for two months before and after childbirth, time at work to breast-feed, and prohibition of child labor and night work for women. The early months of the revolution also saw legislation to bring in equality between husband and wife, civil registration of marriage, easy divorce, abolition of illegitimacy, and the ending of the wife's obligation to take her husband's name and share his domicile. Under Kollantai's directorship in particular, the women's section of the Party, the *Zhenotdel,* saw itself as a force to represent women's interests in the party and to transform society. In Central Asia, it organized mass unveilings of Muslim women and ran literacy classes. (As we shall see, this was attempted fifty years later in South Yemen and Afghanistan.) All this followed from the view that the emancipation of women was an essential part of the socialist revolution, and that this was to be accomplished through "the participation of women in general productive labor," as socialists put it, and through the socialization of domestic duties. Lenin's views on the subject of women, revolution, and equality were sometimes expressed in rather forceful terms:

> Woman continues to be a domestic slave, because petty housework crushes, strangles, stultifies and degrades her, chains her to the kitchen and to the nursery, and wastes her labor on barbarously unproductive, petty, nerve-racking, stultifying and crushing drudgery. Enlightenment, culture, civilization, liberty—in all capitalist, bourgeois republics of the world all these fine words are combined with extremely infamous, disgustingly filthy and brutally coarse laws in which woman is treated as an inferior being, laws dealing with marriage rights and divorce, with the inferior status of a child born out of wedlock compared with that of a "legitimate" child, laws granting privileges to men, laws that are humiliating and insulting to women.[16]

The Bolsheviks also stressed the need for the political participation of women, or as Lenin put it:

We want women workers to achieve equality with men workers not only in law, but in life as well. For this, it is essential that women workers take an ever increasing part in the administration of public enterprises and in the administration of the state.[17]

The Bolsheviks took the initiative in calling the First Communist Women's Conference and prepared the position paper for the occasion, *Theses of the Communist Women's Movement.* Apart from its commitment to the political equality of women and the guarantee of their social rights, the *Theses* included an attack on housewifery and "the domestic hearth." The document reflected the Engelsian view that female emancipation would be a twofold process, incorporating both the entry of women into the national labor force and the socialization of domestic labor.

Like the French revolutionaries before them, the Bolsheviks strongly supported "free union," and therefore legalized divorce. But in other matters they parted company with the French revolutionaries. Debates on sexuality reflected the Bolsheviks' commitment to gender equality and their critique of the family. The liberation of peasant women could come about only through a massive change in the mode of production, as well as a revolutionary transformation of social values and practices. The implementation in the 1920s of the land code and the family code, with their emphasis on individual rights and freedoms—including women's rights to land and for maintenance—was an extremely audacious act that challenged centuries of patriarchal control. It also undermined the collective principle of the household, the very basis of peasant production, and was thus strongly resisted. In Soviet Central Asia in the 1920s, where there was virtually no industrial working class, Bolshevik strategists directed their campaigns at women because they were considered the most oppressed social category.

Material scarcity weakened the Bolshevik vision of liberation, although jurists and party officials maintained their commitment to the "withering-away" of the family, and the Women's Congress in 1927 showed the potential of an active socialist women's organization. This potential was cut short in the 1930s with the consolidation of the power of Stalin and his associates, who ushered in a more culturally conservative era. This led to the decision to disband the *Zhenotdel,* to end open discussions of women's liberation, and to resurrect the family. The earlier critique of the family was replaced by a strong emphasis on the "socialist family" as the proper model of gender relations. Family responsibilities were extolled for men as well as for women.

The Bolshevik Revolution and communist legislation inspired socialists and feminists throughout the world, and for many decades. It was truly an exemplar of the "women's emancipation" model of revolution. Other revolutions in which "the Woman Question" assumed a prominent position in revolutionary discourse and in the policies of the new states include the socialist and populist revolutions of China, Vietnam, Democratic Yemen, and Nicaragua (see Table 1). At least one "bourgeois revolution" also conforms to the women's emancipation model: Kemalism in Turkey in the 1920s and 1930s.

The Case of Turkey

If the Woman Question was the Achilles Heel of the European Enlightenment, it was central to the Turkish Enlightenment and the Kemalist Revolution. To the Turkish reformers, the women of Turkey were both participants in the nationalist and political struggles and symbols of the new Turkey. Kemal Atatürk viewed women's equality to men as part of Turkey's commitment to Westernization, secularization, and democracy.

Toward the end of the nineteenth century, opposition to the sultanate was manifested in the Young Turk movement, officially called the Committee of Union and Progress. One of the principal tenets of the Young Turks was the need for modernization; they were also unabashedly for Westernization. Closely linked to the need for modernization through Westernization was the emancipation of women.

World War I hastened the break-up of the Ottoman Empire and the emergence of a new group from among the Young Turks which advocated the building of a modern Turkish national state that was republican, secular, and non-imperialist. Mustafa Kemal, an army captain, set up a revolutionary government in Ankara in 1920 and oversaw the establishment of the Turkish Republic in 1923, with himself as president as well as leader of the Republican People's Party. The Kemalist reforms were far-reaching in both intent and effect. Atatürk—Father of the Turks—as he came to be known, furthered the process of Europeanization through economic development, separation of religion from state affairs, an attack on tradition, Latinization of the alphabet, promotion of European dress, adoption of the Western calendar, and the replacement of Islamic family law by a secular civil code. By 1926 the shari'a (Islamic legal code) was abolished and the civil and penal codes thoroughly secularized.

Turkish women obtained the legal right to vote in 1934, many years before French women did. Legislation mandating compulsory education, enacted in 1924, provided for equal access of girls to schooling. Not only Atatürk, but Kemalist feminists such as the nationalist fighter and writer Halide Edip and Atatürk's adopted daughter Afet Inan, author of *The Emancipation of the Turkish Woman,* played major roles in creating images of the new Turkish woman. Various Turkish writers stressed the harmful individual and national effects of the subordination of women. Stories and essays depicting individual women who suffered from subjugation, children who suffered because of their mother's ignorance, and households that suffered because women could not manage money properly highlighted the need for education for women. Writings depicting women who descended into abject poverty when their husbands or fathers died underscored employment for women as the solution. Other stories sought to show that society and progress suffered when women were kept illiterate and subordinated to men. Turkish national identity seemed to have a practically built-in sexual egalitarianist component. In this sense the image of the emancipated Turkish woman was in line with the "true" identity of the collectivity—the new Turkish nation.

Why was the question of women's rights so strategic to the self-definition of the Turkish reformers? It would appear that women's emancipation was necessary for purposes of economic development and social progress, which were high on the agenda of the Kemalists. Women's emancipation was also a way to distance the new Turkey from the old.

Another reason was that Mustafa Kemal had been highly impressed by the courage and militancy of Turkish women during the Balkan wars and World War I. Turkish women had taken up new avenues of public employment as nurses on the war fronts and had worked in ammunition, food, and textile factories as well as in banks, hospitals, and the administrative services. The occupation of various parts of Turkey by European troops in 1919 aroused protests in which women joined, and women in Anatolia were part of Mustapha Kemal's army in its war against the invaders. In his speeches in later years Kemal constantly referred to the role played by Anatolian women in the nationalist struggle. In a speech at Izmir in 1923 he said, "A civilization where one sex is supreme can be condemned, there and then, as crippled. A people which has decided to go forward and progress must realize this as quickly as possible. The failures in our past are due to the fact that we remained passive to the fate of women."[18]

In the 1935 elections, eighteen women were elected (4.5 percent of the Assembly), the highest number of women deputies in Europe at that time. Clearly the Turkish case exemplifies the women's emancipation model of twentieth-century revolutions.

THE NICARAGUAN CASE

Nicaragua is also an example of feminist attempts to influence the process of revolutionary transition. Many urban feminists, like many poor and rural Nicaraguan women, supported the Sandinista Revolution, viewing it as offering Nicaraguan women their best chance to obtain full equality. The revolution occurred in the period after the upsurge of the "new feminism" of the late 1960s, at a time when Latin American women were mobilizing around feminist demands in such countries as Mexico, Peru, and Brazil. In 1977, the Association of Women Confronting the National Problem (AMPRONAC) was formed, and combined a commitment to overthrow the Somoza regime with that of struggling for women's equality. Unlike many of its counterparts elsewhere, the Sandinista Front (FSLN) did not denounce feminism as a "counterrevolutionary diversion." When they came to power, sections of the Sandinista leadership recognized the legitimacy of and need for women's liberation in Nicaragua, as well as support for the objectives of the feminist wing, renamed AMNLAE. As in many other countries, however, the Sandinistas and the AMNLAE had to contend with deeply entrenched sexist attitudes and hostility to the idea of women's emancipation. Consequently, the Sandinistas began to build popular support for AMNLAE's campaigns, including an ideological attack on machismo. The government's own emphasis was on legal reform and the political participation of women.

In a social context of high rates of male desertion, migrancy, and serial polygamy which had contributed to the emergence of impoverished households maintained by women alone, new laws were enacted to strengthen the position of women within the family, to clarify the responsibilities of each family member, and to promote family cohesion. Improvements were made in the working conditions of women workers, and rural women workers were given the legal right to receive and control their income themselves. Women's political participation was also encouraged, and a substantial number of highly visible women came to occupy high-level party and government positions as heads of provincial governments, party officers, head of the police, and minister of health.

AMNLAE took a radical turn in the early 1980s and assumed a more feminist stance. It made proposals to the Council of State (the precursor of the National Assembly) on gender issues and used the print and electronic media to stimulate public debate. AMNLAE agitated for the inclusion of women in the draft, and made extensive efforts to promote international solidarity with women from other countries. But AMNLAE did not succeed in having women included in the draft and in legalizing abortion. Birth control was legal and available through public health clinics and private pharmacies, but difficult to obtain. Eventually, the growing numbers of female deaths due to botched abortions brought the abortion controversy out into the open.

The reproductive rights controversy in Nicaragua signaled some of the emerging new divisions within the movement and in the society. While no one was against some form of women's emancipation, understandings of what constituted this emancipation varied considerably, from a limited, traditional protection of women and their mobilization behind certain national campaigns (employment, defense of the revolution, mass education, and health), to policies informed by feminism which saw an alteration of gender relations and the full implementation of reproductive rights as the goals towards which the revolution should be moving. This dynamic debate in Nicaragua today is one of the strengths of the Nicaraguan revolution.

CONCLUSIONS: REVOLUTIONS, STATE-BUILDING, AND GENDER

Revolutions are a special case of social change and collective action that entail attempts to rapidly transform political and economic structures, social relations, and societal institutions to conform to an ideal or an ideology. The twentieth century has been called the century of revolutions, and two sets of scholarship have examined revolutionary change. In one set, standard social-science studies have emphasized the international context as well as class, status, and power within a given society, but have ignored gender as an analytic category in revolutionary transformation. In the other set, feminist studies have revealed the significance of gender dynamics and their links to political, economic, and ideological processes, including constructions of national identity, in times of social transformation. In this essay I have tried to show that women and gender issues figure prominently in political discourses, state ideologies, legal policies, and the construction of a national identity. Although revolutionary transformations are shaped by preexisting gender systems, changes in societal values and ideologies and in economic strategies brought about by revolutions also affect gender relations.

At times of regime consolidation, state-building, and identity formation, questions of the construction of gender, the family, and relations between women and men come to the fore. Cultural representations of women, changes to family law, and legislation on reproductive rights and women's rights reflect the importance of gender in politics and ideology and signal the political agenda of revolutionaries and regimes. Whether political discourses support women's emancipation and equality or whether they glorify tradition, morality, the family, and difference, the point remains that political ideologies and practices are gendered and that social transformation and state-building entail changes in gender relations as well as new class configurations and property relations.

In my reading of twentieth-century revolutionary transformations, two models of womanhood have emerged. One model, which I have called the woman's emancipation model, draws its inspiration from the Enlightenment, the socialist tradition, and the Bolshevik Revolution. This model is more consistent with feminist demands for equality and empowerment of women. The patriarchal model, which I have called the woman-in-the-family model, seems to occur where revolutionaries draw from their own cultural repertoire, frequently in reaction to external modes of control. The cases of revolutionary transformation discussed in this essay, and others not discussed but included in Table 1, confirm the strong links among social transformation, state-building, and laws about women and the family. Revolutionizing society and transforming women are two sides of the same coin.

The differentiation of revolutions by gender outcomes shows that gender is indeed an integral dimension of the revolutionary process and should be accorded conceptual value by sociologists of revolution. Future research in the sociology of revolution, or in analyses of other types of social transformations, should examine more closely the articulation of gender with class, ethnicity, state policies, and world-systemic processes. Research should also attempt to situate gender issues, in a more systematic manner than I have been able to do, in the various stages of a revolution, including the prerevolutionary conditions, proximate causes, the course of the revolution, and its short-term and long-term outcomes. A fruitful line of inquiry could also be whether or not feminist discourses and the growth of women's movements worldwide will reduce patriarchal outcomes in future instances of social transformation.

REFERENCES

1. Rowbotham (1972); Davies (1983).
2. Reynolds (1987a).
3. Tétreault (1994).
4. Papanek (1994).
5. Moghadam (1993), Chapter 3. It should be noted that I use the term "patriarchal" in the strict sense of a form of social organization or an ideology which confines women to the role of wife and mother under male guardianship.
6. Molyneux (1986), pp. 283–84.
7. Ibid., p. 297.
8. Mies (1986), p. 199.
9. Molyneux (1986); Chinchilla (1990).
10. Labao (1990).
11. Urdang (1989), p. 28.
12. Quoted in Reynolds (1987b), p. 113. The similarities to the discourses of the Iranian Revolution are quite striking.
13. Cited in Kelly (1987), p. 127.
14. Applewhite and Levy, (1990), pp. 17–19.
15. Habibi (1995).
16. Marx et al. (1977), pp. 56, 59.
17. Ibid., p. 61.
18. Quoted in Kandiyoti (1989), p. 142.

Dictatorship or Democracy:
Outcomes of Revolution in Iran and Nicaragua

JOHN FORAN AND JEFF GOODWIN

In 1979, revolutions in Nicaragua and Iran overthrew U.S.-supported dictators: General Somoza in Nicaragua and Shah Reza Pahlavi in Iran. Both of the new revolutionary regimes also came into conflict with the United States: in Nicaragua over the regime's socialist ideology and support for revolutionaries in El Salvador, and in Iran over the regime's Islamic nationalism and capture of hostages in the U.S. embassy. Yet the unfolding of these revolutions, despite similar starting points, followed different paths. Iran's revolutionary regime defeated all its foes and by 1990 had consolidated its power over state and society. By contrast, in Nicaragua the Sandinistas held—and lost—free and open elections in 1990, becoming just another political party in a truly competitive democracy. Foran and Goodwin show how these contrasting outcomes developed, highlighting the importance of the post-revolutionary competition for power, the reactions of the United States, and the ideologies of the revolutionary leaders.

A THEORY OF REVOLUTIONARY OUTCOMES IN THE THIRD WORLD

In this article, we present a theory of revolutionary outcomes in the Third World and apply it to the cases of Iran and Nicaragua. Most successful revolutions in poorer, dependent countries have been characterized by the formation of broad, multi-class coalitions in opposition to highly repressive dictatorships that have been supported (and perhaps installed) by foreign powers. Furthermore, the success of these broad coalitions in actually toppling such regimes has been made possible by, among other factors, a permissive international context that is characterized above all by the suspension of external support for the dictatorship. With the fall of the old regime, however, the original revolutionary coalition typically begins to fragment, as the common enemy that once held the coalition together has disappeared. Such fragmentation has led to a sometimes bloody scramble for power among former allies following the overthrow of the old regime. The outcomes of this type of revolution are largely explained by which political leaders within the original revolutionary coalition are able to hold on to state power after the overthrow of the old regime, and by what that leadership is willing and able to do with that power.

Revolution thus requires rebuilding of state institutions that have typically been shattered with the fall of the old regime, especially the army and civil administration. It may also require political and social changes in order to win or maintain the support (or at least neutrality) of various sectors of the population that have been mobilized during the revolution. Certain revolutionary initiatives may be more or less compromised, if not undermined altogether, by the struggle to consolidate state power in the face of opposition from other social groups. Outcomes may also be affected by certain legacies of the old regime, including the state's limited administrative capacities and material resources, and its dependence upon the capital and skills of domestic elites. This accounts for the often-noted fact that the outcomes of revolutions are hardly ever those intended by the new revolutionary leadership, let alone those intended by other groups in the original revolutionary coalition.

From Theory and Society, *vol. 22, 1993, pp. 209–247. Copyright © 1993 by Kluwer Academic Publishers. Reprinted with kind permission of Kluwer Academic Publishers.*

Furthermore, as Susan Eckstein has argued [see the next essay in this chapter—Ed.], the underdevelopment and dependence on the world economy that characterize much of the Third World may severely constrain attempts to transform socioeconomic structures radically unless the new leadership is able to link up with a powerful foreign sponsor—which, of course, only recasts the problem of dependency in a different guise. The overthrow of the old order also invites external intervention since foreign powers—especially, in the post–World War II context, the United States—generally attempt to manipulate the new regime for their own economic and geopolitical purposes.

In short, struggles over state power following the overthrow of old regimes in Third World societies—which largely determine the outcome of such revolutions—typically occur in a context characterized by (1) the fragmentation of the original revolutionary coalition, (2) limited state capacities, (3) economic underdevelopment, (4) external aggression, and (5) continued dependence on the world economy or domestic elites. An adequate account of the outcomes of Third World revolutions needs to show the specific effects of each of these factors on struggles to reconsolidate state power.

Although the control of state power thus stands at the center of our analysis, we wish to qualify this approach to revolutionary outcomes in two specific ways. First, the requirements of rebuilding effective state institutions do not *strictly* determine such outcomes; indeed, these requirements are themselves subject to interpretation and struggle and thereby leave plenty of "play" for the ideology and popular commitments (if not the personal whims) of the new revolutionary leaders. In other words, the exact nature and extent of the transformation of state and society are partly determined by the social base and political ideology of the new revolutionary leadership.

Second, we must not overlook the fact that revolutionaries have other goals and commitments besides controlling state power. In the wake of the 1990 elections in Nicaragua, which we analyze below, we are now in a better position to see that revolutionaries will not do anything and everything in order to maintain state power.

We have chosen to examine Iran and Nicaragua because, despite important similarities, these are revolutions that have had dramatically different outcomes. The Iranian revolution has produced an authoritarian theocracy, whereas the Nicaraguan revolution has given rise to a pluralist democracy. An adequate theory of revolutionary outcomes ought to be able to account for both the similarities *and* the differences.

THE OUTCOMES OF REVOLUTION: IRAN

The revolution against the Shah in 1977–79 was the work of a broad coalition including clerics (the *ulama*) and middle-class intellectuals in leadership positions, as well as a massive base of striking industrial workers, hard-pressed merchants and artisans of the bazaar economy, students, office workers, professionals, and urban lower-class women and men from the shantytowns of the major cities.

Our analysis focuses on the dynamics of the coalition that made the revolution, to explain how one group—the *ulama*—came to prevail after 1979. It also attempts to explain why the *ulama's* hold on the Iranian state and society has ultimately proven stronger than that of the Sandinistas in Nicaragua.

INTERNAL POLITICAL STRUGGLES

The struggle for power in the Iranian revolution did not end with the fall of the shah and the triumphant return of Ayatollah Khomeini from exile in February 1979, but rather with the rise to ascendancy of the clerical wing of the revolution by the end of 1981. The more than two years between these events was the decisive period in the shaping of the new state and its institutions. They witnessed the severe fracturing of the broad coalition that brought down the shah, as first liberals and then the left (both secular and Islamic) were forced into confrontations that the militant *ulama* handled very astutely. By the end of this period the leaders of the new regime were well on their way to consolidating their particular vision of an Islamic state in Iran, despite intense internal challenges and external pressures.

The *ulama* won this struggle for power due to a variety of advantages: its opponents were crucially divided among themselves; it was better organized and better equipped for violent confrontations; it gained control over significant economic resources; it appropriated some of the enormous prestige of Khomeini as well as the popular appeal of his version of a militant Islam; and it skillfully manipulated a series of external crises.

The first revolutionary government of Prime Minister Mehdi Bazargan was composed of Muslim and secular middle-class professionals and intellectuals. It set about trying to restore a semblance of order to the economy and polity in the midst of a highly mobilized population. A critical juncture arose in the summer of 1979 when acrimonious debates over a new draft constitution prompted Khomeini to summon the *ulama* to create an Islamic basis for the new state. This was ultimately enshrined in the constitutional provision for the so-called "rule of the jurist" giving Khomeini far-ranging veto powers over the parliament (the *majlis*) and making legislation subject to conformity with Islamic law. In this period the repression of secular progressives such as the left-of-center National Democratic Front began under the new security forces, the Revolutionary Guards. The onslaught against secular and middle-class women began as early as International Women's Day on 8 March 1979, when a huge rally was attacked by Muslim street toughs known as *hizbullahis* ("partisans of God"). The seizure of the American embassy on 4 November 1979 by radical Muslim students led to the resignation of Bazargan, partly out of frustration at the turn of events and partly due to his association with American officials just prior to the crisis.

The fall of Bazargan did not immediately bring the fundamentalist clerics to the fore, but rather the left-of-center Muslim politician Abul Hasan Bani Sadr, a close associate of Khomeini. In January 1980, Bani Sadr won the first presidential elections. The *ulama* quickly regrouped, however, and dominated the March 1980 elections for the *majlis*, gaining over half the seats; only a small minority of sympathizers and independents supported Bani Sadr, who lacked a political party of his own. The next eighteen months saw a complex and protracted struggle between Bani Sadr's supporters and the *ulama*, against the backdrop of yet another external crisis, the war that began with the Iraqi invasion of September 1980.

Bani Sadr drew support from the merchants of the bazaar, the secular middle class, and elements in the regular army, of which he was commander-in-chief. But he lacked a large base of support. The *ulama*, by contrast, mobilized supporters from the urban lower class, religious students, the state bureaucracy and mass media (both of which it increasingly controlled), and its parallel military force, the Revolutionary Guards. Intellectuals and industrial workers were badly divided, with some supporting communist parties, and others supporting Khomeini, but all opposing Bani Sadr, who was seen as too moderate.

In June 1981 the parliament, under control of the *ulama,* stripped Bani Sadr of the presidency and forced him into hiding and, eventually, exile in France. The *ulama* then skillfully consolidated their hold on society by remaking the institutions of the Iranian state in an Islamic mold. The legal system was brought under religious jurisdiction, radio and television were harnessed to the propaganda needs of the party, and the universities were closed for two years in order to remove secular teachers and "Islamicize" the curriculum. The Revolutionary Guards were strengthened as a military force, and the regular army was supervised by political-ideological commissars; the size of the armed forces grew from 390,000 in 1976 to more than 1.1 million by the mid-1980s, including the regular army, the Revolutionary Guards, and reservists. The state bureaucracy was purged several times and staffed by loyal supporters. Furthermore, large sectors of the economy also came under the state's control, giving it vast material resources with which to reward the faithful.

The untroubled political succession after Khomeini's death in June 1989 gave further testimony to the solidity of the new state institutions. Ayatollah Khomeini may have been an enormously charismatic leader, but the power of the new Iranian regime was clearly based on much more than his popular appeal alone.

In summary, the revolutionary *ulama* emerged as the ultimate arbiters of power in Iran due to the disunity of their opponents, their more effective mobilization of mass support, their control over vast state revenues, and their ability to turn external crises into opportunities to rally the nation under the banner of their version of Islam, which spoke to the dignity of the oppressed and exploited Iranian masses. As a result of all these factors, opposition to the revolutionary *ulama* was basically eliminated from the scene, and a new theocratic state was able to consolidate a strong grip on society.

WORLD-SYSTEMIC PRESSURES

Iran's "special relationship" with the United States was dealt a fatal blow after the November 1979 seizure of the American embassy by radical students, acting independently of the Bazargan government. The students initially planned to hold onto the hostages only for a few days, but the massive demonstrations of public support for their action and the discovery of considerable amounts of intelligence data inside the embassy convinced them to broaden their demands to include the return of the shah from the United States to stand trial, and the repatriation of $24 billion of his wealth taken outside of the country.

As noted above, the liberal Bazargan government fell immediately after the embassy's seizure, and, as the crisis wore on into 1980, the left-of-center administration of Bani Sadr was weakened by its inability to settle the confrontation (as was the Carter administration in the United States), whose prolongation Khomeini supported. Though the shah and his wealth were never returned (nor were the billions of dollars of Iranian assets that had been frozen by Carter), the crisis neutralized U.S. pressure on Iran in the post-revolutionary period and dramatically severed the web of political, military, financial, and economic ties to the U.S. established under the shah. The militant Islamic ideology of the ruling clerics also received a boost in the public's political consciousness at the expense of liberals, moderates, and conservatives.

The regime also turned to its advantage a still greater external threat, the war with Iraq (1980–1988). Iraqi dictator Saddam Hussein had several motives for his September 1980 invasion of Iran: he feared the export of Islamic revolution to Iraq's large Shi'a population; he sought political leadership in the Arab world; and he calculated that Iran's own Arab minority in the oil-rich Khuzistan province adjacent to Iraq would welcome him, while Iran's demoralized regular army would be ineffective. In this last supposition he proved grossly mistaken. The army and the Revolutionary Guards fought well, and the Iranian public rallied behind the war effort. By 1982 Iraq was on the defensive; Khomeini, his domestic opponents now cowed, decided in turn to prosecute the war into Iraq, demanding the overthrow of Saddam Hussein and sponsoring an Iraqi government-in-exile.

Khomeini's plans, however, proved as futile as Iraq's ambitions. The conflict dragged on for eight years, producing some of the worst devastation since the World Wars, including human-wave attacks by Iran, the use of chemical weapons by Iraq, and the bombing of cities by both sides. When Khomeini accepted the "bitter poison" of a cease-fire in July 1988, neither side had won much territory. Instead, Iran had suffered at least 160,000 dead (other estimates claim 300,000 or more) and some $450 billion in damage to cities, villages, ports, and oil facilities. The country had been set back a generation in terms of human and material development, a third of the government's budget having been devoted to the war effort. Balanced against the undoubted grief and war-weariness of the population, however, were the strengthening of the regime's coercive institutions and its undeniable ability to mobilize support for its war aims, at least up to a point. As Khomeini declared, "War enables us to fight the counterrevolutionaries." The war also kept public attention focused on Iran's external enemies and justified the revolution's slow progress in meeting demands on other fronts.

The Limits of Revolutionary Transformation

Despite the considerable political achievements of the *ulama* in consolidating a stable regime, the Achilles' heel of the Iranian revolution has been its limited achievements in the economic sphere. The state came to control banks, insurance companies, construction firms, and commercial, agricultural, and industrial enterprises that employed approximately 370,000 industrial workers. Yet state industry generally operated at a loss, with mismanagement at times compounded by shortages of spare parts and other Western inputs. Much of Iran's foreign trade also passed through state hands. Only small and medium industry remained the domain of a private capitalist sector.

Oil was the linchpin that provided the *ulama* with the means to buy popular support, enact welfare measures, finance the war, and project itself as a regional power. On the other hand, the availability and seeming abundance of oil revenue also allowed and perhaps even encouraged inefficiencies in other economic sectors, and periodic shortfalls of such revenue eroded the state's social welfare and developmental capacities.

The government was able to penetrate the countryside to a degree through road-building and literacy and electrification campaigns. However, food production stagnated in per-capita terms as demand and population grew, forcing the creation of a rationing system that benefited the urban poor, but also requiring continued food imports of some $4 billion per year. Massive migration to the cities continued apace in this context, overburdening the urban infrastructure as Tehran's population swelled dramatically from 4 million in 1979 to 11 million by 1991.

The urban marginal population, which provided the "shock troops" of the revolution, has benefited from food rationing, and some tens of thousands have experienced a sort of upward mobility, however dangerous, through the Revolutionary Guards. Nonetheless, the urban poor still number in the millions and continue to suffer appalling privations as a class.

Members of the middle class have had varying experiences—dismissal from their jobs for some (especially westernized, professional women who held highly visible jobs in business, media, and government), along with adaptation and advancement for others of a more acceptable ideological stripe. The initial gains of the working class evaporated by 1981 as independent factory councils were taken over by the state and workers were massively mobilized into the war effort at the expense of their living standards. High rates of inflation (a serious problem since wages are not indexed to inflation), significant unemployment (despite the huge size of the army and state sector), and a housing crisis have eroded the quality of life of the urban population as a whole.

In drawing up a provisional balance sheet on the outcome of the Iranian revolution, both the political accomplishments and economic limitations of the revolution stand out. From the viewpoint of the clerical state, of course, the outcome has been a fairly clear-cut success: the theocracy has maintained its hold on power against external pressures from Iraq and the United States, and it has eliminated its organized opponents with no strong internal challenge on the horizon. On the other hand, these achievements serve only to highlight the revolution's failures in the realms of civil and political freedoms and economic development.

The legitimacy of the clerical state remains limited due to its inability to bring economic development, and the "pragmatists" who dominate the new government under President Khatami are looking to create political and economic reforms. However, whether they will be able to make major changes in the face of clerical opposition remains a dubious proposition.

THE OUTCOMES OF REVOLUTION: NICARAGUA

The armed insurrection against the regime of Anastasio Somoza Debayle (1967–1979) that was led by the Sandinista Front for National Liberation (FSLN) was supported, like the Iranian revolution, by a very broad multi-class movement that included students, artisans, tradespeople, blue- and white-collar workers, professionals, priests, and members of Christian-based communities. Unlike the revolutionary coalition in Iran, the anti-Somoza movement also drew support from peasants and agricultural workers (although the insurrection of 1978–79 was primarily urban-based). Somoza's flight from the country, after his 7,000–10,000 member National Guard was gradually spread thin by multiple urban uprisings coordinated by the Sandinistas, resulted in the triumph of a broadly based movement and a provisional government with both Sandinista and elite representation. As in Iran, this set the stage for an increasingly intense conflict within the anti-Somoza coalition *after* the Sandinistas triumphantly entered Managua on 19 July 1979.

As in the Iranian case, an explanation of the outcomes of the Nicaraguan revolution must focus on the consolidation and use of state power in a context characterized by the fragmentation of the original revolutionary coalition, external aggression, and continued economic weakness. For Nicaragua, however, we must not only explain the manner in which a particular political leadership—the Sandinista Front—consolidated state power after the fall of the old regime, but also why this same leadership subsequently lost power (at least partially) in the elections of February 1990. The Sandinistas' electoral defeat calls for an explanation of both their unwillingness, unlike the *ulama* in Iran, to eliminate effectively their domestic opposition as well as their creation of a democratic constitutional framework in which they *could* lose power to this opposition. We must explain, in other words, the comparatively pluralist and democratic outcome of the Nicaraguan revolution.

INTERNAL POLITICAL STRUGGLES

After the fall of Somoza, the Sandinistas faced little or no opposition. They were thus able to establish control over the new government and dominate the policy-making process while avoiding the use of openly authoritarian tactics.

Within a few months, the Sandinistas nationalized exports and banking and expropriated more than 180 industrial and commercial enterprises and about one-fifth of all arable land in the country. The Sandinistas also initiated a number of popular social programs designed to improve the population's health and welfare, including a literacy crusade, the construction of new schools and health clinics, and the subsidization of retail food sales. A major agrarian reform was implemented. And, in order to consolidate further their political base among the lower classes, the Sandinistas vastly expanded a number of mass organizations for youth, women, and urban and rural workers. With the complete collapse of the National Guard, the new Popular Sandinista Army (EPS) was built up around a core of FSLN guerrilla veterans and Sandinista-led popular militias recruited during the insurrection.

Even with these dramatic changes, however, the Sandinistas made it clear that they would not expropriate the bourgeoisie—the owners of large private farms and companies—so long as they continued to use their property productively. There would be no quick transition to socialism à la Cuba. And while the Sandinistas consolidated their control over the state apparatus, oppositional political parties and media were generally tolerated. The Sandinista strategy was to consolidate a new regime in which the bourgeoisie would be encouraged to play an important role in the economy, but would be essentially excluded from political power.

The Sandinistas recognized that the bourgeoisie was the key to friendly economic and diplomatic relations with the West, particularly the United States, which would be necessary to reconstruct the economy from the devastation of the insurrectionary period. Of course, if a foreign power had offered the Sandinistas an alternative source of the requisite technical personnel and financial aid necessary for nationalizing the economy, the Sandinistas might very well have expropriated the bourgeoisie after seizing power, like the guerrillas who seized power in Cuba twenty years earlier. However, neither the Soviet Union nor any other regime was willing or able to play this role. Consequently, the mixed-economy model that evolved under the Front is closer to that of post-revolutionary Mexico (at least since the 1930s), Bolivia, and Chile under Allende than it is to Cuba or Vietnam.

Nonetheless, by the end of 1980 a series of sharp disputes between the Sandinistas and the bourgeoisie over the sanctity of private property and representation on the new Council of State had effectively sundered the original revolutionary coalition. The bourgeoisie was anxious and uncertain about the Front's position on nationalizing large properties. Also, the Front expanded the representation of mass organizations in the Council of State, a legislative body based on representation of various anti-Somoza groupings, to give the Sandinista bloc a one-vote majority. Soon thereafter, the Superior Council of Private Enterprise

(COSEP), the bourgeoisie's principal organization, withdrew its representatives from the Council of State.

In November 1980, COSEP vice-chairman Jorge Salazar was killed in a shoot-out with the state police; the Sandinistas soon produced evidence that Salazar was involved in a conspiracy to overthrow the government, although, for the bourgeoisie, Salazar's death appeared to be nothing less than a gratuitous act of state violence. The bourgeoisie thenceforth increasingly distanced itself from the government, attacking the Sandinistas with ever harsher rhetoric.

The Catholic Church hierarchy also broke with the Sandinistas during this period. During the controversy concerning the Council of State, the Catholic bishops suddenly demanded the resignation of those priests who held cabinet positions. Unlike the Iranian revolution, then, the Nicaraguans would not enjoy the blessing, let alone the guidance, of the country's leading religious figures. And in Nicaragua, unlike Iran, an internal basis for U.S. intervention remained after the overthrow of Somoza in the form of the Church hierarchy and especially the bourgeoisie.

WORLD-SYSTEMIC PRESSURES

The fragmentation and polarization of the original revolutionary coalition was reinforced by the policies of the United States. In 1981, U.S. President Ronald Reagan authorized the CIA to assist anti-Sandinista groups and conduct covert operations against Nicaragua. After two bridges were destroyed in northern Nicaragua in March 1982 the Sandinistas declared a national state of emergency—limiting civil liberties, including press freedoms and the right to strike—that would remain in force for most of the next eight years.

The Reagan administration not only organized and financed (with and without Congressional approval) a counterrevolutionary army—the so-called *contras,* commanded primarily by former members of Somoza's National Guard—but also formed a civilian leadership, allegedly in control of this army, from some of the leading figures among the bourgeois opposition. At the same time, Washington sought to isolate Nicaragua politically and economically at the international level. The Sandinistas' forced relocation of peasants in conflict zones, including Miskito Indians in the Atlantic Coast region, and the Sandinistas' conflict with the Church and the worsening economic crisis of the 1980s (see below) also benefited the *contras.*

The Sandinistas eventually responded to the *contra* insurgency with an integrated military and political strategy. A military draft was begun, and the army was expanded from 13,000–18,000 in 1980 to over 40,000 by 1984; local militias numbered another 60,000 to 100,000. Most importantly, perhaps, agrarian reform was accelerated: plots of land and land titles were granted mainly to individuals, and less emphasis was placed on establishing state farms or even cooperatives. This policy was clearly intended to preempt sympathy for the *contras* among the rural poor, whose land hunger had not been systematically addressed by the Sandinistas. Eventually, the Front's counterinsurgency proved quite effective. The *contras'* momentum was broken, and their troop levels peaked at about 15,000 in 1985–86. The *contras* were never able to hold even a small town for more than a few hours, and they certainly never managed to incite a generalized anti-Sandinista revolt.

A different strategy, however, would be necessary to end the opposition of the United States and the bourgeoisie. The centerpiece of that strategy was the elections of 1984:

> The decision to hold elections, announced in December of 1983, two months after the United States invaded Grenada, clearly came in response to growing fears that Nicaragua would be next. If the elections were going to establish enough international legitimacy to stymie the United States, the FSLN realized, Nicaragua's opposition parties would have to take part.[1]

Accordingly, after much debate, the FSLN decided to "replace the Council of State with a National Assembly constituted by political party representatives," a decision that "drastically undermined the role of the mass organizations in shaping the course of the revolution."[2] In fact, the representative democracy inaugurated in Nicaragua in 1984 and written into the 1987 Constitution represents a compromise of sorts that was partly intended to placate the bourgeoisie and the United States.

The principal opposition candidate in the 1984 election, Arturo Cruz, eventually withdrew, claiming that the conditions for a free contest did not exist. Still, six diverse opposition parties ran against the Front, winning one-third of the vote and gaining 35 of 96 seats in the National Assembly. The elections were judged generally free and fair by observer teams from the British House of Commons and Lords, the Irish Parliament, the Dutch government, the Socialist International, and the Latin American Studies Association.

Neither the 1984 elections nor the "strategic defeat" of the *contras,* however, ended the opposition of the United States and the bourgeoisie to the Sandinista government. In January 1985, the U.S. vetoed a $59.8 million loan to Nicaragua from the Inter-American Development Bank for a large-scale agricultural project. In May 1985, President Reagan imposed a trade embargo on Nicaragua, banning virtually all commercial contact between the two countries. Scattered *contra* attacks also continued as the *contras* continued to receive so-called "humanitarian" aid right through the 1990 elections.

All told, externally supported aggression took an enormous toll on Nicaragua during the 1980s. Approximately thirty thousand Nicaraguans were killed and tens of thousands wounded as a result of the *contra* war. Government estimates of the economic costs of the war range from $1.5 billion to $4 billion, the equivalent of almost three years of gross domestic product. By 1987, over sixty percent of government expenditures (nearly one-third of GDP) were required for defense.

The economic limits of the Sandinista revolution were reflected in the Front's decisive defeat in the February 1990 elections at the hands of the National Opposition Union (UNO), a coalition of fourteen diverse mini-parties. As Carlos Vilas has argued,

> The outcome of the elections was conditioned in its most fundamental aspects by a decade of counterrevolutionary war that left thousands dead, wounded and crippled, the economic and social infrastructure in ruins, hundreds of thousands of people displaced—drafted into military service, relocated to refugee camps, forced to flee to the cities to escape attack—and basic goods in desperately short supply. The people voted against that.[3]

In response to this economic morass, the Sandinistas implemented "shock" austerity measures in 1988 and 1989, including massive and repeated devaluations of the currency, the lifting of price controls, cuts in government spending, and increases in credit to the private sector. But these actions created massive inflation. Real wages fell from an index of 29.2 in February 1988 (1980 = 100) to 6.5 in June 1989 and to 1 by December. Tuberculosis and malaria spread widely, and during the first trimester of 1989 infant mortality due to diarrhea was double that of a year earlier.

Not surprisingly, polling during the 1990 electoral campaign indicated that the economy (52%), the war (37%), or both (8%) were viewed as the decisive issues in the election. And while a majority of those polled (52%) blamed Nicaragua's economic problems on the *contra* war or the U.S. economic embargo, 61 percent felt that UNO would be able to "reconcile" Nicaragua with the United States, while only 50 percent felt that the FSLN could do so, and fully 36 percent were convinced that the FSLN could *not* do so. The anti-Sandinista vote, in other words, apparently "reflected a decision by a significant number of Nicaraguans to believe that the United States would *not* accept a Sandinista victory and [was] a rational choice, under those premises, to bring an end to the war, the embargo, and the destruction of the economy."[4]

A provisional balance sheet of the outcome of the Nicaraguan revolution, like that of Iran, would have to emphasize both its political accomplishments and economic limits. First and foremost, a brutal, personalist dictatorship has been overthrown and replaced with a broadly legitimate pluralist democracy. Nicaraguan civil society, moreover, has been immensely strengthened over the past decade; a broad spectrum of political parties, media, trade unions, and other mass organizations is more vigorous than at any previous time in Nicaraguan history.

These achievements notwithstanding, Nicaragua is actually further from socialism today than it was in 1979. Although there has been some redistribution of land, productive forces have been reduced to levels characteristic of the 1960s, and poverty has increased.

SUMMARY AND CONCLUSIONS

Despite their evident differences, a number of striking similarities between the outcomes of the Iranian and Nicaraguan revolutions have been noted here, three of which merit special emphasis. First of all, both revolutions produced stronger, more bureaucratic, and more mass-mobilizing states, a finding that accords well with Skocpol's state-centric account of revolutionary outcomes. In this respect, the Iranian and Nicaraguan revolutions have not differed from the "classic" revolutions in France, Russia, and China nor, indeed, from state- and nation-building revolutions elsewhere in the Third World.

Secondly, and largely as a result of the preceding outcome, both regimes were able to fend off external military assaults. Such aggression, however, produced severe economic problems in both countries and thereby eroded the popularity of the ruling groups, bolstering the fortunes of more moderate leaders. In Nicaragua, especially, a country that is smaller, poorer, and much more vulnerable to economic and military aggression than Iran, the U.S.-backed counterrevolution helped to produce an extremely severe economic crisis that led to the defeat of the Sandinista Front in the February 1990 elections. Iran's rentier state, by contrast, which could finance its war efforts with oil revenues, proved rather less vulnerable to external aggression.

A third similarity between these two revolutions—and one that we have particularly emphasized in this article—is their limited success in transforming the economic structures of Iran and Nicaragua. Neither revolution has been particularly successful in promoting industrialization or in limiting dependence on external commodity or financial markets. Furthermore, while the landed upper class has been weakened, it remains economically intact and currently has a measure of political influence in both countries—an outcome that distinguishes Iran and Nicaragua from most other social revolutions in the Third World.

Notwithstanding these similarities, we would emphasize five critical differences between the outcomes of the Iranian and Nicaraguan revolutions. First of all, the new leaderships in Iran and Nicaragua differed in both their social base and their political ideology. Although the new leaderships in both countries had strong ties to the urban lower classes, the *ulama* in Iran were also closely tied to merchants and large landowners; they had no such ties to either the industrial working class or the peasantry. The Sandinistas, for their part, lacked strong ties to either merchants or landlords, but had quite strong connections to peasants and agricultural workers.

Even more importantly, perhaps, the political ideologies of these leaderships differed in fundamental ways, despite the "populist" and nationalist themes in their discourses. Iran's *ulama* aspired first and foremost to an "Islamic Republic" guided by the Koran (as they interpreted it), while the Sandinistas envisaged a secular (but religiously tolerant) revolutionary government based on an alliance of workers and peasants. We have noted how these ideologies, as Goldstone and others have suggested, are crucial determinants of revolutionary outcomes in Iran and Nicaragua.

Secondly, the *way* in which power was initially consolidated differed in these revolutions. The outcome of the Iranian revolution was not firmly "settled" until 1981, and only then after a violent struggle between the *ulama* and their opponents. In the course of this struggle any effective opposition in Iran was essentially eliminated. In Nicaragua, by contrast, the Sandinistas were quickly able to assert their political dominance in the immediate postinsurrectionary period, and they were willing and able to do so in a nonviolent fashion. The Sandinistas' internal opponents were tolerated for the most part so long as they did not oppose the regime through extra-legal means or economic sabotage.

A third difference in the outcomes of the Iranian and Nicaraguan revolutions is that although neither radically transformed economic or class structures, there can be no doubt that the Sandinistas, at least initially, attempted and to some extent achieved much more substantial socioeconomic change than their Iranian counterparts—a difference clearly linked to the ideology and social base of the new revolutionary leaders. In their attempt to improve the quality of life for the poor majority in Nicaragua, the Sandinistas launched ambitious literacy and public health campaigns and, perhaps most importantly, implemented a far-reaching agrarian reform. While the new regime in Iran did implement literacy and rural improvement campaigns, no equivalent agrarian-reform initiatives were attempted. An early attempt at land reform was essentially blocked due to opposition from landowners and conservative *ulama.*

The great irony here is that the new political leaders in Iran, given their control of a resource-rich rentier state, always had a much freer hand than their counterparts in Nicaragua to institute sweeping social changes. That they failed to do so is due both to the relative weakness of any impetus "from below" on the part of their own social base—in part because of the prominence of merchants and landowners within that base—and to the conservative economic views of many, indeed probably most, *ulama*.

A fourth difference between these revolutions is the fact that the political leadership that initially consolidated power has retained it in Iran but lost it, at least partially, in Nicaragua. The defeat of the Sandinistas in the February 1990 elections, we have argued, was determined in the first instance by the severe economic crisis in Nicaragua, a crisis that a majority of Nicaraguans believed was the result of the direct and indirect forms of economic and military aggression waged by the United States. Given the policies of the United States, voters quite rationally concluded that this crisis could not be resolved as long as the Sandinistas remained in power. In a very important sense, however, the Sandinistas lost power because, unlike the *ulama* in Iran, they created a type of political regime in which they *could* lose power.

This brings us to a final, and perhaps the most important, difference in the outcomes of these revolutions, namely, the nature of the new political regimes that were eventually consolidated. In Iran, the revolution has given rise to a remarkably illiberal theocracy that recognizes few civil or political rights (especially for women and religious and ethnic minorities) and that periodically stages mass executions of those who have opposed the regime. To be sure, a specific sort of "democratization" has accompanied revolutionary state-building in Iran—democratization understood not as an extension of political liberalism but as an enhancement of popular involvement in national political life. However, political debate and electoral alternatives inhabit a very narrow range of the political spectrum.

In Nicaragua, by contrast, the revolution has produced a pluralist, representative democracy that generally respects civil and political freedoms (including the freedom of religion) and that has abolished the death penalty; political organizations from the far right to the far left actively participate in the political life of the country. Indeed, in 1990 the Nicaraguan government became the world's first to come to power through a revolutionary struggle and then transfer power to its opposition voluntarily after free elections.

These differences in regimes arose from the dynamics of struggle within the revolutionary coalitions, as influenced by the leaderships' particular goals, the nature of the country's economy, and the existing international context. In Nicaragua, political pluralism and contested elections were viewed as essential for obtaining the political and economic cooperation of the national bourgeoisie, undermining the legitimacy of the U.S.-backed counterrevolution, and obtaining aid and credit from foreign governments and multilateral agencies.

In Iran, by contrast, the *ulama* were more ruthless with their opponents, in part because none of their opponents were viewed as indispensable for economic recovery or international legitimacy. The domestic and international costs of eliminating oppositional forces were perceived as much lower in Iran than in Nicaragua.

We have argued that both the similarities and differences between the Iranian and Nicaraguan revolutions are largely explained by the outcomes of the struggles over the control and deployment of state power in contexts characterized by the fragmentation of the original revolutionary coalition, external aggression, and continuing dependency on the world economy or domestic elites.

Both revolutions produced striking political accomplishments, but limited economic progress. For revolutions in poor and middle-income societies, facing powerful international opposition, these may be the limits of transformative possibilities. Indeed, in such contexts, there may be more "limits on revolutionary possibilities than prospects for revolutionary development."[5] Nonetheless, the differences in political outcomes also suggest that even within these limits, pluralist democracy can emerge.

REFERENCES

1.   Vickers (1990), p. 23.
2.   Ibid., p. 23.
3.   Vilas (1990), p. 11.
4.   Conroy (1990), p. 27.
5.   Vickers (1990), p. 27.

The Impact of Revolution on Social Welfare in Latin America
SUSAN ECKSTEIN

In this detailed study, Eckstein examines the progress made both in countries that did have revolutions (Mexico, Cuba, Bolivia, Peru) and in comparable countries that did not have revolutions (Brazil, the Dominican Republic, Colombia, and Ecuador) in the areas of inequality, land reform, economic growth, and social welfare. Eckstein makes four major points. First, the outcome of a revolution may depend on what kind of revolution has occurred: from above or below, capitalist or socialist. Second, both those countries that have had revolutions and those that have not are constrained by their position in the world economy and their own internal resources. Therefore, the economic course of events may be similar in countries with similar positions in the world economy whether or not a revolution has occurred. For example, although Mexico has made greater progress than Brazil on land reform, largely due to the Mexican Revolution, both countries, in trying to industrialize from a semi-peripheral position in the world economy, have had similar experiences in economic growth, inequality, and social welfare. Third, socialist revolutions allow certain options that may not be open in countries whose postrevolutionary regimes remain capitalist. Thus, Cuba, although its performance in economic growth since the revolution has been weak, has been able to provide a much higher level of routine health care than most Latin American nations. Eckstein suggests that this is possible because Cuba's health care system does not operate as a private-sector, profit-making endeavor; therefore, it can place a greater emphasis on such low-profit activities as routine and preventive medical care. Fourth, in all the revolutions studied, whether capitalist or socialist, peasants benefited most in the decades immediately following the revolution, when the new government was being consolidated and needed popular support. Later, the pursuit of industrialization tended to increase inequality and to turn the government away from peasant concerns.

How do postrevolutionary societies differ from societies with no revolutionary history? What variations are there in the outcomes of revolutions associated with different class alliances and different modes of production, and of revolutions occurring in countries with different resource bases? This essay examines the specific effects of four revolutions on social welfare standards in Latin America: Mexico (1910), Bolivia (1952), Cuba (1959), and Peru (1968).

These countries which experienced revolutions were integrated into the world economy under the Spanish Colonial empire. The *conquistadores* reorganized the indigenous agricultural economics into *latifundios* and established mining enclaves. With imported slaves, they made Cuba a major sugar exporter. Despite a common colonial heritage, the political economies of these four countries differed in important respects at the time of their respective upheavals. In comparison to the other countries Mexico had a more diversified and developed economy. It had a network of roads and railroads, industries, an agricultural base that could support an urban population, and an educated "middle class." By contrast, Bolivia, at the time of its revolution, had one of the poorest and least developed economies on the continent. It had the second lowest GDP (Gross Domestic Product) and the third lowest GDP per capita in South America, and only one other South American country had a manufacturing sector contributing a smaller share to GDP than Bolivia's. A small tin- and land-based oligarchy ruled the country. Its mine sector, which employed about 3% of the labor force, operated as an enclave oriented toward the export market. Most Bolivians lived humbly off the land, primarily as tenant-farmers and sharecroppers; in 1952 they still retained much of their pre-Columbian heritage. Peru, like Bolivia, had a large Indian population in the highlands associated with *latifundios*. But by the 1960s its coastal farms employed wage labor, and its industrial base and export sector were more developed and diversified than Bolivia's. Cuba was the only one of the four countries to have an agricultural economy that was heavily capitalized and dominated by foreign companies. By Latin American standards its industrial base was also well developed at the time Castro seized power.

All four countries experienced revolutions in the sense that political groups assumed control of the state apparatus through extralegal means, and, at least in the countryside, destroyed the economic base of the then dominant class so as to restructure class relations somewhat. Peru experienced a "revolution *from above*" in that the extralegal takeover and the initiation of the social transformation were organized and led by high-level state functionaries with negligible mass participation. Peru's revolution was initiated by General Velasco Alvarado, the army's top-ranking officer. After usurping power by a *coup d'etat,* he used the powers of the state to obliterate the rural property base of the oligarchy, to expropriate foreign-owned companies in the export sector, and to modify social relations and ownership in part of agriculture and industry.

Mexico, Bolivia, and Cuba, on the other hand, experienced "revolutions *from below.*" The three upheavals began as "middle class" reform movements for free elections and enforcement of electoral results, but the destruction of the *anciens régimes* rested on peasant and worker rebellions. In Cuba the nationalization of most of the economy eliminated the capi-

Abridged from an article with the same title originally published in Theory and Society, *vol. 11, pp. 43–49 (1982). Reprinted with the permission of Elsevier Science Publishers, B.V., Amsterdam.*

talist class and most of the independent petty bourgeoisie. In contrast, in Mexico and Bolivia, as well as in Peru, even though the state's role in the economy increased, opportunities also were created for nationally oriented bourgeoisie and petty bourgeoisie in private enterprise.

Thus the four cases involve: (1) revolutions from "above" and "below"; (2) revolutions instituting socialist and capitalist modes of production based, respectively, on state and private ownership of most of the economy; and (3) revolutions occurring in countries at different levels of economic development and in countries differently integrated into the world economy.

No study has systematically explored what impact these three variables have on outcomes of revolutions. Yet each is likely to be important, for different reasons. The role of the three forces can be formulated as hypotheses, and cross-national patterns that would verify each can be specified.

> *Hypothesis I:*   Postrevolutionary social welfare developments are shaped by the position of countries within the *world economy*.

World economy theory suggests that countries' relative position in the world economy limits their possibilities after revolution. According to Wallerstein,[1] there exists a single, capitalist world economy. Wallerstein also claims that countries' productive and political strength and their capacity to appropriate surplus vary with their core, semi-peripheral, or peripheral status within the world economy. Core countries are strongest and peripheral states weakest, but semi-peripheral countries have considerable potential to increase their share of the world surplus. He recognizes that revolutions may help countries modify their role in the world economy, but he views prospects for less developed countries as not very great, especially in the periphery.

If Wallerstein is correct, developments after revolution should differ in the *periphery* and *semi-periphery* because the two sets of countries assume different roles within the world economy, and accordingly have different resources available for internal use. Other analysts also distinguish between countries with different productive resources, but they view development from a national, not a global point of view. To test the world economy thesis I will trace, where possible, the relationship between internal and global processes. Wallerstein's criteria for classifying countries are not well defined, but Bolivia, with one of the poorest and least diversified economies and one of the most unstable governments in Latin America, was without question peripheral in 1952. Mexico had a growing industrial sector (largely foreign owned) and a strong, stable government at the eve of its revolution. While it was one of the economically most developed Latin American countries at the time, it probably still constituted part of the "periphery." By the time of the other revolutions, however, it had developed to the point of inclusion in the "semi-periphery." Peru and Cuba are more difficult to categorize; they had "peripheral" and "semi-peripheral" characteristics when their respective *anciens régimes* collapsed, although neither had so large an economy as Mexico. When Castro came to power Cuba's manufacturing sector accounted for as large a share of the national product as Mexico's then did. Yet its economy was exceptionally tied to the export of a single agricultural commodity, sugar, and much of its industrial production was sugar-related. Because of its extreme dependence on a single export item, and on one for which international demand varied greatly from year to year, it was limited in its capacity to influence world relations in its favor. Peru's export sector was more diversified than Cuba's and its economy was more productive and developed than Bolivia's. By the 1950's, then, we would class Mexico as semi-peripheral, Bolivia as peripheral, with Cuba and Peru in the middle, having some peripheral and some semi-peripheral characteristics. The world economy thesis thus would lead us to expect qualitatively different patterns in Mexico and Bolivia by the time of the upheaval in the latter. It would also lead us to expect postrevolutionary development possibilities in Cuba and Peru to be similar in important respects, despite their contrasting dominant modes of economic organization.

Hypothesis II: Postrevolutionary social welfare developments are shaped by the *class base* of insurrections.

Another line of argument suggests that outcomes of upheavals depend on which groups partake in the overthrow of the *anciens régimes*. Elites involved in "revolutions from above" might use state power to advance interests of classes other than their own, but if the socioeconomic base of political movements matters, peasants and workers should share more in the fruits of victory when they actively participate in insurrections; that is, peasants and workers should benefit more from "revolutions from below" than from "revolutions from above." If the class base of upheavals affects subsequent societal development, then peasants and workers in the three countries experiencing "revolutions from below"—Mexico, Bolivia, and Cuba—should enjoy benefits unavailable to their counterparts in Peru, since Peru is the only one of the four countries to have had a "revolution from above."

Hypothesis III: Postrevolutionary social welfare developments are shaped by the *dominant mode of production* instituted, and the *form of property ownership* associated with it.

According to this third line of argument, the dominant mode of production should have a decisive effect on societal developments after revolution. Governments in societies based primarily on *capitalist* and *socialist* organizing principles, that is, on *private* and *state* ownership of the economy, may be equally committed to development and distributive goals, but the former may be constrained in ways that the latter are not. When private ownership is the rule, governments must provide sufficient incentive to induce individuals and corporations to invest locally. They therefore cannot readily implement policies favoring labor at the expense of capital. Because socialist regimes assume direct responsibility for production and accumulation, they are not faced with the same constraint. In principle, they are better able to award workers a bigger share of the product of their labor than are governments in capitalist societies. In practice, however, their allocative policies are likely to depend on trade-offs between consumption and investment. If the main form of ownership has a significant bearing on developments after revolution, then we should find major differences between Cuba on the one hand, and Mexico, Bolivia, and Peru on the other hand. Cuba, as noted above, is the only one of the four countries to have socialized ownership of most of the economy.

A problem arises in attempting to assess the relative importance of the three sets of factors in the countries under study: the upheavals occurred in different years. Consequently, differences among the countries could reflect different global conditions at the time of the outbreak of each, and the different time lapses since each transformation occurred. For this reason, a fourth hypothesis will be considered.

Hypothesis IV: The *historical epoch* in which revolutions occurred and the *time lapse* since the upheavals affect postrevolutionary social welfare options.

The timing of the revolution might be important for two reasons. First, at different historical junctures, options for revolutionary regimes might vary. The capacity and desire of powerful global and domestic forces to resist change is likely to depend on the international economic and political environment. Powerful nations would be unlikely to intervene when their economies are in recession and when they are engaged in major wars elsewhere in the world. Second, social welfare outcomes might vary over time, for the longer the time lapse since upheavals, the more opportunity revolutionary processes have had to be played out. But time also permits nonrevolutionary and counterrevolutionary forces to assert themselves and to redirect the course of revolutions. Were the longevity factor important, the impact of revolution should be most apparent in Mexico, and least apparent in Peru, as the time lapse is *longest* since the Mexican insurrection and *shortest* since the Peruvian. Because longevity might erode revolutionary accomplishments, trends in each country must be watched over time. Developments after revolution do not necessarily evolve in a linear manner.

The longevity factor, in addition, raises a more general problem: how to assess which developments are byproducts of the class transformations, and which might have occurred in the absence of revolution. This problem is addressed by comparing developments in the four countries with developments during the same time period in societies that did not have revolutions. As shown in Table 1, each of the countries will be compared with the Latin American country it best resembled at the eve of its upheaval. Bolivia will be compared with Ecuador, Peru with Colombia, Cuba with the Dominican Republic (DR), and Mexico with Brazil. The rationale for the paired comparisons can also be formulated as an hypothesis:

Hypothesis V: As a result of changes in the class structure and class relations, *social welfare developments differ in societies that have and have not had revolutions.*

The specific aspects of social welfare on which this study focuses are land ownership, income, and health care and nutrition. (Figures presented throughout this essay should be viewed as approximations. They undoubtedly contain a margin of error.)

LAND DISTRIBUTION

In societies where much of the population is involved in agriculture, land ownership constitutes an important component of social welfare. Consequently, land distribution patterns in the countries under study are analyzed, including how and why distribution patterns changed since the respective upheavals.

If land rights were a concern of the rural labor force, and if the class base of political transformations has a decisive bearing on revolutionary outcomes, then the Mexican, Bolivian, and Cuban "revolutions from below" should have resulted in a more widespread redistribution of land than Peru's "revolution from above." If, however, the dominant mode of production is the primary factor affecting land distribution, land redistribution should be greater in Cuba than in the other countries. Should world economic linkages further affect how production is organized and property distributed in agriculture, then land ownership patterns

Table 1   GDP Per Capita, Manufacturing Share of GDP

	BOLIVIA	ECUADOR	PERU	COLOMBIA	CUBA	DOMINICAN REPUBLIC	MEXICO	BRAZIL
	GDP per capita (in constant dollars of 1980)							
1950	423	415	604	470	851	423	710	478
1960	383	499	808	479	887	518	907	651
1970	477	597	1014	647	867	646	1306	924
1980	568	1040	1101	922	1455	960	1863	1652
	Manufacturing share of GDP (%)							
1950	15	16	15	16	n/a	17	21	20
1960	14	14	18	18	45	17	19	18
1970	13	18	21	18	48	17	23	25
1976	14	19	23	19	41	17	24	26

should change in the four postrevolutionary societies provided that profits from trade can thereby be increased.

In addition, the timing of the upheavals might affect land allocations. First, land reforms might take time to implement. If so, the most land should have been distributed in Mexico and the least in Peru. Second, land policies might be shaped by *general* global political and economic trends. There might, for example, be little resistance to reforms implemented when there is a world depression and when industry becomes a leading economic sector (especially if large landowners have diversified into industry). Comparisons between the matched countries will help us ascertain whether general historical trends are shaping land policies independently of forces associated with the revolutions.

As indicated in Table 2, land ownership was highly concentrated before the respective upheavals. Mexico had the highest GINI index value of land concentration on the continent, even twenty years after the demise of its *ancien régime*. (The GINI index measures inequality on a scale from 0 to 1; 0 is complete equality; 1 is extreme inequality.) Bolivia had the second highest index of land concentration at the eve of its revolution, and Peru scored only slightly lower. Ownership in Cuba was least concentrated; by regional standards it was moderate. At the eve of the Mexican upheaval less than 3% of Mexican landholders owned more than 90% of the productive land. The proportion held by Mexican peasants had declined in the late nineteenth century, after the Porfirio Díaz administration encouraged large surveying companies and private businessmen to purchase or appropriate land traditionally held by peasant communities. In 1950 in Bolivia, 6% of the landowners held 92% of the land, and in pre-Velasco Peru about 2% of the Peruvian farmowners monopolized 69% of the farmland. In prerevolutionary Cuba, 8% of the farm population controlled 71% of the land.

All four countries announced land reforms shortly after their respective political upheavals. The land reforms transformed rural class relations, encouraged efficient land use, and ushered in more equitable land distributions. They reduced the number of large privately owned farm units and the portion of the land area held by private farmers. Between

Table 2   GINI Index Values
for Land Ownership Concentration

Mexico (1930)	0.96	Peru (1950)	0.88
Brazil (1950)	0.84	Columbia (1960)	0.86
Bolivia (1950)	0.94	Cuba (1945)	0.79
Ecuador (1950)	0.86	Dominican Republic (1950)	0.79

the latest prerevolutionary and the latest postrevolutionary year for which there are data, the private land area in large farms changed most in Cuba, least in Bolivia. In Bolivia the large farms of the landed oligarchy were broken up soon after the promulgation of the agrarian reform, but subsequently big tracts were awarded to market-oriented producers. The privately held land in independently-owned farms of 1000 or more hectares dropped from 92% to 65% in Bolivia, from 69% to 42% in Peru, and from 82% (in 1923, after the breakdown of the *ancien régime* but before widespread land distribution) to 32% in Mexico. In Cuba most holdings over 67 hectares were outlawed after 1963. Consequently, by 1967 approximately 5% of the land in private farms was in units over 67 hectares, and by 1981 only about 9% of the arable land on the island remained in private hands.

Still, the land reforms did not resolve the problem of *minifundismo;* plots of less than 5 hectares that are considered "sub-family" in size. Since the respective upheavals the proportion of farm units with 5 hectares or less increased in Mexico and Cuba (though it decreased between 1950 and 1960 in Mexico); in Bolivia the proportion declined by less than 3%. No data are available on Peru. *Minifundismo* becomes especially problematic when successive generations of land reform beneficiaries subdivide already small parcels.

In no country did all rural laborers gain access to land. The percentage of farm families without land has varied in each country over the years, depending on population growth, migration, and the extent to which the government has distributed new land. The percentage of farm families who are either *minifundistas* or landless farm laborers, according to available information, appears first to have decreased and then to have increased in both Mexico and Bolivia.

Thus, in these four countries revolutions, irrespective of their class origins or the political economy to which they give rise, were associated with land reforms. Yet the four paired countries also promulgated agrarian reforms in the 1960s. Whereas it might therefore appear that land redistribution programs do not distinguish countries which have and have not had revolutions, the different impact of the reforms in the two sets of countries is striking. According to available data, the proportion of the farm population receiving land and the proportion of the farmland redistributed as a result of the reforms has been far greater in the four countries that had revolutions (see Table 3).

Although the land reforms were implemented in Mexico, Bolivia, and Cuba before they were in their paired countries, the different time lapses do not account for the cross-national differences. The Velasco reform was the last to be implemented, yet it had a greater impact than Colombia's, the DR's, Brazil's, and Ecuador's. Nor do differentials in land concentration before the respective upheavals account for the cross-national variances. The data in Table 2 show that the GINI index of land concentration was greater in Mexico in 1930 than in Brazil

Table 3   Proportion of the Male Farm Population Benefiting from Agrarian Reforms and the Proportion of Farmland Distributed or Confirmed by 1969

	YEAR REFORM INITIATED	% MALES BENEFITING	% LAND DISTRIBUTED OR CONFIRMED
Mexico	1916	46.5	35.1
Brazil	1964	0.4	0.4
Bolivia	1955	39.0	29.7
Ecuador	1964	3.7	2.5
Cuba	1959	63.7[b]	—
Dominican Republic	1963	2.0	2.0
Peru 1961–69	1961	2.4	4.8
Peru 1973[a]	1969	21.0	30.0
Colombia	1961	4.0	10.4

[a] For Peru, 1973 data are included, showing the impact of the Velasco reform.
[b] Approximate percentage of farm units eligible for *individual* land rights in conjunction with the 1959 Agrarian Reform.

in 1950, and greater in Bolivia at the time of its upheaval than in Ecuador, but Peru's GINI index was only slightly higher than Colombia's and Cuba's was identical to the Dominican Republic's. Rather, in the four countries which have not had revolutions the landed oligarchies have thus far been successful in resisting pressure for land redistribution.

In sum, no single factor accounts for land distribution policies after revolution, but postrevolutionary societies contrast with societies that have not had revolutions in the extent to which they implement agrarian reforms. The political biases of the ruling elite are also important. For example, the national leadership in Colombia never redistributed land on the scale that Velasco did in Peru even though the Colombian countryside had been plagued by violence since the 1940s and the country was industrializing. The cross-national comparison also reveals that land distribution patterns after revolution depend in part on the dominant mode of production instituted. Mexico, Bolivia, and Peru reduced the number of big farms and the proportion of land area such farms control, but not nearly so much as did socialist Cuba.

INCOME DISTRIBUTION

As societies urbanize and agriculture is capitalized, land ownership becomes a less important determinant of overall welfare. Concomitantly, financial wealth assumes greater importance. It affects people's capacity both to invest and to consume. And the more equitable the distribution of wealth, the more an entire populace can share the benefits of a society's riches. Income is the best available measure of wealth, although it underestimates the economic worth of people with assets. Because revolutions, by definition, involve class transformations and because wealth tends to be class-determined, revolutions should alter the

Table 4   Estimates of Share of National Income Held by Percentile Groups

| | Percentile Groups | | | | | | |
	POOREST 0–20	21–40	41–60	61–80	81–90	91–95	RICHEST 96–100
Bolivia							
1968 [H]	4	13.7	8.9	14.3	59.1	—	35.7
1975 [E]	—	13[a]	—	26	61.0	44.5	—
1975 [H]	—	14[b]	—	29	58.0	41.7	—
Ecuador							
1960 [E]	4	—	—	—	—	—	42
1970 [?]	2.5	8.9	5.6	14.5	73.5	—	42
Mexico [H]							
1950	5.6	7.5	10.9	16.7	59.4	45.5	35.1
1963	3.7	6.8	11.2	20.2	58.1	41.6	28.6
1970	3.8	8.0	13.7	18.7	55.8	39.2	27.7
1975	1.7	6.0	11.5	20.0	60.2	43.4	—
1977	3.3	7.7	12.9	21.1	55.1	38.0	25.5
Brazil [E]							
1960	3.9	7.4	13.6	20.3	54.8	39.6	28.3
1970	3.4	6.6	10.9	17.9	61.9	46.7	34.1
1972	3.2	5.9	9.5	16.5	64.9	50.4	37.9
Cuba [E][c]							
1953	2.1	4.1	11.0	22.8	60.0	38.5	28.0
1960	8.0	12.5	14.5	17.0	48.0	31.0	17.0
1962	6.2	11.0	16.3	25.1	41.4	23.0	12.7
1973	7.8	12.5	19.2	25.5	35.0	19.9	9.5
Dominican Republic							
1960 [E]	—	—	—	—	—	—	—
1970 [E]	5	—	—	—	—	—	26
Peru							
1961 [E]	2.5	5.5	10.2	17.4	64.4	49.2	39.0
1972 [H]	1.9	5.1	11.0	21.0	61.0	42.9	—
Colombia							
1960 [E]	3	—	—	—	—	—	—
1964 [H]	2.2	4.7	9.0	16.1	68.1	—	40.4
1970 [?]	3.5	5.9	12.1	19.1	59.4	—	33
1974 [H]	3.6	7.2	11.0	18.1	60.2	45.1	32.8

[a] Poorest 10% received 3% of the national income.
[b] Poorest 10% received 3.1 % of the national income.
[c] Since the nationalization of small business in 1968, about 7–8% of the labor force remains outside the state sector.
[E] Economically active population.
[H] Households.

distribution of economic resources among socioeconomic groups. Accordingly, income distribution patterns should differ in the countries that have and have not had revolutions. But which aspects of revolutions affect income allocations? If groups benefit in income-producing ways from participation in revolutionary movements, then peasants and workers in Mexico, Bolivia, and Cuba should have improved their earning power more than their counterparts in Peru and their paired countries. But if the dominant mode of production that is instituted after revolution has a decisive bearing on people's income opportunities then income distribution patterns should be similar in all the capitalist countries and different in Cuba. A major structural constraint of governments in capitalist societies is absent in societies where ownership of production is socialized: in capitalist societies businesses must expect sufficient profits or they will not invest. Partly to ensure investment, governments in such societies support inequitable income distributions. By contrast, in socialized economies individual investments need not be governed by profit considerations, especially by returns to owners and managers; consequently, to induce investment socialist governments need not skew income distribution. Accordingly, there is reason to expect that popular groups would be less able to increase their income share after capitalist than after socialist revolutions. Governments in capitalist societies, regardless of whether they had revolutions, would be expected to repress distributive pressures "from below" that threaten capital accumulation.

But capital accumulation exigencies could depend on the way in which economies are integrated into the world economy. This is not to say that distributive patterns are necessarily identical in semi-peripheral countries with different ownership patterns, but that the options in all semi-peripheral countries should differ qualitatively from those in peripheral countries. The success of semi-peripheral countries at industrialization, for example, rests partly on low wages allowing high returns to capital.

Finally, income distribution might depend on the time lapse since upheavals. There is no *a priori* basis, however, for predicting the effect of longevity. The income equalizing effects of revolutions might well vary over time with shifting political and economic priorities of regimes, somewhat independently of the class base of regimes, the dominant mode of production, or global economic dynamics.

Unfortunately, available data do not permit a systematic comparison of income distribution before the respective upheavals. It therefore is impossible to assess the full impact that each revolution has had on the apportionment of income. The data on the postrevolutionary periods, however, reveal that the dominant pattern of ownership most affects income allocations. In Table 4 we see that since the social transformation in Cuba the share of the national income of the poorest 40% increased from 6% to 20% while that of the richest 5% dropped from 28% to 9.5%. The poor have come to earn a larger share and the wealthy a smaller share in Cuba than in any of the other countries surveyed, whereas before 1959 Cuba's lowest income earners received the smallest share of the national income. Yet the data also reveal that the dominant mode of production is not the only factor shaping income allocations after revolution, for distributive patterns have changed *within* each country since the upheavals. They have changed as the economies have diversified and international and internal class pressures have shifted.

After World War II, postrevolutionary governments became increasingly committed to capital-intensive industrialization. The pace of redistribution, however, has slowed down and the main beneficiaries of income redistribution from top income earners after 1960 have been middle income groups: skilled industrial workers, technicians, professionals, and owners of small businesses. Family farmers and unskilled workers were excluded from opportunities in the modernizing sector. Cuba was the only exception in this regard, as the socialist government restrained professional salaries and sharply restricted small private businesses, while allowing farmers to gain relatively high incomes.

The available data for the paired countries suggest not only that the dominant mode of production most affects income distribution patterns, but also that low income earners' share of the national product tends to decrease with industrialization in capitalist countries (except in Colombia). The data also suggest that income is not necessarily more equitably distributed after revolution, at least in the long run, if the dominant mode of production remains capitalist.

In support of the industrialization thesis, as Brazil rapidly industrialized in the 1960s, income distribution deteriorated: the share of the national income accruing to the poorest 40% of the economically active population decreased while the share to the wealthiest 20% increased. The industrial expansion resulted largely from an influx of foreign capital, after the military took power in 1964. Yet the Brazilian-Mexican comparison reveals that political forces may indeed modify the impact of capitalist economic dynamics. Although the share of the national income accruing to the poorest 40% deteriorated both in Mexico and Brazil in the 1960s, it deteriorated less during the decade in Mexico. Moreover, whereas the income share going to the top 5% declined during the 1960s in Mexico, it increased in Brazil. The Mexican social transformation, and the civilian regime to which it gave rise, appear to have helped the petty bourgeoisie and organized labor (who fall within the top 2–3 decile groups) appropriate a larger portion of the national income than their counterparts under Brazil's military rule. The more egalitarian trend in Mexico, compared to Brazil, suggests that internal class dynamics and not merely semi-peripheral status affect income distribution patterns.

In sum, the experiences of the countries under study here suggest that revolutions in capitalist societies do not necessarily give rise to more egalitarian income distributions than societies experiencing no class transformation, that socialist revolutions improve income distribution more than capitalist revolutions and that low income groups benefit most from class upheavals, even under socialism, when the new regimes are in the process of consolidation. In all countries here surveyed, except Colombia, the share of income accruing to the poor diminished with the expansion of the economies. The Mexican-Brazilian comparison, however, shows that in the semi-periphery middle and low income groups benefit somewhat more and the elite somewhat less from industrialization when a postrevolutionary society institutionalizes a civilian regime than when a regime excludes popular groups from power.

HEALTH CARE AND NUTRITION

Well-being depends not only on material comforts but also on good health. Good health requires a well-balanced and adequate diet, including high levels of calorie and protein consumption. It also requires access to a medical delivery system that provides quality health care. The scope of the delivery system is reflected in the per capita supply of physicians, nurses, and hospital beds. The quality of health care, in turn, is reflected in life expectancy

Table 5   Health Care

	BOLIVIA	ECUADOR	PERU	COLOMBIA	CUBA	DOMINICAN REPUBLIC	MEXICO	BRAZIL
Population per physician								
1958	—	—	—	—	2839	—	—	—
1960	3700	2800	1800	2170	—	—	2200	2400
1970	2300	2500	1440	1950	1400	2100	1920	2160
1976	2120	1570	—	1650	1100	1870	1580	1820
Population per nurse								
1958	—	—	—	—	8262	—	—	—
1960	—	2280	2650	—	—	—	3640	3520
1966	—	—	—	—	786.5	—	—	—
1970	2730	8630	1570	3300	581.9	3930	3200	1040
1975	—	—	—	—	443.8	—	—	—
1976	3520	—	—	—	—	1330	—	—
Population per hospital bed								
1958	—	—	—	—	239	—	—	—
1960	580	520	590	275	—	440	490	580
1970	490	430	930	260	215	350	470	450
Infant mortality (per 1,000 live births)								
1940–44	101.1	114.3	119.3	164.7	—	69.6	116.5	152.0
1945–49	123.1	101.8	104.5	117.5	38.9	87.6	108.6	141.8
1950–54	98.8	81.8	91.8	107.3	—	79.7	99.9	113.3
1955–59	81.8	80.4	77.9	107.6	32.4	83.5	98.8	100.9
1965	76.5	70.6	60.7	—	38.4	72.7	74.0	82.4
1970	—	66.6	68.5	110.0	38.4	50.1	65.1	91.3[a]
1973	—	59.1	52.0	—	28.9	38.6	—	—
1976–77	158.0	—	65.0	62.0	23.0	—	—	98.0

[a] 1969 data.

rates, including infant mortality rates (deaths of infants less than one year old per 1000 live births.)

THE HEALTH CARE DELIVERY SYSTEM:
THE SUPPLY OF DOCTORS, NURSES, HOSPITAL BEDS

According to information on the countries here surveyed, as long as the dominant mode of production remains capitalist, revolutions appear not to have any predictable effect on the health care delivery system (see Table 5). Whereas per capita medical personnel and hospital facilities have tended to improve in each country that experienced a social transformation, the per capita supply of each has not come to be uniformly higher and it has not consistently improved more in the postrevolutionary societies than in the paired countries. The factor most affecting the availability of health care, and how the delivery system is organized, is the dominant mode of production. Cuba has the largest supply of doctors, nurses, and hospital beds per population. Because its supply of medical personnel is much greater than Mexico's and Brazil's, and because Mexico has the worst per capita supply of hospital beds of any of the countries under study, the level of development of societal productive resources does not account for cross-national differences in health care facilities.

Postrevolutionary Mexican medical outlays not only are limited, but they also vary greatly by socioeconomic group. In the post-World War II period private and public medical assistance has been concentrated almost exclusively in urban areas, especially in the largest cities. In 1970, for example, 54% of all doctors—private practitioners and state employees—worked in the four largest cities, which contained only 18% of the population.

The expansion and reorganization of the health care delivery system in Castro's Cuba have been so great and so different from the other countries' as to suggest that socialization of the economy provides options private ownership of the economy does not. Given that half the country's doctors emigrated in the first five years of Castro's rule, Cuba's current supply of doctors is especially impressive. The Castro regime sponsored a massive campaign to attract students to medicine. With all graduates guaranteed jobs and with nearly all doctors government-employed, the expansion of the medical profession is a direct reflection of the state's commitment to upgrading health care. Cuba has expanded its per capita supply of doctors to the point that it can export them, with less cost to the domestic economy, than can most Latin American countries.

Just as Mexican governments modified their medical care priorities over the years, so too has the Castro regime. But the two countries have promoted increasingly different health care coverage. Whereas the Castro government initially invested in a costly and elitist doctor-based medical system, once it replenished its supply of doctors it began to invest in paramedical care. It promoted new types of personnel, such as medical and dental assistants (against some initial opposition of the medical and dental professions), and it upgraded established low prestige professions such as nursing. As a result, the population–health care personnel ratio dropped from 2,838 : 1 in 1958 to 171 : 1 seventeen years later. And the nurse–population ratio, which had been between two to three times lower in Cuba around the time of the revolution than in the capitalist countries for which we have information, by 1970 was between approximately two and fifteen times higher. Moreover, nurses, nurse assistants, and auxiliary personnel seem to have more clinical responsibility in Cuba than do their counterparts in capitalist countries.

In sum, the qualitative and quantitative changes that the Castro regime alone initiated suggest that governments in socialized economies are apt to invest more in health welfare, and to allocate funds differently, than governments in capitalist societies. Whereas state ownership of the means of production in itself provides no *guarantee* that medical outlays and health standards will improve, it creates possibilities that private ownership does not. The inferior health care delivery system in postrevolutionary Bolivia is undoubtedly attributable in part to market dynamics and the limited public revenues governments there have had. But the different developments in Castro's Cuba on the one hand, and Mexico and Brazil on the other, demonstrate that capital resources are not the only issue.

Infant Mortality

Infant mortality is the one aspect of social welfare that appears not to be affected by any of the revolutionary-linked variables under study (refer back to Table 5). Because Cuba has a much lower infant mortality rate than any of the other countries, it would appear that soci-

Table 6   Nutrition

	BOLIVIA	ECUADOR	MEXICO	BRAZIL	CUBA	DOMINICAN REPUBLIC	PERU	COLOMBIA
Per capita caloric supply (percentage of requirements)								
1960	69	81	107	102	—	92	97	94
1970	77	89	110	109	—	91	98	97
1974	83	91	121	118	107	109	92	96
Per capita protein supply (total grams per day)								
1960	43	46	65	61	—	50	61	46
1970	46	49	65	64	64	51	62	50
1974	47	47	66	61	—	50	53	50

eties with socialized economies have more effective health care systems than capitalist countries. But because island rates were significantly lower already before the 1959 upheaval and because, according to the data, the infant death rate during the first decade of Castro's rule was higher than when Batista fell, socialism alone cannot be the cause. Possibly, health care deteriorated under Castro until the new generation of doctors replaced the physicians who emigrated. The increase, however, may reflect an improvement in data collection, not a deterioration in health care: in 1969, for example, 98% of all deaths were reported, whereas in 1956 only 53% were.

The level of overall economic development and the position of countries within the world economy, in turn, show no consistent relationship with mortality rates. Through 1970, Brazil had the highest infant mortality rate of any of the countries under study, despite its large resource base.

NUTRITION

Whereas, in the countries under study, infant mortality rates appear to be unaffected by revolution or the overall wealth of societies, according to our indicators nutrition standards tend to vary with the level of development of economies (see Table 6). Between 1960 and 1974 caloric and protein intake was generally lowest in Bolivia and Ecuador and highest in Mexico and Brazil. Peru is the only country where protein and caloric consumption, according to available information, declined after the revolution. It declined probably because only a limited portion of the rural population benefited from the land reform, because other agrarian policies (e.g., credit and pricing) did not favor the peasant sector, and because the earning power of the country's poor has deteriorated.

In Mexico, nutritional patterns appear to have changed over the years. Food consumption of low income groups, especially in the countryside, improved most under Cárdenas, who led Mexico's limited land reforms. Under Cárdenas peasant consumption depended as much on subsistence agriculture and informal exchanges among neighbors as on goods purchased in the market. But as rural communities were progressively integrated into the money economy after World War II, peasant food consumption came to depend on market purchasing power. With the impingement of market forces, informal networks for food distribution eroded and peasants became economically weaker and agrarian capital stronger. Consequently, even though farm output significantly improved after 1940, most peasants have not benefited from the gains. In the 1960s, Mexican upper and middle income group consumption of fruits, vegetables, and protein improved, while low income consumption deteriorated. The earning power of many Mexicans deteriorated to the point that by the end of the 1960s 40% of all farm families and 26% of all nonagricultural families were believed to earn below the minimum needed to assure an adequate diet. Although the government in the early 1970s implemented several programs to improve low income nutritional standards, the programs have thus far had little impact.

The other "revolution from below," in Cuba, also modified food consumption patterns. According to available data, however, the changes have not on the whole thus far been uniformly positive. Data on island consumption of 35 food items reveals that per capita acquisitions of 24 items dropped between 1966 and 1970. During the following four years consumption of approximately two-thirds of the products did improve, but consumption of only half the items was higher in 1974 than in 1966. Yet with basic goods rationed, low income groups may have improved their intake, even during the period when per capita food consumption declined. By contrast in the capitalist countries, where most food is allocated through market channels, consumption of low income groups may not have improved even when per capita consumption rose; post—World War II Mexican data confirm this hypothesis.

Thus, policies of governments after revolution *may* shape societal dietary patterns. But as new regimes become institutionalized in capitalist societies, nutritional standards tend to vary with the overall level of development of the economy and socioeconomic status. The situation in Castro's Cuba reveals that islanders, as a whole, fare no better under socialism than people in the more economically developed capitalist countries. Low income groups, however, may consume more calories and protein on the island than in the other countries, because the Castro government guarantees all Cubans a basic low-cost diet. The state in Cuba is freer than in the other countries to counter market tendencies, and it has used its power accordingly.

In conclusion, this analysis suggests that only in socialized economies is the health care system likely to change in ways that would otherwise be unlikely. Since the respective revolutions, Cuba's health care delivery system has been more extensive, it has expanded more, and it has been organized differently than have the delivery systems in the other countries. Furthermore, both the delivery system and policies affecting nutrition are least class-biased in Cuba. By the second decade of Castro's rule the changes appear also to have had a positive effect on infant mortality, but possibly not before then. Whereas health trends in other postrevolutionary societies have tended to be positive as well, the same is true in the paired countries. Thus, capitalist revolutions have no distinctive impact on the aspects of health welfare under investigation.

CONCLUSION

The foregoing analysis assessed ways that revolutions affected the social welfare of Latin Americans. It compared differences between societies of roughly similar levels of economic development that did and did not have revolutions, revolutions ushered in by different class alliances, revolutions instituting different modes of production, and revolutions occurring in countries differently situated within the world economy.

The class transformations in Mexico, Bolivia, Cuba, and Peru gave rise to more egalitarian societies than they displaced, but low income groups in each country gained most during the new regimes' consolidation of power. Subsequently, the interests of the popular sectors were sacrificed to those of middle and upper income groups. The rural masses benefited from revolution mainly in conjunction with agrarian reforms. Agrarian reforms have been promulgated in all the countries under study, but a much larger proportion of the agrarian population and a much larger proportion of the farmland has been redistributed in the four countries that had political upheavals than in the paired countries that did not.

The level of development of the economy and the way the societies have been integrated into the world economy historically limit what Third World revolutions can accomplish, quite independently of how the upheavals originated. Global constraints have also been one factor restricting labor's ability to improve its earning power and influence over the organization of production. Labor did benefit from the upheavals, but as the postrevolutionary governments became concerned with attracting foreign investment and foreign financial assistance, and with improving profits from trade, labor was marginalized. The Mexican-Brazilian comparison, however, suggests that the "middle class" and the small proportion of workers employed in the modern industrial sector benefit more, and the richest 5% less, in societies where civilian groups have been incorporated into the political apparatus as a result of revolution. Thus revolutionary-linked forces may modify the income generating effect of capitalist industrial dynamics, though not to the advantage of the lowest income earners.

The dominant mode of production instituted under the new order is the aspect of revolution most affecting patterns of land and income distribution and health care. To the extent that ownership of the economy is socialized the state has direct access to the surplus generated. Although the Cuban state has not consistently allocated the resources it controls to low income groups, because the Castro regime need not provide a favorable investment climate it can more readily redistribute wealth "downward" than can the capitalist regimes. It accordingly has also been freer to redesign the health care delivery system in accordance with societal needs rather than business interests and market power. But the Cuban experience suggests that the distributive effects even of socialist revolutions can be limited. Although socialism allows certain allocative options that capitalism does not, the capacity to improve the welfare of Third World people by any revolutionary means is constricted by the weak position of less developed nations within the global economy, by investment–consumption tradeoffs, and by internal political and economic pressures.

REFERENCE

1.   Wallerstein (1980a).

Counter-Revolution

FRED HALLIDAY

Revolutions seek to overturn a country's government, but that is not their only foe. Typically, there are also other forces that seek to defeat, or reverse, the revolution, both inside the country and abroad. Halliday discusses the sources and processes of counterrevolution that are generally triggered during revolutionary conflicts.

REACTION ACROSS FRONTIERS

If revolutions are international in their causes, programmes, and consequences, the same is equally true for attempts to overthrow or prevent them. The fear of such an overthrow haunts all revolutionaries. Two months after the Bolshevik seizure of power, Lenin wrote to Trotsky, "This is a moment of triumph. We have lasted a day longer than the Paris Commune."[1] Counterrevolution, a universal accompaniment of all revolutions, is as international as revolution itself: it is, as much as revolution, a constitutive element in the modern history of international relations. Like revolution, counterrevolution often has international causes. Moreover, it is international in that it seeks to affect politics across state frontiers.

The term "counterrevolution" refers to a policy of trying to reverse a revolution, and, by extension, to policies designed to prevent revolutionary movements that have already gained some momentum from coming to power. It denotes, therefore, both reversal or overthrow, and what has been referred to, variously, as suppression and containment. Like so many terms in the modern political vocabulary, it has its origins in the French revolution, in the movement that developed in the early 1790s, partly within France and partly amongst royalist emigres outside France, which sought to restore the monarchy to power. Counterrevolution cannot turn the clock back, it cannot restore in full measure that which was there before: the passage of time, the very impact of revolution, prevents replication. Just as revolution claims to reject the past, but cannot entirely do so, so counterrevolution cannot realize its claim to restore that which was overthrown. The restoration of Louis XVIII in 1815 did not reestablish a stable Bourbon monarchy in France. Counterrevolution can, however, overthrow the political system created by the revolution and restore the main political and social elements of the previous order.

The French, like later counterrevolutions, involved *both* domestic *and* international forces. The first stirrings of counterrevolution came from *within* France, from dissatisfied politicians and conservative peasantry; the course and success of all counterrevolution involve a combination of these two aspects. Of particular relevance here is that a purely external movement is much less effective. The record of exporting counterrevolution is as long on rhetoric, and short on achievement, as is that of revolution itself.

VARIETIES OF COUNTERREVOLUTION

Counterrevolution is not, however, a single phenomenon, any more than is revolution. In the first place, "counterrevolution" may refer to the overthrow of a revolutionary regime by opponents working within the country and with external support. "Counterrevolution" also refers to movements or policies that are not designed to overthrow or corrupt an existing revolutionary regime, but rather to prevent a revolutionary movement from coming to power. Thus coups designed to prevent revolutionary groups from coming to power, or to prevent reforming regimes from pressing on to more radical measures, can be termed "counterrevolutionary"—the Spanish nationalist coup led by General Franco in 1936, or the Chilean coup of Augusto Pinochet in 1973, being cases in point. By extension, social and political measures, including reforms, that have as their goal the blocking of more radical policies can qualify: the land reforms carried out by the USA in the post-1945 period, first in the Far East, then in Iran and Latin America, were designed to pre-empt peasant revolution.

The most direct international involvement in counterrevolution is that of states who deploy their resources to oppose revolutionary regimes. This is conventionally presented, in the literature on international relations, as "intervention," a term that denotes something more than diplomatic or military pressure, but usually something short of outright invasion; it suggests at least the principle that the sovereignty and separate identity of the state in question will endure. Intervention is coercive: it involves military activity of some kind and violation of the orthodox norm of sovereignty, and has a goal of altering if not the regime itself then at least its policies. Thus the military involvement of the Allies in Bolshevik Russia in 1918–20, and of the USA in Vietnam from 1965 to 1973, are cases of intervention. In such cases troops from the counterrevolutionary power were directly and publicly involved in military activities in another state. However, intervention can take indirect forms—support for guerrillas and sabotage, harassment along the frontiers, financial backing for opposition groups within the revolutionary state. More broadly, it may involve the deployment of propaganda resources and of economic sanctions designed to undermine the revolutionary regime and lessen its ability to meet the aspirations of its people.

Such intervention, overt or covert, accompanies almost all revolutions. Intervention is justified by the counterrevolutionary state on the grounds that it is a response to the international activities of the revolutionaries. On the other hand, it is used by revolutionaries to justify their own international activities. So central is this recurrence of both revolution *and* counterrevolution that it has come to be one of the dominant themes of modern international history. Time and again states have sought to limit, "contain" and overthrow revolutions, using a variety of mechanisms.

THE INCOHERENCES OF COUNTERREVOLUTION

However, the mixed record of such efforts points to ambiguities in the process of counterrevolution itself. Unless it can be carried out swiftly and at acceptable cost, the commitment to counterrevolution is a limited one. Indeed, on closer examination, what one sees time and again is the *incoherence* of the counterrevolutionary commitment.

This is first evident in the uncertain reactions of status quo powers to revolutions. In retrospect it may appear inevitable that such powers would come into conflict with revolutionary regimes: their own conceptions of order, national and international, and the very commitment of revolutionary states to a radical internationalism, would alone have ensured that. But this is not what the historical pattern indicates. There is usually a "period of grace," which revolutionary regimes enjoy once they have come to power. The whole world does not rush to suppress them, but rather waits, gives them some tentative benefit of the doubt, and hopes for an accommodation.

Even when they do respond, however, the counterrevolution is less directed, less mobilized, and in the end less effective than might appear at the time. For what recurs time and again are attempts at counterrevolution that are, in many ways, half measures. They are enough to show something is being done, enough certainly to antagonize the revolutionary state, but well short of what is required to destroy the revolutionary regime.

The twentieth century gives many examples of this incoherence. Certainly, there were cases of successful counterrevolution. Some of these were decisive military interventions to crush revolutionary regimes—Hungary in 1919, the Dominican Republic in 1965, Grenada in 1983. Others, equally decisive, and in the short run "successful," were the Soviet interventions in Hungary in 1956 and Czechoslovakia in 1968. But the examples of incoherence are equally, if not more, compelling. Thus the Allied intervention in Russia in 1918–20 ended with the withdrawal of the armies of the eighteen states that had sent troops on to Russian soil, and the defeat of the White armies backed by the Allies. The eighteen states sending troops into Russia deployed only a fraction of their available military resources, and were divided in aim. In Vietnam, in 1954, and in Algeria, in 1962, a militarily overwhelming France was forced to yield to nationalist opponents and withdraw.

In the Indochinese wars of the 1960s and 1970s the U.S., with backing from some allies, sustained heavy losses in trying to stem the Vietnamese revolutionary movement, but in the end withdrew, and after an interval of two years saw its allies in Saigon defeated. For all the commitment of troops, money and prestige, the U.S. was far from deploying its full might in this endeavor. It never invaded North Vietnam, or bombed northern cities, nor could it sustain its allied regime in the south which, for all its shared anticommunism, was riven with factionalism, military and political. In Vietnam the U.S. was not defeated *militarily,* yet it sustained the greatest *political* defeat in its international history.

Four years later, the USA faced equally striking, and even more absolute defeats, when it was unable to help its beleaguered allies in Iran and Nicaragua. The rise of a popular revolution against the Shah in the last months of 1978 prompted debate in Washington about what to do. But there was sharp division among Carter's advisers about how to respond; no one seriously thought any form of direct US intervention could save the Shah's regime. A few months later, the same dilemmas played themselves out in Nicaragua, as the Somocista National Guard, retreating in the face of the Sandinista uprising, crumbled and fled.

When it came to the fight back, to the "Reagan Doctrine," a similar incoherence prevailed. In the 1980s the USA began to undermine the Sandinista regime in Nicaragua. But throughout this period of US counterrevolution in Nicaragua there was no clarity as to what the USA was doing. Large sections of the US state—including Congress and the State Department—were against the US policy, and the President was forced to resort to devious and illegal means to fund the *contra* effort. At the time there was widespread uncertainty, and debate, about what the US agenda and its goals were. In one sense, this may not have mattered: it did not take much for the powerful and proximate USA to inflict damage on a nation of three million people.

A similar incoherence could be detected on the Soviet side, with the case of Afghanistan. The decision to send troops to Kabul in December 1979 was taken by a small group of leaders, without even the processes of consultation among military and civilian leaders that had become practice on some other issues. The regime it was committed to supporting in Kabul was, as much as that which the Americans had sustained in Saigon, riven with factions. When, six years later, in November 1985, a decision in principle to withdraw was taken, it exposed the lack of clarity of purpose in intervention, or in withdrawal.

LIMITS ON POWER

The record of counterrevolution is therefore one in which the almost universal incidence of attempts to prevent revolutions is matched by the comparatively limited, and often unsuccessful, outcome of such endeavors. In the whole period from 1789 to 1989, counterrevolution defined as *the coercive overthrow of an established revolutionary regime* was achieved on only two occasions: once, through defeat in inter-state war, at Waterloo in 1815; secondly, through the use of overwhelming military power against a state that had lost the support of its people, in Grenada in 1983. Counterrevolution defined as *violent suppression of revolutionary movements* had a more successful record, but even here what is striking is the limitation, as much as the success, of such policies.

The reasons for this limited response, and for the incoherence, are several. In the first place, counterrevolutionary states have to deal with opinion within their own countries. Patriotic sentiment may be strong when a state is confronted with an attack on its own territory, or allied territory; it is generally less willing to sustain loss of life, and expenditure of money, when it comes to intervening to change the regime in another state. If interventions are rapid and successful they may succeed in getting public support. If not, as the Americans found in Vietnam, then such support erodes.

Intervention also entails costs at the international level. Other states not directly involved in the conflict may oppose the intervention, and, while not intervening themselves on the side of the revolutionary state, may provide assistance to it. The more the counterrevolutionary power intervenes, the more other states will be likely to increase their own commitment. France aided the USA in its War of Independence, Russia aided Vietnam.

These constraints, whether domestic or international, have been *political,* and this applies equally to the very relation involved in a conflict of revolutionary and counterrevolutionary powers. Such a relation is, in military and economic terms, profoundly unequal, or *asymmetric.* The counterrevolutionary power has the advantage. Yet in political terms it is the revolutionary power which has, or potentially has, superior assets. This is so in three respects. Within the country at war, it can mobilize large numbers of people in long, demanding, conflict situations in a manner that the counterrevolutionary power cannot. Moreover it can, in both political *and* military terms, turn the asymmetry to its advantage, wearing down the political will of the opponent in the field, and eroding the political constituency for counterrevolution in the metropolitan state itself. It can, moreover, mobilize international support and, beyond that, opinion in its favor.

As in any conflict, the outcome of counterrevolution is not pre-ordained. Examples abound of the failure of revolutions, rebellions, guerrilla wars, and the like. Yet the recurrence of cases in which revolutions *have* succeeded, against the counterrevolutionary efforts of states much more powerful in military and economic terms, draws attention to a potential for victory that conventional assessments of power fail to comprehend.

REFERENCE

1.   Quoted in Taylor (1980), p. 141.

Revolution and War

STEPHEN M. WALT

This paper examines the following questions: Why do revolutionary states fight foreign wars almost immediately after gaining power? Are revolutionary regimes inherently aggressive, or are they simply victims of other powers? Are these conflicts a direct result of the revolutionary process, or is the association between revolution and war largely spurious? Walt argues that because revolutions raise the level of uncertainty and perceived threats, both on the part of new revolutionary regimes and their neighbors, there is a strong likelihood that the appearance of new revolutionary regimes will unsettle old balances of power and expectations, leading to international conflicts.

Revolutions are deadly serious contests for extremely high stakes. The collapse of internal authority places all members of society at risk: until a new order is established, conflicts can be resolved only by tests of strength and no one's interests and safety are assured. Winners will take all and losers may lose everything; as a result, mass revolutions are almost always bloody and destructive.[1]

A revolution is more than the replacement of one set of rulers by another: "a complete revolution involves the creation of a new political order."[2] By definition, a revolutionary state rests on new principles of legitimacy, displays new symbols of authority and identity (names, flags, anthems, etc.), adopts new rules for elite recruitment, and creates new political institutions and governmental procedures. In short, revolutions *redefine* the political community within a given territory by creating a "new state" that rests on principles and procedures that are a sharp departure from those of the old regime.

Abridged from "Revolution and War," published in World Politics, *vol. 44, pp. 321–68 (April 1992). Copyright © 1992 by Johns Hopkins University Press.*

The process of revolution generates two factors that affect international relations: new ideologies and new uncertainties.

REVOLUTIONARY IDEOLOGIES

Revolutionary leaders energize their supporters through revolutionary ideologies. To this end, revolutionary ideologies tend to emphasize three key themes:

"ENEMIES ARE EVIL AND INCAPABLE OF REFORM"

Revolutionary groups usually portray their opponents as intrinsically evil and incapable of meaningful reform: if the current system is unjust and cannot improve, then efforts at compromise are doomed, leaving revolution as the only morally possible alternative. Lenin broke with the "Economists" in Russia and with Social Democrats like Karl Kautsky over the possibility of reforming tsarism and capitalism, and Mao Zedong told his followers that "'imperialism is ferocious.' . . . [I]ts nature will never change, the imperialists will never lay down their butcher knives, . . . they will never become Buddhas."[3] Similarly, the Ayatollah Khomeini opposed compromise with the Shah by warning Iranians that "if you give this fellow a breathing spell, neither Islam nor your country nor your family will be left for you. Do not give him the chance; squeeze his neck until he is strangled."[4] In each case reform and compromise were rejected in favor of a radical solution.

"VICTORY IS INEVITABLE"

Unless potential supporters believe their sacrifices will eventually bear fruit, a revolutionary movement will not get very far. Revolutionary ideologies are thus inherently optimistic: they invariably portray victory as inevitable despite what may appear to be the overwhelming odds against it. Furthermore, the ideology may reinforce this belief by irresistible or divine forces to justify faith in victory. Marxists, for example, saw the "laws" of capitalist development as leading inexorably toward proletarian revolution and the emergence of socialism. Khomeini and his followers rested their optimism on religious faith. Revolutionaries may also invoke the successes of earlier movements to sustain confidence in their own efforts; thus, the Sandinistas saw Castro's victory in Cuba as evidence that their own efforts in Nicaragua could succeed.

Optimism can also be encouraged by depicting one's enemy as a paper tiger. Mao Zedong argued, for example, that "reactionaries" were "paper tigers" who "in appearance . . . are terrifying but in reality . . . are not so powerful," and Marshall Lin Biao asserted that "U.S. imperialism is stronger, but also more vulnerable, than any imperialism of the past."[5] Lenin's assessment of imperialism was similar: as the "highest stage of capitalism," imperialism contained both the power to dominate the globe *and* the seeds of its inevitable destruction at the hands of the proletariat.[6] The method is an obvious way to sustain commitment: however hopeless things appear to be, success is nevertheless assured if only the revolutionary forces persevere.

"Our Revolution Has Universal Meaning"

Although exceptions do exist (such as Kemalist Turkey, revolutionary Mexico, or the Meiji restoration in Japan), the ideologies of most revolutionary states contain strong "universalist" themes. Specifically, the principles of the revolution are believed to apply to other societies as well. In the extreme case, the ideology may go so far as to reject the nation-state as a legitimate political unit and call for the eventual elimination of the state system itself.

During the French Revolution, for example, the pro-war faction led by Brissot de Warville called for a "universal crusade" of human liberty, arguing that the "liberty of the entire world" was worth a few thousand deaths. Orthodox Marxists saw the "inevitable" triumph of socialism as a worldwide process that would bring about a classless, stateless commonwealth of peace. Chinese officials emphasized that the thought of Mao Zedong belonged not only to China but had international implications as well. And Khomeini's version of Shiite theology foresaw the eventual establishment of a global Muslim community (*ummah*) following the abolition of the "un-Islamic" nation-state system.

That revolutionary ideologies tend to include universalist elements should not come as a surprise. Such views promise adherents an additional reward for their sacrifices: a revolution is good not only for one's own country, but it will be beneficial for others as well. Moreover, if the failures of the old regime are the result of external forces (such as "capitalist imperialism"), then action beyond one's own borders may be necessary to eliminate these evils once and for all. Finally, in order to attract popular support, revolutionary ideologies tend to portray new political ideas as self-evident truths—which creates a bias toward universalism. How, that is, can a self-evident political principle be valid for one group but not for others? Could the Jacobins argue that the Rights of Man applied only to the French? Could Marx's disciples in the Soviet Union claim that his "laws of history" were valid in Russia alone? Could the Iranian revolutionaries argue that an Islamic republic was essential for Persians but not for other Muslims?

These ideological themes are neither necessary nor sufficient conditions for revolutionary success, and one or more of these elements may be missing in certain cases. Still, it is hard to imagine a mass revolution succeeding without an ideological program that both justified revolt and gave participants some reason to believe they would win. Indeed, it is a striking fact that the ideological programs of revolutionary movements as varied as those of the American Founding Fathers, the Russian and Chinese communists, or the Iranian fundamentalists all incorporated variations on these three principles.

REVOLUTIONS AND UNCERTAINTY

Despite the certainties expressed in revolutionary ideologies, revolutions actually increase the level of uncertainty in the international system. Such uncertainty raises the likelihood of war.

WHY REVOLUTIONARY STATES TEND
TO ENTER CONFLICTS WITH OTHER STATES

Revolutionary states are prone to international conflicts for several reasons. First, a revolutionary regime will be unsure about the intentions of other states simply because it has little or no direct experience in dealing with them. Lacking direct evidence, it falls back on ideology, and, as discussed above, the ideology of most revolutionary movements portrays opponents as hostile. Thus, even a mild diplomatic dispute is likely to escalate and concessions may be viewed with suspicion, because conflict is seen as inevitable and because compromise is viewed as naïve or even dangerous.

Second, a revolutionary movement may harbor suspicions based on its own experience. Eager to redress past wrongs (as is often the case), the revolutionary movement will be especially wary of any foreign powers that it sees as responsible for them. Thus, Mao Zedong's suspicions of the United States were based in part on past Western interference in China, and revolutionary forces in Mexico, Nicaragua, and Iran were preoccupied with the possibility of U.S. intervention for much the same reason.

Under such circumstances revolutionary regimes tend to assume the worst about other states and to interpret ambiguous or inconsistent policies in a negative light: threats or signs of opposition confirm the hostile image, whereas concessions or signs of approval are seen as insincere gestures masking the opponent's true (hostile) intentions. And indeed, the policies of other states are virtually certain to be ambiguous, if only because it takes time for those states to decide how to respond to the new situation. This problem is compounded by the difficulty in understanding how a new political order works, by ignorance about the beliefs and background of the new regime, and by the absence of reliable information that accompanies a revolution. Even when foreign powers are not especially hostile, therefore, some of their actions and statements will reinforce the suspicions of the revolutionary regime.

Third, conflict is more likely if the elite (or a faction within it) exaggerates a foreign threat in order to improve its internal position, that is, by rallying nationalist support for the new leaders or to justify harsh measures against internal opponents. Such efforts are especially effective when there is some truth to the accusations, for example, if foreign powers had been allied with the old regime and if they are clearly suspicious of the new government. This tactic can be dangerous if it magnifies a conflict that might otherwise have been avoided or minimized. The risk can be contained, however, if the revolutionary elite remains aware that it is engaging in a purely domestic gambit, so that its actual policy decisions are based on its true assessment of others' intentions rather than on the myth it has manufactured.

But maintaining such fine control is difficult. Although their creators may know that these are myths, the campaign may be so convincing that it becomes the basis for policy. Moreover, efforts to enhance domestic support by exaggerating external threats can be self-fulfilling: if foreign powers do not recognize the real motive behind such a campaign, they may take the revolutionary state's accusations and threats seriously. And if they then react defensively—as one would expect—it will merely confirm the bellicose image that others already hold.

Why Revolutionary States Are Insecure but Overconfident

To begin with, the inherent optimism of most revolutionary ideologies can encourage them to overstate their military capabilities. Thus, the Brissotin faction that led France to war in 1792 argued that the Revolution had created a power that would crush its enemies easily. As Brissot told the National Assembly: "Every advantage is on our side, for now every Frenchman is a willing soldier! . . . [W]here is the power on earth . . . who could hope to master six million free soldiers?"[7] This sort of argument is difficult to challenge without appearing unpatriotic; if opponents are destined for the "ash-heap of history," expressing doubts about the certainty of victory betrays a lack of confidence in the revolution itself.

The optimism of revolutionary states also rests on the belief that citizens in other countries will rise up to support them. This hope reflects the universalism common to many revolutionary ideologies and implies that their opponents, lacking popular support, will be unable to fight effectively. The Brissotins used this argument to great effect: Brissot claimed that "each soldier will say to his enemy: Brother, I am not going to cut your throat, I am going to show you the way to happiness." And his associate Maximin Isnard predicted that "at the moment that the enemy armies begin to fight with ours, the daylight of philosophy will open their eyes and the peoples will embrace each other in the face of their dethroned tyrants and an approving heaven and earth."[8] Many Bolsheviks believed similarly that their success in Russia would spark the long-anticipated revolution in Germany and a cascade of upheavals in the rest of Europe. Even Lenin, who had rejected this view in 1917, supported the Russian invasion of Poland in 1920 because he believed it would trigger an uprising by socialist forces there. Mao's claim that "a single spark can ignite a prairie fire" conveys a similar faith in the catalytic effects of revolutionary action. Thus, the overconfidence of revolutionary states is fueled by the faith that the irresistible spread of revolutionary ideas will undermine their opponents.

Revolutionary states can be further misled if they give too much credence to the testimony of foreign sympathizers. The latter, desirous of external support, are prone to exaggerate the prospects for revolution back home. In 1792, for example, the National Assembly in Paris was bombarded with optimistic reports from foreign emissaries claiming that their countrymen cried out for liberation and that the old regime would collapse quickly if attacked.

Furthermore, successful revolutionary leaders may be convinced that they can triumph over seemingly impossible odds. The strength of this factor is likely to be affected by the ease or difficulty with which the revolutionary struggle was waged. The unexpected collapse of royal authority in France may have encouraged the Brissotins in their belief that their ideas would attract universal acceptance, just as the relative ease of Castro's final campaign against Batista convinced Ché Guevara and others that revolutionary forces in Latin America could triumph even when conditions were unfavorable. By contrast, both Lenin and Mao tempered their optimistic proclamations with repeated warnings that revolutions must be conducted cautiously. Mao explicitly warned his followers to avoid both "right deviations" (passivity and fear of struggle) and "left deviations" (overconfident recklessness). Similarly, although Lenin was optimistic about the long-term prospects for world revolution, once in power he usually rejected direct efforts to promote this end. In his 1920 pamphlet "'Left-Wing' Communism: An Infantile Disorder," he warned against ill-timed efforts to seize power, and his speech to the Second Comintern Congress in the same year emphasized long-range revolutionary prospects rather than immediate efforts to foment revolutionary upheaval in other countries. Having personally led prolonged revolutionary struggles, both Lenin and Mao had learned that success was often elusive and never easy.

This discussion suggests that revolutionary states are more likely to resist impetuous efforts to export the revolution if the leadership is experienced and unified and the movement highly disciplined. Thus, the Soviet Union and the People's Republic of China behaved prudently in most cases, despite their inherently optimistic ideologies and the fact that prominent members of both regimes favored a more assertive approach. By contrast, the factional infighting in France and Iran encouraged extremists to use foreign policy—and specifically support for the export of revolution—as a litmus test for devotion to the revolution itself. In the absence of a strong central authority, those who opposed such a policy risked appearing disloyal to the universalist ideals of the revolution and thus could not contain those who advocated a more aggressive foreign policy. The radicals in turn were overconfident regarding their ability to export the revolution and to overcome the opposition such efforts were certain to provoke.

Finally, and somewhat paradoxically, the very vulnerability of a revolutionary state may create additional incentive for aggression. Already fearful that their hold on power is fragile, revolutionary leaders view domestic opponents as a potential fifth column. (In light of foreign support for counterrevolutionary groups in France, the White armies in Russia, the Kuomintang in China, and the *contras* in Nicaragua, such worries are hardly fanciful.) Exporting the revolution by striking first may be seen as the only way to preserve power at home: unless opposing states are swiftly overthrown, the argument runs, they will eventually combine to crush the revolutionary state. Thus, the Bolsheviks who advocated greater efforts to export the revolution did so in part because they believed that capitalist states would join forces and destroy the new Soviet state unless they were swiftly overthrown by the spread of socialism. (At a minimum, the revolutionaries may hope that the mere threat of revolutionary subversion may deter attacks and force opponents to adopt more conciliatory policies.) This general argument was also a potent ingredient in the Brissotin recipe for war in 1792. After describing France as beset by a conspiracy of foreign powers and internal traitors, Brissot told the Assembly, "It is not merely necessary to think of defense, the [counterrevolutionary] attack must be anticipated; you yourselves must attack."[9]

WHY FOREIGN POWERS ARE INSECURE BUT OVERCONFIDENT

Other states will fear the spread of revolutionary ideas—especially when those ideas challenge their own form of government directly. But they also tend to view this as an easy problem to solve. To begin with, the disorder that accompanies a revolution encourages other states to view the new regime as weak and vulnerable. For example, most Europeans believed that the Revolution had reduced French power considerably, leading Edmund Burke to describe the French as "the ablest architects of ruin . . . in the world." When war broke out in 1792, both France and its opponents expected an easy campaign. Where the French deputies believed that "despotism was in its death throes and a prompt attack will precipitate its final agony," a Prussian diplomat commented that "France is without disciplined armies, without experienced generals, without money, and the highest degree of anarchy reigns in all departments." Another official predicted that "the comedy will not last long. The French army of lawyers will be annihilated in Belgium and we shall be home by the autumn." As T. C. W. Blanning remarks, "With all three combatants believing their side to be invincible and their opponent(s) to be on the verge of collapse, the scene was set for the final lurch into war."[10]

This tendency to overestimate the vulnerability of the revolutionary state is not surprising, given the inherent difficulty of calculating its ability to fight. By definition, revolutionary states rest on novel forms of social organization, and revolutionary movements succeed because they devise a formula for mobilizing previously untapped sources of social power. Unfortunately, the novelty of these institutions makes it difficult for others to assess their effect on national capabilities. As Clausewitz recognized, it was not surprising that the European states underestimated the military power of revolutionary France, because in large part it was based on ideas and institutions—best exemplified by the levée en masse—that were previously unknown. Similar problems led outsiders to expect the rapid collapse of Bolshevik power and prevented an accurate assessment of Iran's military potential after the revolution there. Ideological biases may compound this tendency because states based on different political principles may find it difficult to believe that a revolutionary government could be popular or effective. This problem seems to have affected U.S. perceptions of China, for example. Because U.S. leaders believed that communism was illegitimate and immoral, they saw Mao's government as an artificial Soviet satellite rather than as an independent regime commanding substantial popular support. Thus, Assistant Secretary of State Dean Rusk believed that China's "foreign masters" had forced it to intervene in Korea and that Mao's regime was "a colonial Russian government. . . . [I]t is not Chinese."[11] The belief that a revolutionary state is inherently unpopular inclines status quo powers to exaggerate their own ability to confront it successfully.

Foreign powers also exaggerate the threat of subversion because the appeal of revolutionary ideas is impossible to measure in advance and the extent to which they are spreading is difficult to determine. Having witnessed an unexpected revolutionary upheaval, mindful of the confident proclamations of the revolutionary forces, and aware that some members of their own society may harbor similar ideas, other states overstate the threat of contagion. Thus, Burke saw revolutionary France as a mortal danger because "it has by its essence a faction of opinion and of interest and of enthusiasm in every country. . . . Thus advantaged, if it can at all exist it must finally prevail." For Burke, the only option was to eliminate the source of infection. In a similar vein Winston Churchill justified the Anglo-French intervention after the Bolshevik Revolution by describing the new Soviet republic as "a plague-bearing Russia . . . of armed hordes not only smiting with bayonet and cannon, but accompanied and preceded by swarms of typhus-bearing vermin." The main threat was ideological subversion: "to make soldiers mutiny, . . . to raise the poor against the bourgeois, . . . the workmen against the employers, . . . the peasants against the landowners, to paralyze the country by general strikes."[12] Although Churchill's pleas for full-scale intervention were ultimately rejected, "the decisive factor in bringing about a continuation of . . . limited [Allied] intervention [after World War I] was the fear . . . that Bolshevism . . . might spread to other European countries."[13] Similar fears accompanied the Chinese, Cuban, and Iranian revolutions as well. The universalism of most revolutionary ideologies compounds these worries, because other states fear a growing alliance of revolutionary powers that would leave them increasingly isolated in a hostile ideological sea.

Even in the absence of evidence that the revolution is spreading, other states cannot be completely confident that subversive movements do not lurk beneath the surface. European fears of a Jacobin conspiracy and the U.S. Red scares of the 1920s and the 1950s illustrate the tendency for foreign powers to exaggerate the ideological appeal (and therefore the offensive power) of revolutionary states. Because the threat these states pose is not simply a function of material capabilities, revolutions often seem even more dangerous than they are. And the same logic applies in reverse to counterrevolutions. Even when there is no hard evidence, a revolutionary regime cannot be completely certain that foreign powers are not conspiring with its internal opponents.

The tendency to exaggerate the threat from a revolutionary regime and its susceptibility to pressure from outside is also exacerbated by testimony from self-interested émigrés, who, as one would expect, portray the revolutionary state as both a dangerous adversary and a disorganized, unpopular, and vulnerable target. R. R. Palmer has shown, for example, that the belief that revolutionary France headed a vast international conspiracy was a myth manufactured by counterrevolutionary ideologues, several of whom were prominent in émigré circles. According to Nita Renfrew, Iraq's invasion of Iran was encouraged by Iranian émigrés who exaggerated the unpopularity and military weakness of Khomeini's regime. Cuban and Nicaraguan émigrés fed U.S. fears of Castro and the Sandinistas, while encouraging the belief that these regimes would collapse once the United States applied pressure. The warning should be clear: reliance upon "evidence" either from counterrevolutionary émigrés or from prorevolutionary sympathizers is likely to entangle one or both of the adversaries in a destabilizing web of fear and overconfidence.

Taken together, the possibility of revolutionary expansion and the belief in revolutionary weakness create strong pressures for war. Because revolutionary states tend to grow stronger over time, their opponents have a temporary "window of opportunity." Thus, England's decision to enter the war against France in 1793 was based in part on Prime Minister Pitt's belief that war was inevitable and the sooner it was begun the better. Similarly, Iraq attacked Iran in 1979 because it feared the spread of Shiite fundamentalism and because it believed the revolution had weakened Iran's military capabilities. The Somali invasion of Ethiopia in 1977 reflected the belief that Ethiopia's revolutionary government was beset by internal divisions. And U.S. efforts to overthrow Castro in Cuba and the Sandinistas in Nicaragua were justified on the grounds that each would promote revolution elsewhere in Latin America and that it would be easiest to eliminate them before they had the opportunity to consolidate their positions. In all of these cases, the belief that delay would make the job more difficult encouraged opponents of the revolutionary state to take action.

To summarize: revolutions exert far-reaching effects on the balance of threats. Each side tends to view the other as a serious challenge, yet neither can estimate the danger accurately. Lacking reliable information about the magnitude of the threat or their ability to overcome it, both sides are therefore more susceptible to self-interested testimony from émigrés or from other revolutionaries, particularly when this advice confirms preexisting beliefs. Thus, on the one hand, each side fears the other, and on the other hand, each is also likely to believe that the threat can be eliminated at relatively low cost. In short, the belief that opponents are both hostile and vulnerable works in support of a policy of preventive and preemptive war.

WHY BOTH SIDES ARE WRONG

When a revolution topples an apparently viable regime, it is not surprising that other states fear that they might be next. Similarly, if the revolutionary state has suffered extensive damage and faces continued internal opposition, its leaders have reason to fear that their success will be short-lived. Yet revolutions are a relatively poor export commodity, and although counterrevolutionary efforts face somewhat better prospects, efforts to reverse a revolution from outside are usually more difficult than their advocates anticipate. Ironically, then, both sides' perceptions of threat are usually mistaken.

Contrary to the optimistic visions of the Brissotins, for example, the outbreak of war in 1792 did not spark sympathetic rebellions across Europe. To be sure, revolutionary France eventually established a set of "satellite republics" across Europe, and Napoleon expanded this to a sizable if short-lived empire. But these conquests were not the swift and bloodless victories that the Brissotins predicted, nor was the collapse of the monarchy the catalyst for world revolution that conservatives like Edmund Burke feared. Few people anticipated that the outbreak of war in 1792 was the beginning of a quarter century of bloody struggle; neither France nor its various opponents were as easy to defeat as both sides had assumed. Similarly, the Bolshevik Revolution failed to inspire other successes; attempts elsewhere in Europe were abortive. The spread of communism was still nearly three decades off, when the Soviet army imposed similar regimes in Eastern Europe following Germany's defeat in the Second World War. And contrary to the recurring fears that communist revolution would spread swiftly around the globe, containing the Red menace was in fact relatively easy.

Other cases teach similar lessons. The Mexican Revolution had little impact on revolutionary struggles elsewhere in Latin America; Cuba's efforts to promote revolutionary change in the region have been relatively unsuccessful. (True, Cuba was a source of inspiration, advice, and material aid for the Sandinistas in Nicaragua, and for other revolutionaries as well, but a single, short-lived success hardly constitutes a winning record after more than thirty years.) And although fundamentalist movements have become more active throughout the Muslim world, Iran's efforts to export its principles to other countries have proved equally abortive. Irrespective of its specific ideological character, in short, there seems to be little basis for the perennial hope and fear of world revolution.

At the same time, the belief that revolutionary regimes will collapse if attacked is equally dubious. In virtually every case of a major social revolution (France, Mexico, Russia, China, Cuba, Nicaragua, Iran) opponents have argued that foreign intervention could remove the threat at relatively low cost. With the partial exception of Nicaragua, efforts to do so were uniformly unsuccessful. While counterrevolutions from abroad do on occasion succeed, on the whole, the ability of revolutionary states to resist such attempts is striking.

This argument does not mean that the fears harbored by revolutionary states and other powers are groundless. Rather, it means that the threat is usually exaggerated, as is the ease with which it can be eliminated. If the respective fears and hopes were accurate, the struggle would be a swift and decisive triumph for the stronger side. But instead of a wave of revolutionary upheavals or the swift collapse of the new regime, the typical result is either a brief and inconclusive clash (e.g., the Russo-Polish War of 1920) or a protracted and bloody struggle (e.g., the wars of the French Revolution, the Iran–Iraq War, the *contra* war in Nicaragua).

Why are revolutions hard to export and why do foreign interventions fail? First, the universalist rhetoric of revolutionary ideologies notwithstanding, a revolution is first and foremost a *national* phenomenon. A campaign to export a revolution would immediately bring the revolutionary state into conflict with the national loyalties of the intended recipients. And the principle that people who conceive of themselves as a nation are entitled to their own independent state has consistently proved to be a far more powerful social force than any notion of universal revolutionary solidarity. Foreign populations are likely to view efforts to export a revolution as acts of aggression, which makes it easier for the ruling elites to resist the revolutionary forces. Or as Robespierre warned in response to the optimistic predictions of the Brissotins: "No one likes an armed missionary, and no more extravagant idea ever sprang from the head of a politician than to suppose that one people has only to enter another's territory with arms in its hands to make the latter adopt its laws and its Constitution."[14] Moreover, even if conditions in other countries are broadly similar to the circumstances that produced one revolution (and they frequently are not), the special circumstances that enabled one revolution to succeed are unlikely to exist elsewhere. Thus, exporting the revolution is much more difficult than the revolutionaries expect.

Second, a revolution serves as a warning to other states: the more dangerous it appears, the greater the tendency for others to balance against it. Until a revolution actually occurs, other states may not take the possibility seriously. But once the danger has been demonstrated, potential victims will take steps to avoid a similar fate (e.g., through defensive alliances, internal reforms, or more extensive repression). Thus, the Cuban revolution inspired the U.S. Alliance for Progress in Latin America (intended to forestall additional "Cubas" by promoting economic and political development) and encouraged Latin American oligarchies to suppress their domestic opponents more vigorously. Similarly, the Iranian Revolution united Iraq, Saudi Arabia, and the other Gulf states against the danger of revolutionary infection, with tacit or active support from the United States and others. Again, the point is not that revolutions pose no danger; the point is, rather, that other states can and will do a variety of things to contain the threat.

Efforts to export counterrevolutions fail for somewhat different reasons. Revolutionary leaders are usually dedicated, highly motivated individuals who have been successful precisely because they are good at organizing support in the face of impressive obstacles. They are likely to be formidable adversaries, because they can direct those same skills toward mobilizing the nation for war. It is thus no accident that the French levée en masse and the Soviet Red Army were able to defeat their internal and external opponents or that revolutionary Iran managed to rebuild its military power with remarkable speed after the Iraqi invasion in 1980.

Foreign interventions also fail because they provide the domestic legitimacy that a revolutionary regime needs: the same nationalist convictions that make revolution hard to export also work against successful foreign intervention. The Russo-Polish War of 1920 illustrates both tendencies nicely: the initial Polish invasion helped mobilize public support for the Bolsheviks while the Red Army's subsequent counterattack aroused the traditional anti-Russian nationalism of the Poles rather than the proletarian uprising anticipated by Lenin.

The pressure for war produced by a revolution results from two parallel myths: the belief that the revolution will spread rapidly if it is not crushed immediately, and the belief that a reversal of the revolution will be easy to accomplish. Contrary to these expectations, however, is the more typical result: neither a tide of worldwide revolution nor the quick and easy ouster of the revolutionary regime but rather a prolonged struggle between an unexpectedly capable revolutionary regime and its surprisingly resistant adversaries.

REFERENCES

1. Note the following death tolls in modern revolutions: Russia, 500,000 dead; China, 3 million; Cuba, 5,000; Iran, 17,000; Mexico, 250,000; Nicaragua, between 30,000 and 50,000. See Small and Singer (1982).
2. Huntington (1968), p. 266.
3. Mao Zedong (1961), p. 428.
4. Quoted in Arjomand (1988), p. 102.
5. See Van Ness (1970), pp. 40–41; and Lin Biao, "Long Live Victory in the People's War," in Griffith (1966), p. 101.
6. See Lenin (1970), p. 675.
7. Blanning (1986), pp. 108–109.
8. These quotations are from Schama (1989), p. 597; and Blanning (1986), pp. 108–110.
9. Brissot, quoted in Clapham (1969), p. 115.
10. Blanning (1986), pp. 78–80, 115–16.
11. Schaller (1979), p. 125.
12. Quoted in Fiddick (1990), pp. 4–5.
13. Chamberlin (1965), 2:152.
14. He continued: "The Declaration of Rights [of Man] is not like the sun's rays, which in one moment illumine the whole earth: it is no thunderbolt, to strike down a thousand thrones. It is easier to inscribe it on paper, or engrave it on brass, than to retrace its sacred characters in the hearts of men." Quoted in Thompson (1935), p. 207.

The Diffusion of Revolutionary Waves

MARK N. KATZ

Revolutions are an international phenomenon. This is true not only because they often bring military conflict that spreads across borders, but even more because the ideas and goals that inspire revolutions diffuse around the world. When revolutionary ideas spread to other countries where people find them appealing, those ideas can contribute to further revolutions, creating waves of revolutions with similar goals. The democratic revolutions of the United States in 1776, France in 1789, and central Europe in 1848 were one such wave; the Marxist-communist revolutions of Russia in 1917, China in 1949, and Cuba in 1959 were another. In recent years, Islamic fundamentalist and anticommunist revolutions formed additional waves. The power of revolutionary ideas is evident in how widely they spread and in their impact on multiple revolutionary conflicts.

Revolutions upset the existing international order. But not all revolutions upset it equally. The type of revolution that is most disruptive is that which spreads (or credibly threatens to spread) not through invasion, but through one revolution's sparking affiliate revolutions elsewhere. In other words, what is disruptive is not just that an ideological revolutionary regime seeks the establishment of regimes similar to itself elsewhere, but that the revolutionary idea resonates in other countries, and significant forces appear that seek to implement it. For the status quo powers, containing a revolution from spreading via affiliate revolutions can be far more complex than rolling back or containing a revolution that spreads via invasion. For in the former case, it is not sufficient to militarily confront or contain the country in which the revolution initially succeeded. In addition, indigenous revolutionary forces must either be stopped from gaining strength in other countries, or successfully suppressed if they do. The history of the latter half of the twentieth century has shown, however, that the attempt to suppress indigenous revolutionary forces can be extremely difficult—indeed, can fail completely in some countries and thus lead to an even greater revolutionary challenge to the interests of the status quo powers.

While the policy of containment pursued by the United States and its West European allies must be judged a success in terms of deterring a Soviet invasion of Western Europe, it proved woefully inadequate in preventing Marxist-Leninist revolutionaries in Asia, Africa, and Latin America from coming to power and maintaining alliances with Moscow. Similarly, the West was unable to contain Arab nationalist revolutionaries who were inspired by the example of Egypt's Jamal 'Abd al-Nasir from seizing power in several other Arab countries. At present, the United States, Western Europe, and Russia are fearful of the wave of Islamic fundamentalist revolutions that swept to power in Iran, Sudan, and Afghanistan, and that threatens to spread to Algeria, Egypt, and other countries in the Middle East, Central Asia, and elsewhere in the Muslim world.

For purposes of this study, *revolutionary waves* are groups of revolutions with similar objectives. A particular revolution can belong to more than one revolutionary wave. In addition to belonging to a particular "for" wave, it can also belong to one or more "against" waves.

A "for" revolutionary wave consists of those revolutions that established (or earnestly attempted to establish) a particular form of government or socioeconomic system, such as democracy, Marxism-Leninism, Arab nationalism, or Islamic fundamentalism. An "against" revolutionary wave consists of those revolutions that overthrew a particular form of government or socioeconomic system. "Against" revolutionary waves include antimonarchical, anticolonial, anticapitalist, anti-Western, and antidictatorial ones, among others.

Individual "against" revolutionary waves have not been associated with any one particular "for" wave. Antimonarchical revolutions have resulted in democratic as well as a wide variety of nondemocratic regimes, including Marxist-Leninist and Islamic fundamentalist. The wave of anti-communist revolutions in 1989–1991 has resulted in a variety of regimes, ranging from democratic to nondemocratic. Even a revolutionary wave defined as broadly as "antidictatorial" does not imply a particular "for" revolution; some antidictatorial revolutions have resulted in democracy while others have resulted in yet another form of dictatorship.

Similarly, revolutions which have been "for" the same goal have been fought against a variety of opponents. The establishment of Marxist-Leninist regimes, for example, has not been associated with the overthrow of just one type of regime, but of several: monarchies, colonial rule, and other forms of dictatorship. Democratic revolutions have been fought against a variety of regimes as well.

ROLES WITHIN A REVOLUTIONARY WAVE

A revolutionary wave can contain a *central revolution,* which articulates a vision of altering the existing international system by inspiring a series of revolutions similar to its own, and by acting as the center of this group of revolutionary states. In the Marxist-Leninist revolutionary wave, this role was played by the Soviet Union. In the Arab nationalist revolutionary wave, this role was played by Egypt. Iran has played this role in the Islamic fundamentalist revolutionary wave. In these three instances, the central revolutionary states were also the first to experience their particular type of "for" revolution. This need not, however, always be the case. Italy was the first country to experience a fascist revolution, yet it was Nazi Germany that became the central revolutionary state within the fascist revolutionary wave.

In order to play the role of central revolution, a state must have the ability to be a great power on either a regional or global scale. Generally, the central revolution is the strongest state within a revolutionary wave.

But in order for there to be a revolutionary wave, there must also be other actual or potential revolutions. *Aspiring revolutionaries* are inspired by the central revolution, attempt to emulate it, and usually seek its assistance in coming to power. The existence of a central revolution and one or more aspiring revolutionary movements with serious prospects of success is the minimum requirement for there to be a revolutionary wave that spreads primarily via affiliate revolutions.

Not all aspiring revolutionaries, however, are successful. Those that are can have various relations with the central revolution. Revolutionary regimes set up by central revolutions in countries they have invaded are *subordinate* or puppet revolutions. By definition, of course, such subordinate revolutions do not voluntarily affiliate themselves with a central revolution. The existence of one or more revolutions subordinate to a central revolution, however, does not mean that other revolutions elsewhere cannot voluntarily affiliate themselves with a central revolution. Although most of the Marxist-Leninist regimes in Eastern Europe were installed by and subordinate to the Soviet Union, Marxist-Leninist regimes in the Third World voluntarily affiliated themselves with Moscow.

An *affiliate* revolution is one in which the revolutionary government voluntarily aligns itself with the central revolution. Since the affiliation is voluntary, it can occur to different degrees, from tight to loose. A revolution need not occur completely without external involvement to qualify as an affiliate revolution: aspiring revolutionaries often have received military assistance from the central revolution, as well as from other states in their revolutionary wave.

Affiliate revolutions can be either "ambitious" or "unambitious." An unambitious one is allied with the central revolution, but it does not actively spread the revolutionary wave itself. An ambitious affiliate revolution, by contrast, works actively to spread revolution to other countries while maintaining its alliance with the central revolution. Cuba played this role in the Marxist-Leninist revolutionary wave. Whether an affiliate revolution (or, for that matter, a central revolution) is ambitious or unambitious about expanding the revolutionary wave, however, is not necessarily a permanent status: a regime can be ambitious about spreading revolution at one point in time but become unambitious about it later, and vice versa.

SUCCESS OF REVOLUTIONARY WAVES

Revolutionary waves have exhibited different patterns of success over time. Certain waves, once begun, have spread and spread until they have engulfed virtually the entire world. One such "against" wave has been the wave of antimonarchical (or, more precisely, anti-absolute monarchical) revolutions. At the time of the American Revolution in 1776, virtually the entire world was ruled by absolute monarchs. At present, only a handful of absolute monarchies remain. Of course, not all absolute monarchies fell as a result of revolution. Some evolved slowly and relatively peacefully into constitutional monarchies or into some other form of democracy. Antimonarchical revolutions, though, do seem to have helped establish an international norm about absolute monarchy being illegitimate.

Another "against" wave that has enjoyed near-universal success has been that of anticolonial (or, more precisely, anti-European colonial) revolutions. The American Revolution was the first such revolution in the modern era that resulted in colonies establishing independence and being recognized by the status quo powers, including the ex-colonial ruler. Not all colonies achieved independence as a result of revolution: many obtained it peacefully. As with antimonarchical revolutions, though, anticolonial revolutions seem to have been instrumental in establishing what has become a universally accepted norm: European colonial rule without the consent of the local majority is illegitimate.

Some other "against" revolutionary waves have proven more finite. A number of anticapitalist revolutions have sought to either isolate a given country from the international capitalist economy, or, more ambitiously, to create an alternative international economic system. For the most part, these anticapitalist projects came to an end either through the collapse of the revolutionary regimes pursuing them, or, more remarkably, through hitherto anticapitalist regimes' adopting capitalism and seeking to increase instead of decrease their participation in the international capitalist economy (China after 1976 is a dramatic example of this). Antidemocratic revolutions (revolutions overthrowing democratic governments) have proved short-lived in some countries and long-lived in others (most notably Franco's Spain). Antidemocratic revolution has not proven sustainable as a wave. Similarly, the anti-Western nature of many revolutions was often not sustained when, with the passage of time, revolutionary leaders or their successors found cooperation with the West to be desirable.

Among "for" revolutionary waves, the democratic revolutionary wave is the only one that has spread and lasted. The English Revolution of the mid-seventeenth century could be considered the first attempted democratic revolution, though its results were ambiguous. The American Revolution of the late eighteenth century, by contrast, was an unambiguously democratic revolution. Since then, many other states have democratized through either revolutionary or evolutionary means. While there have been setbacks for democracy, especially in countries with little experience with it, by the late twentieth century the number of countries that have adopted and sustained democracy has become impressive. Like the antimonarchical and anticolonial revolutionary waves, the democratic one has also spread widely. Though democracy has been reversed in some countries in the past and there appear to be strong prospects for its being reversed in several countries (especially Russia and others in the former Soviet bloc) that have adopted it recently, the democratic revolutionary wave as a whole appears to be highly durable and is likely to remain so.

PART TWO

COMPARATIVE AND HISTORICAL STUDIES OF REVOLUTION

CHAPTER 5

Republican Revolutions

In the seventeenth and eighteenth centuries, the kingdoms of Great Britain and France faced major upheavals. In the 1640s and 1650s, Britain experienced a great civil war, in which the forces of the English Parliament fought against, and overthrew, the English king. In 1776 the English king again faced revolt, this time from his subjects in the Atlantic colonies who aimed at creating an independent United States. And in 1789, the French monarchy was faced with a revolution that overthrew the traditional rights and privileges of nobles and the monarchy. All of these events produced new republican constitutions and declarations regarding the rights of men as citizens, arguing that men of property (but not yet women) should be considered naturally free, not merely the subjects of divinely appointed kings. These events are considered the first great "liberal" or "republican" revolutions.

What forces led to the overthrow of kings? For a long time, under the influence of the work of Karl Marx (see Chapter 1), historians assumed that these revolutions were due to the rise of capitalism and that it was capitalists (Marx's "bourgeoisie") who made these revolutions. We now know that such a view is too simple. Many complex changes were occurring in these societies—growth in population, an increase in central state power, the expansion of markets. In addition, many of the changes produced by these revolutions unfolded in the course of the revolutions themselves, as different groups influenced one another and developed new positions that they had not anticipated earlier. The story of these revolutions, like that of the revolutions since them, is that a *combination* of changes produced intensified political conflicts that overwhelmed existing institutions.

In the following essays, Jack Goldstone lays out the role of population changes in contributing to the English Revolution of the 1640s, John Markoff shows how the interaction of peasants and notables produced the development of the French Revolution of 1789, and Gordon Wood shows how much the American Revolution of 1776 had in common with the other two great republican revolutions in overturning privilege and social inequality.

The English Revolution: A Structural-Demographic Approach
JACK A. GOLDSTONE

Marx and Engels often suggested that the English Revolution of 1640 was a "bourgeois" revolution, in which the growth of capitalism in trade and agriculture overturned a feudal, backward-looking monarchy. The following essay examines the causes of the English Revolution and finds that the evidence does not support the Marxist model. Instead, the essay offers an alternative structural analysis, stressing the impact of population changes on the key social relationships of early modern England—between Crown and landlords, between landlords and peasants, and between members of the landed elite.

In 1640 Scottish troops crossed into England. The king of England and Scotland, Charles I, had angered the Scots by attacking their religious organization and the privileges of their nobility. The king had also claimed title to Scottish noblemen's lands and asked them to pay new taxes. Charles asked the English Parliament for money for a settlement with the Scots. Yet instead of money the king received attacks on his ministers and a long list of complaints about royal misgovernment. While king and Parliament locked in debates over the king's authority, riots broke out in London and in the English countryside, and a full-scale revolt began in Ireland. The king left London to raise an army to reassert his authority; his opponents in Parliament raised an army to defend themselves. Drawing on the wealth of London and the support of a broad range of landowners, farmers, small merchants, and artisans, the Parliamentary army led by Oliver Cromwell defeated the king and installed a revolutionary government.

Marx and Engels called these events a "bourgeois" revolution: The emergence of capitalism brought the rise of bourgeois classes—capitalist farmers among the landlord "gentry" and merchant capitalists among the growing overseas trading companies—who chafed at the restrictions on their activity which a still largely feudal aristocracy allied with the Crown imposed. Conflict between the rising capitalist classes and the older feudal classes thus lay behind the revolution. Identifying the Parliamentary forces as capitalist and bourgeois and the royalist forces as feudal, Marx and Engels saw the victory of Parliament as the victory of capitalist forces over feudalism.

However, historians have challenged this view by demonstrating that political divisions ran through every social and geographic category: Members of the House of Lords and the House of Commons, merchants and urban oligarchs, the gentry of nearly every county in England, and even members of many single families suffered internal division. All these groups included supporters of Parliament *and* supporters of the Crown. Explanations of the Revolution in terms of class conflict have thus largely receded.

Many English historians, particularly the youngest generation of scholars, have simply abandoned the search for long-term social changes as causes of the English Revolution. Instead they have rallied around G. R. Elton's cry that "the failure of Charles's government was not rendered 'inevitable' by deep divisions in society or inherited stresses . . . but was conditioned by the inability of the King and his ministers to operate any political system."[1] Therefore, Charles's choice of policies and advisors precipitated the political crisis of the 1640s. In the words of one younger historian, it was a "crisis of counsel" that formed "the central crisis of early Stuart government."[2]

Yet this interpretation is unsatisfactory for at least two reasons. First, by blaming the Revolution on Charles's missteps, the historians render the enormous scale of the conflict— two civil wars in a decade and the overthrow of all royal courts, the Anglican Church, the House of Lords, and the monarchy itself—a mystery. Indeed, Englishmen had deposed and

Adapted from "Capitalist Origins of the English Revolution: Chasing a Chimera," Theory and Society, *vol. 12, pp. 143–80 (March 1983). Copyright © 1983 by Jack Goldstone.*

even murdered unpopular kings before and after—William Rufus, Edward II, Richard II, and James II—without England's political institutions or the monarchy itself coming under assault. How was it that by 1640, the bumbling policies of a king—in and of themselves—led to popular uprisings, an urban revolution in London, the fracturing of the entire nation, and twenty years of civil war and interregnum?

Second, the research of recent scholars has made it clear that a key reason for the increasingly sharp conflict in 1642, both between king and Parliament and within Parliament, was the spread of popular uprisings throughout England, including both rural tumults and riots in London. Hill is certainly partly correct in stating that "what mattered in the English Revolution was that the ruling class was deeply divided at a time when there was much combustible material among the lower classes."[3] The exclusive focus on Charles's bumbling precludes an understanding of why so much "combustible material" existed in England in the 1640s. Without having some plausible answer to this issue, the course of the mid-century upheaval is hard to explain.

Neo-Marxist sociologists have taken another road. Barrington Moore, Jr., Perry Anderson, and Immanuel Wallerstein, have—to varying degrees—revised the Marxist view of the capitalist origins of the English Revolution by putting aside the notion of a distinctive bourgeois "class" as the necessary spearhead of revolution. Instead, these scholars have argued that the diffusion of capitalist economic and legal relations throughout society—shown by the agricultural improvements associated with extensive enclosures, and a vast increase in overseas trade—gradually undermined traditional English life and sharpened conflicts throughout the nation. In particular, the emergence of capitalist economic practices intensified conflicts between landlords and tenants, multiplied the misery and poverty of the peasantry, and motivated the popular protests that marked the sixteenth and early seventeenth centuries. At the same time, the greater dependence of England's economy on capitalist international trade left the nation highly vulnerable to cyclical downswings that significantly increased tensions both within the ruling gentry class and between the gentry and the Crown.

Unfortunately, both the neo-Marxist view and the view of the new generation of political historians with its narrow focus on elite politics and the failings of Charles I run into difficulties when confronted with the evidence. As an alternative I suggest a structural analysis of the origins of the English Revolution, one that stresses political conflicts but highlights long-term causes for such conflicts. In particular, I draw upon recent research in demographic history to suggest that the long-term causes of England's political crisis were mainly *demographic* changes, and that many of the effects mistakenly attributed to the growth of capitalism in early modern England were in fact changes in the scale, or the distribution, of traditional occupations, practices, and incomes, due to the rapid population growth of the years 1500–1640.

THE NEO-MARXIST VIEW OF THE CAPITALIST ORIGINS OF THE ENGLISH REVOLUTION: A CRITIQUE

According to the Neo-Marxist view, in the sixteenth and early seventeenth centuries landlords deprived small farmers of their land. Landlords denied villagers their traditional rights to use village common lands, assembled their property into large commercial farms or sheep pastures, enclosed them with fences or hedges, and turned their former tenants and farmers away. Enclosing landlords thus created a landless proletariat whose members spread unrest through the countryside; enclosers also brought to agriculture a new capitalist spirit that was at odds with the conservative spirit of the monarchy. Struggles between enclosing lords and tenants thus contributed to the conflict between landlords and the Crown. At the same time, England's expanding overseas trade, exploiting the growing capitalist world-system, supported new interest opposed to the Crown's control of commerce. These commercial forces added their weight to that of the landlords in the conflict with the monarchy. Instead of a distinct "bourgeoisie" facing feudal landlords, the neo-Marxist view ascribes the Revolution to commercial elements *within* the ruling landlord class, who created a landless proletariat and in so doing came into conflict with the "traditionalist" Crown. The Revolution was then fought between the commercial elements of the gentry, with help from the merchant and manufacturing interests in London, and the king and his aristocratic loyalists.

This story is told, in varying forms, by Moore, Wallerstein, and Anderson. Thus Moore:

> During the sixteenth century the most significant [enclosures] were encroachments made by lords of manors or their farmers upon the land over which the manorial population had common rights. . . . The peasants were driven off the land; ploughed strips and common alike were turned into pastures. . . . Those who promoted the wave of agrarian capitalism, the chief victors in the struggle against the old order, came from the yeomanry and even more from the landed upper classes. . . . [C]ommercially minded elements among the landed upper classes, and to a lesser extent among the yeomen, were among the main forces opposing the King and royal attempts to preserve the old order, and therefore an important cause . . . that produced the Civil War.[4]

Wallerstein and Anderson are even more forceful. Thus Wallerstein: "Encroachment led to the abandonment of villages and migration," as yeomen "usurped (by enclosure) the lands" of their laborers. The spread of the new practices and market orientation within the gentry led to a conflict of interests within the ruling landlord class "between the new capitalists and the old aristocrats."[5] And Anderson: "The English monarchy was felled at the center by a commercialized gentry [and] a capitalist city" which faced in Charles I's absolutism the attempted "political refortification of a feudal state."[6]

Undoubtedly the English economy underwent a profound change between the fifteenth and the eighteenth centuries. In the fifteenth century, though local commerce and marketing were well established, England was primarily a nation of small farmers producing for local consumption, towns with more than a few thousand inhabitants were rare, and overseas trade was modest. By the late eighteenth century, though a substantial number of family farms remained, large parts of England's agricultural output came from the efforts of wage laborers on farms producing for regional or national markets, the urban sector had expanded massively and provided a substantial share of production and consumption, and large segments of the economy depended on overseas trade. The issue is not whether these changes occurred— that is indisputable—but whether these changes adequately account for the conflicts that led to the English Revolution. In the neo-Marxist view, precisely these changes led to increasing conflict and set the stage for the revolutionary crisis. To evaluate this view, we need to look closely at the course of agricultural change in the sixteenth and seventeenth centuries and then examine the hypothesized links between such change, and also changes in manufacturing and overseas trade, and the Revolution.

ENCLOSURES, AGRARIAN CAPITALISM, AND RURAL UNREST

In parts of England the medieval pattern of landholding was for copyholders and other tenants to hold scattered strips of land in open fields with large areas set aside for common use for grazing. In the fifteenth century areas of the open fields and commons began to be enclosed with hedges or fences.

Yet the type of enclosure that was held to have important social and political consequences—the enclosure by a landlord of common fields in order to turn out tenants and create sheep pasture—in fact constituted only a small portion of enclosures and occurred over a limited time span, primarily from 1450 to 1550 and from 1650 to 1750. The largest amount of such enclosure seems to have occurred before 1510; by the 1530s enclosures were generally used for intensive grain farming or mixed sheep and corn husbandry.

Also significant is the fact that in this period enclosures were rarely the work of the manorial lord who possessed all or virtually all of the enclosed lands. Instead, the tenants usually agreed on enclosures to increase the intensity of cultivation. The Chancery rolls of the sixteenth and seventeenth centuries reveal that tenants initiated scores of enclosures by agreement that benefited all concerned. By 1580 the enclosure movement was as much a movement of small farmers and copyholders as of large landlords.

Sharp's study of the enclosure of the Western Forests nicely traces this pattern. The traditional view was that these enclosures and the riots that accompanied them constituted an arbitrary extinction of the common rights of small farmers and tenants (in England called yeomen, copyholders, husbandmen, or freeholders), who rose to defend their immemorial rights. Yet a close examination of the legal proceedings and participants involved completely overturns this view.

> The disafforestations, rather than being arbitrary enclosures, were excellent examples of enclosure by agreement: substantial freeholders and copyholders were asked to grant their consent to the enclosure and the consequent extinction of their rights of common in return for compensating allotments of land. Contrary to accepted opinions . . . the property rights of . . . freeholders and copyholders claiming rights of common on the forest were scrupulously protected in quite elaborate legal proceedings.[7]

Protests against the enclosure came not from dispossessed copyholders and yeomen cultivators but from already-landless squatters in the forest, primarily artisans who relied on grazing, game poaching, and gathering wood for construction, woodworking, and firewood to supplement their incomes.

In addition, much enclosure in the sixteenth and seventeenth centuries was land newly reclaimed from the swampy fens or the forests. Therefore, many enclosures were made on land where common rights had never been important.

The verdict that enclosures were disruptive came from cries against enclosures that first appeared in the sixteenth century. Yet experts have since shown that this outcry was largely a case of scapegoating. In fact, "the great outbursts of public outrage against inclosure [sic] in the century before the Civil War probably do not tell us much about the progress of conversion, for most coincided with runs of bad harvests, in which unease about the food supply [created] an uproar."[8] To better understand the effects of enclosures on tenants, we must look at recent detailed studies of rural unrest throughout sixteenth and early seventeenth century England.

In the far northern counties of Cumberland and Westmoreland, Appleby's studies of enclosure show that population pressure and not the growth of capitalism created a landless and rebellious agrarian proletariat. As population grew, landlords could have profited by enclosing the common, converting it to arable lands, and renting out these new lands to a more numerous tenantry, but they did not do so. Instead, they carefully guarded the common rights of their tenants to maintain the vitality of their patronage relationships. But this protection did not free their tenants from difficulties:

> [E]ach customary tenant . . . had security of tenure on his small tenement or cottage holding. Each tenant also enjoyed the right of pasture on his manorial common. . . . In other words, the tenant retained all his old rights and privileges. But this was no longer enough. . . . The great population surge of the sixteenth century had added too many men to the rural structure, straining it to the point of collapse.[9]

Tenements were fragmented and the traditional commons overburdened as "all competed for limited land and pasture."[10] Younger sons, unable to secure new arable land on the manor lands, became landless migrants or squatters who made piecemeal enclosures in the adjacent forests.

As for the far South, Peter Clark, studying agrarian riots in Kent between 1558 and 1640, found that attacks on enclosures were usually by artisans and pastoral forest dwellers on woodlands newly enclosed for grain and not attacks by displaced cultivators on sheepfolds. Moreover, most riots were not attacks on landlords but on corn merchants in times of high prices.

> It was within the grain producing regions which in normal harvest years produced a surplus which went to feed other areas, notably the larger towns, that grain riots were most likely to occur. . . . [R]iots in Norfolk, Essex, Kent, Sussex, Hertfordshire, Hampshire, and the Thames Valley were commonly provoked by the fear of the siphoning off of local grain supplies to meet [London's] demand. . . . Elsewhere, urban demand played a similar role in provoking disorder.[11]

As for the West, Buchanan Sharp's studies of rioters in the Royal Forests of western England also stress that higher food prices generated disorders. Copyholders protesting loss of land did not cause the majority of disturbances in this region; established and skilled rural artisans, long exposed to the market, whose protests were keyed to shrinking wages, high unemployment, and food scarcity, were the culprits. Food riots, far more common than enclosure riots, recurred in 1586, 1594–1597, 1622, 1629–1631, and 1641–1642.

As for the East, Walter's study of the 1629 grain riots in Essex mirrors Sharp's results. His analysis of the participants in the riots shows they were artisans, chiefly clothworkers, suffering from unemployment and high prices, who directed riots against grain merchants exporting corn from the county. Walter carefully delineates the riots' political overtones. Disorder followed a series of peaceful petitions to the king asking him to relieve the distress of the clothworkers; yet "the inability of those in authority (for all their promises) to relieve the poor threatened the implicit contract between rulers and ruled."[12] Not the failure of the Crown to protect cultivators from enclosure but its failure to provide relief to workers in times of unemployment and rising prices produced the disorders.

Even the great peasant revolts of the sixteenth century, such as Kett's rebellion in East Anglia in 1549, that experts once widely attributed to enclosures, have recently received a reinterpretation in which enclosures have played a lesser role. Cornwall's detailed study of Kett's rising concludes that "It might have been possible to assimilate the new ways in agriculture, had they been the only problem. But from the third decade of the sixteenth century at least, the situation became bedeviled by two further crises which had infinitely more immediate and universal effect: population growth and price inflation."[13]

In sum, we can no longer characterize the agrarian structure of England before the Revolution as being the result of an "enclosure crisis" due primarily to the spread of capitalist commercial farming. The sixteenth and early seventeenth centuries were a period of significant enclosure, but largely of virgin lands, largely by agreement of yeomen and tenants, and largely for the purpose of more intensive grain farming. A far greater portion of rural unrest in the sixteenth and early seventeenth centuries consisted of food riots by rural artisans concerned about unemployment, high prices, and food shortages.

Moreover, we must take a closer look at the enclosure of Crown lands. *The monarchy too* participated in the enclosure movement, particularly the enclosure of waste and fen; in fact its efforts to turn a greater profit from the Royal Forests and fens made the Crown probably the single largest encloser of the early seventeenth century. Pressed by growing financial needs, the Crown spearheaded enclosure projects, often in conjunction with local gentry, splitting the profits from enclosure and rental of reclaimed fens and forests. For example, in Lincolnshire in the 1630s a group of gentry joined the Crown in a fen drainage project; the same gentry emerged as the core of the royalist faction in the county in the Civil War. In the north, the Crown led the way after 1600 in raising rents and entry fines, positioning itself in the forefront of the region's movement toward free market rents. If enclosure for improvement, leasing, and profit is a mark of commercial progressiveness, then in light of the Crown's activity we cannot attribute the seventeenth century crisis to a conflict between a commercial, progressive gentry and a conservative, feudal Crown. In fact, in the relations between landlords and the Crown by the early seventeenth century enclosures were more often a source of cooperation than of conflict.

In short, the gradual increase in enclosures for commercial, capitalist farming in the sixteenth and early seventeenth centuries cannot be held accountable for most of the increase in rural disorders. Rising food prices, shortages of land due to population pressures, and a growing population of urban consumers drawing grain from rural areas seem to have been far more important factors. In addition, examining enclosure practices shows few differences between landlords and Crown. Enclosures evidently were not the source of conflicts that lay behind the revolution.

Can we say the same of the growth of trade and manufacture?

THE GROWTH OF MARKET RELATIONS

Marx had argued that the growth of English trade led to new relationships and new commercial interests that joined the opposition to the king. Yet we must look closely at the growth of English trade and marketing. For the increase in marketing and trade generally did not stimulate the growth of new and distinctively capitalist relationships but did encourage the expansion of traditional markets and trades. Indeed, most of the growth in market relations was simply an increase in scale as the English economy struggled to adjust to its increased numbers.

The most important factor in the growth of market relations was the growth of towns, particularly of London. As surplus rural population streamed to the towns to seek employment, the number of people who had to buy their daily bread on the market sharply increased. The crowds who harried the bishops, signed petitions, and overthrew the Common Council were struggling guild artisans and apprentices in the traditional crafts.

Similarly, the significance of the expansion of the domestic cloth industry prior to 1640 was not the creation of a distinctive proletariat or a distinctive capitalist merchant interest. Mere numbers of traditional workers were the critical problem. Parish relief systems designed to cope with modest numbers of workers simply broke down in the face of ever-larger crowds of artisans dependent on trade. By the seventeenth century, in the major cloth-producing areas, "depression [in the cloth trade] spawned unemployment on a scale which the individual parish was not really designed to encounter, let alone solve."[14]

Moreover, the merchants themselves were not a united opposition; they were divided between the large merchants dealing in overseas trade and the smaller domestic traders and even within income groups between the merchants of the outer ports versus those of London. For the most part, the wealthiest merchants, who profited from monopolies on overseas trade granted by the king, supported the Crown in the Civil War. It was chiefly smaller merchants, hurt most by royal monopolies on trade and royal taxes, who supported Parliament.

The great significance of the expansion of manufacturing and markets was the simple demographic fact that as population growth outran employment opportunities in agriculture, more and more people depended on nonagricultural employment. Such people depended more on the vicissitudes of markets and the predations of rising food prices and falling wages than did agriculturalists. With their increased numbers driving up food prices and making employment harder to find, the lot of almost all workers and artisans was sharply deteriorating.

England's commercial expansion did produce pockets of more modern, larger-scale enterprises: glassworks and ironworks grew substantially before 1640, and coal production underwent spectacular growth. Yet the role played by these ventures in the economy as a whole was minor. And ironworkers or coal miners did not play any significant role in the events of 1640–1660; the prime actors among the populace were the yeomen of the countryside and the artisans, traders, shopkeepers, and apprentices of London. Indeed, a closer look at urban politics provides another curious irony. A center of truly modern capitalist enterprise in seventeenth century England fed industrial markets by production with wage labor: the enormously expanding coal trade centered in Newcastle. Yet as a recent study of its Civil War politics shows, "Newcastle . . . provides a clear case in point of a commercial and industrial center that sided with the King rather than with Parliament."[15]

AN ALTERNATIVE VIEW

Why then did England have a revolution in 1640? Three questions need answering. First, why did the gentry come into conflict with the Crown? Second, why were England's elites so divided among themselves that the political conflicts of 1640 led to civil war? Third, why did so much "combustible material" which made popular disorders likely to accompany the breakdown of the central government exist among the populace?

The conflict between the Crown and the gentry was not over enclosure or commercial practices. The main problem was one found in most pre-revolutionary situations: the attempt of the central government to wrest more money from the elites by raising taxes and attacking elite privileges. The English Crown, like the French monarchy, faced a landed elite that held strategic positions in government and resisted royal attempts to reform taxation. According to England's customary constitution, the English Parliament, composed of land-lord representatives, had to give its consent to all new taxes. English landlords also controlled local law enforcement as Justices of the Peace. In addition, local landlords served the Crown as tax collectors and tax assessors. However, they generally took advantage of these roles to set their own assessments unrealistically low and so avoided taxation. The Crown could overcome this resistance only by reducing landlords' role in local and national government and attempting to reform the system of taxes and elite privileges.

From 1600 to 1640, the Crown began to sell royal offices and elite titles on a large scale. It sold monopoly rights to groups of wealthy merchants to trade with certain regions and to sell certain products. The king also sought to reform and raise taxes without Parliament's consent and interfered more and more in local county government—the traditional preserve of county gentry—in order to raise more revenue. Thus in 1640, when Charles's attempts to raise money in Scotland triggered a rebellion and he asked Parliament to levy taxes for a settlement with the Scots, Charles received not money but angry complaints against his abuses of England's constitution and traditions.

Why did the English Crown need to increase its revenues? In her study of the French, Russian, and Chinese Revolutions, Skocpol suggested that traditional governments often come under economic and military pressure from more economically advanced states abroad. This cause will not explain England's problem, however, for by 1640 England was already one of the most economically advanced states in Europe. In England the need for the Crown to increase its income came partly, as elsewhere, from the expense of waging war. Yet fiscal pressures came even more strongly from rising prices, largely a consequence of England's growing population.

In the fifteenth century, England's population was making a very slow recovery from the Black Death of the 1340s. Restoring the population levels of the early 1300s probably took nearly two hundred years. During this period of population stagnation, prices were extremely stable. From the 1380s to the early 1500s prices went almost unchanged, decade after decade, differing merely 5 percent by the first decade of the 1500s from their level in the last decade of the 1300s. During this period, the Crown amassed land and established its tax base; by 1510 Henry VII was able to tell Parliament that, except in case of war, the Crown revenues were sufficient for him "to live of his own," without need for taxes.

Yet the situation soon changed. England's population, which in 1520 was probably roughly the same as it was in 1320, suddenly began to increase. From 1520 to 1640, England's inhabitants increased from just over two million to well over five million. Increased demand, pushing on a slowly improving agricultural economy, drove up prices. Prices doubled and then doubled again. By the late 1630s prices had risen to six times their level of 1500–1510.

This sustained rise in prices drained royal finances, leading the Crown first to sell its lands, then to sell monopolies, offices, and honors and later to raise taxes ruthlessly and to assault the financial privileges of the elites. The main issues in the struggle between the king and gentry were thus the scope of the Crown's authority, royal taxes, and royal interference in the counties. On these issues, the vast majority of the gentry could agree to oppose the king.

Yet one of the striking aspects of the English Revolution is the manner in which the gentry, fairly unified against the king in 1640, suddenly fractured in to a host of national and local factions in 1642. Why were various county and national conflicts so much sharper and more intense than they had been in the days of Elizabeth or than they were in the later seventeenth and early eighteenth centuries? Certainly part of the reason is the extent of the political crisis posed by the Crown's bankruptcy, the Scots invasion, and uprisings in Ireland, in London, and throughout the countryside. But at least part of the answer also lies in the extraordinarily strong personal competitiveness and insecurity that afflicted the gentry in the early seventeenth century.

The rise in prices drained some gentry fortunes and created opportunities that produced others. Prudent investments by smaller gentry and many yeomen propelled them upwards in wealth and status. On the other hand, gentry and noble families who spent freely or neglected their lands and other investments sank deeply into debt and eventually lost their lands and social position to newcomers. The sixteenth and early seventeenth centuries were thus a period of massive shifts of individual fortunes with families entering and leaving the gentry and nobility at unprecedented rates. In many counties in 1640 over half of the leading gentry families were "newcomers" who had become established after 1500.

Nor were these economic effects the only consequences of rapid demographic growth. For rapid growth meant more families and more surviving children among the gentry, which increased even more rapidly than the population as a whole. From 1540 to 1646, the number of gentry families increased roughly from 5,000 to 15,000. Faced with a relatively limited system of land, civil and church offices, and royal patronage to sustain them, these greater numbers brought a sharp increase in the competitiveness and insecurity of elite society. The competitiveness showed in a flood of applicants to the universities and the Inns of Court who hoped to qualify for posts in the Church or State administration and in increased demands for royal patronage. Stone has gone so far as to assert that "the hostility of the majority of the Peers to Charles I in 1640 can be ascribed in large measure to the failure of the king to multiply jobs to keep pace with the increase of titles."[16] And the increased numbers of gentry and nobles intensified hostility on the part of the Royalists as well, for many of the king's supporters showed the same desperation:

> The situation [in 1642] seems to have been aggravated by the remarkable surplus of landless younger sons in the King's armies, with no estate to root them in the countryside, no career but the army open to them, and little to support their pretensions to gentility.[17]

Under conditions of increasing competitiveness and insecurity, the discipline and high deals of Puritanism increased their appeal to many of the gentry. But to others, insecurity and competition seemed to call for an increase in the order and hierarchy of the established Church of England. Thus religious conflicts further sharpened elite differences.

It appears that the recomposition of the elites, due to great rates of individual mobility occurring in the wake of massive changes in prices and the reproductive behavior of elites, had the effect on the elites *as a whole* of increasing insecurity and sharpening local rivalries and national divisions. Lacking a written constitution and an established bureaucracy, the English state depended on consensus among its elite for its stability. Yet the recomposition of the elites made such a consensus elusive in the face of the mounting political crisis of 1640–1642. Confronted with the pressing problems of royal bankruptcy, religious divisions, and popular disorders, the myriad divisions among the elite gave rise to adversary politics that paralyzed the government. Reluctantly, the English gentry found recourse to open conflict increasingly necessary to resolve both its conflict with the king and its own divisions and rivalries.

Still, we must explore the causes of popular unrest. For the popular uprisings in London and to a lesser degree in the countryside proved a catalyst in the conflicts with the king and among the gentry. In 1640 when the king called Parliament to ask for increased taxes, instead he received demands that he refrain from interfering with gentry privileges, gentry independence, and gentry local government. Yet when the lower and middle classes of England began rioting in London and the countryside, the gentry became divided. Some felt that popular uprisings, especially the urban revolt in London, offered an opportunity for people to frighten the king into concessions. Others felt that popular uprisings threatened gentry dominance so that it was now necessary to rally around the king as the symbol of traditional authority. Thus Parliament, united against the king in 1640, gradually separated into Parliamentarian and Royalist camps in 1641–1642.

The chief source of popular unrest was the vast increase in the portion of the population that depended on wages. In the countryside, rural laborers and artisans protested rising food prices and attacked grain merchants. In the capital, the flow of the landless into London depressed wages and provided recruits whose discontents with grain shortages and unemployment, the elites, in their conflict with the king, could exploit.

In examining whether population growth or the action of enclosing landlords was the main factor behind this growth in "combustible material" among the lower classes, we need to answer two questions: (1) What do studies of English villagers show regarding how they lost their lands? and (2) Could population growth alone have led to the precise changes in property-holding that occurred?

Village studies in Cambridgeshire by Spufford show unambiguously that, while middle-size property disappeared and dwarf holdings multiplied prior to 1640, actions by manor lords were *not* responsible: "Vulnerability to seigneurial action and legal factors did not underlie the change."[18] Rather, in each case, husbandmen had divided family plots among their progeny while holders of such diminished properties often sold out to other copyholders during times of economic difficulty.

Thirsk and Everitt have shown that in Suffolk, Bedfordshire, and Lincolnshire, husbandmen commonly divided property among surviving heirs, leading to shrunken holdings: "As the number of labourers increased, . . . small holdings were either divided up amongst children, and subdivided again till they shrank to mere gardens, or else bequeathed to the elder son alone, so that the younger children were left propertyless."[19] Thirsk cites Edward Lande, an octogenarian of Dent, who in 1634 declared:

Table 1   Patterns of Landholdings of English Laborers
c. 1540–1640

(a) Data: 447 holdings on 28 manors (percentage of holdings of each size)

PERIOD	COTTAGE	< 1 ACRE	1–1¾	2–2¾	3–3¾	4–5
Before 1560	11	31	28	7	11	11
1600–1610	35	36	13	6	5	5
After 1620	40	23	14	8	7	7

(b) Simulation: 100 families in 1535, population growth 20%/yr, partible inheritance (percentage of holdings of each size)

PERIOD	COTTAGE	< 1 ACRE	1–1¾	2–2¾	3–3¾	4–5
c. 1540	11.0	31.0	28.0	7.0	11.0	11.0
c. 1600	31.6	28.5	21.9	8.1	4.9	4.9
c. 1630	41.1	26.3	18.9	7.0	3.3	3.3

Source: Data in (a) from Alan Everitt, "Farm Laborers," in The Agrarian History of England and Wales, *ed. H. P. R. Finberg, 8 vols. (Cambridge: Cambridge University Press, 1967–), vol.4 (1967): 402.*

> If a customary tenant died . . . without having [a] will, then it descended to all his sons equally to be divided amongst them. . . . By reason of such division of tenements, the tenants are much increased in number more than they were, and the tenements become so small in quantity that many of them are not above three or four acres apiece.[20]

As to the likelihood that population growth alone could account for the size of the observed shift in landholding, let us look at the available data. Table 1(a) presents data compiled by Everitt on the shift in size of 447 holdings on 28 manors. Experts have sometimes cited the marked reduction in the size of holdings shown in this data as evidence that landlords were depriving tenants of their lands.

Yet simple subdivision by inheritance can account for the observed shifts as well. From 1540 to 1630, England's population increased by three-fourths. Assuming roughly thirty years per generation, finding out what effect this growth rate would have on landholdings is simple. To increase by three-fourths in three generations, the population must have a net reproduction rate of 1.2. This means that for each generation, 80 percent of the fathers have only one surviving son; 20 percent have two surviving sons. Let us make the simplest possible assumption: that for those 80 percent of fathers with one surviving son, the property is handed down intact, while for those fathers with two surviving sons, the property is divided equally between them. Table 1(b) presents the results of a simulation of the pattern of landholdings that would result from this growth rate and inheritance pattern.

As can be seen, this simplest possible demographic model provides a nearly exact fit. Given the result of such simple demographic simulations, and the results of local studies, it is likely that demographic changes were primarily responsible for the shifts in property seen in the century before the Revolution.

The reduction of holdings and the growth of landlessness, the marked rise in prices and unemployment, the fall of real wages, and the massive expansion of urban centers form a complex pattern we might call the "rapid population growth" syndrome. These factors sharply differentiate the period of rising conflict in the century before the Revolution from the succeeding, more stable century. In the century prior to 1640, while population almost doubled and prices rose several-fold, real wages fell by half, and London grew at an annual rate of 1.5 percent. By contrast, from 1640 to 1740, England's population grew by no more than 10 percent; grain prices leveled off and then declined; London's growth rate fell to .6 percent per annum; and real wages rose by more than a third.

Unlike the French or Russian peasants, English peasants lacked the autonomous village communities that could have sustained a successful revolt against landlords. By 1640 English peasant villages were generally loose settlements of small farmers, tenants, and laborers under the close supervision of local landlords. Local landlords' control of militias for law enforcement allowed them quickly to put down most threats to their authority, and in only a few counties did lower and middle class groups take over local government from landlords. For the most part, peasants and workers were conscripted into Royalist and Parliamentary armies, led on both sides by landlords, before they had a chance to organize for themselves. Only in London, which swelled enormously from perhaps 60,000 inhabitants in 1520 to 400,000 in 1650 with the flow of migrants from the overburdened countryside, did popular discontents give rise to a major revolt.

Still, the widely scattered riots of 1640–1641 played an important role in unsettling Parliament and splitting the gentry. And the urban revolt in London was crucial to Parliament's early assault on the king's authority. Of course, the small merchants and artisans who rebelled in London supported Parliament not through love of Parliament, but because of hatred of the king's monopolies and taxes as well as anger against rising prices and falling real wages. When Parliament itself began to levy similar taxes on the city to finance its war with the king, Londoners again rebelled, this time against Parliament, and only the action of the Parliamentary army restored order.

CONCLUSION

Let us review and compare the effects of emergent capitalism and population pressure on the various conflicts that contributed to the revolutionary crisis.

The Marxist view stresses enclosure as leading to conflict between landlords and peasants and between Crown and gentry. The Marxist view also explains conflict among the elites in terms of conflict between commercial (Parliamentarian) and noncommercial (Royalist) forces. Yet these views do not fit the details of the revolution well.

Not enclosure but population growth and rising prices led to the massive growth of London and to popular unrest. Not enclosure but conflict over taxation and Crown interference in local government led to conflict between Crown and gentry. Finally, we cannot simply identify Parliamentarians as capitalists and Royalists as feudal. Many royalist gentry had cooperated with the Crown in enclosure projects and royal monopolies of overseas trade. Many large merchants and commercial centers (such as Newcastle) supported the king. The division between Parliamentarians and Royalists depended much more on who had benefited from royal policies and cooperation with the Crown in the 1620s and 1630s and who had been left out, as well as on attitudes of individual members of the gentry toward popular uprisings and royal authority.

Rising population and consequent rising prices and widespread fiscal distress were hardly uniquely English. These pressures were felt in many places in seventeenth century Europe and generally increased conflict over taxation and state authority. What gave the English Revolution its particular character was the structure of English society at the time of these increased pressures—a Crown that faced an entrenched gentry elite able to resist increased taxes; a greatly expanded capital city flooded with small merchants, artisans, and workers oppressed by royal monopolies and tax increases; and a peasantry that lacked strong community organization and was closely supervised by local landlords. The result was a revolution dominated by landlord opposition to the king and urban revolt in London, with only scattered and unsuccessful uprisings in the countryside.

In sum, demographic pressures and structural weaknesses help to explain the origins of the English Revolution. This structural-demographic explanation appears more accurate than the Marxist view and more satisfying than a simple emphasis on the incompetence of Charles I. Moreover, paying attention to demographic pressures and structural weaknesses may help to explain the origins of other revolutions far removed from seventeenth century England.

REFERENCES

1. Elton (1974), p. 160.
2. Sharpe (1978), p. 42.
3. Hill (1980), p. 129.
4. Moore, Jr. (1966), pp. 9, 11–12, 14, 19.
5. Wallerstein (1974), pp. 25, 116; Wallerstein (1980b), p. 142.
6. Anderson (1974), p. 142.
7. Sharp (1980), p. 127.
8. Holderness (1976), p. 54.
9. Appleby (1975), p. 580.
10. Ibid., p. 580.
11. Walter and Wrightson (1976), p. 27.
12. Walter (1980), p. 74.
13. Cornwall (1977), p. 18.
14. Walter (1980), p. 73.
15. Howell (1979), p. 112.
16. Stone (1965), p. 743.
17. Everitt (1969), p. 49.
18. Spufford (1974), p. 85.
19. Everitt (1967), p. 399.
20. Thirsk (1961), p. 70.

The French Revolution: The Abolition of Feudalism

JOHN MARKOFF

Until the French Revolution of 1789, French society—like most European socie-ties—was a hierarchy of privilege, often loosely called "feudalism." The king was at the top, closely allied to two privileged groups, or "estates": the nobility and the clergy. Everyone else—lawyers, bankers, doctors, merchants, shop owners, craftsmen, laborers, and peasants—was simply considered to form the "Third Es-tate." There were many influential and wealthy commoners—these were gener-ally called the "bourgeoisie," because they were concentrated in the cities, or *bourgs*. Yet they remained, in terms of their status and legal standing, in the "Third Estate" with all the other commoners. Some of them purchased titles of nobility, or were given a grant of personal nobility for their services to the king, but they were often still regarded as "Third Estate," as for many purposes, only people whose nobility was inherited and had been in their family for three or more gener-ations counted as truly being in the nobility.

The French Revolution of 1789 began with a state financial crisis, which led the king to call together assemblies throughout France to recommend reforms to taxation. These assemblies were organized locally and by Estates so that each elec-toral district in France—encompassing rural villages, small and large towns—had assemblies of nobles, of clergy, and of the Third Estate. These assemblies were asked to prepare notebooks (in French, *cahiers*) detailing their grievances and recommen-dations for reform. The notes were then forwarded to Paris, where the national representatives of the Estates would convene as the Estates-General of the nation.

While the goal of the process was to improve the efficiency and justice of tax-ation, tax collection—like every other state and legal issue in the old regime—was bound up with the system of privileges for various groups. Every noble family, every province, and even many towns had their own set of distinctive tax privi-leges. Among the privileges of the nobles were precedence in selection for military and government posts and exemptions from taxation; among the privileges of many landowners (especially the church and landowning nobility) were *seigneurial* privileges over the peasants who lived or worked on their lands. These seigneurial privileges included the right to levy special fees and dues on peasants, to require them to labor for the lord, or to give the lord special monopolistic privileges over their goods and actions. When called to deliberate on tax reform, the various as-semblies, each in their own way, expanded their attention to question the entire range of privileges that defined the society of the old regime.

John Markoff has undertaken a detailed study of the *cahiers*. Focusing on the "legislators"—the leading members of the Third Estate who came to Paris to de-liberate on and enact reforms—and the peasants, who expressed their interests with direct action against landlords, Markoff shows how the French Revolution gradually developed into a total attack on all seigneurial privileges. Beginning as an effort at reform, the legislators' criticism of privilege induced peasants to attack and dismantle the operation of seigneurialism in the countryside. In their efforts to satisfy the peasantry, the legislators continually pushed further to end the legal structures that were bound up with privilege. Through this interaction of Paris and the countryside, the Revolution was swept forward to the abolition of feudalism.

THEORIES OF REVOLUTION

Revolutionary peasants and revolutionary legislators together ended the seigneurial regime. How was this antiseigneurial convergence achieved? In the historical literature, there are two principal grand narratives of Revolution within which this conjoining of forces has an important place, a Marxist story and a Tocquevillian one. In the Marxist account, changes in the material conditions of existence are held to bring about new patterns of class interests. These interests align people in new patterns of conflict as they come to have a sense of their commonalities of interest with some and their antagonistic interest in relation to others. The sense of identity that thereby develops is deepened to the extent that people organize themselves for the purposes of advancing the interests of their group against others.

In the Marxist analysis, the advance of the marketplace as an organizing principle for social relations provided one of the most important frameworks around which group interests, group allegiances, and group antagonisms formed in early modern Europe. Within this framework, an antifeudal alliance of a cramped bourgeoisie and a threatened peasantry was forged. In Albert Soboul's version, a wealthy and cultivated urban bourgeoisie came to occupy "the leading position in society, a position which was at variance with the official existence of privileged orders."[1] An enormously active and prosperous class of financiers, merchants, and manufacturers were poised to take advantage of economic change. Material transformation had a cultural counterpart: a critique of the existing order was elaborated on behalf of individual rights, property, equality before the law, rationality, progress, and freedom. The whole movement came to resent the multiple injuries of what was left of feudalism: its limitations on property rights and individual initiative, its deleterious effect on agricultural progress, its identification with the irrational past rather than the rationality of the future.

The peasantry were equally if differently hostile to seigneurialism. Although there were important differences of interest within individual peasant communities and important regional differences in the social structures that developed in the rural world, there was a broad unity in distress at the high levels of burden imposed by state, church, and lord, among which the claims of the lord were the most resented. In the eighteenth century lords, moreover, utilized the structures of seigneurialism to enhance their capacity to take advantage of the development of the market. Exactions were tightened to force peasants to sell out so that the lord's holdings could be rationalized and enlarged; communal rights of various sorts came under attack as lords aimed at increasing their incomes still further. As for the chief beneficiaries of the old order, the nobility, they were in the deepest disarray. Some embraced the new forms of economic activity being opened up and championed liberal reform; still others, however, reacted to change by more scrupulously collecting their traditional sources of income at peasant expense and by reasserting their traditional claims.

Prepared for this volume by John Markoff.

De Tocqueville, too, saw a coincidence of peasant and bourgeois interests against seigneurial rights, but he located the source of this alliance in the enlargement of state power and authority. The long process of central state development, de Tocqueville argued, eroded the basis on which others would accept the positions of nobles and lords in French society. To the extent that noble lords furnished protection from violence, maintained the roads, policed economic transactions, succored the poor, supported the true Church, and dispensed justice among the contentious, the privileges of the nobility and of the lords could be seen as so many deserved benefits. The lords' social role was substantial, they bore the costs of performing that role, and they were, perhaps, seen as indispensable. But as these functions passed into the hands of the central state, the entire justification for noble and seigneurial privilege evaporated.

Yet even as the nobles' public responsibilities were being whittled away, royal policy tended to leave their privileges intact in the hope of obtaining their assent to the changing institutions of France. Indeed, the more powerful and potentially dangerous nobles were often granted privileged access to government jobs and government subsidies.

As for the peasantry, erosion of the lord's role had turned a once-genuine protector into an exploiter. The increasingly effective bureaucratic state undermined traditional clientistic rural relationships. De Tocqueville wrote that for peasants in the Middle Ages, "the nobles enjoyed invidious privileges and rights that weighed heavily on the commoner, but in return for this they kept order, administered justice, saw to the execution of the laws, came to the rescue of the oppressed, and watched over the interests of all. The more these functions passed out of the hands of the nobility, the more uncalled for did their privileges appear— until at least their mere existence seems a meaningless anachronism."[2]

Both interpretive frameworks make sense of a peasant–bourgeois alliance against the lords. But neither grapples with the Revolution itself as a political process. Certainly the market and the state both expanded in significance and became increasingly weighty in village lives. Nonetheless, there are limitations to the explanatory power of an exclusive focus on long-term structures. Although the development of the state and the market may have decreased the tolerance of many for the lord's prerogatives, in themselves these structural changes did not bring either urban notables or peasants to the point of totally overthrowing the seigneurial regime. The intricate dance by which peasants came to make their chief target the seigneurial rights while legislators revamped their enactments had to be invented. It was in no way given at the outset.

THE PEASANT–BOURGEOIS ALLIANCE

We have examined the *cahiers* in order to identify the place of the seigneurial rights on the agendas of the country people, the urban notables, and the nobility. The three faced the Revolution differently. While all had in common considerable attention to the broad questions of taxation, the nobility were quite distinctive for their attention to the constitutional issues posed by the advance of the central state. They were sensitive to issues of civil liberties and the rule of law. The nobles also put forth the concept of a personal sphere on which the state is not to intrude: property.

The most distinctive aspects of the Third Estate's agenda were its concerns with privilege and with market hindrances. Where the nobility tended to focus on issues of liberty in the sense of freedom from an arbitrary state, the Third Estate tended to focus on freedom to participate in the market, unconstrained by state, communal, or seigneurial barriers. To eliminate the nobility's privileged, even monopolistic, access to high-level careers would mean that those with skills could trade those skills for income and responsibility in a sort of job market ("the career open to talent"). Rather than an image of a society composed of hierarchically related corporate groups with distinct rights and obligations, whose structure was given by God and tradition, and which was supervised by the state, the new society would be seen as composed of formally equal individuals who could invent and reinvent their relationships through freely consented contracts and to whom the state was responsible.

The peasants' agenda is far simpler to characterize. They were not particularly concerned with constitutional arrangements; they were focused on the details of the claims upon them by state, church, and lord. Nearly half of their grievances expressed in the village *cahiers* involve one or another burden.

The potential for an antiseigneurial alliance of peasants and legislators was there; its elements are evident in the *cahiers*. But only the potential: far more peasant attention in the spring of 1789 was given to matters of taxation. Moreover, the antiseigneurialism of the urban notables—the more well-off urban members of the Third Estate, the lawyers, physicians, and merchants—was far from identical to that of the peasantry; aspects of the notables' position were antithetical to the interests of significant rural elements. When we compare the reform strategy of different groups, we are struck by how frequently the legislative leaders of the Third Estate endorsed some sort of legal procedure, while the peasantry, often rejecting being swallowed up along the legal route, mounted thousands of insurrections to directly dismantle seigneurial rule in the countryside.

The peasants' actions and grievances are utterly inconsistent with any simple notion of a mindless countryside, in thrall to either an unthinking tradition or an unreflective radicalism. Peasant communities seem to have distinguished carefully among rights according to their possible value to the community as well as the feasibility of compromise, including a payment to the lords to compensate them for the loss of their rights. It seems that peasants engaged in careful and rational considerations of costs and rewards, privilege by privilege; that they had a sense of fairness as well as burden; that they had an abstract conception of a seigneurial system rather than limiting their thinking to their own particular lord. They appear to have had a certain acceptance—however resignedly that might have been—of state authority (as indicated by how rare in the *cahier* are demands to abolish the tax system altogether, compared to demands for reform). Plainly, the battle for the hearts and minds of the country people was still up for grabs at the onset of the Revolution.

While a basis for a peasant–bourgeois alliance against feudalism existed at the onset of revolution, the work of forging it was not yet accomplished. That required moving beyond the positions taken at the Revolution's onset to the ensuing dialogue of legislators and peasants.

Let me stress how small a portion of revolutionary events from the summer of 1789 to 1793 was constituted by anti-tax actions. It appears that paying taxes was less unpalatable in the revolutionary years than was paying seigneurial dues. I contend that the *cahiers* show a certain acceptance of the state in the countryside—and a contrasting intolerance for the further existence of seigneurial rights. The pattern of the peasants' insurrectionary actions is consistent with such a view.

Nonetheless, action against the lords, in anything like the concentration reached during the Revolution, was utterly without precedent. The central thrust of peasant uprisings in the seventeenth century was anti-taxation; in the relatively peaceful eighteenth century, subsistence issues were added as significant. In the summer of 1788 subsistence events were overwhelmingly dominant and antiseigneurial events were nearly non-existent. Attacks on the rights of the great lords began to rise in the late autumn of 1788. The great rural uprising of July 1789 was nearly one-third composed of antiseigneurial events. By the burst of insurrectionary action in the winter of 1789–1790, antiseigneurial events had become the dominant component of peak periods of rural mobilization and remained so through the spring of 1792. By the wave of late summer 1792, however, the antiseigneurial focus was beginning to fade: the proportion in September 1792, for example, was a little over one-third. Beyond this point, attacks on the rights of lords fell off rapidly: the late fall minipeak in peasant uprisings was dominated, as in the early phases of the Revolution, by subsistence events; the spring 1793 peak was overwhelmingly made up of counterrevolution—actions resisting novel revolutionary legislation regarding the Church and conscription. If any sort of peasant action can be said to have initially opened the way for later developments, then, it was the subsistence events which dominated from summer of 1788 through summer of 1789. But an anti-seigneurial movement grew strong from the summer of 1789 through the autumn of 1792. Thus, although antiseigneurial actions clearly dominated the first few years of the Revolution, they were the historical exception in France's history of peasant revolts.

How then did it come about that so many peasant insurrections at the beginning of the Revolution were directed, first and foremost, at the lords and their privileges? The presence of a specifically antiseigneurial thrust within the early revolution is not well explained by structural conditions. Peasants could have equally well revolted against the state and its taxes as against the lords and their seigneurial dues. Why didn't the French peasants remain focused on taxation and subsistence issues, the main concerns of most rebellious peasants in the seventeenth and eighteenth centuries?

I would argue that the critical factor precipitating the wave of antiseigneurial actions was the manner in which the actions of revolutionary peasants and revolutionary legislators opened possibilities for each other. As rural communities discovered the strengths of antiseigneurial sentiment in the upper Third Estate during the campaign to choose the leaders of the Estates-General, and within the subsequent National Assembly which met in Paris during the summer of 1789, the seigneurial regime stood revealed as highly vulnerable. In turn, when peasants focused their rebellious actions on seigneurial privilege—attacking manor houses and seizing and burning the books that stipulated the seigneurial dues and exactions that they were required to pay, defying the lords and ignoring their claims—the legislators in the National Assembly yielded to the message of peasant attacks. A great deal of what propelled the Revolution in the countryside was the interplay of peasant and legislator. Peasants and legislators altered their actions in response to the other. The peasants grew more bold in attacking the seigneurial regime as the legislators criticized it and proposed reforms; the legislators grew more radical in their criticism and more willing to wholly abolish the seigneurial system as the peasant uprisings increased. In the actions of legislators and peasants, we have a dialogue, not two monologues.

The legislators ultimately let the relatively united peasant communities push them much further than they had originally intended on seigneurial rights. Revolutionary legislators had, perhaps without intending it, encouraged revolt with their rhetorical attacks on privilege; peasants forced the legislators to live up to the simple promises of their own rhetoric.

In the course of ultimately yielding to the countryside, the revolutionaries disseminated one of their most profound conceptual constructions: the sense of "revolution" as a willed rupture of the fabric of history, of a total repudiation of a past on behalf of a better future, an image of the time of the lords as a social order totally overthrown.

THE COURSE OF THE REVOLUTION

In fact, by 1793, the battle of peasants against lords was largely over. Yet the Revolution continued as a battle of the new revolutionary state to defend itself and to extend its ideals throughout Europe. Foreign powers, many of whose own kings feared for their power, and whose nobility often continued to depend on seigneurial rights, were alarmed that the Revolution might spread. They thus took up arms against the new regime. France's need for loyal armies then led French legislators to aim at satisfying what they thought were the peasantry's most severe grievances, and thus to go further than they had initially intended in abolishing the seigneurial regime, and in championing the ideals of liberty and equality for all mankind.

From 1792 onwards, war with the traditional powers of Europe—Prussia, Austria-Hungary, Holland, England, and Spain—led to dramatic change. In 1793, the king and queen, found to have committed treason by conspiring with the revolutionaries' foreign enemies, were executed. Under the new revolutionary leaders Maximilien Robespierre and Georges Danton, a reign of terror followed attacking not only nobles, but anyone suspected of being an enemy to the revolutionary regime. Although in 1789, after the fall of the royal stronghold of the Bastille in Paris, the legislators had adopted a "Declaration of the Rights of Man and Citizen," which proclaimed that "Men are born free and equal in their rights. . . . These rights are liberty, property, security, and resistance to oppression," such rights were not readily extended to those proclaimed as "enemies of the people." Yet the attacks reached an intolerable pitch, and Robespierre and Danton themselves were led to the guillotine in 1794.

In the meantime, Church lands were seized and sold to pay for the military effort. And an opportunity arose for a talented junior officer to rise through the ranks, and eventually become the leader of revolutionary France and her armies: Napoleon Bonaparte. Napoleon at first managed one striking victory after another, until all of Europe excepting only Britain and Russia were beyond French control. However, in 1812, Napoleon invaded Russia, where the long winter and vast distances proved his downfall. Although he made an attempt to reclaim control of France in 1815, Napoleon was defeated by the forces of England and Prussia at the battle of Waterloo, effectively ending the French Revolution.

Yet France would never be the same. Although after Waterloo the Bourbon monarchy was returned to power, popular and elite pressures for greater equality and democracy continued to burst forth. A series of lesser revolutions, centered in Paris, continued to transform France throughout the nineteenth century. In 1830, France became a constitutional monarchy. In 1848, it again became a republic, and in 1851, another Napoleon—Bonaparte's nephew, Napoleon III—again became Emperor of France. Finally in 1871, following another war with Prussia, France finally became a stable and democratic republic.

Although it thus took almost a century for the political aims of the Revolution to be achieved, in one respect it gained dramatic success very quickly. That was the abolition of feudalism, which was basically completed in the years from 1789 to 1793. It was this sudden and complete overthrow of a system of rights and privileges that created the enduring image of the French Revolution, an image that has continued to permeate the past and the present in the social sciences.

REFERENCES

1.   Soboul (1975), p. 14.
2.   de Tocqueville (1955), pp. 32–41.

The American Revolution: The Radicalism of Revolution
GORDON S. WOOD

In 1776 the British subjects in the American colonies launched a revolution against British rule. Spurred by discontent over taxes thought to be unfairly imposed, and over British governors seen as obstacles to the colonists' right to frame their own destiny, the colonies chose to defy Britain and then fight for their independence. This conflict is usually seen mainly as a political struggle over whether the colonists would have the right to rule themselves. However, Wood shows that even greater principles were at stake, principles regarding the nature of the social order and citizenship. Wood demonstrates that the American Revolution was indeed, in its essential character, one of the great revolutions in seeking not only political renewal but also wide-ranging social change.

We Americans like to think of our revolution as not being radical; indeed, most of the time we consider it downright conservative. It certainly does not appear to resemble the revolutions of other nations in which people were killed, property was destroyed, and everything was turned upside down. The American revolutionary leaders do not fit our conventional image of revolutionaries—angry, passionate, reckless, maybe even bloodthirsty for the sake of a cause. We can think of Robespierre, Lenin, and Mao Zedong as revolutionaries, but not George Washington, Thomas Jefferson, and John Adams. They seem too stuffy, too solemn, too cautious, too much the gentlemen. We cannot quite conceive of revolutionaries in powdered hair and knee breeches. The American revolutionaries seem to belong in drawing rooms or legislative halls, not in cellars or in the streets. They made speeches, not bombs; they wrote learned pamphlets, not manifestos. They were not abstract theorists and they were not social levelers. They did not kill one another; they did not devour themselves. There was no reign of terror in the American Revolution and no resultant dictator—no Cromwell, no Bonaparte. The American Revolution does not seem to have the same kinds of causes—the social wrongs, the class conflict, the impoverishment, the grossly inequitable distributions of wealth—that presumably lie behind other revolutions. There were no peasant uprisings, no jacqueries, no burning of châteaux, no storming of prisons.

Of course, there have been many historians who have sought, as Hannah Arendt put it, "to interpret the American Revolution in the light of the French Revolution," and to look for the same kinds of internal violence, class conflict, and social deprivation that presumably lay behind the French Revolution and other modern revolutions.[1]

But the social conditions that generically are supposed to lie behind all revolutions—poverty and economic deprivation—were not present in colonial America. There should no longer be any doubt about it: the white American colonists were not an oppressed people; they had no crushing imperial chains to throw off. In fact, the colonists knew they were freer, more equal, more prosperous, and less burdened with cumbersome feudal and monarchical restraints than any other part of humankind in the eighteenth century. Such a situation, however, does not mean that colonial society was not susceptible to revolution.

Precisely because the impulses to revolution in eighteenth-century America bear little or no resemblance to the impulses that presumably account for modern social protests and revolutions, we have tended to think of the American Revolution as having no social character, as having virtually nothing to do with the society, as having no social causes and no social consequences. It has therefore often been considered to be essentially an intellectual event, a constitutional defense of American rights against British encroachments ("no taxation without representation"), undertaken not to change the existing structure of society but to preserve it. For some historians the Revolution seems to be little more than a colonial rebellion or a war for independence. Even when we have recognized the radicalism of the Revolution, we admit only a political, not a social radicalism. The revolutionary leaders, it is said, were peculiar "eighteenth-century radicals concerned, like the eighteenth-century British radicals, not with the need to recast the social order nor with the problems of the economic inequality and the injustices of stratified societies but with the need to purify a corrupt constitution and fight off the apparent growth of royal prerogative power."[2] Consequently, we have generally described the Revolution as an unusually conservative affair, concerned almost exclusively with politics and constitutional rights, and, in comparison with the social radicalism of the other great revolutions of history, hardly a revolution at all.

If we measure the radicalism of revolutions by the degree of social misery or economic deprivation suffered, or by the number of people killed or manor houses burned, then this conventional emphasis on the conservatism of the American Revolution becomes true enough. But if we measure the radicalism by the amount of social change that actually took place—by transformations in the relationships that bound people to each other—then the American Revolution was not conservative at all; on the contrary, it was as radical and as revolutionary as any in history. Of course, the American Revolution was very different from other revolutions. But it was no less radical and no less social for being different. In fact, it was one of the greatest revolutions the world has known, a momentous upheaval that not only fundamentally altered the character of American society but decisively affected the course of subsequent history.

It was as radical and social as any revolution in history, but it was radical and social in a very special eighteenth-century sense. No doubt many of the concerns and much of the language of that premodern, pre-Marxian eighteenth century were almost entirely political. That was because most people in that very different distant world could not as yet conceive of society apart from government. The social distinctions and economic deprivations that we today think of as the consequence of class divisions, business exploitation, or various isms—capitalism, racism, etc.—were in the eighteenth century usually thought to be caused by the abuses of government. Social honors, social distinctions, perquisites of office, business contracts, privileges and monopolies, even excessive property and wealth of various sorts—all, social evils and social deprivations—in fact seemed to flow from connections to government, in the end from connections to monarchical authority. So that when Anglo-American radicals talked in what seems to be only political terms of purifying a corrupt constitution, eliminating courtiers, fighting off crown power, and, most important, becoming republicans—they nevertheless had a decidedly social message. In our eyes the American revolutionaries appear to be absorbed in changing only their governments, not their society. But in destroying monarchy and establishing republics they were changing their society as well as their governments, and they knew it. Only they did not know—they could scarcely have imagined—how much of their society they would change.

To appreciate the extent of change that took place in the Revolution, we have to re-create something of the old colonial society that was subsequently transformed. In important respects this premodern society still bore traces of the medieval world of personal fealties and loyalties out of which it arose. To be sure, new ideas, new values, were emerging in the English-speaking world, but the past was tenacious. Like all Englishmen, the colonists continued to embrace deeply rooted assumptions about the order and stability needed in a monarchical society.

Living in a monarchical society meant, first of all, being subjects of the king. This was no simple political status, but had all sorts of social, cultural, and even psychological implications. Monarchy presumed a long train of dependence, a gradation of degrees of freedom and servility that linked everyone from the king at the top down to the bonded laborers and black slaves at the bottom. The inequalities of such a hierarchy were acceptable to people because they were offset by the great emotional satisfactions of living in a society in which everyone, even the lowliest servant, counted for something. In such a society it was inconceivable, unnatural, for inequality not to exist. The hierarchy of a monarchical society was part of the natural order of things.

By the time the Revolution had run its course in the early nineteenth century, American society had been radically and thoroughly transformed. One class did not overthrow another; the poor did not supplant the rich. But social relationships—the way people were connected one to another—were changed, and decisively so. By the early years of the nineteenth century the Revolution had created a society fundamentally different from the colonial society of the eighteenth century. It was in fact a new society unlike any that had ever existed anywhere in the world.

The Revolution did more than legally create the United States; it transformed American society. In place of a society of subjects, where natural inequality kept ordinary people subordinate to a privileged "aristocracy" tied to the king, the Revolution created a society of equal citizens (even if initially only open to free adult men). Instead of kings and royal governors and courtiers, it became "We the people," as the new Constitution would specify, who defined their social and political order by their voluntary choices and relationships to each other.

Because the story of America has turned out the way it has, because the United States in the twentieth century has become the great power that it is, it is difficult, if not impossible, to appreciate and recover fully the insignificant and puny origins of the country. In 1760 America was only a collection of disparate colonies huddled along a narrow strip of the Atlantic coast—economically underdeveloped outposts existing on the very edges of the civilized world. The less than two million monarchical subjects who lived in these colonies still took for granted that society was and ought to be a hierarchy of ranks and degrees of dependency and that most people were bound together by personal ties of one sort or another. Yet scarcely fifty years later these insignificant borderland provinces had become a giant, almost continent-wide republic of nearly ten million egalitarian-minded, bustling citizens who not only had thrust themselves into the vanguard of history but had fundamentally altered their society and their social relationships. Far from remaining monarchical, hierarchy-ridden subjects on the margin of civilization, Americans had become, almost overnight, the most liberal, the most democratic, the most commercially minded, and the most modern people in the world.

And this astonishing transformation took place without industrialization, without urbanization, without railroads, without the aid of any of the great forces we usually invoke to explain "modernization." It was the Revolution that was crucial to this transformation. It was the Revolution, more than any other single event, that made America into the most liberal, democratic, and modern nation in the world.

Of course, some nations of Western Europe likewise experienced great social transformations and "democratic revolutions" in these same years. The American Revolution was not unique; it was only different. Because of this shared Western-wide experience in democratization, it has been argued by more than one historian that the broader social transformation that carried Americans from one century and one kind of society to another was "inevitable" and "would have been completed with or without the American Revolution." Therefore, this broader social revolution should not be confused with the American Revolution. America, it is said, would have emerged into the modern world as a liberal, democratic, and capitalistic society even without the Revolution. One could, of course, say the same thing about the relationship between the French Revolution and the emergence of France in the nineteenth century as a liberal, democratic, and capitalistic society; and indeed, much of the current revisionist historical writing on the French Revolution is based on just such a distinction. But in America, no more than in France, that was not the way it happened: the American Revolution and the social transformation of America between 1760 and the early years of the nineteenth century were inextricably bound together. Perhaps the social transformation would have happened "in any case," but we will never know. It was in fact linked to the Revolution; they occurred together. The American Revolution was integral to the changes occurring in American society, politics, and culture at the end of the eighteenth century.

These changes were radical, and they were extensive. To focus, as we are today apt to do, on what the Revolution did not accomplish—highlighting and lamenting its failure to abolish slavery and change fundamentally the lot of women—is to miss the great significance of what it did accomplish; indeed, the Revolution made possible the anti-slavery and women's rights movements of the nineteenth century and in fact all our current egalitarian thinking. The Revolution not only radically changed the personal and social relationships of people, including the position of women, but also destroyed aristocracy as it had been understood in the Western world for at least two millennia. The Revolution brought respectability and even dominance to ordinary people long held in contempt and gave dignity to their menial labor in a manner unprecedented in history and to a degree not equaled elsewhere in the world. The Revolution did not just eliminate monarchy and create republics; it actually reconstituted what Americans meant by public or state power and brought about an entirely new kind of popular politics and a new kind of democratic officeholder. The Revolution not only changed the culture of Americans—making over their art, architecture, and iconography—but even altered their understanding of history, knowledge, and truth. Most important, it made the interests and prosperity of ordinary people—their pursuits of happiness—the goal of society and government. The Revolution did not merely create a political and legal environment conducive to economic expansion; it also released powerful popular entrepreneurial and commercial energies that few realized existed and transformed the economic landscape of the country. In short, the Revolution was the most radical and most far-reaching event in American history.

REFERENCES

1.   Arendt (1963), p. 49.
2.   Bailyn (1967), p. 283.

CHAPTER 6

Marxist Revolutions

In the seventeenth and eighteenth centuries, revolutions were concerned mainly with political liberties. Political liberties gave the landed, professional, and business elites a role in government, made commoners into citizens, and protected everyone from the abuse of power by kings and emperors. In the nineteenth and twentieth centuries, the rise of large factories and of an industrial labor force raised the issue of the protection of workers from the abuses of capitalists who owned the factories where they worked. Karl Marx and Frederick Engels (see Chapter 1) preached revolution as the way to liberate workers from such abuses. They predicted that advanced capitalist states would be overthrown by communist, worker-led revolutions.

Yet, in one of the great ironies of history, it was not the most advanced capitalist countries but relatively backward ones that responded to the Marxist call for revolution. In Russia, China, and Cuba, where most people remained peasants and capitalists were relatively weak, intellectual leaders such as Lenin, Mao, and Castro reshaped the Marxist vision to appeal to both industrial workers and peasants who were seeking freedom from capitalist or landlord control. Lenin, Mao, and Castro all created revolutionary parties to spearhead their political movements, and when the crumbling of the old regimes allowed them to seize power, they remolded the state and society to eliminate private capitalists *and* private landowners, and placed their own communist parties in total control of society.

The Russian Revolution of 1917: Autocracy and Modernization
TIM McDANIEL

Huntington pointed out that modernization creates strains on traditional regimes that can lead to revolution. Tilly replied that modernization leads to revolution only if it results in weakened states and the rise of new challengers who mobilize against the regime. McDaniel applies these insights to the Russian Revolution of 1917, showing how efforts to modernize Russia's autocratic regime led to revolution. Tsar Nicholas II's ministers attempted to reform Russian society, creating a new Parliament (the Duma), reorganizing peasant communities, and building an industrial work force. Yet making these changes reduced the state's authority and produced new challengers. In a few years, the Tsar faced uprisings from the Duma, the peasantry, and industrial workers. These uprisings overwhelmed the old autocratic regime and provided an opportunity for radical intellectuals—the Bolsheviks, led by Vladimir Lenin—to seize power and embark on building the world's first communist society.

THE AUTOCRACY OF NICHOLAS II

Nicholas II was the thirteenth Romanov monarch, the inheritor of a long tradition of autocratic rule that had deep roots in Russian society. The autocracy was not simply the bulwark of order, but the embodiment of the people's political and spiritual unity. Nicholas believed that he alone was responsible for the destiny of Russia and that he would answer for this trust before the Almighty.

What were the key institutions through which Nicholas II sought to rule Russia as an autocrat? The most important organs of government were the ministries, especially the Ministry of Finance and the Ministry of the Interior. These were enormous bureaucratic agencies, with professional staffs, formal hierarchies, and immense resources and responsibilities. Yet their effectiveness was undercut by the autocratic system of rule. The tsars tended to put their trust in men, not in institutions. They thus placed a great deal of weight on the high officials who served purely at the tsar's discretion. In the last decades of Nicholas II's reign, ministerial turnover was astoundingly rapid, in some years taking on comic-opera proportions. It became difficult to find competent people who would serve; nor was competence always Nicholas's main criterion of selection.

The tsarist autocracy also depended on the police and army; the latter, by the 1897 census, had over 1 million men, most of them peasant conscripts. The top officers were naturally selected by the tsar himself. Yet it was inevitable that the tsar's command could not be so authoritative in a relatively modern army of so vast a size. In addition, the policy of using army troops to quell civil disturbances, including strikes and peasant rebellions, called into question the loyalty of the troops, who often sympathized with the rebels. It also violated the sense of professional competence and dignity of many officers. For this reason, the army was not necessarily a trustworthy protector of the old regime; indeed during the 1905–1906 revolution, when Russia swarmed with strikes and peasant uprisings, many soldiers mutinied when it seemed that the regime might collapse.

Of broader significance were the limitations to autocratic power imposed by the creation of the new parliament, the Duma, in 1906. The Duma was a weak and not very democratic legislature. Most of the deputies were chosen through indirect elections, propertied groups were favored disproportionately, and the weight of the urban vote was grossly diminished. Women were denied the vote. The Duma's measures had to be approved by an upper chamber, the State Council, dominated by the tsar, and the tsar retained an absolute veto on all actions. The tsar could also issue emergency decrees when the Duma was not in session (it was required to meet only two months a year), and all ministers remained appointed by and responsible to the tsar alone.

Yet the tsar never reconciled himself to any diminution of his authority. Although proponents of the Duma hoped that it would lead to a constitutional monarchy, Nicholas opposed it at every turn, dissolving the first two Dumas and demanding election changes to produce

---

From Autocracy, Modernization, and Revolution in Russia and Iran *by Tim McDaniel. Copyright © 1991 by Princeton University Press.*

a more pliant assembly. The Third Duma was more conservative, but hopelessly divided. Thus, despite some trappings of constitutionalism, the Russian regime remained an autocracy as it pursued the rapid modernization of the country, with consequences fatal for itself.

RUSSIAN INDUSTRIALIZATION AND AGRARIAN REFORM

The state's primary motivation for economic change in Russia was to enhance national strength in order to be able to compete with the West. Sergei Witte, Nicholas II's minister of finance, accepted the idea that the strength of a great power in the modern world depends on industrialization. He became convinced of the need for an active state role in promoting modern industry, and state sponsorship of industrialization became the central goal of government policy.

Heavy taxation of the peasants helped to provide the necessary funds for industrialization; but they were not sufficient. The government also protected, subsidized, and rewarded private entrepreneurs, and encouraged foreign capital and foreign entrepreneurship.

The industrialization of the period 1890–1914 achieved considerable success. Although Russia's industry was highly concentrated in just a few places—the capital cities of Moscow and St. Petersburg, and the Urals mining region—and strongly emphasized heavy industry, in terms of total output, by 1914 Russia was a great industrial power. Nonetheless, Russia was already a large and populous country, and in terms of industrial growth *per capita* it ranked below Italy and Spain, and was even further behind the more developed western European countries such as England and Germany.

The concentration of industries in the cities spurred tumultuous urban growth. St. Petersburg added over a million inhabitants between 1890 and 1914; Moscow at the turn of the century was one of the world's ten largest cities, and the fastest growing among them. Factory workers came to be a significant social and political presence in the cities. In St. Petersburg, for example, the number of factory workers increased from 35,000 in 1867 to 200,000 by 1913.

The urban middle class also underwent a notable expansion. Industrial growth increased the demand for white-collar workers such as clerks and accountants, and brought opportunities for physicians, lawyers, and journalists. The state also sponsored a vast expansion of primary education, raising spending twenty times over, and greatly increasing the number of teachers and universities to train them. Literacy, though still low by European standards, increased from perhaps 20 percent to 40 percent of the population.

Some of these changes were the direct result of government policies, but others, such as the development of new political identities among emerging social groups, were neither intended nor advantageous for the regime. How would these new groups fit into the old patterns of Russian social and political life?

Outside of the cities, Russia also sought to modernize its enormous rural spaces. Russia's peasantry had gained its freedom from serfdom only in 1861, as a result of Tsar Alexander II's emancipation. The emancipation had legalized the peasant communal village (the "commune") as the dominant institution of rural Russia, and had tied the individual peasant to it in a multitude of ways. Communes, not individual families, owned the majority of peasant-held lands; indeed they controlled roughly half the farmland of European Russia. Peasants paid taxes collectively, through an allotment of tax responsibilities among members of the commune, and they could not leave the commune without permission from the village authorities. Land within the commune was periodically redistributed to its members according to family size and labor capacity. In general, there was little incentive for families to make agricultural improvements, for the land belonged to the commune regardless.

Certainly the most significant experiment in social engineering for the sake of modernization during Nicholas II's reign was the agrarian reform sponsored by Prime Minister Peter Stolypin beginning in 1906. The reforms sought to turn communal land into individual private property and to weaken the hold of the commune over its members. However, many peasants petitioned for rearrangements of communal patterns rather than outright individual ownership, and the government was willing to accommodate them. The reform thus proved far less radical in practice than in theory. This tendency toward reform, not abolition, of communal patterns may have strengthened internal village unity and cohesiveness in many cases, as the peasants worked together to shape their own land-holdings.

Progress toward privatization did occur—it is estimated that by 1916 somewhat less than half of the peasant households in European Russia still belonged to communes. In the short run, however, the economic achievements of the reform were limited and the vast majority of the rural population remained land poor, partly because of rapid demographic growth. Indeed, Russia's population was growing so rapidly in the nineteenth and early twentieth century that major investments and gains in productivity, not merely redistribution of land, were necessary to prevent land hunger and poverty.

In both its economic and social aspects, the tsarist model of modernization exhibited deep inner tensions. The autocracy decided to wager on the capitalist entrepreneur, the factory worker, and the independent peasant. These new social groups were supposed to be compatible with the maintenance of the autocratic political system, for these new social groups would define themselves not politically or ideologically, but only in terms of their own economic self-interest. They would be politically quiescent, and trust in the state. Yet these new groups, and their interests, were not as compatible with the autocracy as the tsar and his ministers had hoped.

DILEMMAS OF MODERNIZATION

While Russia was moving toward becoming a modern, capitalist society, Nicholas II was moving in the opposite direction, returning to old Muscovite symbols of patriarchal authority, and becoming ever-more distant from society. The events surrounding the massacre of 9 January 1905, remembered in history as Bloody Sunday, testify to the hollowness of the tsar's patriarchal pose, and to the confusion it brought to workers. The workers (from fifty to sixty thousand strong) who marched to the Winter Palace to deliver a petition to the tsar regarding working conditions surely regarded themselves as loyal subjects presenting legitimate grievances to their protector. However, their "little father" did not even bother to be present at the palace, much less receive the workers either in person or through a high official.

If the workers had been acknowledged, even if nothing had been granted, it is almost certain that bloodshed could have been avoided. As it was, the workers were stunned to be met with gunfire, resulting in numerous deaths and serious injuries. Two days later, when a meeting between Nicholas and a delegation of workers took place, the tsar blamed the violence on traitors to the country, but told the workers that he believed in "their unflagging devotion to me, and therefore I forgive them." This, for many, was the demise of the image of the tsar as the patriarch of his people.

The tsar's reaction suggests a more general contradiction in the autocratic pattern of development: the regime staked the success of its modernization program on private initiative, but by its authoritarian nature it stifled it. In the case of some groups, the regime smothered their initiative quite consciously out of fear of overt opposition. For example, the tsar had no intention of permitting an independent trade union movement even if its suppression entailed worker disaffection both in the factory and in society at large.

The middle classes were also held down. The tsarist regime wanted to incorporate industrialists into the policy process but not as an organized interest with guaranteed rights. They were permitted to offer advice, but the tsar was not interested in sharing his authority.

The results were a growing tension, indeed even a "surreal" quality to Russian life. The tsar offered constitutional reforms, but refused to share or limit his authority. Nicholas claimed to be the protector of workers and peasants, but in practice showed no interest in them except to suppress their voices and their actions. The professional middle classes and bureaucratic elites who might have offered help and shared in preserving the social order while adapting to industrialization were ignored. This growing breach between announced policies and outcomes, between ideology and accomplishments, between appearances and reality, polarized society. The coming revolution would therefore be radical in its attempts to resolve these tensions.

REVOLUTION IN THE CITIES

Many specialists have identified the countryside as the decisive locus of revolutionary action. Skocpol and Trimberger [see Chapter 3] have put the case most baldly: the success of social revolutions from below has been determined by "the class struggles of peasants against dominant landed classes and . . . regimes." Yet generalizations of this scope—applied to all modern social revolutions—have little hope of hitting the mark. In the broad sweep of global change, the decisive revolutionary actors will vary with the nature of the old regimes and with variations in the process of modernization. In Russia, where industrialization was focused in, and transformative of the cities, urban centers were the critical locus of revolutionary mobilization. The momentous events of 1917, from the February revolution to the April and July crises and on to the October seizure of power by Lenin, all took place in the cities. The Bolshevik party and its major social base, the workers, were both overwhelmingly urban.

The key to urban politics in Nicholas II's Russia is the unique combination of political autocracy and rapid capitalist development. The autocratic regime resolved to sponsor the capitalist industrialization of the country, privileging private domestic and foreign entrepreneurs, and oppressing worker organizations. Consequently, as would become evident in 1917, workers increasingly identified the political oppression of the tsarist state with the class oppression of the industrialists.

Marxism spread widely among Russian workers, in part because they were accustomed to the idea that state authority should control and regulate industry. However, they wanted a state that would do so for their benefit, not for that of private and foreign entrepreneurs. Since the tsarist state repressed strikes and trade unions, and intervened between workers and capitalists, workers developed no means for bargaining, representation, and negotiation. Marxism taught them that workers were at the forefront of social progress and that to fulfill this responsibility the working class must fight for political rights in an organized way. For workers, the alternatives were clear: either a worker or a tsarist state.

Matters came to a head in the wake of World War I. From 1914 through 1916, the tsar's armies suffered disastrous defeats. Discouraged and discredited, in February 1917 the tsar abdicated to a regent, who was quickly overthrown by a liberal coalition of middle-class professionals, opposition politicians from the Duma, and reformist bureaucrats. These reformers established a Provisional Government, and for a few months, workers and peasants were willing to suspend judgement. Yet the overthrow of the tsar set in motion revolutionary processes that eventually culminated in the victory of the Bolsheviks in October 1917.

The details of the Bolshevik assumption of power are enormously complicated; but beneath all the instability of the months from February to October, an underlying social logic gives coherence to the events. Throughout 1917, confronted with deteriorating economic conditions and the continuation of the war, the urban working class increasingly came to regard class conflict as irreconcilable. The workers therefore rejected compromise and opposed any government that sought to reconcile the interests of workers and industrialists. By October, in their overwhelming majority they were willing to support the only party, the Bolsheviks, that advocated a workers' government to rule in their interests. Following the leadership of Trotsky and Lenin, the workers councils, or soviets, overthrew the Provisional Government and began their march to state socialism.

REVOLUTION IN THE COUNTRYSIDE

If 1917 was partly the outcome of the failure of the Russian government and industrialists to create an industrial order recognizing and imparting rights to a new stratum of industrial workers, it also stemmed from a long-term crisis in rural Russia. This crisis was expressed in the simmering violence between an increasingly threatened gentry and a peasantry unwilling to abide the prevailing distribution of land and power. The attempts of the autocratic regime to shape property relations and rural institutions did little either to shore up the old Russia, as was sometimes its goal, or to hasten the emergence of a dynamic and productive rural society. Peasant discontent with the remnants of the old regime was a constant in the last decades of imperial Russia; they rebelled whenever circumstances seemed propitious.

Despite attempted reforms, the Russian countryside remained poor and backwards. Peasant cultivation was highly inefficient, frequently based on the medieval-style three-field system of tillage instead of modern crop rotations. Peasants lacked access to credit, and hence to sufficient fertilizer or tools to increase productivity. Especially serious was the rapid population growth rate, which was largely responsible for a 45 percent reduction in the size of holdings per peasant household from the 1860s to 1900. In Siberia and other frontier areas, where population density was lower, there were areas of relative peasant prosperity. But in the core European provinces of the Russian empire, many peasants were desperately poor; the villages were overpopulated; and the countryside was afflicted with hunger, and at times famine, as well as by ignorance.

The rural nobility, who had once anchored the Russian countryside, were almost as hard-hit as the peasantry; no serious scholarly work disputes the overall pattern of continuing economic decline of the gentry under Nicholas II. Many had fled their estates after the peasant revolts in the unsuccessful Revolution of 1905. Other landlords preferred to rent their land to the peasants rather than run their estates themselves. In 1905–1906, during the tsar's losing war with Japan, peasants turned on local landowners, seizing noble lands and sometimes burning and looting their estates. Only brutal repression by the army restored order, leaving fear and resentment in its wake. The tsar's ministers pondered whether it might be wise to expropriate the landholdings of rural nobles, and turn them over to the peasantry to secure order in the countryside. But the regime was unwilling to turn against its traditional rural social base. Nonetheless, the peasants became convinced that the tsar intended to transfer the land to them.

The weakening of the rural nobility, combined with increasing intrusion by the autocracy into running rural affairs, created an absolute illegitimacy of the landlords in the eyes of the peasantry. The peasants wanted the gentry's land and the right to run their own affairs without outside influence. Peasants generally relied on the commune to run their own affairs, and it was in those areas where communal organization was most widespread that peasants showed the highest degrees of militancy.

A rural elite without legitimacy; a polarized rural society composed of mutually antagonistic groups; and a state seeking reform but unable to bring about far-reaching change: all these factors, in the context of a backward agriculture and immense peasant poverty, generated a potential for social explosion whenever the government was weakened. Although the challenges to the tsarist regime first emerged in the cities, they inevitably ignited the countryside as well.

THE OCTOBER REVOLUTION

The authority of the Provisional Government, which had taken power in February 1917 following crushing military defeats, widespread strikes, and the abdication of the tsar, was tenuous from the beginning. The Provisional Government, composed largely of members of the former liberal opposition, had no significant social base, and their fundamental outlook on the revolution was inconsistent with that of the workers and peasants, who had their own perspectives and aspirations based on their experiences under the tsarist regime. In particular, as we have seen, neither peasants nor workers accepted the legitimacy or property rights of the upper classes, and they quickly lost patience with these liberal reformers bent on compromise. More than any other party, the Bolsheviks were willing to accommodate their policies to the impatience of the masses, born of both long-term grievances and circumstantial deprivations. By October Lenin's party could act with the confidence that it had gained the overwhelming support of the workers and that its land program—expropriating and distributing noble lands—would be enthusiastically received by the peasantry.

The Bolsheviks also possessed an ideology, that of scientific Marxism, that fit extremely well with the cultural and political circumstances of late Imperial Russia. This provided a totalistic mobilizational ideology that, although imported from western Europe, was easily adapted to the needs of the Bolsheviks and their revolution.

Marxism claimed to possess a store of knowledge largely unknown to ordinary men and women yet vital to the comprehension and ordering of human affairs. In the hands of Lenin, this was made the basis for a vanguard party, drawing on the old Russian tradition of a privileged intelligentsia, that would act on this knowledge to lead workers and peasants into a better world. Marxism also opposed the truth of its view to the falsity of all other doctrines. This polarized view of a righteous elite with an exclusive claim to truth and virtue fighting against an evil enemy also was familiar to Russian society from the similarly exclusive claims that had traditionally been made on behalf of the tsar and the Russian orthodox church.

Marxism had two other features that molded Bolshevik policies, and contributed to their appeal: a transhistorical mission focused on revolution as the means to create a radical break in human history, and a claim to universality. The transhistorical nature of the mission devalued all current political, social, and economic institutions. Everything could be destroyed to clear the path to the future. The universality of Marxist socialism meant not only that its vision of the future applied to all countries; it was also universal in the sense that it ultimately touched on all aspects of individual and social life. Under socialism individual morality, work, the family, culture, and politics will all be transformed. Together, the transhistorical and universal qualities of Marxism have contributed to a characteristic feature of Marxist revolutions: a willingness to ruthlessly destroy all traditional and historical features of a society in order to thoroughly refashion the life of every person and every institution in society.

CONCLUSION

Throughout this essay, I have argued that an autocratic regime's attempt to give birth to urban industrial society involves the state and the society in a web of intractable contradictions. These contradictions, in turn, foster the emergence of revolutionary situations that, depending on the correlation of events, may culminate in revolutions. Sadly, these contradictions are not fully resolved by revolution. In Russia, autocratic control of society meant that critical knowledge vital to rational decision making on the part of individuals and social groups was masked. Workers had no real sense of what support for the Bolshevik party implied. Among many other vices, this legacy of ignorance was one of the most tragic consequences of autocratic rule, for it ensured that the new regime—in its struggles for power—would recapitulate many of the worst features of the regime that it had successfully displaced.

The Chinese Communist Revolution

MARK SELDEN

In the course of the twentieth century, China experienced a series of major revolutions. Up until 1911, China had been ruled for more than two thousand years by an imperial bureaucracy, in alliance with powerful landowners who wielded enormous local influence. In the eighteenth century, Imperial China was at the center of an East Asian regional system that achieved world-leading levels of technology, trade, and prosperity. By the nineteenth century, however, the ruling Qing dynasty was at low ebb, and European powers forced their way into China, demanding acceptance of free-trading privileges and imposing humiliating conditions on the Chinese government and people. Disenchanted with the ineffectiveness of the old imperial system, students, businessmen, military leaders, and officials overthrew the dynasty and created a republic. Students and military leaders pressed for the adoption of modern science and technology as a means of strengthening China and reestablishing its power and independence.

However, the Republic was stillborn, and within a few years China was divided into regional warlord-states. In the 1920s, one modernizing general, Chiang Kai-shek, sought to reunify the country. Building both a modern military force and a political party—the Nationalist Party, or Guomindang—Chiang incorporated leading warlords and established his own regime in China. Chiang faced competition for power from the recently founded Chinese Communist Party, which sought to organize workers for a Soviet-style revolution in Shanghai. After first allying with the communists, Chiang turned on his erstwhile allies and conducted harsh repression in the late 1920s, forcing the communists out of the cities deep into the interior mountains of China. The communists survived only by adopting a new peasant-based strategy combining guerrilla warfare with rural revolution against local landlords while building the party's strength in remote rural base areas.

Yet Chiang's victory was short-lived. Since World War I, Japan had been developing its possessions in Shandong and southern Manchuria, parts of China it had acquired in the war. In 1931 the Japanese seized full control of Manchuria, and in 1937 Japan launched an invasion of China proper. Japan quickly drove the Guomindang forces out of the coastal cities and into the interior. There, the Guomindang and the communists entered into an uneasy united front in the effort to drive out the Japanese. A long stalemate ensued, but Japan was finally defeated in 1945 after overextending its forces throughout East Asia following the attack on Pearl Harbor and the U.S. counterattack. Japan's withdrawal in 1945 was the signal for a renewed civil war between the Guomindang and the communists. By 1949, with their vast peasant base of supporters, the communists succeeded in driving U.S.-backed Guomindang forces out of mainland China and onto the island province of Taiwan. The communists took control of China and proclaimed the foundation of the People's Republic of China in October 1949. Yet the Chinese Communist Party continued to face many challenges in its efforts to bring economic prosperity to China and still hold on to complete political power.

THE HISTORICAL SETTING: CHINA AT LIBERATION

At the founding of the People's Republic of China, Communist Party Chairman Mao Zedong proclaimed that "the Chinese people have stood up." Indeed they had, and if formidable challenges lay ahead, we can be sure that Mao had in mind the following accomplishments, among others:

- Communist-led defeat of Japanese imperialism in China in one of the first successful people's wars.
- The defeat of the United States-backed Guomindang forces in the 1945–49 Civil War, the establishment of the People's Republic, and the elimination of the privileged position of foreigners in China.
- The completion of the land revolution throughout North China, destroying the power of the landlord class by a mobilized peasantry and the achievement of basic equalization of land and wealth.

Whatever its achievements, and they were impressive, the new leadership, which had gained experience in the course of more than two decades of guerrilla warfare and the administration of regional bases, well understood that the Chinese nation now faced a staggering range of problems. The poverty and distress of a war-ravaged agrarian nation, its territory the battleground for competing foreign and warlord armies for a century and more, posed the most immediate challenge.

The first half of the twentieth century in China had been marked by slow growth in population and national income—both grew at approximately 0.5 percent per year—leaving per capita national income roughly constant at about U.S. $60. In 1949, however, in the aftermath of World War II and the Civil War, heavy industrial production had fallen to about 30 percent of the previous peak level, and agricultural and consumer goods output had fallen to about 70 percent of their previous peaks. Hyperinflation had ruined the value of the currency, and economic exchanges were increasingly reverting to barter. The fighting had left the transportation system a shambles, and the Soviet Union, which had declared war on Japan in the closing days of World War II, systematically looted Manchuria of its most modern equipment, removing in all approximately two billion dollars (U.S.) worth of heavy industrial equipment or about half of the capital stock in what had been the leading center of heavy industry in this predominantly agrarian nation.

From The Transition to Socialism in China *edited by Mark Selden and Victor Lippit. Reprinted by permission of the author.*

The problems of wartime disruption overlay more basic structural problems. An arable land area of perhaps 300 million acres had to provide food for a population of more than 500 million. Even before the war-induced declines in production, the entire modern sector had accounted for only 7 percent of national income and could scarcely provide the material inputs—fertilizer, improved seeds, farm machinery—that the modernization of agriculture would require. As a result, traditional production methods prevailed in agriculture, productivity per person was low, and some 80 percent of China's labor force was needed to provide food and other agricultural products. Transportation links were weak even prior to the wartime disruption, and vast areas of the hinterland were served by only the most rudimentary dirt roads. Outside of Japanese-occupied Manchuria in China's northeast, industry had grown in only a few coastal treaty-port cities that were often more closely linked to foreign economies than to the interior in their external economic relations. The disarticulated economy that these conditions define magnified the problems of economic reconstruction.

These and other problems were exacerbated by the fact that from its birth the new nation, like many revolutionary regimes before and since, faced the antagonism of powerful external enemies. The United States, which since 1946 had thrown its weight behind the Guomindang and against the communists in the Civil War, now sought to perpetuate a divided China by backing the Chiang Kai-shek splinter regime on Taiwan as the legitimate government of China. Within less than a year of the founding of the People's Republic, a U.S.-led blockade deprived China of access to trade, capital, and technology. China was barred from assuming its place in the United Nations and denied recognition as well as trade by most other nations within the orbit of American power. Most critical was the fact that beginning in 1950 China was locked in combat with the United States in Korea. Self-reliance was a virtue born of necessity.

The embattled new state enjoyed three important advantages. First, successful leadership of war and revolution over the preceding decade had earned the Communists a national mandate for change. Coming in the wake of a century of national humiliation and the undermining of confidence in Chinese values, that mandate rested in part on the widespread conviction that the earlier Guomindang regime had betrayed the interests of the Chinese people. New policies were clearly in order. Moreover, the Chinese Communist Party had sunk deep roots in rural communities throughout the countryside, positioning itself to stand in the forefront of social and economic change as it had already done in the initial rounds of China's land revolution.

Second, China enjoyed the support of the Soviet Union, support which received concrete expression in the 1950 Sino-Soviet Treaty of Friendship and Cooperation and the subsequent extension both of a Soviet nuclear umbrella (of vital importance at the peak of U.S. hostility toward China) and of economic, military, technical, and planning assistance as China embarked on the path of industrialization.

Finally, the new government could build on the residual strengths of a society which, to be sure, had been humbled and shattered over the preceding century of war and disintegration, but which nevertheless had embedded in its collective experience and psyche traditions of productive labor, nationhood, sometimes explosive resistance to oppression, and patterns of cooperation rooted in family, lineage, and village experience. The Party's leadership of the peasant-based anti-Japanese resistance demonstrated the capacity of the peasantry to organize, to mobilize, and to grow in the context of a movement which respected its subsistence needs and which attempted to locate the foundations for change on such common practices as rural mutual aid and the cohesiveness of village structures.

THE LEADERSHIP'S VISION OF A NEW CHINA

In late 1947, as the Communists prepared for the major offensive that would bring them to the threshold of state power, the leadership delineated a strategic direction that was to prevail over the next five years. How would it be possible to achieve the goals for which they had fought for more than twenty years, goals of assuring national independence and building in a poor and backward peasant society a prosperous and equitable nation free from class exploitation? The Central Committee statement, "On the Present Situation and Our Task," drafted by Mao, sought to respond to this question and establish the parameters for social change. We see here clearly articulated for the first time a concept of stages of development, which proved to be one of the seminal concepts guiding the transition to socialism in China. The resolution set forth measures designed to elicit broad popular support for programs of controlled social change in both rural and urban areas.

In the countryside, "our policy is to rely on the poor peasants and unite solidly with the middle peasants to abolish the feudal and semifeudal system of exploitation. . . ." While stressing the satisfaction of poor-peasant demands for land, the Party sharply criticized ultra-left tendencies which threatened to infringe on middle-peasant interests, policies which would not only create deep rifts within the ranks of the people, but would also conflict with the effort to promote economic growth. Similarly, the document asserted that the essence of a new democratic industrial policy is to "confiscate monopoly capital" and "protect the industry and commerce of the [Chinese] national bourgeoisie." The Party thus initially adopted a moderate strategy, aiming to support poor and middle peasants against the demands of large landlords, and to protect China's small entrepreneurs against the competition of foreign capital. However, the larger heavy industrial facilities (such as steel and machinery factories, the railways, coal mines, and power plants) were placed under the control of the Communist regime. Without proclaiming the initiation of a socialist development strategy at this time, the leadership was preparing the ground for the transition.

With the state controlling the commanding heights of industry following the nationalization of the larger enterprises, and with the party in firm control in the villages from 1947, policy makers saw benefits to be reaped from the carefully monitored development of smaller enterprises owned by the national bourgeoisie, petty handicraft production, and the middle- and rich-peasant economy, which would provide resources for accumulation besides contributing to bringing prosperity to the countryside.

By 1949 publicly owned means of production (much of it previously nationalized by the Guomindang regime) may have accounted for as much as 80 percent of China's capital stock, and the state took a central role in banking, trade, and transport, but the great majority of small enterprises remained in private hands. Similarly, the land revolution program of "land to the tillers" was oriented toward the creation of independent commodity producers in the countryside. The goal of collectivization remained, but the Central Committee saw the transformation of the agrarian economy as developing step by step from individual ownership to collective. The strategy for the transition period was one of controlled revolutionary change by stages, each resting on a broad base of popular support and active participation, and each involving testing at the grass roots level to devise measures appropriate to Chinese conditions and popular consciousness.

THE TRANSITION TO SOCIALISM IN CHINA

In the years 1947–1952, China basically completed its land revolution throughout the countryside along with economic recovery from a century or more of war. Only with the completion of these tasks, and the ending of the Korean War with the July 1953 armistice, did the Party proclaim the end of the new democratic phase and the inauguration of its program for the transition to socialism. In August 1953 Mao succinctly set forth the tasks for the new period in the form of "the general line for the transition to socialism":

> The party's general line or general task for the transition period is basically to accomplish the country's industrialization and the socialist transformation of agriculture, handicrafts and capitalist industry and commerce over a fairly long period of time.[1]

In this statement the Party highlighted two pressing tasks for the early phases of the transition. The first was economic development, centered on industrialization, to overcome the legacy of poverty and economic stagnation. Second was the long-term, phased transformation from private to socialist ownership of the means of production. Both of these projects were already under way. Both would be accelerated with the inauguration of the general line. Both left open the larger and more difficult long-term tasks of ensuring that the new public and collective institutions would indeed be responsive to the authority and interests of the immediate producers, a task which may properly be regarded as the core of the transition process.

At the heart of the first goal was the First Five-Year Plan for Development of the National Economy, spanning the period from 1953 to 1957. That plan, drawn up on the basis of Soviet advice and predicated on extensive Soviet technical and financial assistance, emphasized the dynamic role of large, centralized heavy industrial complexes (notably steel) in initiating China's industrial transformation. In this respect it paralleled early Soviet five-year plans. Simultaneously, however, the socialist transformation of ownership was to proceed with the staged formation of progressively larger and more advanced cooperative forms in agriculture and the gradual extension of state ownership in industry. Here we find the Chinese leadership drawing on its own experience in leading the peasant movement over the preceding decades and charting a path quite different from that which the Bolsheviks had pioneered in the Soviet Union.

Both elements, the change in ownership systems and economic development, are central goals of socialist development in underdeveloped countries in general and China in particular. The transition in ownership involves the transfer from predominantly private ownership to cooperative, collective, and state forms of ownership of the major means of production. Stated differently, socialist societies incorporate a mix of private, cooperative or collective, and state ownership forms, and socialist development implies the progressive restriction of private ownership in favor of cooperative or collective and state ownership. The development of collective and state ownership forms, besides eliminating the exploitation and inequality rooted in unequal ownership of the means of production, makes possible (but does not assure) equitable implementation of the socialist principle "to each according to one's work." It also provides a framework within which economic planning can be implemented, allowing an increasing share of resources to be rationally allocated in accord with society's needs and interests rather than hoping that this end will be served as a by-product of competitive and profit-maximizing behavior.

Socialist development does not require the immediate elimination of all forms of private ownership or of the market, but rather their progressive restriction as cooperative and state systems and planning networks develop the capacity to expand their scope and effectively serve popular needs. These strictures are essential if the transition to socialism is to rest on foundations of broad majority support and if it is to contribute to the economic well-being of the great majority. Here we pose again the case for stages of development within the transition. The history of socialist experiments and, above all, the collectivization of agriculture has been littered with the corpses of premature or miscalculated ownership changes which can result only in large-scale coercion to maintain the system, economic reverses, or abandonment of the changes.

Changes in ownership and economic planning also involve the creation of a substantial state bureaucracy to pursue socialist goals and implement planning. Here we touch upon the central question of the socialist state. We may pose this question: If the old exploiting classes (landlords, capitalists, etc.) no longer exist as classes as a result of expropriation or other forms of transformation of ownership, and no longer control the means of production, what interests other than those of the immediate producers might be served by the socialist state? The answer of course is the interests of those who control the levers of power of the party-state—that is, cadres, managers, and officials at all levels. Once ownership and control of the principal means of production pass to collectives and the state, then the most important social cleavages in society can no longer be comprehended in ownership terms as conventionally defined. They come to center rather on the question of differential access to the wealth and power associated with the state, the party, and the collective. Moreover, the importance of this potential state–society cleavage is accentuated by the fact that the transition to socialism has everywhere strengthened the power of the state through the unification of economic and political authority in its hands.

In short, both the central promise and the central contradiction within societies engaged in the transition to socialism center on the role of the state, which can serve at once as a vehicle for advancing and concentrating the interests of the direct producers in socialist society, and as a roadblock for preventing the articulation and expression of those interests.

In addition to those contradictions concerning the state, a set of interrelated contradictions concerns the economy. For without economic development, even the most ambitious of social reforms in a poor and backward nation will be doomed to create a poor and backward socialism.

The Party's strategy for the socialist transition in the countryside, for the creation of new social relations and institutions as the first step in overcoming stagnation and exploitation, centered on the formation of progressively larger and more advanced forms of agricultural producers' cooperatives. The cooperatives were to be based on the voluntary participation of members who, with state support, embraced cooperative agriculture and created organizational forms appropriate to their needs. The problem, however, lies precisely in the realm of continuing conflicts among individual (and household), collective, and state.

This conflict becomes manifest, for example, in conflicts over the allocation of surplus as the households strive to expand their consumption, the collective to secure access to the surplus for local accumulation, and the state to appropriate the surplus for national accumulation and other public purposes.

In the early to mid-fifties, state—society conflict in the countryside centered on the question of the pace and process of cooperative transformation. This process was governed in significant part by the ability of the new cooperative institutions to provide increased security and incomes for the majority of the peasantry and, on this foundation of rising productivity and progress toward material well-being, to generate support for the expanded scope and scale of cooperation. For only on such foundations could cooperation become anything but an organization of the state imposed on the peasantry. However, at a critical moment in the transformation of agriculture, the party-state intervened decisively to impose nationwide collectivization in ways that challenged basic principles of the mass-line process. The race to collectivization associated with the 1955–56 "high tide" of socialism short-circuited the process of gradual, voluntary transformation.

For the first time in the post-1949 period, the Party set in motion a process that can perhaps best be comprehended as social engineering from above in the sense that social change lacked broad-based support. The setback to the democratic promise of the socialist transition was profound.

If this analysis is correct, there is a pattern of congruence between Chinese and Soviet collectivization processes. And not only of collectivization. At critical conjunctures thereafter, notably during the socialist high tide, the Great Leap Forward, and the Cultural Revolution period, certain striking similarities between Maoist and Stalinist politics may be observed: particularly the insistence by power holders from the center on implementing policies that directly conflicted with the material interests of large numbers of people, including a substantial portion of the peasants and workers.

THE ECONOMICS OF THE TRANSITION

By 1952, China had completed, in the main, a remarkably successful period of reconstruction, bringing output in nearly every industry back to pre-1949 peaks, restoring agricultural production in the wake of land reform, and bringing inflation under firm control. The time had come to turn from reconstruction to construction, bringing to the fore the question of where to find the savings to finance a greatly stepped-up pace of capital formation. Since the ultimate meaning of saving is not consuming, the problem may be rephrased as one of finding sectors of the economy where consumption can be temporarily depressed below the level of output. Accounting for only seven percent of national income, the entire modern sector was scarcely large enough to fill this role.

Only the rural agricultural-based economy had the potential to supply the initial resources for accumulation. A conservatively estimated 19 percent of national income had flowed to rural property owners—landlords, rich peasants, and moneylenders mainly in the form of rent—prior to the revolution, constituting a potential fund for development finance. Since these income flows were in exchange for no productive service, they could in principle be rerouted to serve social purposes without adversely affecting production. Diverting these flows to the state would have made them available to finance capital construction, but the land revolution did not in the first instance divert them to the state. Rather, in dividing landlord holdings among poor peasant households and eliminating rent payments and debt obligations, it had the immediate effect of increasing income for the rural poor. The problem for public policy then became how to extract a *portion* of these peasant gains to finance economic development.

In fact, the state succeeded in extracting slightly over one-half of these gains through taxation and control over the terms of trade between industry and agriculture, still leaving the rural beneficiaries of the land revolution, primarily the poor peasant strata, with substantial improvements in personal income. The contribution of the agricultural sector to development finance, however, did not end with the land revolution. The extraction of surpluses from the village has remained the single largest and most consistent source of investment finance since the founding of the People's Republic.

If the agricultural sector bore the burden of modernization, sustained efforts were directed to find supplementary forms of development finance, new sources of accumulation in a nation with slender financial resources. The "Great Leap Forward" (1958–1960) strategy, for example, rested on a massive mobilization of labor in the countryside for a host of ill-conceived development projects, from small-scale iron smelting to water projects. The key to the Great Leap Forward was the concept of mass effort and accumulation in a bold but abortive attempt to turn mobilized labor into capital, particularly industrial capital. However, these efforts simply drew labor away from the necessary tasks of farming and harvesting. Thus the Great Leap failed. In the end, it produced not the desired breakthrough in accumulation and productivity but the gravest economic and social crisis that the People's Republic of China has experienced, in the form of famine that took the lives of an estimated fifteen to thirty million Chinese, nearly all of them rural people.

Surveying the results of China's monumental effort to intensify rural labor and increase accumulation, one fact stands out: for over twenty years from collectivization and the Great Leap Forward, rural output and income, measured on a per capita basis, failed to increase significantly. Not until 1978 did per capita food production reach the level attained in 1957. And whereas income from collective labor in the rural areas was 57 *yuan* (the Chinese currency unit) in 1957, it rose only to 65 yuan in 1977, about half in food and half in cash. At 1 yuan = $0.65, the gain in cash income was only $2.60 (U.S.) per capita over a twenty-year span, or 13 cents per year, scarcely enough to meet the income and consumption needs of a rural population still desperately poor. Moreover, if this return is measured against labor time expended, given the increased labor demands of collective and commune members, the results reveal a decline over twenty years.

For industrial workers too, the pattern of frequent wage increases during the First Five-Year Plan was broken for two decades after 1957, with real wages remaining essentially flat over that span. If the surplus extracted from the countryside was not going to the workers, where was it going? In essence, it was going into a rising volume of investment, which from the late fifties reached extremely high levels—except for the 1960–65 period when the economic dislocations resulting from the failure of the Great Leap Forward forced a temporary reduction in the investment rate. The high rate of investment, however, did not bring a commensurate increase in the rate of economic growth. With incentives to labor falling as a result of the combination of mobilization and state extraction of much of the rural surplus, and a rapidly-growing labor force looking for productive work, the number of dollars needed to produce each additional dollar of output rose sharply in China, so that an ever-greater volume of resources was needed to sustain a given rate of economic growth. This meant that practically all of society's incremental output had to be reinvested to sustain economic growth, leaving little or nothing to increase personal incomes.

Between 1952 and 1978 industrial output in China grew by an average of 11.2 percent per year and agricultural output by 3.2 percent. Given the difficult initial conditions, the industrial performance measured by this yardstick can be considered excellent and the agricultural one creditable. Together, growth in the two sectors drove the Chinese economy forward at an average annual pace of 4–6 percent in real terms, or 2–4 percent per capita if the average annual population growth of about 2 percent is taken into account. Yet because an increasing share of national income was going into accumulation to sustain this growth, real wages and peasant incomes languished from the late 1950s.

During the First Five-Year Plan period (1953–1957), China devoted 24.2 percent of its material output to investment. At the height of the Great Leap Forward in 1960 this figure reached an extraordinary 39.6 percent, and after dropping in the early sixties it rose again, reaching an average of 33 percent during the period 1970–78. Yet industrial growth in the seventies was slower than it was in the First Five-Year Plan period, reflecting the fact that each new dollar of investment was yielding smaller returns in added output.

The reasons for this are familiar to students of centrally planned economies. The rigidity of economic decision-making, the hoarding of raw materials, uneconomic vertical integration (so that plant managers could assure themselves of supplies), and the inflexibility of the system tend to grow disproportionately as the economy expands, decreasing its efficiency and increasing the waste of manpower and resources.

THE CULTURAL REVOLUTION

In 1966, Mao and some of his key supporters came to believe that the Revolution was losing momentum, with bureaucratic and economic goals overshadowing the idealism and efforts of building socialism. Mao thus encouraged students, workers, and peasants to attack bureaucrats and managers deemed insufficiently radical, in the name of a continuing "Great Proletarian Cultural Revolution." However, the result was to unleash a host of conflicts that had been building in city and countryside since the Great Leap Forward, and to produce something like civil war. After three years of conflict that mounted to national chaos, the military stepped in to restore order and rebel movements were for the most part crushed, even as the rhetoric of Cultural Revolution continued for another half dozen years.

The Cultural Revolution offered an apparent escape from the dilemma of the party-state. Proponents of uninterrupted revolution and continued class struggle did in fact develop a cutting critique of the dangers of bureaucratism, of statist tendencies to monopolize and abuse power. Ironically, however, the power of the party-state increased dramatically during the Cultural Revolution. This was the result of processes which included carrying to dizzying heights a cult of Mao Zedong; the failure of the Cultural Revolution to create institutional processes which could provide effective expression to worker demands (one of which would surely have been an end to the twenty-year freeze on real wages); the rejection as "revisionist" of proposals that would have decentralized power to the enterprise level or given greater latitude to collective institutions; and the destruction of the few existing vehicles (however weak) for expressing worker demands such as trade unions. Ironically, line managers and Party officials in the factories gained unchecked powers in a movement that had begun as an attack by activist workers on bureaucracy.

CHINA AFTER MAO

After Mao's death in 1976, a short power-struggle ensued. It was won by the pragmatic wing of the Chinese Communist Party, under the leadership of Deng Xiaoping. Deng introduced market-based reforms in both the agricultural and industrial sectors in the belief that the combination of institutional reform, and opening China to the world economy, would help improve economic conditions.

Beginning in 1980, Deng introduced a series of reforms in agriculture, industry, and trade. In agriculture, control of the land was taken from collectives and returned to peasant households. Peasants were encouraged to produce and sell whatever they wished, as long as they met their stipulated contributions to the state. In industry, Deng inaugurated processes that would lead to partial privatization of state enterprises and created special economic zones, primarily along the southern and eastern coast, that focused on expanding trade and welcomed foreign investment. These special zones, linked to the world economy through surging exports, soon made China a world leader in exports and a magnet for foreign investment, much of it coming from Hong Kong, Taiwan, and Chinese overseas capital. Rural townships played a dynamic role in the new economy through township and village enterprises (a legacy of the former collective economy), as did private and household enterprises. These enterprises produced a wide range of consumer goods, supplying long suppressed domestic consumption needs and fueling an export boom in everything from textiles to fans, bicycles, refrigerators, and furnishings. These post-Mao reforms were a reaction to the excesses of the Great Leap Forward and Cultural Revolution and to pressures from below to expand the scope of the long suppressed household and market sectors of the economy. The legitimacy of material concerns in a population that was still quite poor by international standards was recognized, and material incentives and individual rewards for productive contributions were reinstated as core elements in the new development strategy. In purely economic terms, the reforms achieved substantial success. China's economy has grown at a rate of 8–10 percent per year in the two decades since 1980, among the highest growth rates achieved anywhere in the world. This growth has lifted significant portions of the population out of poverty, especially those living in the cities and the industrializing coastal areas that have been the center of export-led development.

At the same time, however, the Communist Party has kept a monopoly on political power, prohibiting any organizations not under Party control, and continuing to appoint all national, provincial, and city and county-level officials even as it introduced modest elections in rural township governments. The major industrial and financial pillars of the economy—banks, steel, railroads, electricity, machinery-production—remain dominated by state-owned enterprises, many of them losing money but continuing to employ millions of urban workers. Yet substantial privatization of manufacturing and service enterprises, together with foreign and joint venture capital, have shifted the dynamic of development to the private sector while producing layoffs of tens of millions of former state sector workers, many of whom face a bleak future of unemployment and marginal jobs. Inequality between the poorer rural and interior regions and the booming coastal zones has sharply increased, as has urban unemployment as numerous loss-making state-owned enterprises have closed, privatized, and/or sharply cut back their work forces.

The growth of market relations can contribute to enhanced economic efficiency and improved living standards. Yet it can also give rise to many of the contradictions that inspired the earlier Chinese revolution: class inequality and the formation of a substantial population of marginal workers and peasants excluded from the benefits of economic growth.

The market, then, appears as a necessary but dangerously volatile instrument in the socialist transition. Its dual nature constitutes one of the many contradictions that socialist countries inevitably confront in the transition process. The market must play a significant role in China's economy to increase efficiency, check bureaucratic power, and extend the scope for initiative and responsibility among the immediate producers. The challenge for socialist planners and citizens is to strike an appropriate balance that reduces the disruptive potential of the market, while permitting appropriate scope for the market in expanding income and consumption and mediating state power.

REFERENCE

1.   Selden (1979), pp. 281–82.

The Cuban Revolution, 1959–1961

THOMAS M. LEONARD

In terms of longevity, Fidel Castro is one of the most successful revolutionary leaders of all time. Castro came to power in a guerrilla revolt against the dictator Fulgencio Batista in 1959; as of 2002, 43 years later, Castro was still in power. While some view his long personal rule with concern, he has been able to keep his nationalist heroic appeal to most of the Cuban people for these decades. Leonard describes the origins of the Cuban revolution, its tribulations, and its consequences.

Fidel Castro's revolution in Cuba was not the first in Latin America, nor would it be the last. Latin America's twentieth-century experience is replete with oligarchical or military dictatorships and with calls to cure the consequences of unequal wealth distribution and social immobility by revolution. Prior to Castro, examples include the Mexican Revolution, which began with the ouster of Porfirio Díaz in 1911, and the Bolivian experience under Victor Paz Estensarro from 1944 to 1954. Subsequently, the Sandinista Revolution in Nicaragua (1979–1990) had many parallels to the Cuban experience. Like Fidel Castro in Cuba, the revolutionaries in Mexico, Bolivia, and Nicaragua claimed their desire to end elitist-controlled and corrupt political systems and to provide for greater economic and social opportunities for the downtrodden masses.

In Cuba the ideals of Castro's revolution were not new. During the 1890s José Martí, often described as the father of Cuban independence, not only called for an end to Spanish political and economic domination but also for improvement in the quality of life for the Cuban masses. In the post–World War II period, Eduardo Chíbas repeated Martí's call for democracy, economic opportunity, and social justice. But it was not to be.

Since its independence from Spain in 1898 until Castro's march into Havana, the Cuban government was controlled by the nation's elite, wealthy landowners and merchants who used political power to serve their own purposes. The elite viewed government employment as an opportunity for self enrichment, rather than an opportunity to serve in the best interests of the nation. Corruption and nepotism characterized Cuban politics during the first half of the twentieth century as middle and lower socioeconomic groups had no effective voice within the system.

U.S. economic interest in Cuba predated 1898 and only intensified thereafter. The United States became the major market for Cuban sugar, citrus, tobacco, and raw materials and became the chief supplier of goods essential to the Cuban economy—machinery, spare parts, railroad harbor equipment, communications technology, and consumer goods. American companies dominated every aspect of Cuba's economic life. The economic linkage produced a bond between the Cuban white elite and the American business community. Each sought to maintain the existing political and social structures for its own benefit. They had no interest in meeting the demands of the working classes.

Economic stagnation amid the Great Depression of the late 1920s into the 1930s combined with pent-up anger over economic injustices and political repression to ignite protests in the early 1930s. Student-led protests and demonstrations intensified and attracted elements of the white middle class to demand an end to the corrupt machine of President Gerardo Machado, who was finally deposed in August 1933. A month later a "Sergeants' Revolt"

---

led by Fulgencio Batista resulted in the so-called "government of one hundred days" led by Ramón Grau San Martín. Grau Martín, a former university professor, immediately promoted measures beneficial to the working class, including an eight-hour workday, a minimum wage, and the legalization of unions. He also moved toward political reorganization to permit the lower classes access to the political arena. These measures threatened the economic, social, and political order that had served the Cuban elite and U.S. interest since 1898. Grau Martín further aggravated the United States by unilaterally abrogating the Platt Amendment, which had governed U.S.-Cuban relations since 1903. The Platt Amendment prevented Cuba from creating treaties with other foreign powers and granted the United States the right to maintain political order on the island. In response, Cuba's upper class and the U.S. special envoy on the island, Sumner Welles, maneuvered to oust Grau Martín from office. They found a willing ally in Fulgencio Batista and his colleagues in the middle-rank officer corps whose opportunity for promotion was blocked by the elite-based old-line officers. On January 14, 1934, Grau Martín was deposed and replaced by Carlos Mendieta, but Batista was the power behind the throne. The new government negotiated an end to the Platt Amendment and a new economic treaty with the United States.

For the next eighteen years, Cuban politics returned to the corruption and nepotism that characterized the earlier period, and the primacy of U.S. business enterprise remained intact. In his subsequent attack upon the old order, Fidel Castro would point to the Cuban experiences from 1898 through 1958. He correctly described the bankruptcy of politics, the disparities between upper and lower classes, the discrimination against Afro-Cubans, and the economic omnipresence of the United States.

The immediate causes of the Cuban Revolution are found in the March 10, 1952, coup d'état engineered by Fulgencio Batista against President Carlos Prío Socarrás. Batista publicly justified his action on the grounds that Prío intended to extend his own corrupt presidency, an act certain to result in violence. Batista's underlying motive was equally obvious: to regain power for himself and his close associates who had been excluded from the political process for the preceding eight years. Batista gained immediate popular support by promising free elections for November 1954.

Batista's coup caught Cuba's traditional parties—the *Auténticos* and *Orthodoxos*—unprepared, and the subsequent arrest and exile of their leadership made them ineffective. The 1954 elections proved farcical. Running unopposed, Batista captured only 40 percent of the vote and still moved into the presidential palace. Batista's actions set the stage for confrontation.

In addition to political tensions, Cuba's long-standing socioeconomic disparities worsened in the 1950s. At first glance, Cuba enjoyed widespread economic growth during Batista's administration. Thanks to a sugar boom prompted by World War II and the years immediately thereafter, Cuban entrepreneurs intensified the process of "Cubanizing" the sugar industry. On the eve of World War II, Cuban capitalists owned 54 sugar mills that produced 22 percent of the total sugar production. By 1952 Cubans owned 113 sugar mills that accounted for 55 percent of the total production. Cuban capital was also heavily invested in many foreign-owned mills, and the Cuban-owned cattle industry expanded dramatically. Batista also encouraged expansion of foreign investment, and North American firms capitalized upon the invitation in the production of nickel, cobalt, and other minerals and in the development of tourism. The economic expansion provided the Batista administration with the funds necessary to complete long neglected infrastructure projects and build low-cost housing.

Despite the economic growth, Cuba remained dependent upon the exportation of sugar for its wealth. Sugar was subject to the fluctuations of world sugar prices and the import quotas set by the U.S. Congress. By the 1950s the nature of world sugar production had altered so that it no longer could drive Cuba's economic growth. The United States also remained Cuba's major trading partner. In the 1950s, the United States supplied Cuba with approximately 75 percent of its imports and took in nearly 65 percent of its exports.

The postwar economic growth actually exacerbated Cuba's socioeconomic problems. On paper, Cuba enjoyed one of Latin America's highest standards of living during the 1950s, particularly among its middle class. However, because the economy was tied to the U.S. market, North American-made products permeated the Cuban marketplace at U.S. prices. Wages on the island were not high enough for the majority of the Cubans to consume these imported goods. In addition, Cuban wages did not keep pace with the inflationary pressures of the 1950s. As a result, middle-class Cubans experienced a decline in their standard of living in comparison to their U.S. counterparts. At the same time, members of the upper class preferred to invest their wealth abroad because of the volatility of Cuban politics. In the 1950s, urban workers received higher salaries and benefited from social security programs compared to their rural counterparts, but they faced unemployment/underemployment problems, particularly as new workers entered the labor force.

Overall, women and Afro-Cubans did not fare well in the postwar economy. In the 1950s, 65 percent of the working women were employed in the service sector, many at low-wage occupations. To be sure, women were a potentially significant portion of the professional class—in fact, one-third of all Cubans with a college education were women—but women's gains economically remained more promise than reality. Afro-Cubans often lacked even the promise of significant advance. In 1953, Afro-Cubans made up 27 percent of the population. Occupationally, they were overrepresented in the entertainment and service industries and underrepresented in the commercial and professional sectors. Most were laborers, at the lower end of the wage scale, and they also experienced patterns of discrimination in education, health care, and other government services. Understandably, Afro-Cubans played a major role in labor organizations, particularly in the Cuban Confederation of Labor (CTC).

The middle class also lamented the administration's corruption and repressive measures. This was most evident in the new surge of literature decrying the republic's moral decay. In addition to the long-standing themes of nationalism, reformism, and anti-Americanism, an idolization of Cuba's independence leaders, particularly José Martí, also surfaced. Martí's speeches and writings of Cuban destiny and the need for vision and self-discipline contrasted with the current dictatorship and prompted young idealists, journalists, and intellectuals to call for change. Batista responded to such criticism with violence and repression, further inciting the protestors.

Soon after the 1954 presidential election, several revolutionary groups appeared, including the Directorio Revolucionario and Il Frente Nacional del Escambray. But the group that received the most attention was the 26th of July Movement, because of its earlier bold attack upon the Santiago de Cuba military barracks in 1953 and its subsequent revolutionary activities. The Movement was led by Fidel Castro, a young lawyer from Oriente Province. Castro's middle-class background allowed him an education at the prestigious Jesuit

Belén High School in Havana and later at the University of Havana, where he became interested in politics and the need for social reform.

Castro first sought change in Cuba through the political system. He joined the Orthodox party and ascribed to the ideals of party leader Eduardo Chibás. Castro ran as an Orthodox party candidate for the House of Representatives in the aborted 1952 elections. But following Batista's March 1952 coup, Castro determined that the only path to change would be through the violent overthrow of the system. Thereafter, he used the University of Havana campus as a shelter to organize a small group of followers and store ammunition for an attack on the military barracks at Moncada, the army's second largest installation, located in Oriente Province. Castro planned his attack for July 26, 1953, during the annual carnival at Santiago in eastern Cuba. With the carnival in full sway, Castro expected the military to have its guard down. The attack was to be accompanied by a publicity campaign designed to give the impression of an army uprising by pro-Orthodox officers, which in turn would paralyze the army. Undercut from his main prop of support, Batista would resign, and the Orthodox party would vault into political power. In reality, Castro failed to consult the party, informing it of his intended actions only a day before the assault on Moncada. The attack ended in disaster. Most of Castro's troops were killed; Castro, his brother Raúl, and a few of their followers momentarily escaped into the mountains, where the army subsequently captured them. But the daring attack catapulted Fidel Castro into the forefront of the anti-Batista forces and convinced many Cubans that only an armed struggle would bring Batista down.

While in prison awaiting trial, Castro wrote *History Will Absolve Me* (1953), from which he read aloud in court before his sentencing. In it, Castro associated his movement with the ideals of Martí and Chibás; he called for reforms of Cuba's political system, an end to the economic dependency upon the United States, and social justice for all sectors of Cuban society.

Castro served only eleven months of the fifteen-year sentence he received for the Moncada attack. In a general amnesty, Batista released him from jail and banished him to Mexico. In Mexico City, Castro plotted his return to Cuba and a new strategy for reform there. Meanwhile, in Cuba, the Federation of University Students, led by José A. Echeverría, continued to demonstrate against Batista's regime. To counter the increasing student demonstrations, the military stepped up its repressive measures. Unable to gain the support of Cuba's middle sector and refusing advances from the local communist party, Echeverría and his followers determined that the only way to alter Cuba's political course was to bring Batista down by violent means. Toward that end, Echeverría met secretly in Mexico with the Castro brothers and Ernesto "Che" Guevara, an Argentine doctor and revolutionary, whose travels through Latin America had convinced him that only revolution could correct the hemisphere's social and economic disparities.

As a result of the Echeverría–Castro agreement, Castro returned to Cuba. The plan was for Castro and a small band of revolutionaries to land in Oriente Province from the yacht *Granma* on December 2, 1956, while Echeverría's followers conducted diversionary activities in Havana. Alerted to the plan, government authorities squelched the operation. Castro's unit of eighty men was quickly reduced to eighteen, who escaped to the nearby mountains. In Havana, the police rounded up all suspected revolutionaries.

Castro and his followers immediately found themselves isolated in the Sierra Maestra Mountains in southeastern Oriente Province, but there they soon discovered that the patterns of socioeconomic disparity and the instruments of the central government's repression could be used to build a popular resistance movement. The region was home to an estimated 50,000 peasants living in varying degrees of poverty and misery. They worked as low-paid laborers for low-production farmers or squatted on land that belonged to distant landowners and from which they faced constant eviction notices. The government's Rural Guard terrorized the peasants. Angry and desperate, the peasants became many of the earliest recruits for the rebel army, which by May 1957 had overrun key Rural Guard posts at La Plata and El Uvero. News of these insurgent victories brought new recruits to Castro's rebel force. The arbitrariness of the Cuban army's field operations, which became indiscriminate terror by late 1957, provided additional reasons for peasants to support Castro's cause.

To counteract the peasant support for Castro, the Cuban army forced thousands of peasants into hastily constructed camps near Santiago and Bayamo, reminiscent of the Spanish *reconcentrados* constructed in the mid-1890s to isolate the peasants from the rebels. Those not brought into the camps were presumed Castro supporters. Rather than pacify the peasants, the camps served only to swell further the ranks of the *fidelistas* (followers of Fidel Castro). By mid-1957 the Sierra was up in arms.

Throughout 1957 and early 1958, the size of the insurgent force increased, and its field operations expanded. Raúl Castro operated a second front in the north; Juan Almeida opened a third front around Santiago de Cuba; and in April 1958 Camilo Cienfuegos left the Sierra for the Holguín plains, and Che Guevara operated around Turquino peak.

In response to the events in Oriente, the faculty and students at the University of Havana voted to shut down the institution on November 30, 1956. The government used the occasion to close the school until early 1959. The closing did not silence the students but instead propelled them into the country's political dynamics with only one goal: to end the Batista dictatorship. Over the next three years, as the rural insurgency increased, so too did the urban violence. In an attack upon the presidential palace on March 13, 1957, a student group almost succeeded in killing Batista. But the rebels lost before they won. Echeverría was killed in a coordinated attack upon a Havana radio station. The way was open for new rebel leadership that might unite the rural and urban insurgencies.

Thereafter, Castro coordinated the urban underground acts of sabotage and subversions by the 26th of July Civic Resistance. The rebels sought to disrupt the government at every turn and to show the people that the corrupt government could not protect its own interests and by implication had neither legitimacy nor any claim on citizens' loyalty. The rebels exploded bombs, set fires, cut power lines, derailed trains, and kidnapped and killed their political enemies. Batista responded with equal ferocity with the indiscriminate torture and murder of Castro supporters, suspected or real. The violence also led to a series of planned military uprisings against the government. Beginning in April 1956, first-line army officers, then naval officers at Cienfuegos, and later the air force and army medical corps conspired to change governments. Batista not only faced mounting popular opposition but also an increasingly disloyal and unreliable military. The Batista regime became increasingly isolated.

As a result of the rural insurgency and urban violence, the Cuban economy stagnated by 1958, causing a drastic decline in government public works projects and a marked rise in unemployment. Poverty became more visible in Havana and other cities. At the same time, the guerrillas had exacted a heavy toll. They halted the shipment of foodstuffs into the cities, causing prices to soar. Transportation between Havana and the three eastern provinces had stopped; telephone and telegraph service across the island was paralyzed; large sections of highways and railroads were destroyed; and bridges were put out of service. Matters worsened in February 1958 when the 26th of July Movement launched an attack against sugar mills, tobacco factories, public utilities, railroads, and oil refineries and put the torch to some two million tons of sugar.

Amid the worsening economic conditions, reports of graft, corruption, and Swiss bank accounts opened by Batista and his supporters added to the public outrage and fueled the popular determination to oust the dictator. Even Batista's supporters sought to remove him as a way to cool tensions and, they hoped, appease the various rebel forces. The movement for change was now irreversible, and it favored the bold. In July 1958 the opposition groups organized a meeting in Caracas, Venezuela, where the resultant pact established Fidel Castro as the principal leader of the anti-Batista movement and his army as the main arm of the revolution.

The United States helped with the demise of Batista. In March 1958, just prior to the launching of the government offensive against Castro's guerrilla army, the United States placed an arms embargo on the Cuban government. It had a devastating psychological effect, boosting the rebels' confidence while deflating what little hope Batista's supporters had for outside assistance. The United States also forewarned Batista that it would not extend recognition to his handpicked successor, Rivero Agüro, in the 1958 presidential elections. The United States sought to ease Batista out of office in early December 1958, when it covertly sent William D. Pawley to Havana. Not even U.S. Ambassador to Cuba Earl T. Smith was informed of the mission. Pawley, a Republican businessman long connected to Cuba, was not authorized to present himself as a representative of the Eisenhower administration, but rather to explain that he came as a private U.S. citizen representing influential friends in the United States. He offered Batista and his family safe haven in Florida, provided that Batista form a caretaker government acceptable to Washington, which would then turn on the military assistance spigot in order to prevent a Castro victory. Batista refused. Even had Batista accepted the offer, it might have come too late.

In mid-1958 Batista launched a military offensive against the rebels, but the effort collapsed by the end of the summer. Castro responded with a counteroffensive, and towns and villages in eastern Cuba quickly fell to the advancing guerrilla army. By December the guerrilla army had swelled to 50,000, and Batista's army was in total disarray. With Batista's departure to the Dominican Republic, the remainder of the army troops ceased to fight, giving Colonel Ramón Barquín no other choice but to order an immediate cease-fire, a salute to the "Army of Liberation," and then surrender.

A week later, Fidel Castro arrived in Havana to a euphoric welcome. His charisma would prove to be overwhelming. The *fidelistas* came to invoke history, they claimed, and therefore would install Cuban democratic government and social justice. The structures of old Cuba were to be abandoned and in its place a new Cuba created.

The government set up at Havana in January 1959 consisted mainly of moderate civilians, with Dr. Manuel Urrutia as president, José Miró Cardona as prime minister, and Castro as commander-in-chief of the armed forces. It quickly became clear that Castro had no intention of consulting with his colleagues, and Miró Cardona resigned in February. Castro became premier. A few months later Urrutia also departed. Other moderate nationalist reformers soon left the government to be replaced by Castro's more radical colleagues. Castro also instituted a style of *personalismo* by which he dispensed favors and made decisions without consulting the provisional government. Castro, personally, became the focal point of the revolution.

Over the next few months, the regime took on its own characteristics. At home, it discouraged and denounced dissident views, used the army for political purposes, and ruled by decree in order to prepare the people for "real democracy." It described its own actions, which included alterations in the rules on property, as efforts to achieve social justice. While it was linked to revolutions in neighboring countries, the regime denounced the United States for interfering in Cuba's internal affairs. Throughout, Castro and his colleagues rejected any suggestion that they were communist-orientated. While Castro's actions frightened Cuba's middle and upper sectors and policy makers in Washington, his continued call for revolutionary change incited the general populace to demand further political and social reform. The masses supported rapid change, and Castro manipulated such feeling to his advantage in the early months of the revolution.

In the weeks after marching into Havana, the revolutionaries brought many of Batista's more prominent military and civilian leaders before revolutionary tribunals opened to the public and aired on national television. The trials defied any sense of justice and resulted in the summary execution of hundreds of persons. The regime ended the trials only in response to international criticism but continued to confiscate the properties of Batista supporters and collaborators, real or imagined.

Castro's brother, Raúl, used the military and the large civilian militia to rid the country of Batista supporters and to otherwise intimidate the opposition. The traditional Liberals and Conservatives, the *Auténtico* and *Orthodoxo* parties, were isolated from government.

Castro and his colleagues did not see their legitimacy dependent upon the holding of elections. In May 1959 Castro announced that the priorities of the new Cuba would focus upon full employment, expanded health care, extended education, and the need to create a new political consciousness among the people. Elections, he argued, would only interfere with these programs.

Castro's appeal to the lower socioeconomic groups was apparent from the start. Workers, representing all sectors—sugar, railroad, mining, utility—either demonstrated or struck for higher wages, often at the government's encouragement. On many occasions, Castro himself mediated the labor disputes and mandated settlements on behalf of the workers.

Beginning in March 1959 Castro took bolder steps. The government intervened in the telephone company and reduced its rates. Electricity rates were cut drastically. Virtually all labor contracts were renegotiated and wages raised. Cane cutters' wages were increased by a flat 15 percent. Health reforms, educational reforms, and unemployment relief followed in quick order. Property owned by all past government officials, senior army officers, mayors, governors, and members of congress during the 1954–1958 period were confiscated. Through special licensing and higher tariffs, the importation of luxury items was restricted. Although largely symbolic, the action did save Cuba an estimated $70 million in foreign exchange the first year, as the importation of cars and television sets, among other things, plummeted. The new Cuban government also cut its economic dependence on the United States, reducing its trade from $543 million in 1959 to $224 million in 1960.

By far the most sweeping change came with the Agrarian Reform Law in May 1959, which restricted real estate holdings to 1,000 acres, except for sugar, rice, and livestock farms, where the maximum limits were set at 3,333 acres. Estates above these amounts were nationalized and reorganized into state cooperatives or distributed into individual holdings of 67 acres, with squatters, sharecroppers, and renters receiving first claim to the land they had been working.

In February 1960 a Soviet trade delegation arrived in Havana to complete a trade pact. The Soviets agreed to purchase 425,000 tons of sugar immediately and 1,000,000 tons in each of the next four years. In addition, the Soviet Union offered Cuba $100 million in low-interest credits, technical assistance, and crude and refined petroleum. In April 1960 the two nations resumed diplomatic relations, suspended since 1952. With the agreement in hand, in June 1960 an emboldened Castro ordered Standard Oil, Shell, and Texaco to refine Soviet crude oil. On directions from the U.S. State Department, the companies refused, whereupon the Cuban government took them over. In July President Dwight D. Eisenhower retaliated by cutting the Cuban sugar quota to 7,000 tons for the remainder of 1960 and zero after that. Castro was equal to the challenge. In August he nationalized the remaining U.S. properties on the island, including two utilities, thirty-six sugar mills, and branches of American banks. In response, Eisenhower imposed a total economic embargo on Cuba, with the exception of medicines and some foodstuffs. Eisenhower set the cornerstone of U.S. policy toward Cuba for the next two generations: removal of Castro through economic coercion.

The embargo affected Cuba both economically and politically. It thrust the government into managing the economy. By late 1961, approximately 85 percent of the total productive value of the Cuban industry was under state control. The embargo also facilitated the seizure of other Cuban-owned lands. For Cuba's nearly 150,000 managers, clerks, technicians, accountants, and attorneys, the expropriations proved traumatic. Not only were their salaries brought into line with the lower Cuban wage scales, but their jobs were jeopardized if they opposed or did not demonstrate enthusiastic support for the revolution. Also, as a result of nationalization, thousands of Cubans employed in the insurance services, real estate agencies, gambling casinos, and brokers of all types lost their jobs.

Events in Cuba during 1959 and 1960 contributed to an exodus of nearly 200,000 Cubans, mostly to Puerto Rico and the United States. Those adversely affected by Castro's political and economic policies labeled him a communist. The disaffected and displaced Cuban "exiles" abroad came to believe that Castro had to be brought down by sabotage before his power base solidified. Thus, beginning in early 1959, Cuban exiles in the Caribbean and the United States launched isolated, but futile attacks on the island.

At first, the Eisenhower administration reluctantly welcomed Castro's victory over Batista. But soon the mock trials, the elimination of political opposition, and Castro's increased power and social programs raised questions in Washington about his communist tendencies. Shortly after his visit to Washington in April 1959, the Central Intelligence Agency (CIA) began to devise plans for Castro's ouster and replacement with a more friendly government. The initial acts of sabotage conducted by the Cuban exile community received the agency's tacit approval, but their only impact was to increase Castro's intransigence.

The U.S. hesitancy turned to belligerency following the Soviet-Cuban trade agreement in February 1960, Soviet Premier Nikita Khrushchev's subsequent boast that he would use rockets to defend Cuba, and Castro's claim that he would spread revolution in Latin America. Castro's revolution moved onto the Cold War stage. For U.S. policy makers, Cuba now served as a Soviet pawn in the global struggle between Washington and Moscow. Castro had to go, lest the region itself be lost to communism.

The tension reached new heights in January 1961, when Castro demanded that the United States reduce its embassy staff in Havana to eleven persons. Eisenhower seized the opportunity as a pretext to break diplomatic relations. One of the reasons for Castro's belligerence was his knowledge of U.S. preparations for an attack on Cuba. Eisenhower made the decision in late spring 1960 to force Castro out, and he approved the CIA's covert operation to remove him with a brigade of exiles being trained in Guatemala and Nicaragua. When John F. Kennedy became president in January 1961, he continued the scheme.

The CIA argued that Castro's support base was weak and that a small landing of exile forces would result in a large uprising within Cuba. In fact, American intelligence was hopelessly uninformed. U.S. contacts were with the overzealous exiles or the diminished opposition groups within Cuba. When the Cuban exile brigade landed at the Bay of Pigs in April 1961, Castro was prepared to meet the challenge. The invading exiles found themselves stranded as the Cuban Air Force kept the exiles pinned down and destroyed their lone cargo ship off shore. The Cuban army quickly reached the invasion site, where Castro took command. Within three days, nearly 1,500 exile troops surrendered. The invasion was a fiasco that embarrassed the United States and strengthened Castro's hold on the island. The United States could not hide its involvement in the ill-planned attack and appeared weak and unprincipled. Indeed, U.S. prestige suffered throughout the world, especially in Latin America, and the Bay of Pigs invasion convinced Khrushchev that the new president was weak and that Cuba needed more direct Soviet aid. Thus the ground was laid for the later Cuban missile crisis. The United States, in turn, resolved to isolate Cuba further and to launch aid programs, especially the Alliance for Progress, to counter communist appeal in Latin America. And Castro now had the proof of American treachery to justify further stern measures to protect the Cuban revolution. The American attack also allowed Castro to wrap the revolution in the cloak of nationalism and the long-standing desire of Cubans to be free of foreign interference.

Castro used the failed invasion to further tighten his grip upon Cuba. On December 2, 1961, Castro proclaimed: "I am a Marxist-Leninist, and I shall be one until the last day of my life." Cuba set sail on a new course.

Castro quickly pursued a deliberate path to consolidate his personal power. Old-line communists, student activists, and other allies were removed from the decision-making process. Dissent would not be tolerated; political parties were outlawed, except for the Communist Party, which Castro reorganized until he was in firm control of it and could use it to serve his purposes. By 1965 the traditional social pyramid had collapsed and a new one resurfaced. At its apex stood Fidel Castro, with the support of Cuba's army, headed by his brother Raúl. As in many revolutions, a new dictatorship had emerged.

Only the lower social classes remained uncommitted, and Castro implemented programs—health, housing, social security, and the like—to gain their support. Every sector of society was organized to support the revolution, from athletics to women. The state provided every service either free or at minimal cost. To ensure that future generations were imbued with the proper ideological zeal, church schools were closed and the state directed education at all levels. Over time, loyalty to the revolution and membership in the Communist Party became the measuring stick for benefits to be received from the system.

With revolutionary zeal, Castro set out to remake the Cuban economy. In cooperation with his chief economic advisor at the time, Ernesto "Che" Guevara, Castro planned to make

Cuba self-sufficient in foodstuffs and consumer goods. But his zeal was not matched by resources or essential management skills. The revolution resulted in the loss of U.S. capital and prompted the out-migration of Cuba's managers and technicians. The effort to go it alone failed by 1970 when Cuba did not achieve its 10-million-ton sugar harvest. The economy was in disarray.

Castro attempted to conceal the revolution's deficiencies by showcasing its accomplishments in medicine, health care delivery, education, and sports. But he could not hide a decaying infrastructure, inadequate housing, and continued political tyranny.

In the international arena, Castro pursued an aggressive foreign policy in an effort to demonstrate Cuba's ability to stand tall against its historic nemesis, the United States. Castro intended to fan the revolutionary flames in Latin America. His call for the violent overthrow of the hemispheric oligarchies in the 1960s and his support for Maurice Bishop in Grenada, the Sandinistas in Nicaragua, and Farabundo Martí in El Salvador in the 1970s and 1980s illustrated the consistency of his policy. Castro's military adventures in Africa and the Middle East and leadership of the Nonaligned Movement were designed to make Castro a Third World leader deserving of equal treatment by the superpowers.

But the unfulfilled social revolution within Cuba and the world leadership role that Castro so badly wanted unraveled in 1989 as the Soviet Union began to disintegrate and finally collapsed two years later. Without its benefactor, the Cuban economy was hard hit, and Castro struggled to maintain the social programs he had instituted. Despite all the adversity and with his charisma lacking its confident twinkle, still the seventy-one-year-old Fidel Castro promised to stay the course.

The calamity of the 1990s prompted Castro to implement significant changes in Cuba, yet he continued many of his traditional policies. Cuba's dire economic circumstances in the 1990s forced Castro to abandon some of his socialist principles by permitting foreign capital to enter Cuba and repatriate profits; introducing market reforms that have enabled many Cubans to earn money for the acquisition of scarce consumer goods; and relying upon the charitable activities of the Roman Catholic Church to provide the social safety nets that the state can no longer supply. Still, he remains in control of the government apparatus, which refuses to tolerate political or social dissent. And Castro continues to blame the United States for all that has gone wrong in Cuba.

CHAPTER 7

Revolutions Against Dictatorships

Until the twentieth century, revolutions were usually fought against traditional regimes, in countries ruled by kings or emperors. Revolutions were thus considered to be a force of modernization, overthrowing the political systems of the past. However, since 1910, revolutions have acted against a new form of government, the modernizing dictatorship. Often (but not always) founded by military officers, modern dictatorships came to power promising rapid economic development and efficient, technically trained management. Yet as noted in Goldstone's essay in Chapter 3, such regimes not only can fail to deliver on promises of development, but they can also become corrupt, and dependent on foreign support. When they do so, even modernizing dictatorships—like their traditional predecessors—can be vulnerable to revolution. This chapter examines the overthrow of dictators in Mexico (1911), Nicaragua (1979), Iran (1979), and the Philippines (1986).

The Mexican Revolution

WALTER L. GOLDFRANK

The Mexican Revolution, begun in 1910 and culminating in the land reforms of 1934–1940, has a colorful and fascinating cast of characters: the president of Mexico from 1876 to 1911, Porfirio Díaz, who ruled Mexico with a combination of *"pan y palo"* ("bread and a club"); the peasant leader Zapata and the bandit leader Pancho Villa, both of whom led revolutionary armies; the moderate Madero, who raised the first challenge to Díaz; the counter-revolutionary general Huerta, who attempted to reestablish a conservative regime after Díaz's fall; the Constitutionalist generals Carranza and Obregón, whose victory sealed the success of the revolution; and the reforming president Cárdenas, whose land reforms helped fulfill the revolution's promise.

Yet behind the personal victories and tragedies of these historic figures lay complex structural relationships that shaped Mexican history, relationships between Mexico and the international states system, between the Porfirian state and Mexican elites, and between landlords and peasants. In this essay, Goldfrank analyzes these structural relationships and the ways they combined to create a revolutionary situation in early twentieth-century Mexico.

For a long time the Mexican revolution has fascinated lay persons and engaged scholars from different disciplines and many countries. Numerous confusions surround its interpretation. For the most part, attention has been focused on several aspects: on the heroes and villains of the violent struggles of 1910–1920; on the reorganization and reforms instituted by President Lázaro Cárdenas (1934–1940); on the so-called economic miracle of the decades since then (Gross Domestic Product averaged a 6.5% annual increase from 1940 to 1970); and on the victims of that miracle, the children of Sánchez in the cities and their compatriots in the countryside. Yet the great transformation of Mexico began well before 1910, in the last third of the nineteenth century. While not ignoring the dramatic years of armed struggle nor the remarkable changes that have occurred since, this essay concentrates rather on the earlier time. It attempts to account primarily for the outbreak and character of the revolution which, in the long view of the last hundred years, appears to have decisively enhanced Mexican national autonomy, economic growth, and, to a lesser extent, the well-being of the rural and urban workers. Yet these "successes" can be, and typically are, exaggerated: Mexican autonomy is gravely restricted by the country's dependent position in the world economy; Mexican economic growth has greatly profited foreign corporations, left the state with a large foreign debt, and owed much to Mexico's proximity to the U.S.; and the reforms alleged to benefit the working class have neither halted the trend toward increased inequality nor substantially affected a large number of so-called "marginal" persons, serving, rather, as a means of social control.

TOWARD A STRUCTURAL EXPLANATION
OF THE MEXICAN REVOLUTION

To account for the Mexican Revolution, we need a conception that brings together elements which by themselves are insufficient conditions. That is, "x," "y," and "z" may be necessary conditions but will not be sufficient conditions unless they occur simultaneously or in a particular sequence. Substantively, we need to identify those conditions in a way that goes beyond the uniqueness of the particular Mexican case (rendering the Mexican revolution comparable with others). But we need to avoid going so far beyond it as to reduce it to an instance of "collective violence," irregular change of regime, or rebellious movement.

Four conditions appear to be necessary and sufficient, although as these conditions interact and overlap with one another, it is difficult to say exactly where one leaves off and another begins. For any particular national society, they are: (1) a tolerant or permissive world context; (2) a severe political crisis paralyzing the administrative and coercive capacities of the state; (3) widespread rural rebellion; and (4) dissident elite political movements.

Abridged from "Theories of Revolution and Revolution Without Theory: The Case of Mexico" by Walter Goldfrank, originally published in Theory and Society, *vol. 7, pp. 135–65 (1979). Reprinted with the permission of Elsevier Science Publishers, B.V., Amsterdam.*

WORLD CONTEXT

In her work on the major social revolutions in France, Russia, and China, Skocpol has made the case explicitly for the second and third conditions while treating the first and fourth in the course of analyzing outcomes. She has fully appreciated the role of international competition in spurring states to undertake politically difficult modernizing efforts and directly in bringing on potentially revolutionary crises. Perhaps because the cases she has treated are all states with great power ambitions if not great power results, she does not explicitly raise as a causal necessity favorable configurations of the world system as a whole and of the immediate international context. As one moves toward the present temporally and toward the periphery of the world system spatially, this condition becomes increasingly critical.

In the case of lesser and/or more peripheral states, the world system variables assume great importance. The successful independence movements in Latin America in the early nineteenth century reflected the ascent of Great Britain to world hegemony and the decline of Spain, perhaps more than any internal changes. The Cuban revolution depended at first on the division of opinion within the U.S. and later on Cold War rivalry to sustain its momentum. And the Vietnamese revolution was in part clearly a creation of great power configurations: the displacement of the French by the Japanese and the former's attempt to reestablish sovereignty; the U.S. effort to stop the spread of communism; and the Soviet and Chinese capacities to thwart that effort.

In general terms it is sufficient to reduce the variety of favorable world contexts to a single formula. Provisionally, several possibilities can be suggested. First, when the cat's away, the mice will play: the preoccupation of major powers in war or serious internal difficulty increases the likelihood of revolution. This holds both in a general sense for the world system as a whole, and in its specific application to instances of revolution in societies dominated by a single power. Second, when major powers balance one another, especially if that balance is antagonistic, the likelihood of revolution is increased. Third, if rebel movements receive greater outside support than their enemies, the likelihood of revolution is increased. (At the same time, it is worth noting that "outside intervention" in support of the old order may deepen and further the revolutionary process if it comes too little or too late.)

What was the favorable world situation that helped to cause the Mexican revolution? First, the changing balance of world power in the Caribbean region made it progressively less possible for Mexico to continue the diplomatic balancing act of playing off European versus U.S. interests. The U.S. had invested heavily in Mexico, where in 1911, 45.5 percent of U.S. (compared to 5.5 percent of Europe's) foreign investments were. This had two principal consequences: it meant that diplomatic pressure from the U.S. could put the Díaz government in a bind, since it owed its financial prospects to foreign investors but its political support to increasingly nationalistic Mexicans. And it also meant that internal U.S. politics would make a greater difference to Mexico than before.

Second is the shape of U.S. politics in the critical years from 1910–1913. This was a period of domestic realignments in the U.S., such that no clear policy emerged toward Mexico and the initial rebellions. U.S. opinion ranged from the conservatism of most foreign investors to the openly anarchist and socialist sympathies of the more radical workers. At the top, the Republican president faced a Democratic congress in 1911 and 1912, as well as the division in his own party that resulted in Theodore Roosevelt's Bull Moose campaign. Both before and after 1910 domestic political considerations restrained Taft from vigorously suppressing rebels north of the border, as did hopes for pressuring Díaz into reorienting his policies in a more pro-U.S. direction. With the election of Wilson in 1912 came a period of confusion, as the new president preached popular sovereignty and free elections for Mexico while the holdover ambassador in Mexico City abetted the right-wing movement to overthrow the government of Madero.

Third, the increasing U.S. involvement in World War I left Mexico alone for a time. By then the U.S. had settled on the eventual winning side, so that when it helped Obregón mop up pockets of resistance in 1919–1920, the way was clear for renewing U.S. influence and thwarting for almost twenty years—until the Great Depression gave Cárdenas an opening—much of the nationalist impulse of the revolution.

It is not accidental that many other political changes, as well as the Mexican revolution, occurred in the period around World War I, when the great powers were fighting one another: revolution from above in Turkey, leftward movement in Argentina and Uruguay, a spurt of nationalism in India, and of course the beginnings of revolution in Russia and China. But this general world context had to be complemented by a favorable situation in the United States. Otherwise, the Díaz regime might have been more firmly supported in its last days and an orderly succession worked out. Otherwise, sanctuary and arms supplies would have been denied insurgents at several critical junctures. Otherwise, armed intervention could have thwarted the continuation of the revolutionary process. And otherwise, Mexican state bureaucrats and private capitalists would not today share so strongly in the control of Mexico's political economy.

Political Crisis

A second necessary condition of revolution is the breakdown of the administrative and coercive capacities of the state in a political crisis—a revolutionary "situation." For France in 1788–1789 the crisis came with the bankruptcy of the royal treasury and the convening of the Estates General; for Russia in 1917 it was the Tsarist government's failure at war; for China in 1911 it was the Manchu autocracy's inability to manage major reforms without losing control to regional gentry cliques. Each of these crises was determined by a significant disjunction between state and the upper classes.

In Mexico, the rough picture is not dissimilar. The precipitating trigger was the failure of the government to snuff out quickly the initial Madero insurgency (itself a typical Latin American *pronunciamiento*). This failure occurred in the context of a succession crisis, as Díaz himself was eighty years old in 1910, and had been unable through the recently created institution of the vice-presidency to pave the way for a successor. The crisis deepened after Madero took over the presidency in 1912, as he was unable to carry out promised reforms with an army and civil administration held over from the Porfiriato, yet from the perspective of many powerful groups was too open to such reforms and the loss of social power it would entail for them.

What brought the Mexican state to such a critical passage was a set of contradictions inherent in the political economy of the Porfiriato as it developed. The most serious was the relationship of the state to elite groups, though also grave were the political practices strengthening Díaz's personal rule and the difficulties of representing the Mexican nation while relying heavily on foreign capital.

Díaz's rise to power coincided with the great worldwide expansion of industrial capitalism in the last quarter of the nineteenth century, as the competitive search for markets, materials, and investment outlets sent European and U.S. firms into new territories and invigorated their activities in old ones. Mexico in this period experienced rapid growth in mining, commercial agriculture, and manufacturing for the national market. In this economic context, three social groups shared power. There were first the older estate-owners who relied on indebted resident laborers to turn a small profit; Catholic in religion, conservative in politics, this group was conciliated by Díaz but never allowed to exercise influence at the national level. The most important group was the entrepreneurial bourgeoisie, a heterogeneous lot including promoters, import-export merchants, bankers, estate owners who modernized their operations (using more machinery and more wage-labor), and manufacturers. Varied in ethnic origins and regional loyalties, oriented to diverse markets, increasingly differentiated as the economy became more complex, and content with the state's protection of property, these "modern" bourgeois had little incentive to organize as a class, beyond distinct interest groups. The third important group was the political machine of Díaz: governors, generals, local bosses, mostly *mestizo,* socially excluded, culturally distinct.

Before the turn of the century and increasingly after that time, the second group—particularly those with extensive foreign connections—came to dominate economic policy. They also endeavored to institutionalize their future control over Mexico by insisting on a vice-presidency and by forming a political party. Their political rivals, especially in the third group, fought back, with Díaz playing the one off against the other. The ruler in fact became "indispensable," as he feared armed foreign intervention if he handed the government over to nationalistic *mestizo* politicians and even greater foreign economic dominance (and possibly open revolt) if he entrusted the future to the unpopular bourgeoisie. The disjunction between state and ruling class that was a source of leverage for the regime in its heyday weakened it severely in the crisis.

Díaz's political methods were likewise successful in the short run but disastrous in the long run. Fearing the military, he juggled commands, reduced the budget (also helpful for impressing foreign investors), and allowed corruption to flourish; the result was a federal army unable to quickly suppress the Madero insurgency. In civil politics, he destroyed the potentially self-correcting liberal institutions (free speech and press, independent judiciary, meaningful legislative assemblies and elections) that elsewhere regulated conflict within ruling groups and helped them to absorb popular demands—in that period of Latin America typically originating among the urban middle strata. A personal political machine was enhanced at the expense of liberal institutions, while the ideology of liberalism was paid lip service. Thus it is not accidental that the Madero insurgency began as an electoral campaign for the presidency, and that demands for reinvigoration of liberal institutions were the most important points in his program. In addition to concentrating power in his own person, Díaz carried the techniques of discrediting potential rivals to such a point that no strong-man successor was available.

Finally, the Mexican state was weakened by its compromises with foreign capital and foreign governments, particularly the U.S., at a time when business rivalry, imperialist penetration, and the use of U.S. personnel in managerial and highly skilled occupations were generating increasingly potent nationalist interests and sentiments. A number of diplomatic incidents from 1907 to 1910 increased tensions, incurring Washington's displeasure with the Díaz regime. As Díaz was also favoring a British oil firm in its competition inside Mexico with U.S. firms, the U.S. government was even less friendly to him. In the end, Díaz's diplomatic balancing act—attempting to maintain diversified dependence—failed. As the Madero insurgency gathered momentum (in large part from the participation of refugees and sympathizers in Texas), the U.S. government did not move vigorously to help suppress it. Díaz then chose to resign rather than invite a protracted struggle that risked armed intervention by the U.S.

WIDESPREAD RURAL REBELLION

However, a political-administrative crisis and a favorable world context are insufficient conditions for revolution. Rural rebellion is a third necessary condition, interacting with the previous ones. In the French and Russian cases peasant revolts facilitated by the crumbling of royal power furthered its collapse; in the Chinese case the Communist Party was able to mobilize peasant rebellion faster than the Nationalist regime could squash it. In Mexico the rural revolt was neither so widespread as in France or Russia nor so nationally organized and ideologically sophisticated as in China. This relative weakness contributed to the fact that the Mexican revolution was relatively less successful in removing the landed upper class from power. But as in the other cases, so in Mexico it was the country people who fueled the revolutionary process, pushing would-be reformers further than they would otherwise have gone, and preventing the landed class from playing an important role in stabilizing elite coalitions at the national level.

The heterogeneity of rural Mexico increased greatly during the period preceding the revolution. Thus several distinctive rural rebellions accounted for the greater part of revolutionary participation, and the regions and groups that were relatively quiet also showed considerable differences in the nature of cultivation, the organization of labor, and the extent and kind of political organization. In general terms, it can be said that *rural rebellion was strongest where two conditions obtained simultaneously: first, where the newly dynamic capitalist (though not exclusively export) agriculture had most deeply penetrated; second, where the rural labor force enjoyed what Wolf terms "tactical mobility"—meaning village organization and/or relative autonomy from supervision and/or geographical-military advantages.* [See the essay by Wolf in this volume.—Ed.]

Table 1 presents both the array of centers of rural revolt and instances where only one of or neither of the necessary conditions obtained. Yet this level of analytical abstraction is insufficient for capturing important differences among the rebel groups, differences that severely limited their capacity for concerted, as opposed to parallel, political action.

In the thirty years before the revolution, capitalism spread over the Mexican countryside unevenly and in different forms. In the Yucatán, *henequen* plantations were established to grow the raw materials for binding wheat in the U.S. and Canada. Much of the indigenous Mayan population was pushed or fled further and further into the jungle, so that the labor force had to be partly imported from other parts of Mexico, and most notably from the northwestern state of Sonora where other indigenous groups, the Yaqui and Mayo, were defeated by the federal army as part of a land grab. The heterogeneous, brutally exploited plantation workers took no part in the revolutionary events, while a Constitutionalist army took

Table 1   Conditions of the Rural Labor Force in Selected Regions of Mexico, c. 1911

NEW CAPITALIST PENETRATION	TACTICAL MOBILITY	
	HIGH	*LOW*
HIGH	Chihuahua Sonora Morelos	Yucatán
LOW	Oaxaca	Central plateau haciendas

over the state in 1915 and used *henequen* revenues to help finance the struggle against the rural revolutionaries from Morelos and from the North.

In Oaxaca, the peasantry was notably quiet during the revolution. In this case, however, it was more because modern agricultural capitalism had not penetrated the state, and less due to the weakness of the cultivators' organizational and geographical potential for political action. Estate owners were less prominent in the state's political elite, and they encroached little on the lands of Mixtec and Zapotec peasants after 1880. Sugar was grown in small quantities by old methods; where coffee was introduced it was primarily grown by small scale producers.

The third non-revolutionary combination of variables includes neither significant capitalist transformation of agriculture or large degrees of peasant autonomy, organization, and military-geographic potential. This combination describes a large portion of the central Mexican plateau. In most of this region, the conventional *hacienda* predominated with its well known underutilization of land and technology and over exploitation of labor. While scattered estates went over to intensive cultivation of the century plant (a cactus yielding juices fermented into *pulque,* an alcoholic beverage popular with the demoralized urban poor) or to dairying, the majority took advantage of favorable land legislation to expand their holdings without measurably increasing production. One result was that the cultivation of food crops lagged behind the growth in agriculture for export and for domestic processing, not to mention a considerable growth in population. Another result was to incorporate the majority of the formerly autonomous peasant communities into the *hacienda,* and to encourage migration out of the region. Residents, perpetually indebted peons (*acasillados*), comprised the stable labor force, which was supplemented at peak seasons by day laborers and migrants. Probably because they enjoyed the advantage of job security and suffered the disadvantage of close supervision, the resident estate laborers were notably absent from revolutionary participation.

Rural rebellion did arise where both new capitalist thrusts occurred and for one or another reason large numbers of workers were tactically mobile. But the three principal loci of revolt differed greatly from one another, both in the developing patterns of capitalist agriculture and in the organizational structure and capacity of the working population. In Sonora and some others parts of Northern Mexico, small to medium scale commercial farmers rallied against discriminatory taxation, high freight rates on the foreign-controlled railroads, and preferential treatment of U.S. firms and individuals in land deals. The Sonoran rebels were also able to recruit among the defeated Yaqui and Mayo Indians whose lands had been distributed to large-scale agricultural operations and whose compatriots had been deported to the *henequen* plantations. This combination, with provincial professionals as well as commercial farmers in the lead and recently subjugated peasant cultivators in the ranks, readily lent itself to the standard military organization of companies and battalions. Remote from Mexico City, separated from the Northern desert plateau by the Sierra Madre, and bordering on the U.S. so that arms could be rather easily acquired, Sonora was a stronghold of rebellion throughout the decade, once the political changes following Díaz's fall weakened the pre-existing apparatus of coercion. On the other hand, the Sonoran rebels were led by elements of the middle strata who allied themselves with the moderate Constitutionalists after 1914 to defeat the more plebeian armies of Villa and Zapata. They also parlayed their military success into control of the Mexican presidency until the nineteen-thirties.

In other parts of the Mexican North, particularly Chihuahua, capitalist agriculture expanded mainly in cattle ranching, although cotton production and the cultivation of India rubber (*guayule*) were also important. Debt peonage was on the wane in the North, with share-cropping, cash rentals, and wage labor becoming common. The mining and railroad booms stimulated food production for local and export markets. The giant ranches provided spectacular examples of *latifundismo* yet were increasingly modern enterprises well suited to the terrain. Their owners controlled local and state politics, making life difficult for cultivators. They employed hundreds of cowboys — often irregularly employed — and sustained the uncertain livelihood of numerous illegal operators, involved in smuggling, banditry, and cattle rustling. When in 1909 the Northern Mexican economy was hurt as a consequence of a downturn in the U.S., workers returned from across the border only to find stagnation in mining and then drought in agriculture. They were available to join the relatively rootless proto-cavalrymen who eventually formed the core of Villa's army, after first providing the forces that enabled Madero to oust Díaz. Yet the background that made this popular cavalry strong, the development of fierce independence and equestrian skill, was also a limitation: their contempt for settled cultivators made them very parochial in their land policy and their exclusion from civic life rendered them politically inept, unable to consolidate their military gains.

The third major locus of rural rebellion was Morelos, a small state strategically located over the mountains from the capital city. There — and in adjacent portions of Guerrero, Mexico, and Puebla, as well as non-contiguous places like Huaesteca — independent villagers whose livelihoods were being squeezed by the expansion of newly capitalized *haciendas* spearheaded rural rebellion. In Morelos it was the capitalization of sugar cultivation after 1880 that set in motion the squeeze on the villagers. In order to pay for new milling machinery and to reach markets that the railroads put within reach, the *haciendas* that had formerly coexisted with peasant production came utterly to dominate it. Some villagers lost lands and water, others (15% of the state's total) disappeared completely. Villagers turned to stock raising in the mountains, to sharecropping the worst hacienda lands, to day labor in contracted gangs, even to the hated alternative of becoming resident peons. Increased competitive pressure (from beet sugar and other regions) after 1900 pushed the planters to higher investment and greater expansion at the villagers' expense, but the Madero insurgency in the North furnished the occasion for a counter-attack by the villagers. Protected by the mountains, they drew upon a tradition of rebellion stretching back almost a century to the independence war against Spain and organized into a classic guerrilla army defending its homeland. Their pressure on Mexico City helped Madero win in 1911, and when reforms were slow to come, they resumed armed struggle for the better part of a decade while carrying out their own agrarian reform in between extermination campaigns against them. But the village organization that gave their backward-looking egalitarian idealism its awesome tenacity also entailed a localistic orientation that gravely impaired their capacity for political action at the national level. The Zapatistas made agrarian reform a national priority but were shut out of the victorious coalition that would eventually, haltingly, carry it out.

Together these three sorts of rural rebellion made a moderate stabilization impossible, whether under the reformist liberal Madero or the more conservative but by no means reactionary Huerta. From the standpoint of comparative analysis, however, two points deserve emphasis. First, the rural rebellion in Mexico was not a nationwide conflagration, a general rising against landlords or peonage or "feudal" forms of surplus extraction. Except for a few localities, irreversible *de facto* land reform did not occur as in revolutionary France or Russia until the government enacted and enforced it. Second, the heterogeneity of the rural rebels, each set responding to a different form of capitalist penetration, mirrored the heterogeneity of the bourgeoisie. If the latter were unable to agree on programs and policies because of the material, cultural, and regional differences and the absence of mediating institutions at the national level, so the rural workers failed to make a coherent bid for political power. And no party, like the communists in China, came along to do it with and for them.

DISSIDENT POLITICAL MOVEMENTS

The fourth necessary condition for revolution is the existence of dissident urban political groups capable of reshaping the state to achieve or hasten modernizing transformations and to increase its competitive standing in the world system. Dissident movements need not predate administrative breakdown and political crisis, though like the subversive moralists of pre-revolutionary France or the agitational parties of pre-revolutionary Russia they may contribute to such crisis. Nor need dissident groups link up in an organized way with peasant rebellion, as the Chinese Communist Party did. In varying degrees such groups arise and grow as a logical consequence of a revolutionary conjuncture, given the unusual opportunity. And since the victors typically write their own histories, we must be wary of their claims to have cleared their own paths to success.

In the Mexican case, three broad movements can be identified. First, several "precursor" movements came into existence after the turn of the century, spreading conventional liberal ideas at times tinged with anarchism and/or labor grievances. Second, Madero's presidential campaign in 1910 built on the network of liberal "clubs" that had formed in many provincial cities. Finally, the Constitutionalist movement arose to resist Huerta's government after his coup ousting Madero in 1913, then built a coalition whose armies defeated Villa and Zapata, wrote a new constitution in 1917, and became the new government. The first two movements preceded and contributed to the revolutionary conjuncture, while the third emerged from it. The first two were utterly normal political phenomena, different in local detail from protest movements and electoral campaigns elsewhere but clearly part of ordinary politics; their causal necessity can easily be overemphasized. The third was a logical outcome of governmental breakdown at the national level and of widespread rural rebellion, and it insured that neither anarchy nor a return to the *status quo ante* would result.

The "precursors" of the Mexican revolution paralleled three kinds of protest movements current in that era, in varying degrees, in the rest of the Americas, movements that either succeeded peacefully or were absorbed, deflected, and repressed elsewhere. They included civic and electoral reform spearheaded by the professional middle class, agrarian populism, and syndicalist labor agitation. Within them dissident intellectuals formulated overlapping critiques of the regime, focusing on the restoration of constitutionally guaranteed individual and community freedom, an end of favoritism to foreigners, and the elimination of labor abuses. Besides preparing the ground for Madero's electoral challenge in 1910, these movements had the important consequences of increasing the political awareness and abilities of the Mexican refugee communities in South Texas and generating support for reform in Mexico among liberals and the left in the United States generally.

Madero's presidential campaign and subsequent insurrection is conventionally regarded as the beginning of *the Revolution*. While such an understanding makes political sense for the inheritors of Madero's mantle, it misdirects analysis by uncritically taking over the Spanish "revolución" (= armed overthrow). Madero's ascent to the presidency was a temporary solution to the succession crisis of the Díaz regime, orchestrated by high officials so as to defuse incipient local rebellions by instituting an interim presidency and allowing free elections. The solution was temporary because the political freedoms of the Madero presidency facilitated the exacerbation of class conflicts and further weakened the state. Important elements of the old order were entrenched in the military and civilian bureaucracies where they first thwarted implementation of change that would satisfy popular demands. They then carried out the coup under Huerta that damaged the state beyond rescue, provoked rural rebellion and brought forth the dissident movement that would ultimately consolidate a revolutionary outcome, the Constitutionalists.

The Constitutionalists, so called because of their aim to undo the illegal coup against the duly elected Madero, began as a group of provincial landowners and professionals concentrated in the North. They formed a civilian cabinet under the leadership of their "first chief" Carranza, a minor official under Díaz and a state governor under Madero, and they gathered an army comprised of defecting federal troops and rebel groups previously loyal to Madero. Relying first on the middle class agrarians led by Obregón and then on an alliance with urban workers, they put together an army which defeated Villa and contained Zapata. But in the course of the struggle, the civilian liberals were pushed to the side, as more radical elements dominated their army, and, after elections in the provinces they controlled, dominated the 1917 constitutional convention as well. Obregón's assumption of the presidency in 1920 symbolized the shift from liberalism to populism, and the state he and his successors reconstituted fits well the model of the populist state.

Aspects of the revolutionary outcome—an end to debt peonage, the beginning of serious though insufficient land reform, the legal foundation for nationalizing foreign mineral holdings, improvement in the protection and bargaining power of labor—had been discussed before 1910 by dissidents and reformers, but no movement was able consciously to guide the revolutionary process. The "precursor" movements and Madero's electoral campaign and insurrection helped to make a revolutionary conjuncture; the Constitutionalists were finally able to reconstruct the state, though by no means with overwhelming popular support. True, their victory entailed some concessions to the radical demands represented in armed struggle by these elements of the rural poor who rebelled (and Morelos was the first state to see sizeable land reform), but that victory more importantly required the military defeat of those very forces. That the Mexican revolution did not go further to the left is in part explained by the fact that the Constitutionalists made promises to the masses but unlike the Russian or Chinese communists did not develop or practice an ideology requiring cadre self-discipline and urging mass participation.

Analytically, we can suggest that a dissident movement capable of reorganizing the state and restoring order, which the Villistas and Zapatistas were unable to do when militarily they held the upper hand, is a necessary condition for a revolutionary outcome: otherwise, anarchy and/or reversion will occur. Yet such a movement seems in the Mexican case to follow upon the fulfillment of the other three necessary conditions and thus ought to be accorded a less independent causal status.

CONCLUSION

The above analysis identified four conditions as necessary and sufficient for revolution in general and the Mexican revolution in particular: a favorable world context, an administrative and coercive crisis of the state, widespread rural rebellion, and dissident elite movement(s). The first three interact to produce a revolutionary situation; the fourth, given the near-automatic existence of alternative contenders, emerges to effect political and social transformation after military superiority is proved.

The Mexican Revolution hastened the elimination of the reactionary elements of the landed class from national political influence, and led to the establishment of new state machinery strong enough to direct the economy and to regulate class conflict. Yet while the new revolutionary state carried out land reforms in the 1940s, and presided over several decades of strong economic growth from the 1940s and the 1970s, it was unable to eliminate severe inequality or considerable rural poverty. And although the new state machinery incorporated peasants and workers in state organizations, the political leadership did not open the government to democratic control until 2001. The mixed legacy of the Revolution—economic growth but with continuing poverty and inequality, and populism but without full democracy—shapes Mexico's politics and economy to this day.

The Nicaraguan Revolution

THOMAS W. WALKER

The decade of the 1980s was not the first in which the United States fought rebellion in Central America. From 1927 to 1933, U.S. marines occupied Nicaragua to defend the government against a peasant insurrection led by Augusto Sandino. Sandino's guerrillas battled the United States to a standstill, and peace came only when the United States promised to withdraw all troops. However, before withdrawing, the United States established and trained a Nicaraguan National Guard. In 1934 the leader of the Guard, Anastasio Somoza Garcia, arranged the assassination of Sandino.

In 1936 he overthrew the existing president and arranged his own election as president of Nicaragua, beginning the forty-three-year rule of the Somoza family: Anastasio Somoza Garcia (in power 1936–1956) and his sons Luis Somoza Debayle (in power 1957–1967) and Anastasio Somoza Debayle (in power 1967–1979).

The Somozas' rule came to an end in 1979 as a consequence of international pressures, elite opposition, and popular revolts. International pressures came from the United States, which, under President Carter's human rights policy, forced Somoza to ease the repression aimed at his opponents, and from the International Monetary Fund, which forced Somoza to devalue Nicaragua's currency and institute economic reforms. Elite opposition grew from the Somozas' corruption and from Anastasio Somoza Debayle's exclusion of the elites from even their traditionally modest role in Nicaraguan politics. The Sandinista Front for National Liberation (known by its Spanish initials FSLN) organized neighborhood defense committees in the cities and guerrilla units in the countryside to lead the popular revolt. In the following essay, Thomas Walker describes the economic and political background to the revolution. The outcome is examined by John Foran and Jeff Goodwin in Chapter 4.

Located at the geographic center of Central America, with Honduras to the north and Costa Rica to the south, Nicaragua is the largest country in the region. Even so, its 57,143 square miles (148,000 square kilometers) of surface make it only slightly larger than the state of Iowa. Its population of about 2.5 million is slightly smaller than Iowa's 2.8 million. Nevertheless, Nicaragua is an extremely interesting and unique country with an importance that far exceeds its size. Although there have been many revolts and coups d'etat in Latin America, Nicaragua is one of only a handful of Latin American countries to have experienced a real social revolution, by which I mean a rapid process of change in social and economic as well as political structures.

THE ECONOMIC BACKGROUND

There is a profound difference between what is loosely called free enterprise or capitalism in the United States and its counterpart in Latin America. Capitalism in the United States coexists with relatively high levels of social justice precisely because it is dependent on the bulk of the American people as consumers. Most of what U.S. industry produces is consumed in the United States. The economic system, therefore, would collapse if the majority of citizens were exploited to the extent that they could no longer consume at relatively high levels. Quite the opposite is true in Latin America, where the so-called "capitalist" economics are overwhelmingly externally oriented, placing great emphasis on the production of products for export. Under these dependent capitalist systems the common citizen is im-

From Nicaragua: The Land Sandino *by Thomas W. Walker; excerpts reprinted with permission of the publisher, Copyright © 1981 Westview Press.*

portant as a cheap and easily exploitable source of labor rather than as a consumer. Therefore, there is little or no economic incentive for the privileged classes that dominate most Latin American governments to make the sacrifices necessary to improve the conditions of the majority of the people.

While prerevolutionary Nicaragua was not at all unusual as an example of a society distorted by dependent capitalism, it was nevertheless an exceptionally and strikingly tragic case. Unlike certain other countries—such as Bolivia, where natural resources are in relatively short supply—Nicaragua is, and always has been, a land of impressive economic potential. The population / land ratio is very favorable. Not only is Nicaragua the largest of the five Central American countries, it is the least densely populated, with fewer than 20 persons per square kilometer as opposed to 45 for the region as a whole and approximately 210 for El Salvador. The land itself is rich and varied, with different soil, climatological, and altitude characteristics suitable for the production of a wide variety of crops and livestock. The country's many rivers and volcanoes offer easily exploitable sources of both hydroelectric and geothermal energy, and internal waterways facilitate inexpensive domestic transportation and present the possibility of exploitation as part of some future transoceanic-waterway. Nicaragua has both Caribbean and Pacific coastlines, providing direct access not only to the food and mineral resources of the seas but also to the major markets of the world. The country has significant timber resources—from pine forests in the highlands to hardwood stands in the lowland tropics. Among the known mineral assets are silver and, particularly, gold. Finally, the Nicaraguan people, with their relatively homogeneous culture and language and their indomitable spirit and *joie de vivre,* are themselves a very important national asset.

The best way to understand the inequities of the Nicaraguan economic system is to examine its historical roots. Nicaraguan economic history prior to the Sandinista Revolution is divisible into four distinct time spans: (1) the colonial period, from the 1520s to the 1820s; (2) the first half century of independence, from the 1820s through the 1870s; (3) the period of primitive dependent capitalism, from the late 1870s through the 1940s; and (4) the rise of modern dependent capitalism, from the 1950s through the 1970s.

THE COLONIAL ECONOMY

When the Spaniards arrived in western Nicaragua in the early sixteenth century they found a relatively advanced agrarian society. The approximately one million native inhabitants of the region—the descendants of migrants from the Mayan and Aztec civilizations to the north—lived in villages and cities ranging in population from a few hundred to tens of thousands. This was a feudal society, with chiefs, subchiefs, and commoners, in which tribute flowed from the lowly to the lofty. However, land was held collectively and each inhabitant of the villages and cities had access to a designated plot nearby. The rich soils of the region yielded agricultural products in abundance ranging from corn, cassava, and chili to beans, tobacco, and a variety of vegetables. Each population center had one or more local markets at which agricultural products were sold. Though periodic crop failure and intertribal warfare undoubtedly inflicted occasional acute hardship, the economy in general was relatively self-sufficient and self-contained. The market system, intraregional trade, and general access to rich agricultural lands provided the material wherewithal for the satisfaction of basic human needs.

The Spanish conquest had an immediate and devastating impact on this economic system. Superimposing themselves on the existing feudal structure, the *conquistadores* demanded tribute in gold and, when that was depleted, Indian slaves. Within a few decades the near total destruction of the native population through death by contact with European diseases and the export of slaves created a severe manpower shortage that all but destroyed the labor-intensive agricultural base of the region's economy. To be sure, some lands remained under intensive cultivation throughout the colonial period, providing some export products such as corn and cacao and food to meet the region's much reduced internal demand. But, for the most part, the rich lands of Nicaragua reverted to jungle or were exploited for the raising of cattle to produce hides, tallow, and salted meat for sale to other colonies.

In a few decades, therefore, the economy had become essentially externally oriented. In addition to the sale of corn, cacao, and cattle products, the tiny Spanish elite accrued wealth through the exploitation of forest products, shipbuilding, and intermittent gold mining—all to meet external rather than internal demands. The under-population of the colony and the concentration of wealth in the hands of the privileged classes made Nicaragua a prime target for attacks by pirates from England and elsewhere in Europe, further contributing to the region's status as a colonial backwater. The process of underdevelopment had begun.

THE FIRST HALF CENTURY OF INDEPENDENCE

The partial interruption of foreign dominance resulting from the disintegration and eventual collapse of Spanish colonial rule in the early nineteenth century was reflected in important changes in the Nicaraguan economic system. It is true that British traders were quick to provide the landed elite with an outlet for their traditional export products, but the relative political anarchy and international isolation of the first half century of independence also encouraged the growth of a number of other types of economic activity. There was a rapid growth in the number of self-sufficient peasant farms or *huertas*. A fragile, indigenous marketing system was reestablished. And, in the villages and cities, various types of cottage industry began to develop.

For most of the Nicaraguan people this economic system, though certainly not highly developed, was fairly benign. Although he may have been exaggerating slightly, one observer writing in the early 1870s noted that "peonage such as is seen in Mexico and various parts of Spanish America does not exist in Nicaragua. . . . Any citizen whatever can set himself up on a piece of open land . . . to cultivate plantain and corn."

PRIMITIVE DEPENDENT CAPITALISM

The relative isolation of Nicaragua and the gradual development of an internally oriented economy were abruptly interrupted by the coffee boom that hit Central America in the late 1800s. Coffee was probably introduced into the country as an exotic curiosity in the first quarter of the nineteenth century. By 1848 it was being produced commercially on a small scale. In the early 1850s it was a favorite beverage of the twenty thousand or so foreign passengers each month who utilized Cornelius Vanderbilt's Accessory Transit Company route across Nicaragua on their way to California. But it was not until the 1870s that coffee really came into its own. By then the international demand was so strong that the country's ruling elite was motivated to monopolize and redirect much of Nicaragua's productive capacity toward the cultivation of that one export product.

Two factors of crucial importance to the production of coffee are fertile land in the right climatological setting and a large, essentially unskilled work force that can be called upon to offer its services for a few months during the harvest season. In Nicaragua in the early 1870s both were in short supply. The coffee culture had already moved into most of the exploitable lands around Managua, and other promising lands in the northern highlands were occupied by independent peasants and members of Indian communes engaged in traditional subsistence farming. And as the rural masses had access to their own land, there was no pool of vulnerable and easily exploitable peons.

The traditional elite solved both of these problems with ingenuity and speed. In the late 1870s and 1880s they took the land they coveted and created the work force they needed through a combination of chicanery, violence, and self-serving legislation. Individual squatter farmers and Indians working the land through communal arrangements were extremely vulnerable to legal manipulation because, in most cases, these people held rights to the land by tradition rather than by legal title. For several decades the agrarian elite had attempted, through legislation, to abolish communal and squatter landholdings. In 1877, under the presidency of Conservative Pedro Joaquín Chamorro, an agrarian law was passed that outlawed communal holdings and gave individuals the right to buy "unoccupied" national lands. The resulting massive dislocation of Indian communal farmers and individual peasants led inevitably to the War of the Communeros in 1881 in the Pacific and north-central regions of Nicaragua. After a series of cruel battles in which as many as five thousand Indians may have been killed, the new order was imposed on the region. Coffee was free to expand into new land.

The laws that forced the small farmer off the land also helped create a vulnerable rural proletariat. To reinforce this phenomenon the elite-controlled governments also passed laws against "vagrancy" and the cultivation of plantain—the banana-like staple food of the peasants. Forced to buy staples at high prices in the plantation commissaries, many coffee workers had to rely on credit from these company stores. Before long they were trapped into a very effective system of debt peonage. In less than a decade, the self-sufficient peasantry of a large section of the country had been converted into a dependent and oppressed rural proletariat. Most rural Nicaraguans began to lead a life of insecurity, fluctuating between the good times of the coffee harvest, from November through February, and the hardship and unemployment of the *tiempo muerto* (dead period) between harvests.

The growth of the coffee culture also marked the birth of dependent capitalism in Nicaragua. Before this period the economy was based on traditional cattle ranching and subsistence peasant and communal farming. Neither involved a significant use of capital. Coffee, however, was different. First, years before the first harvest, the planter had to make a significant investment in preparing the land and planting and nurturing the seedlings. When the trees began to bear fruit, it was necessary to spend considerable sums of money on manpower and machinery. A large work force was needed for the handpicking of coffee berries, and more people and machinery were employed in weighing, pulping, drying, sorting, sacking, and transporting the product.

It is not surprising, then, that although some small farmers converted to coffee bean production, most of those who went into this new enterprise were large landholders, prosperous commercial speculators, and, in some cases, foreigners. The Conservative oligarchy used its control of the legislative process to pass the Subsidy Laws of 1879 and 1889, which gave planters of all nationalities cultivating more than five thousand trees a subsidy of five cents per tree. Among other things, these laws encouraged foreign colonists to seek their fortunes on the fertile slopes of the central highlands. With them came an infusion of new capital.

Once established as the cornerstone of the Nicaraguan economy, coffee held that position until the 1950s. This is not to say that other forms of agriculture were completely wiped out. Some farsighted peasants chose to flee the new coffee zones entirely, moving on to subsistence farming on land in other regions that were not yet coveted by the landed elite. In addition, the traditional precapitalist cattle *hacienda* (ranch) of the lowlands, though now less important, was by no means completely eclipsed. But overall, coffee was clearly the mainstay of the country's economy.

With the growth of the coffee industry, Nicaragua developed what is often loosely referred to as a "banana republic" economy—one based heavily on a single primary export product. Typically, the benefits of the system flowed heavily to a small domestic elite and its foreign trading partners. Taxes on coffee profits, which might have helped redistribute income to the impoverished majority, were virtually nonexistent. The common citizen was an abused instrument of production rather than a benefactor of the system. The Nicaraguan economy also became subject to periodic "booms" and "busts" produced by the fluctuation of the world price of its single product. In good times the economy grew and coffee planters imported luxury goods and machinery, invested money abroad, and educated their children in the United States and Europe. The first of the Somoza dictators received his U.S. education as a result of such a boom. In bad times, such as those following the onset of the 1929 Depression, coffee prices plummeted and the economy stagnated. Planters hunkered down, lived off savings and investments, and imported fewer luxury items and less machinery.

Typical also of the banana republic syndrome was the fact that throughout most of the period little effort was made by the governments of Nicaragua to see that the economy served the purpose of genuine national development. The notable exception to this rule was the regime of Liberal strongman José Santos Zelaya from 1893 to 1909. Zelaya had no real quarrel with laissez faire economics or with coffee. Indeed, he helped the coffee industry by opening up new lands and improving Nicaragua's transportation network. Nevertheless, he also emphasized education, brought fiscal responsibility to the government, created the rudiments of a modern administrative structure, and insisted on national economic self-determination. His refusal to concede to the United States canal rights that would have diminished the economic and political sovereignty of his country and his subsequent negotiation with other powers for a more equitable canal treaty contributed to the U.S. decision to encourage, and then reinforce militarily, the Conservative rebellion of 1909. After Zelaya, the Conservatives, and later the much-chastened Liberals, provided governments whose economic policies fit the banana republic model closely. Within a few years of their ascent to power, the Conservatives gave their U.S. protectors essentially the same canal treaty Zelaya had rejected. From then until the 1950s virtually no effort was made to alter Nicaragua's established role as a provider of a single primary product.

MODERN DEPENDENT CAPITALISM

The quarter century preceding the Revolution was a time of economic modernization and dependent "development." New products were added to Nicaragua's portfolio of exports, technology and technocrats became faddish, the government bureaucracy grew rapidly, expanding—at least on paper—into various social service areas and the gross national product grew in respectable spurts. But the benefits of this change and growth did not "trickle down" to most Nicaraguans. Their perilous standard of living remained essentially constant as the gap between them and the tiny middle and upper classes widened relentlessly.

One of the most obvious changes to occur during this period was the diversification of Nicaragua's exports. In addition to coffee and beef products, Nicaragua now exported significant quantities of cotton, sugar, bananas, wood, and seafood. The most important new product was cotton. The sharp increase in the world price of this raw material in the early 1950s, flowing out of heightened demand during the Korean War, motivated Nicaraguan planters and speculators to invest in cotton production in the Pacific lowlands. Nicaragua, which had exported only 379 metric tons of cotton in 1949, increased that figure to 43,971 metric tons in 1955. Eventually as much as 80 percent of the cultivated land on the Pacific coast was converted to cotton. Some cattle ranches became cotton plantations, but, as in the case of the coffee boom seven decades earlier, much of the land that went into the production of this new export product was appropriated in one way or another from peasant producers of grains and domestic staples. Once again independent farmers were transformed into a rootless rural proletariat in the name of "progress" and "development" for the privileged few.

Cotton, like coffee, was subject to cycles of boom and bust. The first period of bust began in 1956, three years after the end of the Korean War. Compared with coffee, cotton was a very capital-intensive activity. It required great investments of machinery, fertilizer, insecticides, and labor. In Nicaragua's case, cotton came to account for almost all of the tractors and harvesters, most of the irrigation systems, and more than three-fourths of the commercial fertilizer used in the country. Small-scale production of cotton was simply out of the question.

Another factor that affected the Nicaraguan economy in this period was the birth of the Alliance for Progress in the early 1960s. A U.S.-sponsored response to the revolutionary success of Fidel Castro in Cuba, the alliance was designed to bring about social and economic development in Latin America through politically moderate means. Enlightened reform from above would, it was hoped, defuse the "threat" of popular revolution from below. The Somozas and the traditional elite of Nicaragua found the idea of the alliance very appealing. Not that they were particularly concerned with its lofty objectives of social and economic justice. Rather, they saw it in more practical terms as a legitimizing device and a source of a variety of economic opportunities. In return for rather painless paper reforms and the creation of a modern social-service bureaucracy, they would receive increased foreign aid and technological assistance and have access to numerous new business opportunities.

Nicaragua in the 1960s was typified by a peculiar type of neopositivism reminiscent of Mexico in the days of Porfirio Díaz. Technology, foreign investment, and "development"—as defined in terms of growth in gross national product—were the new articles of faith. A group of highly trained developmentalists known as the technocrats or, less respectfully, the "miniskirts," were elevated to positions of great responsibility. The heart of their operations was the Banco Central in downtown Managua. There the dictator-president, the head of the "miniskirts" (Francisco "Ché" Láinez, the bank's director), and the cream of Nicaragua's technocratic community often met late into the night planning the country's economy as if they were the board of directors of a large corporation. Feasibility studies were ordered, foreign investment was wooed, and joint ventures were embarked upon. Once a year the Banco Central issued an annual report brimming with tables and analyses concerning the national economy. To help train even more business technocrats, Harvard University's School of Business Administration cooperated in the creation of the Central American Institute of Business Administration (INCAE), located in the outskirts of Managua.

A parallel stimulus for capitalist development in Nicaragua, which coincided with the Alliance for Progress, was the birth of the Central American Common Market in 1960. This attempt at regional economic integration provided increased incentive for both incipient industrialization and the diversification of export products. As such it was, for a while, an additional boon to the privileged domestic and international groups who controlled these activities. However, the Soccer War of 1969, between El Salvador and Honduras, brought about the demise of this integrative effort.

The developmentalist optimism of the 1960s proved to be a hollow illusion. Compared with the rest of Latin America, Nicaragua received relatively little foreign investment—perhaps because doing business in that country normally entailed paying off the Somozas in one way or another. Though economic growth did take place, its benefits were concentrated in relatively few hands. The Somozas and their allies simply used their control of the expanded governmental apparatus and the country's new technocratic expertise to increase their own fortunes. Eventually, in the late 1960s and early 1970s, the technocrats themselves were pushed aside as the corrupt and intemperate Anastasio Somoza Debayle replaced skilled administrative personnel with National Guard officers and other cronies to whom he owed rewards for personal loyalty.

GOVERNMENT AND POLITICS

If one had been foolish enough to take seriously the constitutional formalities and stated objectives of the Nicaraguan government during the Somoza years, one would surely have come to the mistaken conclusion that Nicaragua was blessed with a modern democratic form of government that was pursuing praiseworthy developmental goals. According to the constitution, there were free elections, separation of powers, and a full gamut of explicitly guaranteed human rights. To insure minority participation, the largest opposition party was automatically awarded 40 percent of all seats in the legislature and minority representation on boards of government agencies, judgeships, etc. What is more, there were a variety of public agencies and institutions such as the Central Bank, the National Development Institute, the Nicaraguan Agrarian Institute, the Institute of Internal-External Commerce, and the Social Security Institute, which were ostensibly designed to cope with the problems faced by a modernizing society. The stated policies of the government were also impressive.

The major expressed goal was to develop the country through the modernization and diversification of the economy. Accordingly, highly trained technocrats were given important roles in the development process and lofty five-year plans were issued and subsequently endorsed by lists of international agencies.

All of this, of course, was simply a facade. Under the Somozas, democracy was nonexistent, corruption was elaborately institutionalized, and public policy consistently ignored the well-being of the majority of the population.

Nicaragua was a democracy in name only. Although there were constitutional provisions for the separation of power—with a bicameral legislature, an executive, and a judiciary—in reality, all power was concentrated in the hands of the president. The National Guard was the president's private army. His command over the Liberal party—which in turn dominated both houses of the legislature and all government agencies—meant that the president was, in fact, the only decision maker. Mandated minority participation served only to legitimize the system and to co-opt Conservative politicians. There was never any possibility that the opposition would come to power legally since elections were thoroughly rigged. During campaign periods, there was frequent censorship of the press and intimidation of opposition candidates. On election day, there was multiple voting by the pro-Somoza faithful, tampering with the ballot boxes, and, cleverest of all, the use of a translucent "secret" ballot that, even when folded, could easily be scrutinized by government election officials as it was deposited in the ballot box.

Given the hopelessly undemocratic character of elections under the Somozas, party organization and activity were shallow and essentially without meaning. The two major parties, Liberal and Conservative, were crusty relics of the nineteenth century. The original ideological differences between them had long since faded into insignificance. Both represented the interests of a small privileged minority and, by the middle of the twentieth century, both had been co-opted and subordinated by the Somoza system.

Officially, the Somozas were Liberals and their governments were Liberal administrations. In fact, however, throughout most of the period, the Liberal party was simply a cosmetic appendage of a system that depended on brute military force. One apparent exception occurred in the late 1950s and early 1960s when Luis Somoza—who enjoyed the trappings of democracy and party politics—encouraged the Liberal party to have a life of its own. In that period, new Liberal leaders emerged and there was some hope that they might turn into real presidential prospects. In the late 1960s, after the "election" of the less politically minded Anastasio Somoza Debayle, these hopes were quickly dashed. Independent upstarts left or were drummed out of the party as the dictator began to maneuver to perpetuate himself in power, and the Liberal party lapsed into its more traditional cosmetic role.

The official Conservative opposition played an even less dignified role. Since the facade of democracy was so important to the Somozas, it was imperative that there always be an opposition to run against during elections. Enticed by personal bribes and/or lucrative opportunities inherent in mandated minority participation in congress, the judiciary, and government agencies, the leaders of the Conservative party frequently agreed to provide a legitimizing opposition during the rigged elections. Even on those infrequent occasions when the leaders of the Conservative party mustered the dignity to refuse to participate, the dictators were usually able to convince less important Conservatives to carry that party's banner to defeat.

There were a number of microparties during the Somoza period. A few of the more notable were the Independent Liberal party (PLI), composed of Liberals who, from 1944 on, chose to dissociate themselves from the parent party over the issue of Somoza's continuing dominance; the Nicaraguan Social Christian party (PSCN), formed by young Catholic intellectuals in 1957; and the Nicaraguan Socialist party (PSN), which was founded by local Communists in 1944.

One of the more interesting of the microparties was the Social Christian party. Inspired by progressive papal encyclicals, lay Catholic humanism, and Christian Democratic ideas emanating from Europe, this party attempted to take advantage of Luis Somoza's somewhat more open attitude toward competitive political activity. Stressing the importance of platform, ideology, organization, and tactics, the Christian Democrats not only won a significant popular following, but also penetrated the labor movement and came for a while to dominate the national students' organizations. Though many young Christian Democrats freely admitted their admiration for the courage and audacity of FSLN guerrillas, they felt at that time that a peaceful, democratic solution might still be possible. When it became clear in the early 1970s that they were wrong, the more progressive members of the party split from the PSCN to form the Popular Social Christian party (PPSC), which espoused an increasingly revolutionary position.

Mass-interest articulation through legal channels was also a fairly hopeless activity under the Somozas. Peasants and urban labor, for instance, had almost no input into the political system. Ignorant, illiterate, and geographically scattered, the peasantry and rural proletariat were subject to constant abuse by landowners and the National Guard. An agrarian reform program legislated in the early days of the Alliance for Progress had virtually no impact on the misery of the rural poor. From 1964 on, a private Social Christian-oriented organization—the Institute for Human Promotion (INPRHU)—did struggle to organize and raise the consciousness of the peasants, but in the face of government roadblocks, its efforts were largely ineffectual. In the end, clandestine activity proved to be the only viable alternative. In the late 1970s, the FSLN began organizing rural workers and landless peasants in workers' committees. In 1978, these were fused into a national organization—the Rural Workers' Association (ATC). In the following year, as the Revolution neared its successful conclusion, ATC-organized peasants made their contribution by digging trenches and felling huge trees across roadways to block troop movements and by maximizing the first post-Somoza harvest through the seizure and immediate cultivation of *Somocista*-owned lands in the newly liberated areas.

Urban workers were only slightly better off than their country cousins. The organized labor movement encompassed a small minority of all workers and was badly fragmented. In 1977, the major union organizations included the Marxist Independent General Confederation of Labor, with 12,000 members; the government-patronized General Confederation of Labor, with 8,000 to 10,000 members; the AFL–CIO-oriented Confederation of Labor Unity, with 7,000 members; and the Social Christian Confederation of Workers of Nicaragua, with 3,000 members. The right to strike, while formally enshrined in law, was so severely restricted that most of the many strikes that took place in the 1960s and 1970s were declared illegal. Collective bargaining was made all but impossible by Article 17 of the *Regulations of Syndical Association,* which allowed the employer to fire, without explanation, any two leaders of the striking union. In the long run, the only viable option for urban workers, too, was to organize themselves clandestinely, again under FSLN leadership. Significantly, the urban insurrections—which took place almost exclusively in working-class neighborhoods—turned out to be one of the most important ingredients in the overthrow of the dictatorship.

Not surprisingly, given the nearly complete absence of institutionalized popular input into the political system, the Somoza government was virtually oblivious to the interests of the ordinary Nicaraguan citizen. Lofty-sounding social programs—ostensibly concerned with public health, agrarian reform, low-income housing, education, social security, and the like—served mainly as devices to legitimize the system, attract foreign aid, employ the politically faithful, and diversify opportunities for the pilfering of public revenues. Very little of what the government spent actually trickled down to the people. With members of Somoza's family at the head of most government agencies, a large chunk of each agency's assets went directly to satisfy the family's greed. For instance, in the ten years in which he headed the National Institute for Light and Energy, Anastasio Somoza Debayle's uncle, Luis Manuel Debayle, allegedly siphoned off more than $30 million (U.S.). Under the Somozas were layer upon layer of corrupt bureaucrats who were expected and, indeed, encouraged to help themselves. Honesty, a threat to the system, was discouraged.

The problem of corruption had existed throughout the Somoza period. Anastasio Somoza García had encouraged corruption in his subordinates as a way of isolating them psychologically from the people and thus making them dependent on him. In a conversation in 1977, Luis Somoza's close advisor and confidant, Francisco Láinez, the chief of the "miniskirts" during that earlier period, told me an interesting story. One day Luis Somoza, in a pensive mood, asked Láinez to tell him in all frankness what one thing he, Láinez, would do, if he were in Luis's shoes, to bring development to Nicaragua. Láinez thought for a moment and then responded that he would take each of the major categories in the national budget—health, education, etc.—and see to it that *at least half* of that money actually went for the purposes for which it was ostensibly destined. According to Láinez, Luis simply smiled sadly and responded, "You're being unrealistic." This is not to say that, at the highest levels, money was being stolen openly. That would not have been acceptable to Washington—which was footing much of the bill—nor was it necessary, since the Somoza's absolute control of the government gave them the ability to apply a legalistic patina to the flow of public funds. Even after the patent and massive misuse of international relief funds following the 1972 earthquake, the U.S. government, intent on not embarrassing a good ally, was able for several years to produce audits that appeared to refute claims that these funds had been misappropriated. But by the time the dynasty was overthrown the Somoza family had accrued a portfolio worth perhaps a billion dollars, including about one-fifth of the nation's arable land.

The events of the 1970s accentuated the abuses and defects of the Nicaraguan economic system. In the last years of the Somoza dynasty, it had reached a state that, from the point of view of most citizens, was intolerable. For over a century, the country's rich natural resources had been plundered, appropriated, and abused for the benefit of a tiny minority. Millions of Nicaraguans had become economic instruments rather than fulfilled and participating human beings. Public revenues and foreign aid officially destined "to meet basic human needs" had been routinely laundered to end up in the pockets of the ruling family and its allies. The nation's public and private banks had been used first as instruments for the concentration of wealth and finally as conduits for the export of capital as the erstwhile ruling class began to flee into exile. The Revolution of 1978–1979 was as much a product of systemic socioeconomic factors as it was an expression of intense political opposition to a particularly venal dictator.

THE BEGINNING OF THE END: 1972–1977

The half-decade following 1972 was a time of mounting troubles for the Somoza regime. Most of the responsibility for the growing systemic crisis lay in the excesses and poor judgment of the dictator himself. Somoza's first major demonstration of intemperance came in the wake of the Christmas earthquake of 1972, which cost the lives of more than ten thousand people and leveled a 600-square block area in the heart of Managua. Somoza might have chosen to play the role of concerned statesman and patriotic leader by dipping into the family fortune (which, even then, probably exceeded $300 million [U.S.]) in order to help his distressed countrymen. Instead, he chose to turn the national disaster to short-term personal advantage. While allowing the National Guard to plunder and sell international relief materials and to participate in looting the devastated commercial sector, Somoza and his associates used their control of the government to channel international relief funds into their own pockets. Much of what they did was technically legal—the self-awarding of government contracts and the purchasing of land, industries, etc., that they knew would figure lucratively in the reconstruction—but little of it was ethically or morally appealing.

It was at this point that open expressions of popular discontent with the Somoza regime began to surface. When the quake struck, Somoza lost no time using the emergency as an excuse to proclaim himself head of the National Emergency Committee. There were many high-sounding statements about the challenge and patriotic task of reconstruction, but it soon became apparent that his corrupt and incompetent government was actually a major obstacle to recovery. The promised reconstruction of the heart of the city never took place. Popular demand for the building of a new marketplace to replace the one that had been destroyed went unheeded. Emergency housing funds channeled to Nicaragua by the Agency for International Development (AID) went disproportionately into the construction of luxury housing for National Guard officers, while the homeless poor were asked to content themselves with hastily constructed wooden shacks. Reconstruction plans for the city's roads, drainage system, and public transportation were grossly mishandled. As a result, there was a series of strikes and demonstrations as the citizens became increasingly angry and politically mobilized.

It was at this point, too, that Somoza lost much of the support that he had formerly enjoyed from Nicaragua's economic elite. Many independent business owners resented the way he had muscled his way into the construction and banking sectors. And most were angry at being asked to pay new emergency taxes at a time when Somoza—who normally exempted himself from taxes—was using his position to engorge himself on international relief funds. As a result, from 1973 on, more and more young people from elite backgrounds joined the ranks of the Sandinist Front of National Liberation, and some sectors of the business community began giving the FSLN their financial support.

THE FINAL STRUGGLE, 1977–1979

Over the next several years, a growing coalition of businessmen, politicians, peasants, and urban workers called for Somoza's ouster. From 1972 to 1974, the FSLN financed its activities with kidnapping and raids. In response, Somoza declared a state of siege in which savage repression, including torture, strict censorship, and an expanded militarization of society, forced the FSLN to go underground. However, in 1977, amid mounting publicity from Amnesty International and protests from the Catholic Church, the U.S. Congress and President Carter informed Somoza that the United States would stop aid unless he improved his record on human rights.

Somoza grudgingly lifted the state of siege. Allowed slightly more room to operate, the FSLN and elite opposition immediately stepped up their activities. However, Somoza again responded, this time with the assassination of Pedro Joaquín Chamorro on January 10, 1978. Chamorro was a courageous journalist (and relative of a former Nicaraguan president) who had long criticized the Somoza dynasty. The reaction of the Nicaraguan people was massive and immediate; angry crowds attacked Somoza-owned business establishments, and the business community conducted a widespread general strike, closing their stores and offices for two weeks. The FSLN stepped up its attacks on political and military targets throughout the country, including a daring attack in August on the National Palace, home to Somoza's rubber-stamp national congress.

In the face of continued popular uprisings in the cities and the countryside, Somoza continued to operate as if his army was an occupation force in hostile territory. His air force bombed, strafed, and napalmed FSLN strongholds in Nicaragua's major cities, causing thousands of civilian deaths. Instead of strengthening his position, however, such acts led to increased elite opposition and pressures from the Catholic Church and the United States that he depart. In June 1979, another round of planned insurrections in many parts of Nicaragua divided and pinned down the National Guard, while a national strike closed down the economy. In July, Somoza fled to Guatemala, and the Guard began to desert and dissolve, many of its officers and units fleeing to Honduras. On July 19, 1979, the Revolutionary Junta declared control of Managua; the revolution had won.

Countermobilization in the Iranian Revolution

JERROLD D. GREEN

Green provides a detailed account of the breakdown of the Shah's regime in Iran. He notes that the breakdown depended on the weakening of state coercion and on the mobilization of the urban poor under the direction of the religious elite. He also notes that middle-class opponents of the Shah sought an alliance with religious leaders and that the latter's huge organizational network gave them a dominant role in the Revolution.

Countermobilization may be simply understood as mass mobilization against a prevailing political order under the leadership of counterelites. Due to its great magnitude, in certain cases such a process can be virtually irreversible. Reliant upon the mobilization capacity of counterelites, the anti-regime sector of a society may quickly develop the attributes of a parallel state, rendering the prevailing state structure powerless, while itself becoming impervious to attempts to undermine it. It is this process of countermobilization that is the focus of this paper. Particular attention is paid both to the conditions leading to countermobilization and to its attributes.

THE CONDITIONS LEADING TO COUNTERMOBILIZATION

In order to appreciate the antecedents of countermobilization, we should enumerate and apply them to the Iranian case.

The conditions leading to countermobilization are as follows:

1. The declining coercive will or capacity of the state.
2. A simplification of politics.
3. Mass polarization.
4. The politicization of traditionally non-political social sectors.
5. Crisis-initiating event(s).
6. Exacerbating responses by the regime.

The Declining Coercive Will or Capacity of the State

The earliest antecedents to the Iranian Revolution may be traced to a crisis of participation among Iran's most highly socially mobilized sector—the urban middle class. Prior to the 1975 elections the Shah announced his willingness to sanction electoral opposition to the government-controlled Iran-Novin Party. In part, this political liberalization was a response to sporadic terrorism as well as to the economic deterioration (for example, 40 percent inflation rate and housing shortages) resulting from the ill-conceived doubling of the expenditure level of the fifth five-year plan. Frightened by the ensuing scurry of political activity reflecting popular desires for expanded political participation, the Shah backpedaled, put an end to two-party politics, and created a single mobilization party named *Hizb-i-Rastakhiz-i-Melli* (National Resurgence Party). Yet Rastakhiz was doomed to failure from the outset. Iranians had seen parties come and go and greeted the Shah's newest attempt to generate support with ambivalence or cynicism.

By 1977 the Rastakhiz Party was but a political relic while popular dissent grew in scope. Highly socially mobilized Iranians were unable to forgive the Shah for his abolition of two-

From Comparative Politics, *vol. 16, pp. 153–69 (1984). Copyright © The City University of New York.*

party politics. At the same time, the Shah was under pressure from President Jimmy Carter, Amnesty International, and the International Commission of Jurists, all critical of Iran's dismal human rights record. Dissident Iranian students staged well-publicized demonstrations in the United States and western Europe, while Iranians at home were losing patience as the quality of life in the country rapidly and visibly deteriorated. As Tehran was afflicted with extended electricity blackouts throughout the summer of 1977 and the police were engaged in pitched battles with indigent squatters in South Tehran, the Shah spoke loftily of his new campaign to guide Iran towards a "great civilization" and his desire to surpass Sweden by the year 2000!

Inspired by the activities of Iranian students abroad, human rights groups, and even the United States government, various middle class professional and associational groups decided to act. Frustrated by the absence of participatory mechanisms, such groups chose to go outside of the system in order to express their dissatisfaction. According to James Bill, "the middle class in Iran . . . make up over 25 percent of the population."[1] This sector, the one that felt Iran's crisis of participation most keenly, was initially reformist rather than revolutionary in character. It was only later, in coordination with the national religious sector, that opposition groups became sufficiently powerful to seek an end to the Pahlavi dynasty altogether.

Throughout this period, Iran's crisis of participation became most acute, and it is here that the first condition leading to countermobilization, the declining coercive will or capacity of the state, is most crucial. This diminished coercive capacity is reminiscent of Theda Skocpol's findings in her analysis of the French, Russian, and Chinese revolutions where, due to "the incapacitation of the central state machineries," a breakdown in the coercive ability of the state resulted.[2] Frequently induced by pressures from the international system, such breakdowns are not unlike that in Iran. Yet the rejection of the use of violence by the Shah, unlike that in the cases studied by Skocpol, was largely self-induced rather than the result of irresistible external or internal pressures. Consequently, state-sponsored coercion during the revolution was limited to particular types of situations.

In May of 1977, a group of fifty-three attorneys called for an inquiry into the lack of impartiality in the judiciary. In June, the long banned Writer's Association sent an open letter to the prime minister. Signed by forty of its members, the letter demanded greater cultural freedom and the right to reconstitute their organization. Three days later, the National Front sent a similar letter directly to the Shah in which adherence to the national constitution was demanded. The Group for Free Books and Thought was established by publishers seeking the elimination of censorship and severe government restrictions on publishing. A manifesto signed by fifty-six well-known representatives of various groups sought a return to the constitution, a cessation of human rights violations, abolition of single party rule, the release of political prisoners, and free elections. Other groups comprised of bazaaris (merchants), judges, lawyers, teachers, university professors, and students were also active in this period. Mehdi Bazargan, Khomeini's first prime minister, created the Iranian Committee for Freedom and Human Rights. Finally, on the evenings of October 10 through 19, 1977, the Writer's Association sponsored a series of poetry readings at the Goethe Institute in Tehran. The poems, in part, were extremely critical of the current order and attracted thousands of listeners—an unprecedented liberty in Pahlavi Iran.

Although unanticipated even by their most active participants, the above events heralded the earliest stages of Iran's revolution. And given the Shah's historical willingness to employ coercion, often quite brutally, we must ask why such activities were tacitly encouraged through his uncustomary tolerance. In part, the state's acquiescence may be attributed to a modest liberalization undertaken by the Shah in response to international pressure on Iran born of a heightened sensitivity in the West to human rights issues. Other more tangential explanations include the possibility of royal indecisiveness due to the Shah's early bouts with cancer and the attendant lassitude resulting from chemotherapy. Additionally, he may have been unwilling to employ coercion so as not to alienate large segments of Iranian society. Perhaps recognizing that his tenure would be prematurely curtailed, the Shah was conceivably attempting to liberalize his regime in order to facilitate the succession to the throne of his son, Crown Prince Reza. Given the Shah's accession to power at age twenty-three, he was, I suspect, keenly aware of the potential difficulties awaiting his own successor. Although none of these interpretations can be verified with any certainty, it is clear that the liberalization, what some termed the "Tehran Spring," was limited and of short duration. Yet peculiarly, it did herald a pattern of state behavior in which coercion was used in a limited and particularly inefficient manner. For the Shah resorted to coercion in a reflexive rather than preventive fashion, choosing to respond to revolutionary *symptoms* rather than *origins.* Thus, there were innumerable instances of the military repressing processions and demonstrations in which hundreds were killed (for example, at Tabriz, Qum, and Jaleh Square). Yet the Shah's secret police (known as SAVAK) were far less active in this period than usual. And the Shah, even after the imposition of total martial law, never clamped down tightly on the most vocal leaders of the revolution, many of whom, unlike Khomeini, were resident in Iran. Preference for highly public military responses alienated most Iranians while providing a series of heroes in whose martyrdom the revolution's legitimacy lay. Popular revolutionary consciousness was raised while the state never really suppressed the source of opposition to it. Had the regime put down the early middle class challenges, the revolution may have been forestalled somewhat. But it seems that from the very beginning the Shah misread the nature of opposition to him.

On January 7, 1978, the regime went on the offensive, not against its middle class opponents, but instead targeting the most troublesome segment of the religious sector. The Tehran daily newspaper *Etela'at* published a fabricated letter attacking the exiled Ayatollah Khomeini in a vicious and personal fashion. Although historically an opponent of the regime, Khomeini in this period certainly presented no greater threat to regime stability than he had in previous years. Yet ironically, the regime unwittingly designated Khomeini as the "official" head of a heretofore nonexistent national opposition. The popular response was rioting of unanticipated severity in the holy city of Qum by a citizenry outraged by the regime's attack on a respected religious leader. With these riots a cycle of violent protest began, as forty days later a commemorative gathering was held for those who died earlier. This *arba'een* led to protest, further loss of life, and another commemorative gathering forty days later. With the introduction of the religious sector into the fray and the regime's inability or unwillingness to use coercive means to halt a movement that would soon grow to uncontrollable proportions, an important watershed of the Iranian Revolution had been reached.

A Simplification of Politics and Polarization

As an antecedent to full-scale countermobilization, a simplification of politics acted to delineate two crude groupings in Iranian society, a not insignificant development in a country of over 35 million people. The mechanics of this simplification remain as yet unclear. And to attribute it wholly to Iran's oppositional sector grants the opposition greater cohesion, power, and prescience than it deserves. Rather, the simplification of politics served as the early stage of polarization. Such polarization was begun by the Shah's introduction of the Rastakhiz Party in 1975, when he stated: "Those who [do] not subscribe to [its] principles [are] either traitors, who belong in prison, or non-Iranians who [should] be given their passports to go abroad. . . . Each Iranian must declare himself and there [is] no room for fencesitters."

Just as national leaders in such a system create an internal cold war, forbid fencesitting, and try to sanctify politics, counterelites can pursue similar goals. At first glance this may seem counterintuitive, and we must ask whether regime opponents are able even more effectively to employ the same techniques as the political order they oppose. If we remember, however, that revolutions are the products of the very forces they oppose, then such mirror image emulation, often unwitting, seems plausible. Just as elites attempt to reduce politics to their lowest common denominators, counterelites can benefit as well from such an arrangement in which potential participants are presented with two simple choices while less dramatic and/or distracting options are simply filtered out. Given a choice between what appear to be the forces of light and those of darkness, the popular choice is clear from the outset. And a contest between elite and counterelite legitimacy, charisma, and societal integration can emerge. This was the case in Iran with Ayatollah Khomeini besting the Shah on all counts. Confronted with two highly salient and conflictual poles, and little political life in between them, traditional oppositional elements in Iran flocked to the regime's critical pole.

As a society rapidly becomes polarized, in part due to a paucity of political options, its regime will soon find itself in direct competition with its critics for popular support. This competitive mobilization is in itself a de facto form of official recognition as the state chooses to vie with its competitor rather than use coercive means to eliminate it. Gradually, the oppositional pole exercises an undiscerning, almost magnetic pull, passively *attracting* supporters rather than actively recruiting them. Importantly, however, influential counterelites provide the oppositional pole with a rough shape and character while helping to focus and refine grievances against the state. In such a competitive situation, the character of counterelites is all-important. And given the infrastructural attributes and inherent legitimacy of Iran's religious sector, it found itself in an unanticipated and unique oppositional role.

Let us for a moment try to establish the basis for the religious sector's successful countermobilization. Iran contains some 80,000 mosques, 1,200 shrines, and 180,000 mullahs. Among these are roughly 100 ayatollahs, 5,000 *hojats-al-Islam,* and 11,000 theology students. In Tehran alone, there are more than 5,000 shrine attendants. Ironically, Iranian modernization did not weaken but rather strengthened the national religious community. For example, the number of religious pilgrims to holy places in Mashad increased tenfold, from 332,000 in 1966–1967 to 3.5 million in 1976–1977. Rises in income, improved transportation, and expansion of the roadway system, all made what was once a long journey into a relatively simple excursion, highlighting the manner in which the infrastructural attributes of Iran's religious sector were strengthened over time and benefited from national modernization.

The Qum disturbances in response to the Khomeini letter illustrated to opponents and critics of the Shah the mobilization potential of Iran's religious community. For with its introduction into oppositional political activity, the scope and magnitude of what was primarily reformist anti-Pahlavi activity grew dramatically. On January 19 and 20, 1978, the Tehran bazaar closed in response to a joint call for a general strike by Ayatollah Khomeini and Karim Sanjabi of the National Front. Recognizing its inability to generate popular support despite its petitions, letters, manifestoes, and poetry readings, Iran's secular middle class adopted a potentially more fruitful stance by throwing in its lot with the religious sector. The strike of the Tehran bazaar was the first public instance of cooperation between the two groups and illustrates the countermobilization which would provide the revolution's dynamic.

What were the mechanics of Iran's simplification of politics and polarization? Such events as the Qum disturbances and the strike of Tehran's bazaaris brought Iran's incipient revolution within reach of most Iranians, particularly those in the major urban centers. At the same time, the country was flooded with Khomeini's writings as well as taped cassettes of his *khutbehs* (sermons) delivered from his place of exile in Najaf, Iraq. The foreign press avidly followed rising dissent in Iran while the BBC ultimately became an unofficial voice of the revolution. For example, when Khomeini later moved to the outskirts of Paris, his aides would tell the BBC of a general strike called for the following day. Iranians hearing the BBC would thus learn of Khomeini's call and do as he bid. *Elamiehs* (notices) from the opposition covered the walls of Tehran and other cities giving Iranians news of the opposition while listing various demands from Khomeini and his aides. Instructions from the Ayatollah would be telephoned to Iran, while photocopying machines worked overtime reproducing revolutionary materials. For example, while in Tehran in 1978, I obtained a recently received communiqué from Khomeini's supporters in Paris. I went to the clerk responsible for photocopying in the government-sponsored research institute where I was based. I quietly called him aside and asked him to make a copy of it, but he refused. After some insistence, he looked at what I had, derisively said "een copy khoob mist" (this copy's no good), and extracted a better reproduction of what I wanted from a huge pile on his machine. In and of itself this anecdote seems relatively insignificant. Yet actions such as that of a simple clerical worker, when aggregated throughout Iran, indicate a growing revolutionary force of remarkable durability and power. This man, in his own fashion, was a revolutionary. He was never recruited into a formal oppositional structure but rather responded to stimuli rampant in the Iran of 1978–1979. He had two choices open to him, support the Shah or Khomeini. He chose the latter, as did most Iranians, giving in to vague though irresistible instincts by supporting what most Iranians were led to believe was good over evil.

THE POLITICIZATION OF NON-POLITICAL SOCIAL SECTORS

Given the high levels of popular participation which characterize countermobilization and the different effects that political mobilization has on diverse segments of society, we must ask how popular revolutionary consciousness develops. Despite the high levels of political mobilization evident in Iran's urban centers, for example, this process was for the most part restricted to Iran's burgeoning middle class. Thus such mobilization did not reach deep enough into Iranian society to include the large numbers of peasant migrants that swelled the urban sector. Tehran's population doubled from two to four million people between 1966 and 1976. This doubling came from peasants who left the countryside to seek greater opportunity in the national capital. Though fulfilling some of the criteria for political mobilization (such as changes from traditional occupations and exposure to mass media and the products of modernity) these migrants showed little evidence of conventional politicization such as awareness of their national political leadership, membership in political parties, or voting.[3]

Yet the sudden involvement of these migrants in oppositional activities (they were the footsoldiers of the revolution) raises important questions as to their sudden politicization and commitment to oppositional values. The rapid induction of urban migrants into revolutionary action testifies to the pervasiveness of Iran's simplification of politics and attendant polarization. Simultaneously, the persuasiveness of the national religious sector is emphasized as we begin to understand the manner in which local mullahs were able to involve their constituents in revolutionary action.

The rapid politicization of Iran's previously unpoliticized urban masses may be seen in the huge processions of *Tasuah* and *Ashura* where, in Tehran alone, over two million people took to the streets in meticulously organized, peaceful marches against the regime. The procession was led by Ayatollah Talegani and Karim Sanjabi of the National Front, the pinnacle of the coalescence of interests discussed earlier. Individual mullahs led their parishioners through the city in separate groups of men and women, leaving no doubt that even the last socially mobilized segments of Iran's urban centers were committed to the revolution. Thus, the incipient revolution itself politicized such people, albeit in a somewhat less sophisticated fashion than it politicized the middle classes, and only the stimulus of their mullahs was needed to provide a vehicle for their anti-state participation.

CRISIS-INITIATING EVENTS AND EXACERBATING REGIME RESPONSES

The final antecedent to full-scale countermobilization highlights the transition from reformism to revolution. In Iran several events of tremendous national importance contributed to increasingly higher levels of revolutionary consciousness. For the revolution fed itself, with each triumph leading to greater heights of unity and cohesion.

The first crisis-initiating event and exacerbating regime response was the publication of the falsified Khomeini letter and the subsequent military repression of demonstrators in Qum. This led to forty-day cycles of demonstrations, military intervention, and violence in which the state provided opportunities for periodic commemorative gatherings as well as an ample supply of martyrs and heroes.

Among other particularly significant crisis-initiating events was the brief military takeover of Tabriz in February of 1978. This led to a purported shake-up of SAVAK and a censure of the military for its handling of the incident. Further contributing to the upheaval was the mysterious fire at the Cinema Rex in Abadan where 400 people perished. Widely believed to be the work of SAVAK, it was perceived as a graphic illustration of the lengths to which the Shah would go to discredit his opponents, whom he blamed for the tragedy. The religious sector, acting almost as a parallel state, imperiously opened its own investigation into the origins of the fire, helping to formalize popular views of it as a natural and legitimate competitor with and successor to the Pahlavi dynasty.

On September 8, 1978, serious rioting occurred in Tehran with hundreds being killed in Jaleh Square—a day to be known as Black Friday. Attempting to capitalize on the tragedy,

Khomeini announced that Muslims could not kill other Muslims and thus the troops responsible for the massacre were Israeli. This story was given wide credence in Iran, and Black Friday was immediately enshrined in the lore of the revolution, contributing mightily to sentiment in favor of the religious sector and against the state. It also led to martial law in Tehran and in other cities.

Later in this month an earthquake struck the small city of Tabas, resulting in 15,000–20,000 deaths. It was widely believed that the religious sector sped aid to the survivors more quickly and efficiently than did the government. This further hardened opposition to the regime while strengthening the credibility of the religious sector.

On November 4, a large number of students demonstrating at Tehran University were killed by the military; this led to massive rioting. On the following day, the rioting continued, several high officials resigned, total martial law was imposed by the Shah, and General Azhari was named prime minister.

Finally, the solemn religious month of Muharram began, with the overwhelming processions of *Tasuah* and *Ashura*. The religious sector referred to the processions as a referendum against the Shah. This peaceful idiom reflected the tenor of the revolution as a whole.

Exacerbating regime responses to these crisis-initiating events took consistent forms. Demonstrations were put down with violence, except for *Tasuah* and *Ashura,* while other forms of dissent were met with offers of salary increments, lowered taxes, and other financial inducements, as well as symbolic gestures such as the closing of gambling casinos and the dismissal of the minister of women's affairs to mollify the religious community. Yet both the stick and the carrot worked to alienate most segments of Iranian society. While the former tended to emphasize the sacrifices and purity of the oppositionists, the latter served to denigrate them. That is, most regime opponents had little patience with regime attempts to "buy them off." Such cooptative techniques were a time-honored cornerstone of Pahlavi rule and represented for many Iranians what they wanted to change in their society. Additionally, these gestures served to convince the oppositional sector that it was making progress against the state, for otherwise why would the state accede to popular dissatisfaction with such uncharacteristic rapidity and concern?

COUNTERMOBILIZATION
AS A REVOLUTIONARY FORM

Given the high level of support for the opposition, we must investigate those factors contributing to it. Several interrelated causes can be forwarded. Of these, one of the most significant is to be found in the behavior of Khomeini and his immediate supporters in which oppositional rather than initiative issues were stressed with an emphasis on negative rather than positive goals. That is, the religious sector tended to portray itself as Iran's most legitimate and potentially effective anti-Shah force. Thus, it was viewed as an entity in opposition to something rather than one in favor of something else. By keeping its character vague and ill-defined, all anti-state elements could be drawn to it. Whether this was a conscious revolutionary technique or, as is more likely, a consequence of the opposition's inability to keep pace with rapidly changing events, is unclear. Yet the image of Khomeini contained "something for everyone" opposed to the Pahlavi political order. Thus, groups as diverse as the urban middle class and ethnic and religious minorities were able to support him due to a crucial, single-goal consensus focused on removal of the Shah. Commitment by such groups to Khomeini lay in his ability to countermobilize popular revolutionary participation rather than in this role as the architect of what at the time was vaguely defined as an Islamic Republic. For example, during a strike of the predominantly Arab oil workers in Khuzistan, Khomeini asked them to return to the fields in order to provide for domestic consumption. The workers were unimpressed by the Ayatollah's request and returned to work only after the intercession of Mehdi Bazargan, a former director of the National Iranian Oil Company under Mossadeq. Interestingly, it became clear after an interview with Bazargan in Tehran that he himself was not particularly enamored of Khomeini. Presumably, his eventual and short-lived commitment to him was pragmatic, much like that of other groups in Iranian society.

Khomeini's emphasis on his anti-Shah credentials rather than on his goal to create a theocracy in part led to a situation in which coalition-building among diverse and at times conflicting groups was simplified by a diminution in the importance of Iran's traditional ethnic, tribal, socioeconomic, generational, educational, religious, and geographic cleavages. Iran is a multiethnic society in the extreme, with Persians a minority in their own country. Yet traditional rivalries (such as those between Azerbaijanis and Kurds), which manifested themselves after the revolution, were shelved as all segments of society worked towards a common goal. This led to some surprising outcomes. For example, over several weeks Tehran was afflicted by nightly blackouts orchestrated by dissident electrical workers. Blackouts were not engineered, however, on Christmas and New Year's eves out of solidarity with the revolution's Christian participants! Members of Tehran's large and sophisticated intelligentsia quickly supported Khomeini in his goals, their last thought being the creation of a society governed by the mullahs whom they disdained. When the newspapers went out on strike, influential mullahs paid congratulatory visits to newspaper offices while bazaaris collected money to help the striking journalists support themselves. In fact, visceral hatred of the Shah fleetingly brought Iran a degree of unanimity and national cooperation unprecedented in its history and unlikely to recur in its future.

An important aspect of Iranian countermobilization involved the gradual development of coalitions between oppositionalists and those in government. This is a common attribute of revolutions, and in Iran it assumed dramatic proportions due to already high levels of countermobilization. Although on the highest levels many such defections have yet to come to light, we can cite the case of General Hussein Fardust, former chief of the Imperial Inspectorate, which superseded SAVAK, and a close boyhood friend and classmate of the Shah from their days at a Swiss boarding school. Fardust emerged as a post-revolutionary director of SAVAMA, the Islamic Republic's version of SAVAK.

On a somewhat different level, the ouster of the Shah was strongly facilitated by the disintegration of the national bureaucracy, most of whose employees at middle and lower levels went over to the national opposition. Wildcat strikes paralyzed virtually all segments of the government. Anti-regime meetings were held in government offices, while their employees circulated petitions urging individual cabinet ministers to resign. Workers at the Central Bank of Iran provided lists of those Iranians taking large amounts of currency out of the country. Government printing presses and photocopying machines churned out anti-state materials. And, confronted with such internal and external pressures, the apparatus of state crumbled within months.

It is difficult to identify an Iranian revolutionary elite with any precision. The most viable leadership was found in Ayatollah Khomeini and his circle of advisors on the outskirts of Paris. Yet these leaders had important contacts within Iran, as the religious community closed ranks in a rare show of solidarity. Basically, the Iranian Revolution boasted a shifting, amorphous, loosely structured revolutionary leadership with no oppositional center for the regime to crush. In part, this is attributable to the distance separating Khomeini from his followers in Iran. Yet such an arrangement, which favored the Ayatollah's personal security, also entailed severe costs due to the necessity for leadership from afar and for long-range communication. Yet within Iran it would be no exaggeration to argue that countermobilization rendered virtually all of the country's 180,000 mullahs agents of revolution. At the same time, large numbers of bazaaris, professors, teachers, secondary school and university students, lawyers, doctors, and urban migrants were actively engaged in attempts to overthrow the Shah. Support for the revolution was virtually universal in Iran.

Given the extraordinarily high level of revolutionary participation, Iranian countermobilization emphasized nonviolence. This is not to say that the revolution was nonviolent, but rather that the opposition eschewed its employment while the military resorted to coercive tactics in its suppression of various demonstrations, processions, and meetings. The revolutionary sector chose to emphasize idioms of peaceful change which extended to virtually all aspects of the upheaval. The sheer size of the opposition allowed it to oust the Shah while avoiding armed conflict.

A key attribute of countermobilization is its lack of longevity, for mass revolutionary participation is time-perishable and is dependent upon quick gains, high polarity, and a truncated time-frame. Given such traits of countermobilization as a loosely structured leadership, an unwieldy and cumbersome popular following, its inherent ideological vagueness, and its oppositional, responsive character, the underlying simplification of politics which supports it cannot last indefinitely. For a society in the throes of countermobilization is like a rudderless ship. Its only link to "normalcy," the primary factor providing cohesion, is its universal opposition to the prevailing political order. People tend not to work during such an upheaval; food shortages, inflation, and other social ills are exacerbated. Yet, on the other hand, the rare society able to generate high levels of countermobilization is likely to oust a preeminent ruling elite with unanticipated rapidity.

Given these considerations, it is not surprising that, due to unnaturally high levels of unity and revolutionary participation, countermobilization is likely to culminate in rapid demobilization. Once the goal of countermobilization is achieved, disparate social groups will revert to their original niches in society. Compounding this predictable fragmentation as the bond among widely differing entities disappears, is the issue of what shape a postrevolutionary polity will take. Thus, the very factors distinguishing different groups will again become salient at a time when the polity is particularly vulnerable due to the inability of its new ruling elite(s) to consolidate its newfound power. Such demobilization was quite evident in Iran and was characterized by intense disagreements within the religious sector as to the desired character of the "new Iran." At the same time, none of Iran's not inconsiderable ethnic minorities was particularly eager to see the institution of theocracy, instead committing themselves to timeless desires for greater autonomy and cultural freedom. More liberal middle class groups were shocked by the attendant religious authoritarianism, while even the more traditional middle class, the bazaaris, felt threatened by the possible nationalization of enterprises which would adversely affect their pursuit of business. In the two years following the fall of the Shah, well-known supporters of the revolution dropped from sight (for example, Bazargan, Yazdi, Nazih, Ayatollah Shariat-Madari, Bani-Sadr, Ghotbzdeh, Matin-Daftary, Entezzam). And Iranian society was convulsed by futile attempts by the Khomeini regime to exploit unfavorable political developments in order to restore once high levels of popular mobilization (for example, the holding of American hostages, the war with Iraq, the blowing up of the headquarters of the Islamic Republican Party, and political assassinations). The very factors which contributed to the early success of the Iranian Revolution also contributed to its subsequent failures.

REFERENCES

1. Bill (1978–1979), p. 333.
2. Skocpol (1979), pp. 50–51.
3. Kazemi (1980), pp. 69–70.

The Philippines "People-Power" Revolution

RICHARD J. KESSLER

The Philippines Revolution, which overthrew the dictator Ferdinand Marcos, was unusual in several respects. On the one hand, the revolution established an ongoing democracy, in contrast to the authoritarian outcome of most other revolutions. This was its greatest achievement. On the other hand, and most unusual for a popularly supported revolution, the new revolutionary regime engaged in no efforts at social change, engaged in no efforts at land reform, and produced no significant changes in the social and political elites that dominate Philippine society. The revolution failed to address the issues of poverty and inequality, or factional conflicts among the elites. The result is that the people of the Philippines, despite their popularly restored democracy, still struggle with political and economic conflicts.

In 1986, a combination of popular demonstrations, army defections, and pressure from the United States led President Ferdinand Marcos to flee the Philippines. In succeeding years, Corazon ("Cory") Aquino, who led the opposition, sought to build a democratic nation. She

From Revolutions of the Late Twentieth Century *edited by Jack Goldstone. Copyright © 1991 by Westview Press, Inc. Reprinted by permission of Westview Press, a member of Perseus Books, L.L.C.*

had to struggle with a host of obstacles, including attempted military coups, continuing Muslim and Communist rebellions in the countryside, and opposition from the Philippine elite to major social reforms. Although the Philippine Revolution began as an inspiring case of popular triumph over tyranny, a variety of conflicts continue.

PREREVOLUTIONARY STATE AND SOCIETY

The Philippines is an island state still caught in the awkward process of becoming a nation. With over 57 million people packed into about 116,000 square miles, and a population density that exceeds China's, the population is a mixture of Malay, Chinese, Spanish, Negrito, and Caucasian peoples speaking about eighty languages or dialects.

For over 300 years, from 1521 to 1898, Spain ruled the Philippines as a colony. By the end of the nineteenth century, a newly emerging and educated middle class began to challenge Spanish control. An insurrection in 1896 was crushed, but two years later Philippine rebels joined with U.S. troops to end Spanish rule during the Spanish American War. Expecting U.S. support for independence, Filipinos were surprised when in 1898 the Philippines were placed under U.S. colonial rule. Again war broke out, this time between U.S. troops and Filipinos, and before the hostilities ended in 1903, 4,234 U.S. troops and at least 16,000 Filipinos had died.

Despite (and perhaps because of) the brutality of the conflict, the United States indicated its intentions to ultimately grant Philippine independence, forming a legislature in 1902 and describing a development plan that would assure "the Philippines for the Filipinos." In 1934 the U.S. Congress established the Commonwealth of the Philippines and provided for a ten-year transition to full independence. World War II intervened, but the Philippines, though devastated by the war, was granted independence on July 4, 1946.

The government of the newly independent state was modeled on the U.S. system with a president, a Senate, and a House of Representatives. The president could serve a maximum of two four-year terms, but until Ferdinand Marcos won reelection in 1969, no one controlled the presidential residence, the Malacanang Palace, for more than one term.

Marcos's reelection occurred during a period of economic and political turmoil. Although the Philippines had enjoyed economic growth of 5 percent annually in the mid-1960s, it still suffered from great inequality. A sense that the political system was impeding economic progress had led to a popular call for a constitutional convention, which when it met in 1971, focused on replacing the presidential system with a parliamentary one. This was in part a reaction to the 1969 presidential election, in which Marcos's victory was widely seen as fraudulent.

In September 1972, to protect his position, Marcos declared martial law, arresting about 60,000 political opponents, and announced the birth of a "new society" that would cleanse the Philippines of corrupt elements and remove barriers to economic modernization. Marcos ruled under martial law until January 1981, during which time he solidified his political and economic control by using executive decrees to reward his cronies and punish his enemies.

THE ELITE

A national elite began to emerge only in the late nineteenth century, and many members of the current ruling elite are the grandchildren or great grandchildren of this original group. The current elite trace their political heritage to the leaders of the 1896 revolt against Spain, and their economic power either to the agricultural and industrial empires created in the nineteenth century or to the opportunities created when Americans broke up Spanish control of the economy and the Catholic church's landed estates in the twentieth century.

Wealth thus has remained concentrated for several generations. Throughout the latter half of the twentieth century, the top 20 percent of Philippine families controlled over 50 percent of the nation's income. Families created broad-based economic empires, spreading their sons and daughters among agricultural and industrial businesses rather than concentrating their holdings in one sector. Traditionally, politics was a means to acquire more wealth, and was based more on pragmatic alliances to obtain power than on ideologically based issues.

ECONOMIC AND DEMOGRAPHIC TRENDS

The Philippines has traditionally been an agricultural exporter, with sugar, coconuts, and other products grown on large commercial estates. In the 1950s, it began an industrialization policy using import-substitution policies to develop a domestic manufacturing base protected by high tariff barriers and import controls, which led to the creation of a classic dual economy with a traditional agricultural sector and a more modern industrial base.

From 1975 to 1983, the Philippines enjoyed a spurt of strong economic growth, produced by rising demand for its agricultural exports and generous lending by international agencies. However, the growth was badly unbalanced in two respects. First, the growth in exports was not sufficient to compensate for growing consumption and borrowing; total external debt thus increased fivefold between 1975 and 1982. Second, the basic structure of the Philippine economy was little altered; growth was concentrated in the protected industries, and Marcos's policy of favoring a select few "crony capitalists" forced out many other private entrepreneurs. The result was that when demand for the Philippines' agricultural products declined after 1982, the economy quickly crumbled under its load of debt and its concentrated and inefficient industries. In 1984, per capita real GNP fell by 9.3 percent; in 1985 it fell a further 6.3 percent; and in 1986, it declined another 0.9 percent.

The International Monetary Fund (IMF) and World Bank provided an aid program, begun in late 1983, that helped to stabilize the economy. However, servicing the large debt required measures to restrain domestic consumption and spending, including reductions in public expenditures and increases in taxes. These measures weakened public support for the government and encouraged the political opposition.

Continued concerns about political instability prevented the Philippines from resuming growth, and the economic setbacks of the early 1980s were not reversed. By 1985 personal income had fallen to below its level in 1972, when Marcos had declared martial law and begun his rule as a dictator. Poverty and unequal income distribution were maintained by unequal asset ownership, rapid population growth, and lack of employment opportunities.

INTERNATIONAL POSITION

After independence, the Philippines remained closely allied with and dependent on the United States. The United States maintained large military bases in the Philippines, remained the most important market for Philippine exports, and was the source of most foreign capital, accounting for 80 percent of total foreign investment. U.S. aid increased dramatically in the 1970s: in 1966, U.S. development assistance was only $4 million; in 1972, it was $30.5 million; and in 1973, it was $135 million. Yet these amounts remained small in comparison to the Philippines' debts, arising mainly from loans advanced by the World Bank. In 1972, the Philippines owed the World Bank $142 million. By 1985, this obligation had skyrocketed to $2.5 billion.

After 1972, Marcos used foreign aid and foreign affairs to establish his legitimacy. He became an active proponent of regional cooperation in the Association of Southeast Asian Nations (ASEAN); he pursued the non-aligned movement, sending observers to its meetings; he courted the Islamic countries in the Middle East and East Africa; he established diplomatic relations with the Communist bloc countries, especially the Soviet Union and the People's Republic of China; and he periodically threatened the United States with the closing of U.S. military facilities. But while Marcos's often nationalist rhetoric and independent actions were applauded by the elite, they did not add to his credibility and were viewed as cynical attempts to convince the Americans that their financial support should be increased. Ironically, despite dramatic foreign policy initiatives and increased aid, Marcos's legitimacy declined, as did the condition of his country. By 1985, the Philippines was no longer acclaimed, as it had been in the 1950s, as Asia's economic and political showcase for democracy. Its political system was bankrupt, governed capriciously by a dictator in ill health, and an ambitious wife trying to position herself as his political successor.

THE ONSET OF STATE CRISIS

Opposition to Marcos's rule had been stymied when he declared martial law in 1972, partly because considerable public support emerged for his promise of a "new society." Many people had grown disgusted with the political infighting among elites and the violence in the streets, and they had become apprehensive that the Philippines was being left behind economically by the rest of Asia. In 1972, Marcos did the unthinkable by arresting many of the traditional elite's leaders and weakening their economic power by confiscating their lands. Private armies also were disbanded and weapons confiscated, leaving the country, especially the capital, with a sense of calm not experienced in many years. The opposition groups that did exist were negligible and isolated. The Communist-led New People's Army, which then consisted of a few hundred men, retreated to the mountains. The principal military threat came from resurgent Muslim secessionists operating in parts of Mindanao Island. Yet by 1976, the Muslim rebels had been tamed, co-opted by Marcos's deft political maneuvers, and the political opposition—including the popular Senator Benigno Aquino—lived mainly in exile in the United States.

By the late 1970s, however, Marcos's support had begun to weaken significantly. Early expectations that martial law would be a short-term condition followed by the reestablishment of normal political institutions had been disappointed. People began to grow weary of Marcos's extended rule and to be wary of the political dynasty he seemed to be establishing through his wife, Imelda, and three children. The development of "crony capitalism," in which a few of Marcos's favored business people gained monopoly control of major parts of the country's agricultural and industrial sectors, alienated members of Manila's business elite, who initially had supported martial law in the expectation that a more rational and technically sound approach to development would occur.

Continued economic difficulties forced a general retrenchment under guidance from the IMF and the World Bank. Stricter economic policies, however, reduced general government outlays. This retrenchment reduced the funds Marcos could use to win support in the rural areas and to spend on the military, which had been an essential part of his power base since he first entered politics. Marcos's political maneuverability was being limited.

Marcos tried to compensate for this reduction in political space by solidifying his support in Washington, the Philippines' major economic and military ally. He was aided in this tactic by the election of Ronald Reagan, a conservative eager to demonstrate his support for authoritarian leaders loyal to U.S. interests—unlike the Carter administration, which had withdrawn support from the Shah in Iran and from Somoza in Nicaragua. Reagan had a personal relationship with Marcos dating back to 1969 when Reagan had served as President Nixon's special emissary to Manila. Reagan sent a clear signal of support through Vice-President Bush, who visited Manila in 1981 and saluted Marcos, saying "We love your adherence to democratic principle and to the democratic process."

In 1981, Marcos officially lifted martial law, and U.S. officials, including members of Congress, encouraged Marcos to hold elections to normalize the political system and thus provide a needed sign of political stability for foreign investors. Yet rather than stabilizing Marcos's control, these actions encouraged the opposition. The Communist insurgency became more active through the early 1980s as the deteriorating economic situation brought the Communists more recruits. Their attacks soon placed government forces on the defensive, strung out as they were across the many islands of the Philippines. In addition, the solution to the debt problem came only at the great cost of negative growth rates, and economic decline made the people even more disgruntled. The solution to political uncertainty—ending martial law and holding local and national elections—only provided more legitimate venues for the opposition to organize, and more targets for them to attack, as Marcos tried to manipulate the political outcome.

The Catholic Church, led by Archbishop Jaime Sin, also provided support for groups dedicated to social action and political reform. Church opposition to poverty and dictatorship helped to establish the basis for a broad alternative political agenda, and provided the mass support that was needed later to give credibility to the opposition leaders.

In a presidential election in June 1981, Marcos won 88 percent of the vote against two minor opposition candidates. But the elections also gave elite opponents the opportunity to organize and begin mobilizing their own supporters. The reawakening of political activity gave people an opportunity to express attitudes long suppressed under martial law. Senator Benigno Aquino and other leaders formed the People's Power Party (Lakas ng Bayan, or

LABAN). Former Senator Salvador Laurel formed the United Democratic Organization (UNIDO), which became the basis for a surprisingly strong opposition showing in the 1984 elections for the National Assembly.

In 1983, Benigno Aquino returned to the Philippines from his exile in the United States, wanting to personally take part in the political events occurring in Manila. However, he was assassinated while exiting the plane at the Manila airport. His death encouraged a proliferation of opposition groups. Yet the opposition remained divided, unable to agree on a common chieftain or a joint strategy.

Marcos's strategy was to divide and conquer the opposition by offering the opportunity for political participation in the 1984 National Assembly elections, which were recognized as being a precursor to presidential elections later in the decade. He also allowed limited reforms to voting procedures. These tactics did succeed in dividing the opposition. Cardinal Sin and Corazon Aquino—the widow of Senator Benigno Aquino—both favored participation in the elections, while others in the opposition believed that the elections would not be fair, and that only an election boycott could undermine Marcos's control.

But participation was aided by a powerful external force, the United States, which—through congressional hearings, executive branch statements, and emissaries—conveyed the message to Marcos that a credible election process was important if Marcos was to continue to receive support.

Encouraged by the United States but on their own initiative, Filipinos organized the National Movement for Free Elections (NAMFREL) as an independent election oversight group. Led by a Manila business executive, Jose Concepción, and supported by other prominent businesspeople, all of whom retained close ties to the Catholic church, NAMFREL organized in a few months a national system of 150,000 poll watchers to supervise balloting and to produce a "quick count" on election day.

NAMFREL was critical to the opposition's strong showings in the 1984 National Assembly elections and the February 1986 presidential election, and there were both external and internal reasons for this success. Externally, NAMFREL helped energize international public attention. Concepción visited both Europe and the United States to dramatize NAMFREL's work, speaking to policymakers and journalists. The resulting international press and U.S. congressional attention were extraordinarily effective in focusing world public opinion on Marcos and restricting vote fraud. Internally, NAMFREL provided an institutional setting for hundreds of thousands of previously apolitical Filipinos to participate politically without being overtly anti-Marcos.

Thus, although the opposition remained divided, the large-scale public mobilization that occurred after 1983 supplied a source of mass support for the opposition, as Filipinos at all levels of society were politicized. In addition, the formation of NAMFREL and the intervention of outside observers established more reliable criteria by which to judge Marcos's legitimacy.

One of the keys to Marcos's coming fall was the increase in opposition to him by the urban elite and rural poor as a result of the deteriorating economy. Yet although these two groups were united in opposition, their agendas were separate. The poor wanted land reform, improved prices for their produce, basic improvements in living conditions, and personal security from an undisciplined military and a corrupt judicial system. The elites were more interested in wresting political control from Marcos so that they could regain their economic power. They opposed anything but the most superficial land reform schemes and preferred low agricultural prices in order to maintain lower living costs and wages. These differences did not weaken the alliance, but they did suggest that once Marcos was gone, cooperation between the poor and the rich would cease.

REVOLUTIONARY MOBILIZATION
AND THE STRUGGLE FOR POWER

The critical decision that brought the regime down was determined, not by the opposition, but by Marcos himself when he announced on November 3, 1985, his intention to hold early presidential elections the next year.

Although after Aquino's assassination, opposition voices had begun to be increasingly heard in Manila and in Washington, denouncing the regime and exposing its corruption was not the same as overthrowing it. Even though the attacks did increase public sentiment against the government, the opposition had little short-term hope for success. Instead it hoped to take power in the then-scheduled May 1987 presidential elections. Characteristic of the opposition's conservative tactics was the preference of the elites to play by Marcos's rules, within the legal and institutional systems he had forged.

Believing that he still controlled popular opinion and could dominate the political process, Marcos decided to call an early presidential election. He did so for two reasons: First, doing so disrupted the opposition's timetable, hopefully leaving them too sharply divided and without a single leader. Second, he was under U.S. pressure to stabilize the political system by a show of greater legitimacy. Republican Senator Paul Laxalt visited Manila in October 1985 as a representative of President Reagan, and recommended that Marcos hold a snap election. On November 3, Marcos announced this intention in a satellite interview on the David Brinkley television show.

After his announcement, the opposition leaders continued to bicker over whether or not to participate, and over a candidate. Although inexperienced, Corazon ("Cory") Aquino was the one leader whom most could support. Aquino's popularity was derived from her status as a martyr's widow; the drama associated with her husband's death and the personal charisma that surrounded the diminutive widow appealed to the common people. Her close association with the Catholic church, typified by her frequent allusion to the power of prayer and periodic sequestering in a convent, attracted a populace attuned to ritual and miracles. There was something mystical about "Cory's crusade." In addition, the church provided her with an institutional mechanism to mobilize supporters, and her lack of prior political experience made Aquino even more appealing to people who had grown disenchanted with the posturing of traditional leaders.

The fragmentation of the opposition continued up to the last moment of the filing deadline. At first, Laurel—leader of UNIDO and Marcos's major opponent in the recently elected National Assembly—filed separately. Despite the clear majority support for Aquino, Laurel held out, saying he would take the vice-presidential position only if Aquino agreed to run under his party's name. This tactic would assure UNIDO's primary political position in dividing the spoils should they win. The division was not over ideological issues, as they agreed that the only goal was Marcos's removal, but over political supremacy. Only Cardinal Sin's intervention united the opposition. Summoning both Laurel and Aquino to the archbishop's palace in Manila just hours before the final deadline, Sin persuaded Laurel to accept the vice-presidential position and Aquino to accept UNIDO. Both sides were forced to accept the other's demands because both realized that they could not win without the other.

Once the election campaign began, U.S. pressure was considerable. The U.S. Congress held investigative hearings concerning Marcos's hidden wealth and the fabrication of his war record. Republican Senator Richard Lugar played a key role in U.S. public opinion by exposing fraud. All these groups were heavily influenced by NAMFREL's analysis of the election process, which in essence provided the standard by which the fairness and the credibility of the election would be judged.

These actions served to undercut Marcos's control of the election process. Filipinos could even receive broadcasts of U.S. news programs from the U.S. military facilities at Clark Air Base and Subic Bay Naval Base. Aquino and Laurel attracted enormous crowds to their rallies, and enthusiasm spread. Using local citizen-band club radios, business-donated computers, and a national system of 500,000 volunteers, NAMFREL was able to estimate voter turnout and results without having to wait for the "official" returns.

Marcos's final weapon, the military, was also failing him. In early 1985, a military reform group consisting of junior officers, mainly graduates of the Philippine Military Academy affiliated with the defense minister, Juan Ponce Enrile, began plotting a coup against Marcos. This group had become disenchanted with Marcos's rule, angry about the promotion of incompetent officers who were Marcos's personal favorites, and concerned about the growing insurgency. They were fed by Enrile's personal fortune and ambition to replace Marcos with himself. During the vote tabulation for the 1986 presidential election, the wife of one of these plotters dramatically led a walkout of the computer technicians, charging that Marcos was trying to rig the outcome with false data.

The election on February 7 exposed Marcos's fragile hold on the country, but, although condemned both domestically and internationally, he still held on to power, claiming victory in the election vote-count, and bolstered in part by Reagan's refusal to withdraw support. On February 10, Reagan said that despite charges of fraud, there was still evidence of a strong democratic system in the islands and he hoped that Marcos and Aquino "could come together to make sure the government works." Instead, political disintegration continued as both sides dug in their heels. Aquino's supporters held vigils, demonstrations, marches, and rallies around the country demanding that Marcos recognize her victory and resign.

Possibly (although it is unlikely) Marcos could have survived the political crisis despite mounting pressures. But he had become aware of the military plot against him, and while attempting to preempt the plotters by arresting them, he set in motion the very event he was trying to prevent.

On February 22, elements of the military supported by Enrile and the military's vice chief of staff, Fidel Ramos, rebelled. Holed up at the military's headquarters in Manila, this small group called on the rest of the military to join them and appealed to Cardinal Sin to send the people for support. On Radio Veritas, Cardinal Sin called the people out into the streets. Matrons and nuns, workers and executives all flocked to create a human barricade between the rebels and the Marcos loyalists attempting to move within firing range.

Marcos hesitated to counterattack, partly because he was unsure about the extent of rebel support within the military, and partly because the Americans insisted that no violent action be taken, fearing that bloodshed would produce further rifts in the military and the political system. As Marcos hesitated, other units joined the rebel cause. Increasingly isolated in the palace, Marcos equivocated. By the time he finally ordered troops to attack, it was too late; few remained on his side. On February 25, Marcos and his family and aides were airlifted by U.S. helicopters from Malacanang Palace and flown into exile in Hawaii. Cory Aquino was swept into the palace in triumph, and sworn in as president.

In retrospect, clearly no single person or factor was solely responsible for the February 1986 "people-power" revolution. It was the result of a combination of factors (internal, external, social, economic, political, psychological) and individuals that eroded the regime's legitimacy and its responsiveness to change and provided the opportunity for an opposition to emerge and grow. It was almost a "bloodless" revolution.

REVOLUTIONARY OUTCOMES

During her first four years in office President Aquino had three major accomplishments: surviving at least six attempted coups, restoring democratic institutions, and improving the economy.

The coups reflected continuing divisions among the elites, as both Vice-President Laurel and former Defense Minister Juan Ponce Enrile were implicated in efforts to wrest power from Aquino. The first serious coup attempt, led by Colonel Gregorio Honasan, one of the leaders of the anti-Marcos military plotters, nearly succeeded in toppling Aquino's government in August 1987. In December 1989 he tried again, and as before, almost succeeded. After each serious attempt, improvements in military benefits, changes in the command structure, and the arrest of several coup plotters helped quiet the restive military. General Fidel Ramos proved to be Aquino's most important supporter among the military.

The United States strongly supported Aquino. In 1986, she was welcomed to Washington for a state visit, and in late 1987 a group of congressional leaders proposed a special aid package for the Philippines. Aid flowed into Manila from all quarters, so that by the end of 1988, commitments of financial support amounted to over $4 billion. The U.S. also provided military support for the Aquino regime; jets from Clark Air Base overflew the rebels attempting the December 1989 coup, discouraging them from any further action.

With increased amounts of foreign aid, and the successful conduct of elections for a new Philippine Congress and for local offices in 1987 and 1988, the confidence of investors and consumers returned. Buoyed by a spurt in consumer spending, the Philippines' growth rate rebounded dramatically in 1986 and reached almost 9 percent per year in 1988.

Yet foreign support, new political institutions, and a popular president could not mask continued problems within a polity trying to make a political transition to democracy and an economic transition to industrialization. For while the removal of Marcos had meant an end to dictatorship, it had not meant an end to the deep social divisions between prosperous urban centers and stagnating rural areas or between the rich and the poor. Filipinos also struggled to define a renewed sense of national identity; nationalist politicians attempted to build mass support by asserting control over foreign investment and U.S. military facilities—the latter being a symbol of repression by both a foreign power and a fallen dictator long supported by Washington.

Throughout the presidencies of Cory Aquino, and her successor, Fidel Ramos, the alliance across class lines that made the Philippines Revolution was breaking down. It was essentially a Manila-based revolution in which few in the provinces had participated, and it did not directly touch the lives of the majority of Filipinos. Thus it did not bridge the urban-rural chasm.

The most discouraging factor in the Philippines' future remains its poor, whose numbers daily grow larger. By the end of the twentieth century, the Philippines contained close to 100 million people, the vast majority of whom remained poor. There has been little effort by the Aquino government or its successors to respond to this problem, whose dimensions have long been apparent. To do so will require a level of national (and international) commitment that has not yet appeared.

CHAPTER 8

Revolutions Against Communism

Communist regimes were created by revolutions in many countries throughout the twenti-eth century. The Marxist revolutions in Russia (1917), in China (1949), and Cuba (1959) are discussed in Chapter 6. It was rather a shock to many analysts that these communist re-gimes were themselves overturned by revolutions. However, this simply proved that no type of regime is immune to social upheaval; any government that becomes weak, with its elites divided and rebellious, and with its population mobilized for protest, can experience revolutions or rebellions.

In Eastern Europe, many countries became communist following World War II, when the Nazi forces were driven out by the Soviet Union. These regimes remained strongly dom-inated by Soviet influence, and the Soviet Union gave them both economic and military sup-port. China also became communist with Soviet assistance but developed its own type of communist institutions and ideals. By the end of the 1980s, however, the communist re-gimes in Eastern Europe, the Soviet Union, and China all faced multiple problems. Jeff Goodwin and Jack Goldstone describe how in Eastern Europe and the Soviet Union, these problems led to a dramatic revolutionary collapse. In China, as Martin King Whyte dis-cusses, a student protest turned into a major rebellion, but the regime stayed in power, and the rebellion was violently suppressed. Nonetheless, China is also changing, and observers await to see whether China's regime will change in the future by reform or by revolution.

The East European Revolutions of 1989

JEFF GOODWIN

Goodwin shows that the anti-communist revolutions in Eastern Europe had much in common with the Third World revolutions discussed in earlier chapters. In all of these cases, a relatively closed, autonomous state was blamed for poor economic performance and excessive dependence on a foreign power. The result was na-tionalist, anti-regime opposition that came from all levels of society, even mem-bers of the ruling elites. When foreign support was withdrawn, these regimes col-lapsed or were quickly driven from power by popular protests.

If one set out in the spring of 1980 to analyze recent revolutions—inspired, perhaps, by the dramatic events of the previous year in Iran, Nicaragua, and Afghanistan—one's attention would have been drawn inexorably and indeed exclusively to the Third World. At that time, certainly, there did not seem to be anything particularly revolutionary occurring in the "Second World" of the Soviet bloc (and certainly not in the "First World" of advanced capitalist societies). Indeed, opposition movements in Eastern Europe seemed extraordinarily weak or simply nonexistent. The fact that powerful movements within and without the ruling Communist parties had been bloodily suppressed by the Soviet Union in Hungary in 1956 and rather more easily, but no less thoroughly, in Czechoslovakia in 1968 only underscored the apparently insurmountable difficulties in opposing the extant Communist regimes. (The emergence of the Solidarity movement in Poland was still a few months away.)

And yet, little more than a decade later something truly revolutionary had occurred: The Soviet bloc was no more. In 1989 one of the most startling and almost completely unanticipated revolutions destroyed the Communist regimes of Eastern Europe and all that went with them: the political monopoly of the ruling Communist parties; state organizations (including armies and secret police) thoroughly penetrated by these parties; state control over the means of production; and extensive state economic planning. How could this have happened?

Some writers have stressed the role of *economic factors* in the demise of Communism. In this view, Communism collapsed because it represented a form of economic organization that, because of state ownership and planning, was thoroughly inefficient, technologically stagnant, and, accordingly, incapable of keeping pace with the capitalist West. Others view these events as reflecting the triumph of a new "civil society" in Eastern Europe. In this view, the old regime—weak though it may have been—was pulled down by a combination of political dissidents and capitalist entrepreneurs, groups that had emerged within the region's political (and intellectual) underground and the "second" or informal economy, respectively—the interstices, as it were, of the old order. Finally, the events of 1989 have been explained by what Albert Hirschman has aptly described as "a deus ex machina"—namely, Mikhail Gorbachev.[1] In this view, the fall of Communism in Eastern Europe was an inevitable result of the reformist orientation of the Soviet leader and, more particularly, of his refusal to employ Soviet forces to defend the Soviet Union's satellite regimes in that region (i.e., his rejection of the so-called Brezhnev Doctrine).

All of these explanations certainly capture important aspects of 1989, and I shall invoke them in the analysis that follows. And yet they also beg crucial questions. Neither the economic nor the "Gorbachev" explanation for 1989, for example, explains why there was so little interest, as there once had been, in "fixing" or reforming Communism in Eastern Europe as opposed to overthrowing it. (This, after all, was precisely what Gorbachev was attempting to do in the Soviet Union itself.) "Civil society," moreover, was relatively underdeveloped in 1989 (a legacy of Communist despotism felt to this day), more so in some countries than in others, and its generally antisocialist orientation needs to be explained, not simply assumed. Finally, we need to ask why Communist leaders in the region (outside of Romania) did not *themselves* attempt to defend their privileges, through violence if necessary. Why was there so little counterrevolutionary violence in Eastern Europe during 1989? Economic stagnation may explain why people were generally unhappy in Eastern Europe, and Gorbachev's leadership may explain why *Soviet* troops were not employed to suppress their protests, but neither of these explanations adequately explains the rapid and relatively bloodless overthrow of Communist rule in 1989.

An alternative perspective on 1989 is to view the events of that year as a reaction by both political dissidents *and* important elements within the regimes themselves to the decline of an overextended imperialist power. Although certainly a year of democratic revolutions in Eastern Europe, 1989 was also, for that very reason, a year of anti-imperialist revolutions directed against Soviet domination of the region.

The dissolution of empires, formal and informal, has in fact been one of the distinguishing and most consequential characteristics of the twentieth century, and one for which revolutionaries can take substantial credit. The popular struggles for national sovereignty that have helped to destroy empires have sometimes (although certainly not always) been fused with attempts to change radically the socioeconomic institutions inherited from the imperialists. The result of this fusion has been nationalist revolution—or revolutionary nationalism—another phenomenon largely unique to the present century. Eastern Europe is only the most recent example of how imperial domination not only has generated nationalist opposition, but has also unwittingly radicalized it—albeit in a very peculiar way that this chapter attempts to explain. Thus, the Eastern European revolutions of 1989, as Pavel Campeanu has pointed out, had "a dual nature; social, since their goal was to destroy the socioeconomic structures of Stalinism, and national, since they aspired to reestablish the sovereignty of the countries in question."[2]

Were the events in Eastern Europe in 1989 "revolutionary?" "Social revolution" denotes a fundamental and relatively rapid transformation of a national society's state structure, economic institutions, and/or culture; these changes, furthermore, are initiated and/or achieved, at least in part, by popular mobilizations, including armed movements, strikes, and/or demonstrations. While the events of 1989 largely fit this definition, especially in Czechoslovakia and East Germany, the process of revolutionary change in Eastern Europe was certainly unusual compared to most revolutions. To begin with, the undeniably radical transformations that have taken place in Eastern Europe—including the collapse of Communist Party rule, the elimination of longstanding military and economic ties to the former Soviet Union, and the transition to a distinctively Eastern European capitalism—occurred (except in Romania) virtually without armed conflict. In addition, these transformations were at least partly the result of reformist movements or factions within the ruling Communist parties themselves. These distinctive characteristics of Eastern European revolutions obviously require some explanation.

My analysis emphasizes the *similarities* between the Eastern European revolutions, on the one hand (especially the cases of Poland, Hungary, Czechoslovakia, and East Germany), and certain Third World revolutions, on the other (including such cases as Mexico, Vietnam, Cuba, Iran, and Nicaragua).

THE OLD REGIME STATES

The structures and practices of the old-regime states of Eastern Europe share a number of similarities with two particular types of Third World regimes that have proven exceptionally vulnerable to revolutionary overthrow: neopatrimonial, personalist dictatorships, on the one hand (such as once ruled Mexico, Iran, Cuba, and Nicaragua), and racially exclusionary and repressive colonial regimes, on the other hand (such as were once found in Vietnam, Algeria, Angola, and elsewhere). These state structures and practices became the target of an extremely broad nationalist opposition and, by rendering these regimes "unreformable," unintentionally served to radicalize these oppositions as well. In the Second World no less than the Third, in other words, certain types of states helped to construct the very movements that would bury them.

The Soviet-backed communist regimes in Eastern Europe were remarkably independent, or autonomous, from the societies that they ruled. The autonomy of Eastern European regimes, in fact, like that of prerevolutionary Third World states, was predicated on their historic intolerance of "civil society"—independent associations and ideological currents. However, after the 1960s, many of the Eastern European regimes—Romania being the clearest exception—largely shed their totalitarian pretensions, abandoning the goal of ideological conformity among the population, *even among Party members,* and sometimes tolerating small "islands of autonomy" within civil society so long as these did not seem to threaten the regime. This change is nicely captured in the Hungarian leader Janos Kadar's famous reversal of the formula that "He who is not with us is against us" into "He who is not against us is with us." Indeed, "After the Stalinist period, the state accepted an implicit 'pact of non-aggression' with society, allowing citizens to pursue private and egoistic ends in exchange for withdrawal from public life and politics."[3] In other words, there eventually emerged in most of Eastern Europe what scholars have referred to as post-totalitarian regimes.

The post-totalitarian policy of "salamis for submission," as the Czechs called it, suggests that Second World totalitarianism was gradually evolving, at least in certain respects, into a form of rule that was increasingly similar to Third World authoritarianism. The post-Stalinist "social compact," however, even as it opened up some limited space for the development of a civil society, also placed the thin popular legitimacy of these regimes on a new, non-ideological, and, as it developed, even more tenuous basis: If the regime could not provide sufficient salami, it had no right to expect submission. As Valerie Bunce wryly observes, "Regimes that had long castigated capitalism for its short-term horizons and that prided themselves on the long-term vistas enabled by planning, state ownership of the economy, and Communist Party rule were increasingly placed in the position of making decisions in response to a single question: what have you done for me lately?"[4]

The politicized economies of Eastern Europe, in fact, proved increasingly incapable of "delivering the goods," particularly quality consumer goods, during the 1970s and 1980s (although there were certainly important variations in this regard among individual countries). To be sure, these regimes were relatively adept at heavy industrialization through the "extensive" mobilization of ever-greater resources (including labor) during their first two decades, but "intensive" economic growth based on the efficient utilization of such resources and routine technological innovation was systematically undermined by the politicized (and militarized) nature of state-socialist economies. Above all, the "soft budget constraints" of state enterprises that are characteristic of such economies—the practical impossibility, that is, of firms going bankrupt, owing to their receipt of state subsidies—provided few incentives for efficient production, quality control, or the development of labor-saving technologies. In this economic context, moreover, as Katherine Verdery has noted, "many workers developed an opposition cult of *non*-work, imitating the Party bosses and trying to do as little as possible for their paycheck."[5]

Economic stagnation, in fact, led a number of Eastern European states to borrow heavily from the West during the 1970s, which simply compounded problems of external dependence. Economic stagnation in the region also led to a number of experiments with economic liberalization and decentralization during the post-Stalin era. The politicized nature of state-socialist economies, however, impeded the sort of fundamental political and economic reforms that might have increased enterprise efficiency.

Significant economic and political liberalization threatened political elites and enterprise managers with the loss of access to state-centered economic resources. The nomenklatura's loss of *political* authority, in other words, threatened its *economic* authority and privileges. The result was that state-socialist regimes—again, like neopatrimonial dictatorships and racially exclusionary colonies in the Third World—generally proved incapable of reform "from above": "Major reform was as necessary as it was politically impossible."[6]

Since reform was thus unavailable, Eastern Europe's state-socialist regimes—or if need be, their Soviet patron—almost invariably used repression against those who sought social change. As in many Third World countries, however, indiscriminate repression of opposition movements ultimately backfired in Eastern Europe; repression severely impeded overt oppositional activities, to be sure, but at the cost of further undermining the regimes' legitimacy and swelling the ranks of those who identified with an increasingly radicalized (i.e., anti-Communist) opposition. Repression and political exclusion, in fact, predictably strengthened those "radicals" who argued that the entire social and political order was thoroughly bankrupt and must be recast from top to bottom.

OPPOSITION MOVEMENTS

Opposition movements in Eastern Europe in 1989 generally shared five characteristics with most successful Third World revolutionary movements: They were (1) multiclass movements that were unified by (2) widespread anger against state authorities as well as by (3) nationalism or patriotism, and they were (4) led by "radical" leaderships with (5) imitative and "reactive," albeit quasi-utopian, ideologies. Let us examine some of these characteristics of revolutionary oppositions in more detail.

Opposition to Communism was certainly not confined to the poorest or most oppressed segments of these societies; it reached from peasants and workers to intellectuals and professionals and, ultimately, into the nomenklatura itself. This broad opposition to Communism was characterized and indeed "glued" together by a widespread hostility toward political authorities—a broadly shared anger that helped to "paper over" the latent conflicts of interest within this opposition (at least until Communist rule was dismantled). Since the state centrally planned, "owned," and distributed virtually all economic resources and consumer goods, when the public became dissatisfied, it did not (or could not) blame fate, itself, the market, or even local bosses, but generally came to blame Communist Party rule as such.

A similar logic of opposition has been encouraged in the Third World context by neo-patrimonial dictatorships and by racially exclusionary colonial regimes. These regimes are not only characterized by repressive authoritarianism, but also by extensive economic pow-ers and modes of intervention, blatant political and economic favoritism toward privileged clients, and pervasive corruption based on racism and/or "cronyism." Accordingly, these re-gime types and their typical practices also unintentionally focus a wide array of social and economic grievances upon the state (and thence upon its foreign backers), because the suc-cessful resolution of *socioeconomic* conflicts requires a redistribution of *political* power within the state, if not its actual overthrow.

Revolutionary change in both the Second and Third Worlds is linked to the politics of hegemonic powers in yet another way. In the Third World, revolutionary change has been possible when colonial or neocolonial powers at last grew weary of the high costs of empire, although this typically did not occur until after long and bloody wars of counterinsurgency aroused opposition among the metropolitan power's *domestic* population (cases include, among others, the French in Indochina and Algeria, the United States in South Vietnam, and the Portuguese in Africa). In Eastern Europe, similarly, a revolutionary breakthrough at last became possible when the Soviet Union grew weary of the high costs of its empire. Neither Soviet forces in Eastern Europe nor (neo)colonial troops in the Third World were *militarily* expelled; the decision to withdraw them came, rather, after the progressive attrition of their governments' political will to deploy them in the face of continuing, yet by no means over-whelming, nationalist resistance.

As many analysts have noted, moreover, Gorbachev's reform policies at home and his abandonment of the Brezhnev Doctrine abroad both demoralized conservative, hard-line Communist leaders in Eastern Europe and invigorated their opponents inside as well as out-side the ruling parties. Communism in Eastern Europe, in other words, was delegitimated "from above and outside" as well as "from below." The increasingly clear understanding that reformist initiatives would be tolerated and perhaps even welcomed by the Soviet leader-ship certainly helped to fuel popular opposition movements in Eastern Europe through the course of 1989, producing what one observer has termed a "revolutionary bandwagon," as previously hidden preferences for regime change could be openly expressed.[7]

Generally, there were two distinct, and temporally sequential, patterns of revolution-ary change in 1989 in Eastern Europe's post-totalitarian regimes—one initiated primarily "from above" and the other "from below." Where Communist "soft-liners," or reformers in the Gorbachev mold, predominated, allowing for the development of a comparatively strong civil society, the regime initiated round-table discussions with civic groups—in the wake of serious strikes and protests in 1988 in Poland—which led to negotiated transitions (or "pacted transitions") to democracy and, eventually, capitalism. These "negotiated revo-lutions" occurred in Poland and Hungary. However, in those post-totalitarian regimes in which Communist "hard-liners" held sway, and civil society was especially weak, regime intransigence provoked massive (and nonviolent) protests of a more or less spontaneous nature. In these cases (Czechoslovakia and East Germany), the hard-liners eventually capitulated when confronted by popular protest.

This sense of a broad, familiar "us" pitted against an alien "them" has not only arisen under state socialism in the Second World, but also under personalist dictatorships and racially exclusionary colonialism in the Third World. In fact, externally dependent and domestically repressive regimes that are strongly fused with economic authority are the institutional frameworks that have most consistently led to revolution—not capitalism or socialism per se. What collapsed in Eastern Europe was not socialism, but a type of authoritarian socialism—just as what collapsed in the Third World has not been capitalism or even "backward" capitalism, but authoritarian modes of colonial and "crony" capitalism.

REFERENCES

1.   Hirschman (1993), p. 196.
2.   Campeanu (1991), pp. 806–807.
3.   Ekiert (1990), p. 2.
4.   Bunce (1999), pp. 56–57.
5.   Verdery (1993), p. 4.
6.   Bunce (1999), p. 3.
7.   See Kuran (1991), p. 36.

Revolution in the U.S.S.R., 1989–1991

JACK A. GOLDSTONE

From 1985 to 1989, the leader of the Soviet Union, Mikhail Gorbachev, led a campaign to reform communist rule. However, to the surprise of all observers, including Gorbachev himself, his efforts led not only to the end of Soviet communism, but to the end of the U.S.S.R. itself. Gorbachev's reforms spurred the rise of more radical movements to create independent national states, including a new Russian state under Boris Yeltsin. At the same time, there arose a conservative reaction against reform. In 1991, while Gorbachev was vacationing in the Crimea, conservatives attempted a military coup to reverse Gorbachev's reforms, but their coup failed, defeated by popular resistance in Moscow led by Yeltsin. When Gorbachev returned, he found Yeltsin in control of Russia, while the other national states of the U.S.S.R., in the Baltics, the Caucasus, and Central Asia, broke away to form independent states. The Soviet Union and the absolute rule of the Communist Party were no more. Goldstone argues that these events were a major revolution and that behind them lay a causal pattern similar to that in great revolutions of history.

A REVOLUTION IN THE U.S.S.R.

Some observers have likened the events of 1989–91 to the dissolution of the Austro-Hungarian and Ottoman Empires after World War I, when old multinational empires broke up into an array of new nations. However, in those cases the dissolutions were clearly the outcome of war, and the dismemberment of the old regimes was overseen by military victors. In 1989–1991, by contrast, one of the world's military superpowers collapsed without any military confrontation with its chief rivals.

It might be suggested that the collapse of the U.S.S.R. was brought about by the revolts against communism that occurred in Eastern Europe, beginning with the Solidarity rebellion in Poland in 1980. Yet I believe this view reverses the true direction of causality. There had been many efforts to reform or throw off communist rule in Eastern Europe since the 1950s—in Poland and Hungary in 1956, in Czechoslovakia in 1968, and again in Poland in 1970. But each time, such movements were crushed by Soviet command and with Soviet assistance. The great surprise of 1989 was that this time, the rebellious actions of Poles, and shortly thereafter other Eastern Europeans, met with acceptance and even encouragement from Gorbachev's Soviet regime, and that Gorbachev asked Eastern European governments to restrain their repression. This time the Soviet Union felt too unsure of itself to act to maintain its satellites. Thus the essential surprise, the linchpin of events, was not that people in Eastern Europe rose up, but that the Soviet regime was already breaking down.

More optimistic observers have suggested the events of 1989–91 were the beginning of a peaceful democratic reform. Yet while it is true that the communist regime was overthrown without excessive bloodshed in Moscow, it required a confrontation between tanks and ordinary citizens; and seen more broadly, the collapse of the U.S.S.R. involved widespread popular uprisings, and extensive violence in Azerbaijan, Tajikistan, and Chechnya. What occurred, in sum, was the collapse of the communist regime, the dissolution of all Soviet institutions of government and the ideology that supported them, and economic and political chaos as new groups struggled to reconstitute new states. These changes would seem to qualify the events of 1989–91 in the U.S.S.R. as a major revolution.

I have argued that revolutions are not the result of a single primary cause, but will occur only when there is a *conjunction* of several trends. Those trends are a decline in state effectiveness and fiscal strength; increased alienation and conflicts among elites, generally evidenced by clogged routes of social mobility that create heightened competition and frustration among aspirants for elite positions; and an increase in mass mobilization potential, created mainly by declining living standards and increased urbanization.

To see if the Soviet collapse resembled past revolutions in its causes, I suggest that we focus on three questions: (1) Was the Soviet state losing effectiveness in a manner visible to state leaders and Soviet elites? (2) Were the elites of the Soviet state and society experiencing increasing alienation and divisions, due to failures in social mobility? (3) Were declines in living standards and shifts in urbanization so great as to provide a basis for growing mass mobilization potential among the populace? If the answers to all three questions are yes, then I would argue that the sudden collapse of the Soviet regime is not only comprehensible, but in fact conforms to the general causal pattern of major revolutions.

THE DECAY OF STATE EFFECTIVENESS

Michael Mann[1] has suggested that there are four types of power: economic (the power of resources and production), ideological (the power of inspiring ideas), military (the power of coercion), and political (the power of legitimate authorities, particularly when supported by control of complex organizations, to command obedience). Until roughly 1970, the relative success and stability of the Soviet regime rested on all four power forms. But thereafter, the four bases of Soviet power decayed steadily, with the decay accelerating greatly after 1985.

After establishing much legitimacy through its costly victory in World War II, the Soviet regime scored numerous economic and political victories during the next twenty-five years. Economically, steady industrial growth rates of more than 6 percent per annum established centers of modern industrial production throughout Soviet territory. The U.S.S.R. rose to world leadership in the output of oil, steel, and other basic industrial goods. In space and nuclear technology, it became one of two super-powers.

Militarily, the U.S.S.R. and its allies kept NATO and the United States on the defensive throughout the world. The Berlin Wall and the Cuban missile crisis in the 1960s, though seen as Western victories, were only defensive victories that did no more than slightly limit Soviet gains from its increased control of East Germany and Cuba. In Vietnam, the United States suffered a costly defeat at the hands of Soviet-supported opponents. Soviet automatic rifles (the Kalashnikov), tanks, and jet fighters challenged U.S. arms manufacturers for dominance on the battlefield and in world arms markets.

Ideologically, America's civil rights battles, student movements, antipoverty campaigns, and interventions in the Dominican Republic and Vietnam during the 1960s gave the world the impression of a capitalist society that was racist, oppressive, imperialistic, and rife with poverty. In contrast, the socialist ideology of the Soviet Union, which appeared free of unemployment and discrimination and had led Russia's rise in a few short decades to challenge American power, had great international appeal. In 1975, when the United States withdrew in defeat from Vietnam, America's capitalist ideology seemed weak. In Angola and Mozambique, Egypt and Syria, Cuba, and even among significant communist parties in Western Europe, communist ideology seemed to be gaining influence.

Politically, the CPSU (Communist Party of the Soviet Union) under Khrushchev and Brezhnev gradually institutionalized its control of Soviet society. The police state and mass gulags under Stalin were replaced by extensive, but less heavy-handed, political authority, which operated as much by favoritism and incentives for successful managers, scientists, artists, and athletes as by coercion and terror. Political opposition was reduced to a few thousand dissidents, while political allegiance was gained from silent millions who benefited from the extension of industrial amenities and services. From 1958 to 1971, Soviet infant mortality was halved, from 40.6 to 22.9 deaths per thousand.[2]

The strength and stability of the Soviet regime from 1945 to 1970 was therefore evident. But after about 1970, conditions in all these domains began to deteriorate. Economically, Soviet productivity faltered. An economy geared to producing heavy industrial commodities could not make the adjustment either to the next industrial generation of microcomputer technology or to the provision of diversified consumer goods and services. From 1945 to 1970, the Soviet Union increased its economic output by producing increasing numbers of tractors, tons of concrete, and sheets of steel. But by about 1970, the society's ability to absorb basic industrial commodities came into question. Giving a farm two tractors where there had been none greatly increased output. Giving a farm four tractors where there had been two (especially since there were insufficient spare parts to keep even two running full time) did not add to output and thus did not cover the cost of producing the additional tractors. Producing more tractors, concrete, and sheet steel simply meant more goods piled up on railway sidings or severely underutilized in plants and fields.

Thus, during the 1970s the Soviet economy poured enormous resources into basic investments while achieving less and less growth in outputs. Manufacturing and agriculture stagnated, and the U.S.S.R. became more dependent on production and trade of raw materials. Annual industrial growth fell from 6.4−6.5 percent in 1961−70 to 5.5 percent in 1971−75 and then sank to 2.7 percent in 1976−80 and 1.9 percent in 1981−85.[3] In 1955, 28 percent of the U.S.S.R.'s exports to Western Europe had been manufactured goods. By 1983, as a result of shortages in the U.S.S.R. and the inferiority of Soviet manufacturers, that figure had fallen to 6 percent.[4] Shortages of consumer goods, even of basic items such as housing, increased sharply. No more houses were built in the U.S.S.R. in 1984 than had been built in 1960, despite a substantially increased population; thus, the stock of housing relative to the population decreased by 30 percent over these years.[5]

In 1985−86, Gorbachev followed Yuri Andropov's lead in trying to improve the economy mainly by enforcing work discipline and "accelerating" work efforts. But these efforts failed. Following these failures, early efforts at more severe restructuring under the banner of *perestroika* simply disrupted production and led to severe shortages of goods. Finally, attempting to buy rather than force reform, Gorbachev literally bankrupted the Soviet state. Printing rubles to underwrite unrealistic promises of raises and investments in key sectors of the economy, the currency multiplied dramatically. The state budget deficit, stable at 15− 18 billion rubles per year in 1980−85, suddenly rose to 90 billion rubles per year in 1988− 89. The sizable inflation that followed further undermined the legitimacy of Gorbachev's government.

Militarily, after 1975 the tide of Soviet influence began to recede. Vietnam and Cuba became burdens rather than areas of further expansion in Asia and Latin America. Egypt threw off its Soviet alliance, leaving only a badly defeated Syria as the U.S.S.R.'s main Middle East ally. Most critically, the communist regime in Afghanistan faced an internal rebellion in 1979 and looked to Soviet troops to defend it. But following ten subsequent years of unsuccessful warfare, Soviet troops withdrew from Afghanistan, leaving the Afghan rebels in control of the countryside and, three years later, Kabul. In a striking parallel to America's experience in Vietnam, Soviet withdrawal in 1989 marked the most dramatic military failure in Soviet history.

Ideologically, the failure of socialism became most marked in the environmental arena, especially in the wake of the Chernobyl disaster. Capitalism had been castigated as an economic system that exploited and ravaged its workers for the sake of profits for the few. The U.S.S.R. claimed to be a workers' state whose economy operated with the welfare of its workers as its chief aim. Yet the explosion of the nuclear power plant at Chernobyl, and more especially the inept reaction of the authorities, comprehensively undermined the Soviet claims. Because of the Chernobyl disaster's watershed political consequences, it deserves closer examination.

On April 26, 1986, one of the four reactors at Chernobyl nuclear power station overheated, leading to steam explosions and fires that spread highly radioactive materials over the countryside and into the atmosphere. Yet Soviet authorities did not even admit to an accident until three days later, when Swedish authorities who had suddenly detected a major increase in radioactive fallout in their country began to press through private and public channels for an explanation of what had occurred. Although more precise figures are still being developed, even early estimates place the total radiation release as *eighty times* that of the Hiroshima or Nagasaki explosions.[6] Nonetheless, Soviet authorities made no announcement to people in the regions affected by fallout, advocated no precautions. Party leaders ordered schools, shops, and workplaces to remain open, while sending their own families away. May Day parades went on in Kiev (whose 2.4 million residents lived only seventy-five miles from the reactor site) while radiation plumes were still spreading overhead. As the extent of the disaster slowly became clear, Western reports on Radio Free Europe increasingly conflicted with the reassurances of the Soviet authorities. As the truth gradually became known in the U.S.S.R., it became clear to Russians, Ukrainians, Belorussians, and Latvians that the Soviet regime had been encouraging them to feed their children with contaminated foods and left them uncertain about the safety of their homes. The myth that they lived in a society chiefly concerned with workers' welfare vanished, replaced by a cynical reevaluation of the "authorities."

Moreover, the Chernobyl explosion was just the tip of the iceberg of environmental disasters that began to come to light. It raised, for example, concerns about pollution of the Dnieper River, the main source of drinking and irrigation water for the Ukraine. However, a search for possible alternatives revealed that none existed; industrial pollution had already rendered every other major river in the central and southern Ukraine unfit for human consumption.[7] In the port of Ventspils in Latvia, schools periodically had to issue gas masks to children due to the venting of the petrochemical and tanning works in the city. Radioactive wastes, chemical effluents, fertilizer and pesticide misuse, and poorly designed and managed irrigation schemes had left much of the U.S.S.R. and Eastern Europe an ecological nightmare, encompassing some of the most dangerously polluted lands on earth and wreaking destruction of habitats and resources (such as the shrinkage of the Aral Sea and the disappearance of the Volga sturgeon fishery) on an unprecedented scale.

Growing indications of ecological disaster were accompanied by declines in health care and mortality. From its low point in 1960–61 to 1975–76, the Soviet death rate increased 30 percent, from 7.2 to 9.4 deaths per thousand per year. Infant mortality, which had steadily fallen to 22.9 per thousand in 1971, swiftly rose (according to Soviet official statistics) by almost half, to 31.1 per thousand by 1976.[8] Things then deteriorated even further. By 1980–81, adult life expectancy had fallen four full years from 1964–65, from 66.1 to 62.3 years. By 1987 the Soviet health minister admitted that infant mortality in the U.S.S.R. ranked no better than fiftieth in the world, after Barbados and the United Arab Emirates.[9]

Shortages of medical supplies contributed to the decline of public health. Increasing numbers of industrial accidents, as workers suffered with worn-out machinery and deteriorating mines and factories, probably also contributed to greater mortality. Under such conditions, in which public health and mortality sharply deteriorated while party officials evaded responsibility and shielded themselves, any ideological claims about the superiority of socialism and its greater regard for the working man and woman provoked anger rather than assent.

Coming together with great force in the late 1980s, these trends and conditions eroded the CPSU's political authority. Managers complained that central economic directives were unproductive and out of touch with local needs. Military officials, bruised in Afghanistan, questioned national policy priorities. Local party officials sought to defend their regions against pollution excesses. Previously passive miners began to strike for safer conditions. Writers and artists increasingly gave expression to the mounting problems. Under this drumbeat of problems, the formerly cohesive party structure weakened amid a host of evasions of responsibility for the apparent deterioration in every main area of Soviet life.

THE GROWTH OF ELITE ALIENATION AND CONFLICT OVER ACCESS TO ELITE POSITIONS

A top-down view of revolution suggests that unrest and alienation among elites can carry a state far down the path to collapse well before popular mobilizations occur. In the French Revolution, it was the Finance Ministry's admitted bankrupting of the Crown, as well as the rejection of the Crown's proposed reforms by the Assembly of Notables, that precipitated the calling of the Estates General. It was only after the Estates General met that Parisian crowds surged to the Bastille. Similarly, in the U.S.S.R., it was elites inside the party structure that issued calls for reform, and later for the dissolution of the regime.

Elite alienation grew rapidly as the trends discussed above became evident; indeed, the trends were most evident to party leaders and to middle-level and provincial elites. As J. F. Brown has noted, "the communist ruling elite . . . began to lose confidence in its ability to rule, and more to the point, to lose the willingness to use the means to retain its rule.[10] Among middle-level and provincial elites, the change in attitudes was exemplified by the disgust of Leonid Teliatnikov, who had been chief of the Chernobyl Nuclear Plant Fire Station at the time of the accident. Learning that local political leaders neither informed nor prepared to evacuate the affected population, he told the journal *Smena*, "I felt sick in my soul and ashamed that I should belong to the same Party as these people. . . . I stopped respecting many city leaders."[11]

Teliatnikov's reaction was indicative of the attitudes of increasing numbers of technical school graduates. From the 1960s to the 1980s, the Soviet Union experienced an explosion of graduates in engineering and other technical subjects. Yet as the structure of the Soviet economy did not become more information—and skill-intensive but stayed mired in its

Table 1   Social Mobility and Competition in the U.S.S.R., 1930–1989

	(Percentage of Population)					
	1930s	1940s	1950s	1960s	1970s	1980s
Manual	33	37	42	48	51	41
Clerical	6	6	7	10	12	16
Education and services	7	8	9	14	14	19[a]
Professional and elite	2	3	4	5	5	

Source: Data from Gordon and Nazimova (1986), pp. 48–50; Aslund (1991), p. 21; Garcelon (1995), p. 249.

Note: Columns do not add up to 100 because of the exclusion of agricultural and miscellaneous workers.

[a] Education/services and professional/elite categories merged.

heavy industry structure, there were few suitable outlets for the career ambitions of these graduates. Instead of rising in income and influence, these "technical specialists," as they were called, remained subordinate to party officials and a small cadre of enterprise managers, who thwarted their efforts to rise in the system. Much of the support for reform came precisely from these specialists, who joined the more exalted academicians and the upper intelligentsia of writers, television and radio workers, artists, and professionals in thoroughly rejecting the Communist Party.

Table 1 shows trends in the occupational structure of the Soviet Union's labor force from the 1950s to the 1980s. What is most striking in this table, and in marked contrast to trends among North American and European labor forces during the same period, is the utter stagnation in the proportion of the labor force engaged in professional and administrative positions from the 1960s to the 1980s. We see here the U.S.S.R.'s clear failure to shift from an industrial to an information based economy.

This occupational stagnation occurred despite a huge increase in the proportion of the population with higher degrees. The number of those whose jobs qualified them as "specialists" due to advanced technical or college training rose from roughly one million in 1940 to perhaps ten million by 1970. In 1959, only 2 percent of the population had postsecondary degrees; by 1989, the proportion had risen to 9 percent. Yet the decline in the number of auxiliary and unskilled jobs was painfully slow, and the increase in the number of jobs requiring a specialist's training lagged far behind the output of specialists.

The overproduction of specialists produced both economic problems and political frustrations. These aggrieved specialists, numbering in the millions and concentrated in the major cities and industrial centers, represented a pool of energetic, educated, mostly younger people who were frustrated aspirants to elite status and who targeted the Communist Party hierarchy, and the latter's control of the economic system, as the reason for their plight. They provided the core of support for the election of Boris Yeltsin and the Democratic Russia Party in the Russian and all-U.S.S.R. elections. In the 1989 balloting for the Congress of People's Deputies in Moscow, 73.5 percent of the winning candidates were faculty, researchers, artists, engineers and technical specialists, managers, public administrators, and professionals. In the Moscow branch of the Democratic Russia movement, the key popular support group for Yeltsin, more than 75 percent of its members were drawn from the ranks of specialists.

Although the main social divide among the elites ran between the younger, better educated, and more urban artists, writers, academicians, professionals, and technical specialists on the one hand, who supported first Gorbachev and then Yeltsin, and the older, more provincial party careerists and officials who supported the status quo, the split ran through all the ranks of the elite. Even Gorbachev's advisers, the party elite, and the Supreme Soviet were divided over whether the remedy for the U.S.S.R.'s problems lay in strengthening current institutions or in fundamental reform. Even within the Army and the KGB, there were severe splits rather than consensus or overriding loyalty to the regime.

During the attempted military coup against Gorbachev in August 1991, the chief of police in Leningrad immediately went over to the side of the liberal mayor against the coup plotters. General Evgenii Shaposhnikov, commander of the Soviet air force, and General Pavel Grachev, head of Soviet paratroops, supported Yeltsin and sent paratroopers to help defend the Russian Parliament. In sum, the entire elite structure was divided over the best course for Russia and the U.S.S.R.

Nonetheless, what happened in the Soviet Union from 1989 to 1991 was not a mere coup or elite rebellion. The degree of fracture in the party would not have developed, nor its consequences been so great, without considerable mass mobilization for the cause of reform.

MASS MOBILIZATION AND THE COLLAPSE OF THE U.S.S.R.

After what has been said about the deterioration of health, life, environment, and economy in the Soviet Union, the intensification of popular grievances after 1975 requires no further comment. What is remarkable is the extent to which Western observers refused to believe that this deterioration existed or that it affected popular attitudes in the Soviet Union and Eastern Europe.

The marked deterioration in infant mortality was evident to Western demographers, who suggested that the data on its steep rise in the 1970s indicated fundamental problems in the Soviet system. But imported consumer goods on display in Moscow (often purchased with borrowed funds) gave foreign observers a sense that the regime was meeting consumer needs. The drabness and disrepair of East Berlin was often contrasted with the liveliness of West Berlin. But some observers downplayed the import of this distinction, assuming that modern factories lay behind the pockmarked walls and that contented workers lived in the crumbling tenements. Speaking of East Germany, but using words applicable to the entire Soviet bloc, Amos Elon notes that when "Eduard Reuter, head of Daimler Benz, returned from his first thorough tour of East German industrial installations he is reported to have said that the problems there could only be resolved by bulldozers." Elon further observes, "Many now wonder at the apparent willingness of so many governments and 'experts' in the West over the years to swallow as a fact the myth of East Germany as the 'eleventh' industrial world power. The one successful public relations coup of the East German regime—a regime otherwise so disreputable—was to make so many people believe in the myth."[12] One might also add westerners' willingness to believe, as a converse to the bravery of Soviet dissidents, in the myth of the "stoic" Russian people and their immunity to suffering.

Mikhail Gorbachev had come up through the party hierarchy as a talented, ambitious manager. But it was under Yuri Andropov, when he had led an intensive review of the country's situation, that he became a committed reformer. Gorbachev thought the way to overcome entrenched conservative interests was to encourage the population to make apparent the shortcomings of Soviet society and hold guilty authorities responsible. Thus, his policy of *glasnost* was developed as the essential precursor to restructuring, or *perestroika*.

Glasnost, however, led as certainly to state breakdown in the Soviet Union as the policy of the French Crown two centuries earlier when it invited peasants, bourgeoisie, and nobles throughout France to meet in local assemblies to discuss the problems of the nation and elect representatives to the Estates General. Once a far-reaching debate on the problems of the U.S.S.R. was encouraged by the authorities, they could neither set the terms of that debate nor resist the demands for solution of pressing problems that followed. Given an opening, the intelligentsia, who had earlier faced a hard choice between conforming to or opposing the regime, leapt at the chance to highlight myriad problems that had previously been concealed. The vast range of problems that came to light, and conflicts between conservative and reformist elites over their solution, led to policy paralysis. Confronted with inaction and waffling from the central authorities, local and regional grievances quickly blossomed into demands for greater autonomy and later into nationalist separatist movements.

Gorbachev first encouraged the formation of independent social clubs, where citizens could share opinions. Apparently thinking that these would remain amenable to party control, Gorbachev was surprised when these clubs quickly formed cross connections, coalescing into popular fronts in support of reform. When Gorbachev decreed that popular elections would now be required for selecting local leaderships and representatives to the All-Soviet Congress, communist politicians had to orient themselves to winning popular support and the popular fronts quickly became independent political organizations.

What form would these take? While Gorbachev apparently envisaged popular action by Soviet citizens, he failed to realize that local organizations would follow the preexisting lines of local organizations created by the U.S.S.R., which emphasized the national identity of the constituent republics. Led by the Marxist-Leninist belief that only class, and not nationality, would be a lasting source of political divisions, the Communist Party made permanent, and even magnified, nationalist identities in the Soviet Union. The nationalities not only received distinctive passports, and support for traditional cultures and languages; the regime went so far as to provide extended apparatuses of sovereignty, including duplicate republican ministries, scientific and cultural academies, and communist parties. The officially recognized form of political organization alternative to the central Soviet authorities was *territorial and nationalist*. As Branko Milanovic notes, when the center had overwhelming authority, this did not matter. But "when the whole system became shaky, these 'shells' could be easily filled with substance; the proto-states became real states."[13]

The electoral campaigns forced upon local party officials by Gorbachev quickly ceased to become confrontations of corrupt officials by loyal Soviet citizens. Instead, they became true contests based on popular appeal. And given the sense of betrayal and frustration felt by so many with the Communist Party, nationalist alternatives were frequently compelling. The election of nationalist governments seeking autonomy in the Baltic and the Caucasus began the process of making the "republics" real competing centers of power with the Communist Party in Moscow.

The challenge to the authority of the Communist Party from non-Russian nationalist republics was abetted by popular demonstrations in the major cities of Russia. In the years from 1959 to 1989, Russia had transformed itself from being a mainly rural to a mainly urban nation; its urban population almost doubled, from 100 million to 188 million. These urban centers became the focus for popular mobilization in support of Boris Yeltsin and against the communist regime. On February 4, 1990, more than 250,000 people demonstrated in Moscow demanding the end of the Communist Party's constitutionally guaranteed monopoly of power, and almost a year later, on January 20, 1991, 200,000 demonstrated in Moscow against the efforts of the Soviet regime to militarily intimidate the Baltic republics. In March 1991, Yeltsin's supporters held vast demonstrations in support of Russian sovereignty throughout the Republic, with hundreds of thousands turning out in Moscow and tens of thousands in Leningrad, Yaroslavl, Volgograd, and other cities. And during the crucial days of August 19–21 in Moscow, during the attempted coup, perhaps 500,000 turned out at some time in support of Yeltsin against the coup, including perhaps 50,000 or more who took part in the defense of the White House during the crucial night of resistance on August 20.[14]

The efforts of the non-Russian republics to secure autonomy and the efforts of the Russian reformers to throw off communist domination reinforced and fed on each other. As the republics drew away, violence over borders and refugees broke out, particularly in Armenia, Azerbaijan, and Moldova. Interethnic conflict in 1988–91 killed more than a thousand people and created hundreds of thousands of refugees and tens of billions of rubles of damage: "the inability of the U.S.S.R. government to control nationalist violence . . . was one of the major factors leading to the collapse of the Soviet state, reinforcing perceptions of the frailty of Soviet power, . . . impelling some groups toward secession, and provoking a sense of desperation" among conservative elites.[15]

The third element of popular mobilization that contributed to the fall of the Communist Party was strikes, particularly among the coal miners, who provided the essential energy for Soviet industry and heat for Soviet homes. Massive strikes in 1989 and 1991 rocked Gorbachev's authority and provided a base for Yeltsin, who was able to rally the miners' support. The 1989 strike involved more than four hundred thousand workers who organized themselves in new grass-roots unions. The 1991 strike helped persuade Gorbachev to support Yeltsin, a turn that provoked the August coup. And the costs of settling the strikes contributed to the financial unraveling of the regime.

Glasnost had put Gorbachev in an untenable position. Having decided, after Chernobyl, that the policy of covering up errors would lead to further decay, it was clearly necessary to expose faulty state policies. Seeking to undermine party conservatives, it was essential to demand responsibility, support the intelligentsia, and encourage popular representation. But when such actions unleashed increased opposition, Gorbachev could not suppress that opposition without handing power to conservatives and silencing future complaints against the system's faults. In Eastern Europe and the Baltics, in particular, massive armed intervention to suppress autonomy would dash Gorbachev's hopes for increased autonomy and support for his reforms from Soviet society. When mild interventions in the Baltics drew harsh international and domestic criticism, Gorbachev had to decide whether to act like Stalin to preserve the dominance of the party or to leap ahead with still greater reforms. Having begun his career attempting to change all that was associated with Stalin, Gorbachev had little hope but to attempt, like a surfer, to keep ahead of the wave of popular discontent he had aroused, hoping to ride it to greater power and further reform.

Waves ultimately break, overturning the surfer. Gorbachev lost his balance as his own allies in reform in the military and in his ministries saw that his policies were leading to greater disorder and the destruction, not the salvation, of party authority. In their attempted 1991 coup, they admitted the bankruptcy of Gorbachev's party-led reform policy. However, their failure left no authority at all to the party, or to Gorbachev.

It is thus not a serious distortion to say that, while of course manifesting its own distinct elements (as does every revolution), the demise of the Soviet regime in the U.S.S.R. basically followed the script of past major revolutions such as the English Revolution of 1640 and the French Revolution of 1789. As in the past, a key part of the revolutionary dynamic was a split among elites amid a developing crisis or crises—initially economic stagnation, which spurred Gorbachev's efforts at reform, then popular rejection of communist authority under glasnost and perestroika, which polarized elites and left Gorbachev squeezed between Yeltsin and his anticommunist reformers and communist conservatives in the army, the bureaucracy, and the KGB. When Yeltsin proved successful in rallying popular support from a population increasingly mobilized along nationalist lines, the reformers were able to win the struggle, and set out on a revolutionary destruction of the Soviet regime.

REFERENCES

1. Mann (1986).
2. Davis and Feshbach (1980), p. 3.
3. Rostow (1991), p. 62.
4. Aslund (1991), p. 19.
5. Aganbegyan (1989), p. 28.
6. Haynes and Bojcun (1988), p. 44.
7. Haynes and Bojcun (1988), p. 118.
8. Davis and Feshbach (1980), pp. 2–3.
9. Field (1991), p. 79.
10. Brown (1991), pp. 3–4.
11. Quoted in Haynes and Bojcun (1988), p. 51.
12. Elon (1992), p. 36.
13. Milanovic (1994), p. 63.
14. Dunlop (1993), pp. 324, 223; Garcelon (1995), pp. 473, 562.
15. Beissinger (1998), p. 406.

The Social Sources of the Student Demonstrations in China, 1989
MARTIN KING WHYTE

China's politics have shown many twists and turns since the communist revolution of 1949, led by Mao Zedong. Until his death in 1976, Mao fought strenuously to overcome private property, inequality, and individualism, which he saw as elements of the capitalist economies that had, in the nineteenth century, reduced China to semicolonial dependence on Western imperial powers. However, Mao was never fully successful in his quest. After his death, China's new leadership, dominated by Deng Xiaoping, recognized that private property, inequality, and individualism were not merely capitalist errors, but unavoidable elements of a growing economy (see the essay by Kelley and Klein in Chapter 4). Deng thus sought to permit these elements to take root in China, while preserving much of the socialist structure of heavy industry and preserving the dominant political role of the Communist Party.

Deng's reforms have not solved the problem of creating harmony among China's diverse elites and popular groups. Instead, a variety of student, worker, and bureaucratic groups have pressed for greater reforms, including free markets and democratic politics. Against these groups, military and party officials have sought to preserve the Communist Party's control of government and the economy. These divisions burst forth in the spring of 1989, in student-led demonstrations in Tiananmen Square, in Beijing. In this essay, Whyte describes the social and political changes that led to the student demonstration, and the consequences of this event for China's current leadership.

As 1989 began, China could boast a population that was much better clothed, fed, and housed than it had been a decade earlier, when a program of sweeping economic and political reform was introduced. One testimonial to the magnitude of the country's transformation came from Chinese who had the opportunity to travel to the Soviet Union and Eastern Europe at the end of the 1980s. They reported back incredulously that frustrated East European consumers were trying to buy the clothing off their backs, as well as any food items and consumer durables they had happened to bring along. It was almost as if they were visitors from the rich and capitalist West. This was quite a turnabout from the 1950s, when China had taken lessons from her socialist elder brothers. Deng Xiaoping's version of "goulash communism" appeared to be outpacing the original East European version.

The reforms not only improved economic conditions; they also increased cultural diversity. The rigid political restrictions of the Mao era governing acceptable proletarian literature, art, and popular ideas were relaxed, and an increasing variety of cultural forms became available to the Chinese. The "open" policy produced a proliferation of Western cultural products, ranging from politically "rehabilitated" classics (for example, Shakespeare and Beethoven) to newly "liberated" foreign radio broadcasts and translations of the likes of Sigmund Freud, Henry Kissinger, Herman Wouk, and Sidney Sheldon. New imports even included such choice samples of Western proletarian culture as motor-cross racing, Rambo movies, and bodybuilding. With foreign tourists, teachers, and businesspeople streaming into China and with increasing numbers of Chinese going abroad, contact with Western individuals, ideas, and institutions began to reach beyond the small circle of the Chinese political elite.

The relaxation of restrictions based on ideology extended to China's own cultural heritage as well. Temples were restored and monasteries reopened, Confucius and his ideas

From China Briefing 1990, *edited by A. Kane. Reprinted with permission from the publishers. Copyright © 1990 by Westview Press.*

were reexamined, and in general an effort was made to retrieve artistic, musical, and literary products of the past. This revival of tradition was not confined to high culture. The restoration of family farming helped to fuel revivals of ancestor worship, wedding feasts, elaborate funerals, geomancy, and other customs the authorities had earlier branded "feudal remnants." Peasants appreciated the new opportunities these changes offered to pursue family goals and participate in culturally meaningful rituals. The restoration of temples and sacred sites and the new tolerance for religious activity also resulted in revivals of temple worship, religious pilgrimages, and the manufacture of ritual items (for example, spirit incense, sacred charms, coffins), all of which had been banned during the Mao era.

The general relaxation of control in the political sphere, combined with growing incomes and increased leisure, led to a boom in domestic tourism. Foreign travelers accustomed to having a near monopoly on sites such as the Great Wall found themselves increasingly bumped and jostled by throngs of Chinese, who were able to enjoy the sights of their native land.

Better economic conditions and greater cultural diversity were accompanied by social healing. Large numbers of people who had been condemned to political purgatory during the many political conflicts of the Mao era were rehabilitated and allowed to resume normal lives. The system of class labels used to stigmatize individuals and families and to foster class struggle in the Mao era was formally dismantled. Millions of urban youths who had been sent to the countryside were allowed to return to the cities, there to resume interrupted educations, careers, and spouse searches. Many couples separated by arbitrary job assignments or by reeducation campaigns were able to arrange transfers so that they could live together for the first time in decades. Such developments made it possible for individuals to retreat from the scars and battles of public life without apology and devote more time and attention to affairs of the home and family. In general, the frazzled nerves produced by the tumult of the late Mao era began to be soothed.

Given these considerable improvements in the quality of people's lives, one would have expected the reforms, and the post-Mao leadership responsible for them, to be hugely popular. Since no popular elections or referendums on the reforms were held, and since the public opinion polls that began to be carried out during the 1980s were for the most part officially sponsored and rather unscientific, readings of popular opinion can only be impressionistic. Many observers would argue that had a referendum on the reforms been conducted in, say, 1984 or 1985, the result would have been overwhelming approval. Yet by the close of the decade the rule of Deng Xiaoping and his cronies had to be maintained by massive force of arms against widespread public disapproval. To reform-minded Chinese, at least, Eastern Europe seemed to have leapt ahead of China once again.

THE SOCIAL ROOTS OF POPULAR DISCONTENT

Why was popular discontent increasing despite the apparent success of the reforms? In addressing this question I shall distinguish three separate groups within the population: those who felt the reforms had not gone far enough, those who thought that they had gone too far, and those who were generally satisfied. For the sake of simplicity, I shall call these groups the "not far enoughs," the "too fars," and the "satisfieds."

China's post-Mao reforms introduced dramatic changes in society initially; however, increasingly after the mid-1980s the reform momentum stalled, leaving a partial transformation of the system that made nobody very happy. The reasons for rising disaffection in the late 1980s, though, differed sharply between the "not far enoughs" and the "too fars." The social dynamite that exploded in the spring of 1989 was formed by a combination of circumstances that made it possible for social groups holding quite contrary views to overcome their differences and unite in their common hostility to the leadership.

Too Little Reform

The Beijing Spring demonstrations were spearheaded by those who believed that the reforms had not gone far enough. These included not only students but also many intellectuals and a newly emerging group, urban entrepreneurs.[1] In part the "not far enough" reaction of these groups involved frustration that political reforms had been repeatedly placed on the national agenda and just as often taken off without producing any concrete results. For example, Deng Xiaoping's August 1980 speech calling for fundamental changes in China's political structure was republished on three separate occasions in the 1980s, each time stimulating discussion that led nowhere.

Students and their allies found the economic reforms insufficient as well. The slogans and goals of the reformers implied that intellectuals and experts would have a leading role in plotting China's future and that intellectual talent and expertise would play the central role in China's modernization drive. Improved treatment of intellectuals and future intellectuals (that is, students) became a standard slogan voiced by officialdom, and reforms were launched aimed at giving such individuals greater autonomy, more comfortable working conditions, greater rewards, and increased freedom to select where and on what they would work. The idea that the leadership would increasingly rely on the advice of the experts in formulating national policies held enormous appeal for most students and their allies, for whom this notion resonated with ancient ideas about the active incorporation of intellectuals into state service.

When students looked at the society around them, however, they perceived that not much had changed. State investment in education was pitifully low, even compared with many other Third World countries, and the material conditions and prospects of most students remained bleak. Most could look forward to lives earning modest and largely fixed salaries in jobs not of their choosing, under less well-educated supervisors who often did not appreciate their talents and aspirations, and with only limited chances to cash in on the new opportunities created by the reforms. Student optimism about the future was further dampened by a spate of articles published during the mid-1980s claiming that middle-aged intellectuals were not only poorly paid but also had greater health problems and shorter life spans than people in other occupations.

Intellectuals similarly saw a large gap between reform goals and present realities under reform. Instead of being able to work unobstructed and contribute to China's future, many found themselves locked into the same jobs as before. Bureaucratic overseers and constant shifts in the national political atmosphere presented repeated reminders of the Mao era, when intellectuals were presumed to be infected with bourgeois tendencies. Successful and aspiring entrepreneurs faced blatant hypocrisy as well. Instead of competing in a fully developed market, they had to make their way through a minefield of changing regulations and petty regulators. Access to the resources and opportunities they needed to run their businesses was never fully secure. As one bitter description put it, "A 'visible foot' is stepping on the 'invisible hand.'"

Although the specific ways in which the "not far enough" sentiment was felt by these groups varied, they were united in their anger at the hypocrisy involved in the meritocratic vision of the reforms. Although the reforms were supposed to produce a society in which the educated, the skilled, the hardworking, and the innovative would receive the most rewards and prestige, the reality often looked quite different. A few individuals were benefiting disproportionately, even though they had done relatively little to merit such benefits. These included suburban peasants and children of high-ranking officials who happened to be situated favorably in relation to new market opportunities and who had personal access to scarce resources and foreign contacts.

Those groups angered by these inequities found they had little opportunity to vent their grievances or effect change. Their resulting frustration produced increased pressure for political reforms whose general goal would be to create a more equitable society. It is well to keep in mind the distinction between equity and equality. In political terms the "not far enough" groups wanted to reduce the power of the party/state bureaucracy, but their preferred alternative was not in most cases some sort of mass egalitarian democracy. Rather, they were concerned with gaining their own deserved places in the political sun. Many would have been horrified at the idea that an intellectual should have no more say in society than a worker or a peasant. Equity was thus seen as demanding not equality but rather a society in which the educated and technically skilled would increasingly take over from the politically loyal. This frankly elitist picture of the good society is expressed most clearly in the speeches and writings of astrophysicist Fang Lizhi, "China's Sakharov," whose views aroused such indignation within the CCP leadership that he was ousted from the party in 1987 and had to seek refuge in the American embassy during the June 1989 crackdown.

It would be a mistake, however, to see all the discontent of the Deng era in economic or political terms. Perhaps equally important in undermining support for the regime were critiques stressing the loss of cultural and moral cohesion in post-Mao China. China's leaders were seen as jettisoning the cultural and ideological orthodoxy of the Mao era without providing a coherent alternative. A long period during which individuals knew precisely what was good and bad and how they should behave gave way in the Deng era to a confusing variety of cultural practices and moral arguments. Official slogans such as "socialism with Chinese characteristics" provided only the vaguest of guidance.

In this arena of moral confusion, most of those who shared the "not far enough" view came to the conclusion that the institutional reform agenda of the May Fourth Movement (China's other great student-led, Western-oriented reform movement, launched in 1919) should be resumed. They felt that the failures of Maoist socialism represented, in large part, the continuing influence of China's long feudal legacy, and that only a thorough critique of both Marxism-Leninism and the traditional legacy, combined with institutional renewal drawing on modern Western models, could save China. Throughout the 1980s these sentiments led to increasingly sharp and systematic critiques of both China's traditional legacy and its bureaucratic socialism.

Too Much Reform

The sentiment that the reforms had not gone far enough in dismantling the bureaucratic system of state socialism was by no means the dominant view in society at large. In terms of sheer numbers, more people probably leaned toward the opposite view that the reforms had already gone too far. It is one of the persistent dilemmas of reforms in China, and elsewhere, that changes that are not sufficient to satisfy critics threaten and alienate other previously satisfied groups. This tendency makes the task of building popular support for further reform problematic. In China those who were increasingly worried that the reforms were going too far included industrial workers, low-level bureaucrats and party officials, the army, and the police. The members of these groups are much more numerous than intellectuals, students, and entrepreneurs, even if they are not as articulate.

China's workers had seen job and income security as among the greatest achievements of the revolution. Lives that before 1949 were characterized by constant fear of unemployment, inflation, and impoverishment were transformed by the socialist system. Those on the state payroll were provided with permanent employment, compensated with secure wages, and protected by a range of health care and other benefits that were unusually broad for a developing society. Even though opportunities for advancement and wage increases were limited, and were terminated almost entirely in the last decade or so of Mao's rule, the enhanced security provided by state employment made it possible for workers to plan their lives and build families in a more secure environment.[2] The efforts by the reformers to destroy the "iron rice bowl" system of job security in favor of limited-term employment contracts, the right of managers to demote and fire workers, and newly promulgated bankruptcy legislation threatened this proud victory of socialism. Even though these reforms were not fully implemented, the Chinese media came to be filled with accounts of disgruntled workers who retaliated with threats or even violence against those pushing such reforms locally.

Women workers were particularly upset that, as a consequence of the industrial reforms, many enterprises began to selectively lay off female employees or to refuse to hire any but males, using the justification that male workers were less troublesome and more productive.[3] Although advocates of these changes argued that returning women to the home would open up more employment opportunities for young males and provide more nurturance and discipline within families, women employees, accustomed to slogans of the Mao era that said that women "hold up half of heaven," were often hard to convince. The normally sluggish Women's Federation took up this issue and denounced the increasing discrimination against female workers that the reforms spawned.

When in 1988 and 1989 the government experimented with contracting out the management rights over failing state firms to private entrepreneurs, not only many workers but also bureaucrats and even some intellectuals were outraged. Although the justification for this measure was that it would turn failing enterprises around and preserve jobs, it was widely seen by workers as representing a sellout of socialism and a return to dependence upon exploitative capitalists. (Not surprisingly, such experiments were repudiated after the crackdown, despite the claims of China's gerontocrats that the reforms would proceed.)

Workers at least could see that the reforms provided them with new opportunities to increase their salaries and bonus payments. Most other groups in the "too far" camp were not in this situation. Low-level bureaucrats, party officials, soldiers, and police shared with intellectuals the complaint that their modest and mostly fixed incomes prevented them from benefiting as much as others from the reforms. In addition, they perceived that the reforms threatened their power and prestige within their local bailiwicks as well as within society generally. Indeed, in many cases they were being blamed for the abuses and inefficiencies of the Mao era. Subordinates, colleagues, and neighbors who had formerly paid them deference now treated them with disrespect or even hostility. For individuals in these groups who felt that they had followed the call of Mao and devoted their lives to the revolution, the perception that others regarded them as political Neanderthals or worse was particularly galling. In rural areas such sentiments often led grassroots cadres to resign in order to free themselves to concentrate on getting rich, but this was not an option readily available to their urban counterparts. The changes introduced by the reforms created morale problems in organizations such as the army and the police and complicated recruitment of young people into careers in these organizations, careers that had once commanded great respect.

The "too far" groups' vision of the good society was decidedly not one in which party bureaucrats would be replaced at the top of the social pyramid by meritocratic experts. While some of the members of these groups may have yearned for a more ideal socialist society in which the actual producers would be the masters of the state, most were more realistic and assumed that Chinese society would remain sharply hierarchical. However, they were generally more comfortable with "reds" than "experts" in charge at the top. For many this preference resulted in nostalgia for the perceived benevolent concern of Mao Zedong for the problems of workers, peasants, and soldiers. They saw precious little of such benevolence in the policies and pronouncements of the reform-era leadership, and many feared the elitism and arrogance of China's intellectuals. (These groups found the slogans about favoritism toward experts convincing, even if the experts themselves did not.)

The resentments generated in such "too far" groups were aimed at a variety of targets. For some the villains to be blamed for their loss of privileges and prestige were the new entrepreneurs and the well-educated experts and managers who were taking over leadership at the grass roots. However, equally likely to receive blame were the higher-level leaders who were pushing through the changes that left grass-roots cadres and party officials feeling scapegoated and powerless. One of the weak points of a Leninist system is that it substitutes the very visible hand of the state (or the "foot" alluded to earlier) for the invisible hand of the market. When groups feel that they are being treated unfairly, they are not likely to blame fate, their own imperfections, the market, or even rival groups. Their angry glances are quite likely to be directed upward at those who command the entire system.

The increased alienation of the "too fars," like that of the "not far enoughs," had cultural and moral dimensions beyond the economic one. The "too fars" saw the preferred remedy of the "not far enoughs" for China's cultural malaise, Westernization, as precisely the wrong solution. Indeed, when they looked around and saw such things as the revival of open prostitution, an upsurge in Christianity, and a fever among the young for foreign ideas and culture, they could agree with the claim of party conservatives that China was being "spiritually polluted" as a result of the "open" policy. For example, the 1988 documentary television series "River Elegy," with its highly unfavorable comparisons between China's bureaucratic lethargy and the dynamic West, deeply offended many "too fars" on patriotic grounds. But within this group ideas about the preferred alternative to Western culture varied. Some felt the solution to China's problems was to be found in a return to China's Confucian tradition. Such critics of complete Westernization began to produce laudatory evaluations of how Confucian values had contributed to economic development in Taiwan, South Korea, and Japan. Other opponents of the new infusions of Western culture tried to resurrect the democratic spirit of original Marxism from under the distortions introduced by Lenin, Stalin, and Mao, or even yearned for the perceived moral purity of the Mao era.

The "not far enoughs" and the "too fars" saw the world in very different terms. However, they agreed that the economic situation in the late 1980s was unacceptable and that China in the Deng era had become an unsatisfying mixture of cultural confusion and moral decay. Two factors acted together to make the economic frustrations experienced by many particularly severe. First, there were the long years of enforced spartan living of the Mao period, which left every group in society feeling that its just demands for material improvement urgently needed to be met. One effect of this backlog of unmet material aspirations was to make the early post-Mao grass-roots discussions of pay increases particularly angry and tearful. This phenomenon helps to explain why so many raises and bonus payments that were supposed to be distributed to the most worthy ended up being doled out equally to all. The second aggravating factor was inflation, which became increasingly serious after the mid-1980s. Many groups found their hard-won gains in buying power undermined and reversed; for some the fight to stay on top of the inflation treadmill brought back memories of the (much more serious) inflationary spiral of the late 1940s.

Sufficient Reform

The reader may wonder whether there were any groups at all in China who perceived that they were benefiting from the reforms. The answer is yes. Within both the "not far enough" and the "too far" groups there was, of course, diversity of views, and some students, intellectuals, workers, soldiers, and others were quite content with their lot in life. But in addition, there were two groups with particular cause for satisfaction, who felt gratitude rather than hostility toward the reformers.

One such group was the peasantry. Many if not most peasants felt that the reforms had rescued them from years of state-enforced poverty. Rural incomes initially increased more rapidly than did urban incomes and peasants created a boom in construction of new housing and competed with urbanites for the televisions, washing machines, and other new symbols of reform-era prosperity. As noted earlier, the new rural prosperity also found more traditional outlets—in elaborate weddings and funerals, in restoration of local temples and lineage halls, and in pilgrimages and tourism. No doubt the renewed ability of families to escape from the day-to-day supervision of rural cadres and plan their own lives and work activities was also a source of considerable satisfaction. However, satisfaction on this score was tempered by one increasingly severe and unpopular way in which the lives of peasant families were regulated by the state in the Deng era—the mandatory birth-control program which culminated in the one-child policy after 1979. Even among the peasants, of course, views varied widely. In many disadvantaged regions, and among disadvantaged peasant families within every region, there were strong reasons for feeling that the benefits of the reforms were not trickling down the way they were supposed to. Even peasants who prospered under the reforms often felt anger at the shifts in rules and regulations and the demands for "contributions" and bribes that kept them from enjoying their economic success. In addition, localities and families that had prospered in the Mao era often felt threatened by official demands that they disband organizational forms painfully developed over the years in order to revive competition in the marketplace. Both "not far enoughs" and "too fars" could be found in the Chinese countryside, although they were in the minority.

Because peasants make up the single largest group in Chinese society, constituting between 70 and 80 percent of the total, one might have thought that their general satisfaction with the reforms would have provided the leadership with a powerful source of support. However, those peasants who had prospered under the reforms and who felt they could now operate successfully under them did not form a well-organized group that could make its influence felt effectively in support of the leadership. The difficulty of mobilizing peasants, short of revolution, combined with their concentration on local horizons and activities, made them a negligible factor in the political battles that erupted in the late 1980s. Moreover, trends such as stagnation in grain production after 1984, continued state reluctance to invest heavily in agriculture, and budget deficits that required some peasants to be paid for their grain in IOUs rather than cash had, by 1989, eroded support for Deng and his colleagues even in the countryside. Toward the end of the decade, outbursts of anger directed at the state agents became increasingly common in rural areas.

The other major group with cause to be satisfied with the reforms as they were was, of course, the high-ranking bureaucrats and their friends and families. The stalled nature of the reforms made available many opportunities for gaining new riches and prestige without providing a level playing field that would enable all groups to compete for those new opportunities. The continued substantial bureaucratic obstacles that restricted access to resources, information, and opportunities worked to the advantage of those who had the personal connections to take advantage of them, and the official slogans about the desirability of getting rich provided legitimation for their pursuit of gain. Since this small and privileged group was increasingly seen by both the "too far" and the "not far enough" groups as the cause of the problem, its satisfaction with the situation in 1989 was not an effective barrier against growing popular discontent.

FROM DISCONTENT TO MASS DEMONSTRATIONS

The existence of widespread popular discontent in the reform era is not a sufficient explanation for either the student demonstrations or the mass response to them. Widespread popular discontent has existed in many societies, and it certainly existed during a number of periods in the Mao era, without producing anything comparable to the events of the Beijing Spring. A number of other developments were required in combination to produce those events.

One such element was the relaxation of political controls that occurred in the reform era. Political study and mutual criticism sessions in schools and work units were less intense and less frequently held than in the Mao era. As noted earlier, large numbers of individuals and groups were "rehabilitated," and although many of those who lost their negative labels concentrated on lying low and enjoying their restored lives, others began to seek out audiences for the critiques of the system that their years in political oblivion had nurtured. Similarly, former Red Guards who had survived factional battles, years in rural exile, and university entrance exams took their place as teachers of the young and found enthusiastic disciples for their unconventional analyses of the ills of Chinese society. Exposure to China's cultural legacy and to the growing flood of ideas and models from the outside world provided a new awareness of political and cultural alternatives. Images of "people power" sweeping aside Marcos in the Philippines and of the legalization of alternative parties in Taiwan also provided examples of how to organize to bring about desired changes. These concrete models were probably more influential than accounts of the separation of powers in the American political system.

Over the years, as people could see public declarations of formerly heterodox views being raised without those raising them getting into political trouble, the feeling began to grow that dissent and efforts to change the system were safe. By the mid-1980s, avowedly autonomous clubs and associations began to emerge all over China. Even though most of these were apolitical and cautious, they provided a venue within which growing numbers of individuals (mostly urbanites, and disproportionately educated ones) could acquire a sense of being able to organize activities without CCP guidance and control. Although no major changes in the structure of the political system were carried out during the 1980s, the loosening of the political atmosphere created increased opportunities for critical views to be shared beyond the boundaries of family and close friends. China did not produce a fully formed "civil society," but individual grievances found new opportunities to coalesce into group dissent.[4]

Critical voices were more widely heard in the 1980s, and groups sharing common grievances began to emerge. Still, if the political elite had remained united and consistent in opposing any mass political action, the events of the Beijing Spring would not have escalated out of control. The previous rounds of student demonstrations were successfully contained, even though they showed an ominous tendency (from the standpoint of the leaders) to revive each time in enlarged form. What made the situation different in 1989 was the crumbling of unity within the elite and the implicit and explicit encouragement that the more ardent reformers within the leadership gave to students and others to raise critical voices. That encouragement seems to have been motivated by the increasing frustration that Zhao Ziyang and his followers felt over their difficulties in reviving reform momentum. Eventually many students and intellectuals came to feel that mass pressure was not only needed to promote the reform cause within a divided leadership, but that such pressure could also be effective in turning the tide against the conservatives within that leadership. The confidence (misguided, as it turned out) that bold public voicing of discontent not only would not be penalized but might actually produce desired results helped to energize active participation among the students and their allies. To be sure, there were some students who were very pessimistic about the prospects for change and who were willing to risk martyrdom nonetheless for their cause. However, if such pessimism had been generally shared, and if discontented students had faced a united and hostile elite, no escalating mass demonstrations would have occurred.

Even in the presence of widespread popular discontent, an opportunity to share that discontent with others, divisions within the elite, and some high-level encouragement of the demonstrators, the resulting demonstrations need not have gotten out of control. Indeed, given the sharp disagreements between the "not far enough" and "too far" groups, there were considerable opportunities for the leadership to foment conflict between groups as a way of keeping the situation from getting out of hand. In the previous major wave of student demonstrations, in 1986–1987, this is precisely what happened. Leader statements and mass media accounts then portrayed the student demonstrators essentially as spoiled brats, concerned with improving their already privileged lives rather than with the problems of workers and peasants. The student demonstrations at that time attracted only minor public support from other groups in society and were relatively easily squelched.

By 1989 the students had learned the lessons of earlier rounds of demonstrations, although some of this learning occurred only during the course of the Beijing Spring. Initially the students tried to exclude other groups from participating in their demonstrations, and in mourning former CCP general secretary Hu Yaobang, who died on April 15, they tended to focus upon issues (political reform and intellectual freedom) that were mainly of concern to other "not far enough" partisans. However, eventually this exclusionary policy was dropped and replaced by active encouragement of other groups to join them. In good Chinese fashion this participation usually took organized, corporate form, with individuals taking part as members of delegations from their schools or work units, complete with banners and signs, rather than as a heterogeneous mass. The appeals and demands raised by the students increasingly focused on issues that had broad popular appeal—to the "too far" groups as well as the "not far enough" ones. Increasingly the demonstrators' anger focused on inflation and corruption within the leadership, major problems that could unite the two disparate sides in hostility against the national elite.

Still, it took a further dramatic step to overcome the political and cultural gap between the students who initiated the demonstrations and the ordinary workers, cadres, and other urbanites who later joined them. That step was provided by the hunger strike launched in mid-May. The hunger strike testified in a vivid and relatively unconventional way to the students' position that they were not simply trying to benefit themselves but were laying claim to the moral legacy of righteous intellectuals in previous dynasties who were willing to risk their lives in their quest for justice. The dramatic act galvanized popular support for the students and led to a rapid escalation in both the size of the demonstrations in Tiananmen Square and in the number of supportive acts by other groups around the city. During this crucial period, splits within the leadership as well as problems in preparing for the Gorbachev visit prevented the elite from taking timely and forceful action to prevent the alliance between the "not far enoughs" and the "too fars" from being consolidated. Once that consolidation became apparent, a bandwagon effect set in, with more and more casual onlookers and thrill-seekers augmenting the ranks of committed protesters.

The unlikely alliance that had been forged to produce this popular uprising was visible in the symbols carried in Tiananmen Square and in countless smaller squares in provincial cities and towns. It is important to remember that demonstrations were not confined to Beijing. Not only provincial cities but many county seats and even small towns witnessed student demonstrations during the period of the Beijing Spring. Prominent in such demonstrations were Western symbols that conveyed themes favored by the "not far enoughs," such as slogans about freedom of the press and the Goddess of Democracy statue. However, also visible were competing non-Western symbols that reflected the views of the "too fars"—for example, the portraits of Mao Zedong that were borne aloft by many groups of demonstrators.

CONSEQUENCES OF THE BEIJING SPRING

The mass demonstrations of the Beijing Spring were thus a product not merely of popular discontent but of a whole series of forces and contingencies. Furthermore, this chain of developments undermined the ability of the regime to unite the "too fars" and the "satisfieds" to fend off the challenge of the "not far enoughs." Instead, the "not far enoughs" were able to recruit support from the "too fars" in common opposition to the bureaucratic elite despite their many differences, while most of the "satisfieds" (China's peasants, in particular) remained on the sidelines. Under these circumstances, a disaffected and highly vocal minority almost succeeded in overturning the regime.

After the crackdown, the new conservative leadership coalition took a number of steps designed to stamp out organized opposition and prevent something similar from happening again. They ousted Zhao Ziyang and some of his key followers from the leadership and promoted into their ranks new leaders not closely associated in the public mind with the crackdown (notably Jiang Zemin, the new general secretary of the CCP) in an effort to forge an appearance of unity and stability. They increased political study and indoctrination activities, tightened the limits on cultural activities, and tried to stamp out harmful ideas and influences (for example, by jamming Voice of America broadcasts). They reduced enrollments in key universities and initiated mandatory military training prior to enrollment in some institutions in an attempt to inoculate the young against "bourgeois liberal" ideas. They made it abundantly clear that voicing heterodox opinions could still get people into deep political trouble. They instituted measures designed to address the twin problems of inflation and bureaucratic corruption. And they attacked those who stimulated and participated in the demonstrations as unpatriotic, a theme designed to appeal to the nationalist sentiments of both the "too fars" and the "satisfieds."

Although such measures are designed to defuse both the sources of discontent and the precipitating conditions that led to the mass demonstrations, there are reasons to believe that the success of Deng Xiaoping's new conservative coalition in regaining control can be no more than partial and temporary. First, there are questions about how thorough and sustained these measures by the elite can be. Many provinces and localities are participating in the tightening of the political atmosphere only in a perfunctory manner, and even in Beijing many units are carrying out the new political study rituals and group criticism sessions in a formalistic and superficial way. Expressions of discontent are not being totally suppressed. Some individuals who have cooperated actively in the crackdown (for example, by turning in fugitives on the official arrest list) are now being subjected to public scorn. Furthermore, many of the familiar signs of elite disarray—conflicting messages in the mass media, unexplained disappearance and reappearances, rumors about schemes to gain more power—are apparent, making it difficult to persuade the public that the leadership will follow unified and consistent policies in the future. Even with the formal retirement of Deng Xiaoping from his last posts, it is obvious to everyone that the configuration of top leaders formed after the crackdown is of his making and is not likely to survive his death or incapacity. (The shift of mood in China is symbolized by the sad fact that many who in the early 1980s used to pray for Deng's longevity now hope for his early demise.)

All of these phenomena make it very unlikely that the genie of mass discontent can be put back in the bottle of quasi-Maoist controls. In addition to the grievances that existed prior to the Beijing Spring, there are new problems that will make the attempt by the conservatives to assert control highly problematic. There is now a powerful resentment unleashed by the crackdown itself, an outraged feeling that China's conservative leadership coalition has the blood of peaceful protesters on its hands. In addition, the economic situation has turned for the worse since the crackdown, producing new fears about stagnation and unemployment.[5] These new sources of anger are likely to make the reactions of the "too fars," who ordinarily might be expected to support the sort of curtailing of reform measures that has been launched since the crackdown, less than enthusiastic. In addition, the expressed commitment of the current leaders to continue the reforms and the "open" policy has prevented them thus far from formulating policies that would relieve the pre-1989 anxieties and hostility of the "too fars."

China's conservative leaders cannot simply turn back the clock and wipe out all consequences of the Beijing Spring, and the problems produced by the crackdown provide a strong basis for a continued union between "not far enough" and "too far" groups in the future. The Chinese political scene resembles a pressure cooker and is likely to do so for some time to come. Any crisis or rupturing of the enforced unity of the leaders is likely to unleash renewed popular anger, making the present "stability" a very precarious thing.

The paradox presented at the outset of this paper—of mounting discontent amid reform progress—is not so paradoxical after all. Dissatisfaction, pent-up consumer demands, and social tensions left over from the Mao era created extraordinary hopes and pressures that made the task of China's reformers very difficult. The initial progress of the reforms created public relief and gratitude but led to a thirst for more changes among some groups while fostering anxiety about future changes among others. Even in the wake of the June crackdown, the leadership has been unable to find a formula that will defuse popular hostilities and rebuild an effective alliance between those who think the reforms went too far and those who are relatively contented, in order to isolate the smaller but more articulate groups who do not think the reforms went far enough. Unless China's conservative leaders can find ways to defuse the situation, split the alliance of popular forces that oppose them, and rebuild popular support for their program of curtailed reforms, future explosions of mass discontent are quite likely.

REFERENCES

1. This combination is symbolized by the leadership-in-exile that emerged in Paris after the June crackdown, composed of student Wuer Kaixi, intellectual/reformer Yan Jiaqi, and the founder of the Stone Computer Company, Wan Runnan.

2. Of course, greater economic security was combined with increased political insecurity in the Mao period, and individuals who got into political trouble forfeited all claims to the security provided by Chinese socialism.

3. In the Mao era, when enterprises had no power to retain their own profits and could request funds freely to cover any deficits, there was no incentive to economize on either labor costs or fringe benefits. Under the reforms, enterprises can retain a share of their profits for reinvestment or for spending on employees, and this change produces increased incentive to minimize labor costs and fringe-benefit expenditures.

Employers claim that women are more costly due to higher absenteeism, maternity leave, and earlier retirement, and on this basis they may resist hiring and retaining female employees.

4.   Theorists of democratic transition argue that a civil society is a basic precondition for a democratic political system, and this view has been very influential among dissidents and reformers in Eastern Europe. Civil society involves the existence of a wide variety of organizations and associations that operate autonomously vis-à-vis the state. Such associations nourish a sense of citizenship that is protected from state infringement, and they provide vehicles through which group ideas and interests can be articulated and used to pressure the state. For an attempt to apply this concept to contemporary China, see Gold (1990), pp. 18–31.

5.   The picture on the economy is somewhat mixed. Inflation was reduced in the latter part of 1989 and a record grain harvest (in absolute, though not in relative, terms given the continued growth in population) occurred in the same year. However, one of the causes of the decline in inflation is the retrenchment of the economy, and that has led to the closing of many enterprises, reductions in employment, and new efforts to force excess urban personnel to return to the countryside. These latter trends make popular perceptions of the economic situation considerably less than bullish.

CHAPTER 9

Guerrilla and Ethnic Revolts

We often think of revolutions as explosive affairs, with revolutionary crowds spilling through the palace gates. Although the French, Russian, and Philippine revolutions did begin that way, in recent years it has been more common for revolutionary struggles to take the form of slowly building, drawn-out struggles for liberation. The guerrilla warfare of Mao in China and Castro in Cuba inspired many would-be revolutionaries to begin their campaigns against a regime by seeking to build strength in the countryside. This strategy of revolution has been widely used around the world in the twentieth and twenty-first centuries, in Latin America (Cuba, Nicaragua, Colombia, Peru), Africa (Angola, Mozambique, South Africa), East Asia (China and Vietnam), Ireland, and the Middle East.

Guerrilla wars have been especially attractive in wars of liberation from colonial or ethnic oppression, where a relatively powerless populace faces a strong and determined regime and where successful guerrilla warfare makes it too costly for the oppressive power to remain in control. On the other hand, most guerrilla insurrections have been crushed. In the following essays, Wickham-Crowley analyzes the reasons for success and failure among Latin American guerrilla movements, Seidman discusses the interaction between guerrilla efforts and unarmed resistance campaigns in the South African struggle against apartheid, Robinson studies the ethnic and guerrilla conflict between Palestinians and Israeli authorities, and Ahady examines the Islamic guerrilla wars in Afghanistan and their consequences for global terrorism.

Toward a Comparative Sociology of Latin American Guerrilla Movements

TIMOTHY WICKHAM-CROWLEY

Revolutionary movements have had two major sources of popular support—urban workers and rural peasants. Prior to the 1940s, revolutionary peasants were usually led by traditional village leaders. Yet beginning with Mao Zedong's organization of the Chinese peasantry, a new pattern arose of urban middle-class intellectuals moving to the countryside and organizing peasants into ideologically based guerrilla movements. Revolutionary guerrilla movements then spread around the world, to Vietnam, Algeria, sub-Saharan Africa, and other parts of Asia and the Middle East. Yet the Maoist model had perhaps its greatest influence in Latin America, where

Fidel Castro's success in building a guerrilla-based revolutionary movement inspired a flood of guerrilla activity. Wickham-Crowley examines several Latin American guerrilla movements of the 1960s and 1970s, and examines why they arose and why only a few achieved success.

A BRIEF HISTORICAL REVIEW

Following the success and socialist transformation of the Cuban Revolution, guerrilla movements appeared throughout Latin American in the 1960s, but most — such as Che Guevara's efforts to create a radical rural movement in Bolivia — died an early death. A few nations have seen a strong resurgence of such activity since roughly 1975: Nicaragua, Guatemala, Colombia, El Salvador, and Peru.

In Cuba, Fulgencio Batista seized power in a coup in 1952, to stave off probable electoral defeat. In response, one of the disappointed candidates, Fidel Castro, organized a 1953 attack on the Moncada military barracks. Imprisoned, but later pardoned, Castro — following an exile in Mexico — withdrew to the hills of eastern Cuba, where he built a guerrilla movement. Castro's guerrillas began a summer offensive in 1958, eventually forcing the dictator to flee the country at year's end. Castro assumed and consolidated power, instituted reforms, and declared Cuba socialist in mid-1969 following a confrontation with the United States over the nationalization of sugar lands.

In Guatemala, a decade of reformist government ended with the 1954 CIA-orchestrated overthrow of Jacobo Arbenz, who had begun a major land reform. A series of dictators followed. A left-leaning military revolt in 1960 was suppressed, but two young officers escaped capture, later forming the MR-13 guerrilla movement, and later still the Rebel Armed Forces (FAR). The guerrilla groups gained substantial ground in northeastern Guatemala by 1965, but succumbed to an intense U.S.-backed counterinsurgency campaign in 1966–67. After periods of dormancy and urban terrorism, various offshoots of the FAR reemerged in the 1970s, primarily among Indians in the western highlands. After sustained growth to 1982, a violent counterinsurgency campaign under General Ríos Montt again reversed guerrilla fortunes.

In Colombia, a particularly intense period of violence accelerated with the 1948 assassination of populist Liberal leader Jorge Eliécer Gaitán. *La Violencia,* as it came to be called, claimed over 200,000 lives in the next fifteen to twenty years, mostly in rural areas. In response to the violence, Liberals and Conservatives agreed to forego their internecine rivalry, and to form a pact, known as the National Front, in which they alternated the presidency. Government and military forces soon took notice of the "peasant republics" that had formed during *La Violencia* as quasi-independent zones for self-defense and self-administration in agrarian matters. A military campaign retook those areas in 1964 and 1965. The communist-affiliated Colombian Revolutionary Armed Forces (FARC) rose out of the ashes of those "republics." In 1965, another group of proto-guerrillas, returning from a trip to Cuba, formed the Fidelista Army of National Liberation (ELN). The fortunes of the guerrillas waned toward 1970, but waxed anew in the 1970s; by the early 1980s, their combined membership was in the thousands. By the 1990s, the guerrillas had secured agreements with the government of Columbia that gave them "temporary" control of large portions of Colombia's territory.

In Peru in the late 1970s, university professors organized a Maoist guerrilla group, *Sendero Luminoso* (Shining Path), with substantial peasant support. *Sendero* spread and grew in the early 1980s, despite its extreme violence and ideological rigidity. Nonetheless, by the 1990s *Sendero's* leaders were captured and the movement lost much of its rural support.

Working in the wake of Bolivia's 1952 revolution and subsequent land reforms, Che Guevara organized a Cuban-led guerrilla movement in late 1966 in eastern Bolivia to push for a more radical and socialist regime. Forced into premature activity and completely lacking peasant support, Guevara's guerrillas split into two groups and never reunited. Peasants informed on them, and the army destroyed the guerrillas by October 1967; Guevara himself was killed following his capture.

In Nicaragua, because of the dictator Somoza's continued refusal to share real power with any other social groups or parties, by 1978 middle-class and guerrilla opposition coalesced into a semblance of unity. With business and professional groups, urban workers, and rural guerrilla groups joining in demanding Somoza's ouster, insurrection in various forms continued to grow until the regime fell in July 1979.

In El Salvador, an extended period of military rule since 1931 began to decay in the early 1970s. A number of guerrilla groups engaged in irregular warfare against the military. The three largest groups achieved cooperation in 1979–81, resulting in the joint Farabundo Martí Front for National Liberation (FMLN). At the same time, general opposition to military rule grew with the electoral frauds of 1972 and 1977 and the brutality of the Romero government. Guerrilla and mass-organizational opposition increased even after a new "reformist" civilian–military junta seized power in late 1979. A guerrilla "final offensive" in 1981 failed to oust the government from power, and the revolutionaries withdrew mainly to the countryside. Elections for a constituent assembly in 1982 lent some new legitimacy to the central government, as did the later legislative and presidential elections of 1984 and 1985, even though important groups were excluded from the elections. Guerrilla fortunes declined after 1982.

ORIGINS OF GUERRILLA MOVEMENTS

For the 1960s movements, the historical conjuncture of the *international* Cuban "demonstration effect" and a frustrated *national* revolution in each nation produced powerful guerrilla movements in Guatemala and Colombia. In Guatemala, the post-1954 reversal of the Arbenz agrarian reforms of 1952–53 amounted to a virtual agrarian counterrevolution. Peasants awakened by the promise of land reform before 1954 were slow to revert to dormancy thereafter. In Colombia, the social situation during and after *La Violencia* created a milieu of widespread insurrection. Peasant republics were retaken by the military in the mid 1960s, directly leading to the formation of the FARC, the ELN, and other rebel movements.

In both cases, the eruption of guerrilla activity was a reaction to the *reimposition* of non- or counterrevolutionary governments.

In the 1970s, strong guerrilla movements appeared more to be responses to the *persistence* of the old regime. In Nicaragua, Guatemala, and El Salvador, personal or military dictatorships of long duration—reaching back to the 1930s in Nicaragua and El Salvador—persisted in denying any institutional share of power even to "respectable" middle-class opposition parties, let alone the lower classes. In Colombia, political outsiders were excluded from power by the National Front coalition, which may have retained power in 1970 through electoral fraud. In response to a "closed" political system in all four countries, guerrilla movements were initiated in the 1970s, if not before, by disaffected intellectuals and marginal political elites.

Peru remains a special case among the later guerrilla movements: there an extremist ideology proved a "functional alternative" to the political exclusivity found elsewhere in contributing to the creation of revolutionary sentiment. A combination of Marxist dominance of the highland University of Huamanga and a subsistence crisis in the Andes produced the powerful guerrilla movement *Sendero Luminoso,* radically different in many ways from its counterparts elsewhere. The affinity between the Maoist message of peasant war against the cities, and the poor and remote highland conditions typically conducive to peasant millenarian revolt, led to a merger of Maoist and millenarian ideology in a powerful revolutionary movement with apocalyptic overtones.

The nonpeasant founders of these revolutionary movements typically hailed from universities. Latin American intellectuals were singularly well placed (given university autonomy) and well disposed (given their history of resistance to the state) to respond to the "new ideas" of the Cuban revolution. Most guerrilla movements, both failures and successes, were organized and led by university students and professors, or by former students and professors now involved in leftist politics.

In summary, leftist guerrilla movements usually began as glimmers of hope in the minds of revolutionary intellectuals. Strong guerrilla movements appeared in two waves: in the 1960s in response to a reimposition of nonrevolutionary governments, in the 1970s because of the persistence of old regimes. They also occurred in places with rapid enrollment-growth at universities, which typically were havens and birthplaces of guerrilla leadership.

PEASANT SUPPORT AND MOVEMENT EXPANSION

In the rest of this chapter I seek to explain the causes of the *expansion* of guerrilla movements on a base of peasant support, and of the *seizure of power* in just two cases, Nicaragua and Cuba. Not all guerrilla movements succeed in moving beyond their modest beginnings; when they do so, peasant support is critical in the regions where they operate. Yet peasant support is a necessary, but not sufficient, condition for ultimate success; most movements that have garnered peasant support have failed. Those that seize power must meet two other conditions: They must be militarily strong enough to confront the government's armed forces; and they must strip the incumbent government of moral authority and cloak their own movement with that aura, shifting the loyalties of the nonpeasant population to their movement.

We must first consider the question of peasant support. Guerrilla movements have usually appeared as an alliance between an intellectual leadership and a peasant rank and file. The mere attempt to do so did *not* guarantee success in establishing and maintaining such an alliance: the Bolivian debacle is evidence enough to refute that thesis. Available evidence suggests that peasant support depends on several conditions: (1) particular agrarian social structures; (2) particular changes in agrarian systems; (3) the historic rebelliousness of peasants; (4) strong organizational ties linking peasants either to guerrillas or to the status quo.

Agrarian Structures

Revolutionary guerrillas appear to be more readily recruited among peasants who lack secure control over the land that they farm; this condition holds among peasants who are sharecroppers, squatters, or migratory laborers.

The 1960s guerrilla strongholds had markedly higher rates of sharecropping or squatting than did the areas where there were no guerrillas, or where guerrillas got a lukewarm or hostile reception. In Cuba, squatters were the key source of peasant support. They composed more than 22 percent of all landholders in Oriente Province (home of Castro's guerrillas), but less than 3 percent in the rest of Cuba. In Colombia, those places with extensive guerrilla influence in the 1960s contained about 17 percent sharecroppers versus less than 8 percent in the rest of the country. Meanwhile, where sharecroppers or squatters were scarce, so too was peasant support. Such was the case, for example, in Bolivia. Efforts by the guerrilla leadership to seek peasant support there failed.

Moving from the 1960s to the 1970s, in Nicaragua squatters made up 42 percent of the cultivators in all guerrilla *municipios,* but only 10 percent elsewhere in Nicaragua. In the revived 1970s–1980s Guatemalan guerrilla movements, resistance was concentrated in the largely Indian areas of the western highlands. While these areas are not foci of sharecropping or squatting, we do find the prevalence of our third type: the migratory estate laborers, who typically leave their own villages, where land is inadequate for their needs, and migrate to harvest one or more export cash crops, especially coffee. In both Guatemala and El Salvador, one should note, the strongest peasant support for guerrillas after 1970 was found in areas not themselves the center of cash cropping; instead they were in areas that certainly (Guatemala) or probably (El Salvador) provided migratory labor to other zones.

To summarize: For most of the cases reviewed here, we encounter correlations between relatively high rates of sharecropping, squatting, and migratory labor and high levels of peasant support for guerrillas.

Peasant Dislocation

However, agrarian structure alone does not reveal all the correlates of revolutionary peasantries. Evidence suggests also that assaults on the landed security of peasant cultivators lead to peasant radicalism, as in Emiliano Zapata's village in Morelos early in this century. To specify further, peasants embroiled in such changes are more likely to be revolutionary than those peasants who remain secure *or* those for whom this process is now largely an accomplished fact (e.g., the sugar workers of Cuba).

In Cuba, the squatters of Oriente Province in the 1950s [like the squatters in Chiapas, Mexico, in the 1980s—Ed.], also were experiencing an assault on their very landed existence, as landlords increased land eviction cases. In Guatemala and El Salvador in the 1970s, peasant radicalism was largely concurrent with areas in which military elites or commercial farmers were displacing peasants from their lands.

Yet in some cases, peasant radicalism had other, more historical roots.

Rebellious Cultures

Guerrilla movements also disproportionately took root in areas with histories of popular rebellion against national authorities, and often failed where such rebellious cultures were absent. In the Cuban case, Oriente Province had been the locus of slave revolts, anti-Spanish rebellions and civil wars, and antigovernment movements since the early 1800s. No other Cuban region has had such a distinctive pattern. Colombia's ELN guerrillas intentionally began operations in Santander because earlier Liberal guerrillas had operated successfully there during *La Violencia.*

We may contrast Bolivia to those cases just discussed. In the former, despite literally thousands of peasant movements in the past century, few such took place in Che Guevara's guerrilla zone near the Santa Cruz–Chuquisaca border. Thus Guevara concentrated his efforts in a region that lacked a tradition of peasant resistance.

Moving to the 1970s and 1980s, we can observe that the major centers of Sandinista support in Nicaragua were also areas that had been centers of Sandino's own resistance fifty years before. Many residents of those regions continued to keep those memories alive, creating a culture of resistance to Somoza's National Guard. In Peru, *Sendero*'s center of initial support lay in or near the area of Héctor Béjar's guerrilla campaign of 1965, although it subsequently spread to other adjoining regions.

However, in El Salvador and Guatemala we find the opposite of the expected. The area of El Salvador's massive 1932 peasant revolt and subsequent massacre in the western coffee districts was not a center of guerrilla activity. Likewise the Guatemalan east has not seen a strong recurrence of guerrilla activity since the federal terror campaign of 1966–67. These findings suggest that *extreme* levels of terror against peasant movements may have the historically "successful" impact of dampening revolutionary fires.

Access to Peasant Resources

The resource-mobilization view of revolutions [see Tilly in Chapter 2—Ed.] suggests that the kinds of discontent nurtured by social conditions, such as the struggles over control of land just discussed, are *not* enough to generate rebellion.

Discontent is always present in social systems, and the problem instead is to organize people, and to get them to commit their resources—time, money, energy, even their lives—to the goals of the movement, and not to workaday routines. Moreover, resource-mobilization theorists have noted that social movements often appear when outsiders enter a social system and begin to mobilize the resources of those who by themselves might not be able to escape the constraints of everyday life. That is, there are the mobilizers and the mobilized.

If the mobilizers are to mobilize peasant resources in the service of revolution, however, they must have access to the peasantry. Such access is not a given of social structure.

Instead, varied patterns of peasant—outsider social linkages and cultural influence generate different *degrees of access* to peasant resources. Certain features of social and cultural structure channel the peasants and the guerrillas' leaders into alliances, while other features function as structural obstacles to such alliances. Such features include political party influence in a region; kinship and patron—client ties; strategic political alliances against a common enemy; the advocacy or opposition of respected religious personnel; and membership (or nonmembership) in minority ethnic and religious groups. Where impediments are few and facilitation is great, guerrillas have generally been more successful in securing peasant support. Furthermore, much depends on who gets there first with the most to offer: guerrillas will secure peasant support only with great difficulty where *other,* hostile political groups have arrived earlier and themselves forged peasant alliances. Guerrillas thus fare better on virgin soil or friendly terrain than they do on occupied ground.

In Cuba, Castro's guerrilla unit gained squatter support in large part through an alliance Fidel struck with Crescencio Pérez, a squatter leader in Oriente Province. Pérez was a major force in organizing squatters into anti-eviction bands *before* Castro's return from Mexican exile. Pérez placed his extensive kin and patronage network at Castro's service.

In Colombia, the Communist Party had begun to establish ties to certain rural areas as far back as the 1930s. Such areas of influence spread during *La Violencia,* and the Communist Party was certainly involved in forming the FARC guerrilla movement in those regions. Most important, though, the FARC guerrillas had no need "to go to the peasantry"—as guerrillas did elsewhere—for they were peasants themselves. By contrast, Guevara's ELN in Bolivia failed to establish any such channel to the peasantry, and obtained not a single peasant recruit. Che's guerrillas taught themselves the wrong Indian language, a further impediment to making contacts.

We can observe new forms of counterguerrilla influence in the period after 1970. In the 1970s and 1980s in Guatemala and El Salvador, state-formed peasant organizations gave military governments a ready channel to, and some control over, village activity. Nonetheless, the later period also saw new forms of influence favorable to the guerrilla forces as well. Before 1970 the Catholic church hierarchy clearly supported governments in Peru, Colombia, and elsewhere (but not in Cuba, where they requested Batista's resignation in early 1958). After 1970 part of the church shifted in a manner crucial to peasant loyalty. The Medellín bishops' conference of 1968 paved the way for liberation theology, leading local priests, in particular, to view revolutionaries in a far more congenial light. Subsequently, *Comunidades Eclesiales de Base* (CEBs), or Christian base communities, helped to spread liberation theology throughout the region wherever Catholicism was strong. Such influence could now provide an imprimatur for revolution.

Peru's *Sendero* and the Guatemalan guerrillas of the 1980s garnered peasant support through a shift in organizational strategy, directly addressing a failure of their predecessors. Indian recruitment and a partly Indian leadership comprise the key elements of that shift, made possible by a commitment to meeting the indigenous populace in their own languages, such as Quechua and Kekchi. *Sendero* leaders built their base of support from ties to Quechua villages in Ayacucho, and the successors to FARC built on ties to various highland Indian villages in Guatemala. In the latter place, entire villages went over to the guerrillas since the mid 1970s, channeled there by Indian recruits and apparently by CEBs as well.

THE IMPORTANCE OF MILITARY STRENGTH

Yet peasant support alone does not guarantee revolutionary success. The Colombian, Guatemalan, and Salvadoran cases provide striking evidence: by far the largest guerrilla movements Latin America has seen, numbering in the thousands, they have been incapable of ousting their opponents from power. Two additional factors are critical to revolutionary success: amassing sufficient military force, and achieving a mass transfer of popular loyalty to the guerrillas. I shall discuss military strength briefly and then mass loyalty shifts in more detail.

The collective strength of government *or* rebel armed forces depends on (1) external support, (2) internal financing, and (3) the internal solidarity of fighting forces. I shall not discuss the second element in any detail, save to note that post-1970 guerrillas have had far more money to spend than their predecessors, generated largely through kidnap for ransom, bank robbery, and drug trafficking.

External support has varied greatly, with both the Soviet Union and the U.S. providing support to sympathetic guerrilla movements and counterinsurgency assistance to allied regimes. In Latin America, from the 1960s through the 1980s the U.S. often supported regimes against guerrillas, albeit with limited success. In some cases—as in Guatemala after 1954—U.S. support of regimes against guerrillas has been decisive; in other cases—as in Cuba in the 1950s and Nicaragua in the 1970s—U.S. support for dictators was withdrawn, undermining the regime and providing an opening for guerrilla advances.

Internal solidarity is the last critical element in the military outcomes of guerrilla war, whether we refer to the divisions among the guerrillas or the willingness of the armed forces to stand by the regime. Where official military forces show a high degree of loyalty to the government, revolutionary movements are likely to fail. Therefore guerrilla wars are not simply battles of financial resources, but also of morale and solidarity.

Where guerrilla forces have fallen out and become divided, their campaigns have usually failed. In the two Latin American cases of guerrilla victory, the Cuban and Nicaraguan guerrillas never splintered decisively, holding together quite well in comparison to movements elsewhere. What is crucial for the guerrillas is maintaining sufficient military capacity to defend themselves against the regime's forces, while also inflicting intermittent hammer blows of damage against the regime. If the regime's forces become demoralized—as is more likely where the armed forces are corrupt and politicized—then even a small guerrilla force can defeat its opponents.

The morale of the regime and its forces in turn depends on their ability to maintain support among at least a core social base. If loyalty among most of the population or the elites is lost by the regime and gained by the guerrilla forces, then the military effectiveness and the strength of the regime's forces are likely to sharply decline.

THE SHIFTING OF MASS LOYALTIES

In Cuba and Nicaragua, revolutionary success rested on the guerrillas' securing cross-class and multi-institutional allies and support, leading to a final scenario in which they overthrew a dictator bereft in the end of all but decaying military support. In neither case did the lower classes "carry out" a revolution against upper-class resistance, for in the end virtually all Cubans and Nicaraguans supported the end of the dictatorships. In both cases, during their struggle against the regime the guerrillas presented themselves as moderates; they thereby gained alliances not only with urban working-class groups, but also the support of "bourgeois" sectors of the population, including professionals, journalists, educators, and even segments of the capitalist business elites.

The contrasting case of El Salvador strengthens this view. Massive guerrilla and peasant resistance to government there allied itself to often radical working-class opposition, yet failed to come to power. This outcome arose because the Salvadoran business sector either stayed firmly in the government's camp, or moved to the government's right and armed itself to resist change when the government adopted a more moderate, even reformist, stance. With no Somoza-type leader making enemies out of the Salvadoran elites, business and landlord groups remained violently opposed to the programs of the guerrillas and their allies. A unified bourgeois–worker–peasant alliance against the Salvadoran government thus never developed.

In general, in those cases of strong but unsuccessful guerrilla movements, as in Guatemala, El Salvador, and Colombia, the guerrillas failed to shift mass (nonpeasant) loyalties appreciably in their direction. Outside of their rural strongholds, they never approached a situation in which a substantial portion of the populace came to regard them as the rightful authority.

In many cases, this was because the regimes acted to shore up their legitimacy with the populace. Throughout the region, relatively open elections led again and again to the decline of guerrilla fortunes, often acknowledged by the revolutionaries themselves: in Colombia, Guatemala, El Salvador, and Peru. (Of course, corrupt or clearly dishonest elections can instead trigger rebellions, as happened in Mexico in 1910, Bolivia in 1952, the Philippines in 1986, and Somoza's Nicaragua.)

Governments also increased their attention to peasant welfare. Guerrillas typically provided various health, literacy, police, and administrative services to the regions they controlled. Such activities commonly led peasants to accept the guerrillas as legitimate "governments." However, central governments could and did attempt to reduce the influence of guerrilla movements by competing with the insurgents for peasant loyalties. They responded in kind to guerrilla welfare measures by building schools and clinics, digging wells, conducting occasional health checkups, and even carrying out limited local land reforms. The military could also engage in "civic action" by providing assistance and services to peasant communities.

Whereas Batista in Cuba and Somoza in Nicaragua employed virtually no such techniques, other governments proved themselves adept at wielding the carrot as well as the stick. Army violence might produce new recruits for the guerrillas, but military civic action to improve peasant welfare could instead produce supporters of, and collaborators with, the established order. In Guatemala in 1966–67 a combination of terror tactics *and* civic action programs, by the guerrillas' own admission, led to the insurgents' loss of peasant support and even to betrayals to the government.

Where governments were most successful in courting popular support, guerrillas were cut off from urban alliances, and the loss or inadequate development of urban-rural linkages led to the guerrillas' decline. Even where guerrillas appeared to gain an unshakable hold over select rural areas, their critical links to urban areas were often sketchy, and easily broken or unraveled. Where such urban-rural linkages could be sustained—Castro's link to supporters in the city of Santiago, or the Sandinistas' ties with urban resistance in León and Matagalpa—then opposition could grow in both areas, leading to coordinated rural warfare and urban insurrection, generating revolution.

To summarize, where guerrillas have *not* succeeded in seizing power, governments improved their claims to legitimacy through elections, rural reforms, and welfare measures. Guerrilla movements remained strongest where such government activities were most restricted, while guerrillas fared worst where governments actively courted the support of the peasantry and the rest of the populace.

CONCLUSION

Since 1970 elected governments in Colombia, Peru, Guatemala, and even El Salvador have been able to make persuasive claims to popular cross-class support, even though guerrillas continued to receive strong peasant support in areas of all four nations. In Colombia and Peru such areas remained mere "oases" of the armed struggle.

In searching for the causes of the expansion and success of guerrilla movements in Cuba in the 1950s, and in Nicaragua in the 1970s, we have seen that in those countries guerrillas successfully pursued programs and proposed policies to appeal to the great majority of the national populace, while the regimes did not counter with their own programs of appeal. In fact, the reverse was true: Batista and Somoza launched programs of widespread corruption and repression that convinced even urban, professional, and business groups that the guerrillas were more deserving of national authority than their regimes.

Only the Cuban and Nicaraguan guerrillas achieved all three necessary conditions for revolutionary success: strong and sustained peasant support; maintenance of sufficient military strength to endure army attacks and to sustain a more general offensive; and stripping the incumbent government of all legitimacy and replacing it with their own movement as the legitimate, revolutionary alternative in the eyes of the broader populace. Each of these three elements was a necessary condition for the success of guerrilla-based revolution: jointly they were sufficient to seize power.

Elsewhere in the region the tale was different. Governments neutralized peasant—guerrilla ties through military civic action, or actively increased their own overall bases of support through reform programs and elections, while guerrillas pursued or revealed revolutionary socialist programs. Guerrilla movements frequently splintered and lost crucial linkages to urban and other allies. As a result, governments could reasonably claim greater and wider popular support than the insurgents they confronted.

The military strength of regimes and guerrillas, as well as mass popular loyalties, depends *jointly* on the character and actions of both the incumbent government and the revolutionaries. Analysis, therefore, requires attention to both of these actors, and to their activities and their support.

South Africa: The Struggle Against Apartheid

GAY SEIDMAN

South Africa is a wonderfully diverse society. Roughly three-quarters of the population are black Africans; these include many different linguistic and ethnic groups, the largest being Bantu speakers, but even these have marked divisions, of which the major groups include the Xhosa, the Zulu, and the Sotho-Tswana. Less than fifteen percent of the population is white, mainly descendants of Dutch and British settlers. Three percent of the population is Asian, mainly descendants of laborers brought from India by the British, and another nine percent is of mixed racial ancestry ("colored").

However, until 1994, South Africa was one of the most racially divided countries in the world. In 1948 the white South African government adopted a policy of "apartheid" that demanded strict racial segregation. Only whites were allowed to vote, hold office, and hold high positions in government, the military, and private business and social organizations. Most blacks were not even allowed to settle in South Africa's cities, compelled to live either in rural "tribal lands" or sprawling dusty townships outside the major urban centers. South Africans of all races who detested the injustice of this system—known as "apartheid"—worked together in the African National Congress (ANC) and other groups to oppose the white-dominated regime, even taking up arms against it.

In response, the white-dominated government of South Africa banned the ANC, imprisoned or exiled its leaders, and prohibited any expression of support for the ANC or its goals. Thus opponents of apartheid had to found new organizations, such as the United Democratic Front (UDF), which claimed to have no association with the ANC or its leaders and which pursued far more limited efforts to undermine and oppose apartheid. After an international campaign of sanctions and decades of internal resistance, white leaders realized that they could not maintain a modern and prosperous South African nation while oppressing more than eighty-five percent of the population—the need for skilled and educated workers, for domestic peace, and international acceptance led to a reform settlement and a new multi-racial political and legal system. Yet the individuals and groups who emerged to lead the new South Africa—notably Nelson Mandela—were primarily affiliated with the ANC. In this essay, Gay Seidman shows how despite banning and exile, the ANC, and particularly its guerrilla wing, played a crucial role in leading, mobilizing, and sustaining the anti-apartheid resistance. In demonstrating the importance of the armed struggle against the regime, she shows how the ANC led a truly revolutionary movement against apartheid.

South Africa's anti-apartheid movement of the 1980s is frequently presented as a victory for peaceful protest, as if the movement directly paralleled the mainstream U.S. civil rights movement of the late 1950s. The truth, of course, is very different: South Africa's popular movement was deeply entwined with a clandestine guerrilla struggle, as much an anti-colonial movement for national self-determination as a civil rights movement working within an existing legal framework. In South Africa, the armed struggle played a key role: it attracted popular support to the anti-apartheid movement, it demonstrated the persistence of resistance to white supremacy despite repression, and it served as a complicated badge of commitment for anti-apartheid activists. This chapter examines the dynamics of armed struggle, from the mobilization of participants, to variation in types of participation, to the sources of the resources (including weapons and ammunition) that were used.

PROTESTS AGAINST APARTHEID

Sociologists discussing South Africa tend to try to fit the anti-apartheid movement into the framework of western social movement theory. Descriptions of anti-apartheid activism stress the role of student groups, political activists, unions, and women's groups, rarely mentioning the way these groups interacted with, and cooperated with, armed activists within the national liberation movement. However, a broadly-supported armed struggle introduces a host of complex social processes: the construction of a "national" project across disparate ethnic groups or social classes; the decision to take up arms and the mobilization of popular support for a seemingly impossible undertaking; the problems of maintaining discipline and control in a guerrilla army; the logistics involved in providing supplies and infiltrating guerrillas; the relation between guerrillas and local populations.

In South Africa's anti-apartheid movement, moreover, the lines between different types of collective action may be more blurred than the distinction between "peaceful" and "armed" opposition recognizes. As is well known, the turn to armed struggle in South Africa came after several decades in which collective protests against apartheid seemed to have little impact. "Passive resistance" relies heavily on appeals to the oppressor's humanity; by 1960, many South African activists believed the apartheid regime would not listen. The South African government—elected in 1948 by less than half the electorate, in an election basically restricted to the 20 percent of South Africans legally classified as "white"—was firmly committed to maintaining white domination. Far from viewing the 80 percent of South Africans who were not racially classified "white" as citizens, it viewed them as subjects, refusing to recognize their claims to political rights or inclusion. From 1948, South Africa's government intensified its segregationist policies, which were enforced through draconian security legislation. Individuals' racial classification legally determined where South Africans could live, what schools they could attend, what jobs they could hold, even who they could marry; South African society was redesigned to ensure, as a major architect of the system put it, that "natives will be taught from childhood that equality with Europeans is not for them."

From "Guerillas in Their Midst" by Gay Seidman from Mobilization, *6(2), pp. 111–127 (2001). Reprinted with permission of the publisher.*

In the early 1950s, anti-apartheid activists sought to imitate Gandhi's recent successes in India. In 1952, thousands of volunteers joined the ANC's Defiance Campaign, refusing to obey segregationist rules at bus stops, train stations, post offices and so on, generally in an orderly and non-violent manner. In terms of mass mobilization, the campaign was a huge success. Eight thousand people were arrested between June and November, 1952; popular enthusiasm for the campaign swelled the ANC's membership, from about 7,000 to about 100,000. In terms of political achievement, however, the campaign was a dismal failure: the government made no concessions, and took firm steps to crush the campaign. Thousands of volunteers were jailed, and when jails grew overcrowded, the government rushed through new laws allowing judges to sentence resisters to floggings as well as three-year jail terms. Meetings were outlawed; leaders were placed under house arrest. Drawing on the language of the Cold War, the government redefined resistance to racial segregation as "communism," and then charged the campaign's leaders with treason; the government's repression disorganized the resistance and immobilized the campaign.

Over the next decade, repeated attempts to engage in non-violent tactics—bus boycotts, demonstrations, petitions, pass-burning campaigns—provoked violent reactions. The 1960 massacre outside the Sharpeville police station, when 69 people were killed and 178 wounded, shot in the back as they tried to run from a police attack, came to symbolize the government's refusal to permit any kind of peaceful protest. In an earlier era, South African prime minister Jan Smuts had felt compelled to release Gandhi from jail when he led non-violent demonstrations. After 1948, however, South Africa's leaders explicitly rejected compassion; regretfully, a prominent South African proponent of non-violence concluded that it seemed unlikely that South Africa's rulers could "be converted by extreme suffering when they are so strongly confirmed in the ideologies of white domination."[1]

Faced with an intransigent regime at home, South Africans looked beyond their borders for help. From the early 1960s, black South Africans repeatedly appealed to the international community to impose economic sanctions, arguing that they would take up arms unless political and economic pressure from the outside offered a peaceful way to undermine the powerful and repressive apartheid state. But again, South Africans found no audience. In India the British government, and in the American South the U.S. Federal government, had each sought to avoid embarrassment on the international stage, intervening on the side of protesters to overcome the intransigence of local colonial officials, states' rights advocates and white elites. But by the mid-1960s, no western power had direct colonial or federal links to South Africa, and no western power appeared to feel much moral responsibility for ending apartheid. From 1960 to 1990, Britain and the United States routinely vetoed efforts at the United Nations to impose sanctions on South Africa, allowing only a loophole-riddled arms embargo in 1976. In 1961, ANC president Albert Luthuli received the Nobel Peace Prize for his non-violent efforts at social change; but twenty-four years later, when his fellow South African Desmond Tutu won the same Peace Prize in 1985, Tutu was still repeating Luthuli's appeals for international help. In the mid-1980s, when the European community and America finally imposed mild economic sanctions and international banks refused to extend loans, the impact was indeed what sanctions advocates had long predicted: the threat of economic stagnation and isolation quickly undermined white support for strict apartheid, and helped create a climate in which negotiations became possible.

In the intervening decades, however, anti-apartheid leaders argued they could no longer ask their followers to risk their lives in unarmed confrontation. In the aftermath of the Sharpeville massacre, when the government arrested 20,000 political activists and banned political parties that demanded political rights for all South Africans, anti-apartheid leaders concluded they had no choice but to establish armed wings. Despite the arrest in the early 1960s of most major anti-apartheid figures—including Nelson Mandela, a popular political organizer who served as the ANC's first military commander—the ANC managed over the next fifteen years to establish a network of cells and arms caches, linked to camps of guerrillas located farther north, in Angola, Tanzania and Uganda.

It is important to place the ANC's "turn to armed struggle" in its historical context. Discussions in South Africa were clearly influenced by prominent contemporary examples of nationalist struggles, including Algeria and Kenya; parallel discussions were going on in nationalist movements in Angola, the Congo, Rhodesia (now Zimbabwe), and Mozambique. Obviously, the willingness of Eastern European countries, as well as Algeria and later Libya, to support armed nationalist movements with resources and training helped persuade ANC leaders that this turn was a logical one; conversely, in the months immediately after the Sharpeville massacre, the decision by U.S. banks to extend a very large loan to shore up South Africa's capital reserves undermined those ANC activists who would have preferred to appeal to the West.

As decolonization proceeded down the continent in the 1970s, politically aware South Africans recognized new opportunities for guerrilla campaigns. For example, although the 1976 uprising in the black township of Soweto was primarily a protest against the use of Afrikaans as the official medium of instruction in all South African schools, student protestors at the time also celebrated the recent collapse of Portugal's colonial control of Angola and Mozambique, a collapse which removed colonial buffer zones which had protected South Africa's borders from guerrilla incursion. Thousands of black South Africans had left the country after 1960, living for years in guerrilla camps in the forests of independent African countries, or traveling to Eastern Europe for military training. In 1976, student protestors recognized new possibilities for guerrilla infiltration—possibilities that were given substance when the government repressed the student uprising, prompting thousands more young South Africans to leave the country and join the ANC's "external" army.

From the late 1960s on, small groups of ANC soldiers had tried to infiltrate into South Africa through Angola, Mozambique or Rhodesia, but they were usually imprisoned or killed by colonial police before they even reached the border. However, by the early 1980s, the ANC's guerrillas could claim several dramatic attacks: the 1977 downtown shoot-out with South African police; the 1980 attack on a coal-into-oil refinery, Sasol, which created a three-day smoke-plume that could be seen from Johannesburg; a 1983 explosion that destroyed the South African air force intelligence headquarters; and the 1984 rocket attack on an army camp near Pretoria. None of these attacks came close to bringing down the state, but they provided physical evidence of a tangible *potential* threat to the regime—reinforcing the sense, as Nadine Gordimer put it, that "something out there" represented a shadowy threat to the long-term future of white supremacy.[2]

It did not hurt the ANC's popularity, either within the country or internationally, that the Palestine Liberation Organization (PLO), for example, sometimes chose to attack civilians in Israel/Palestine, and to attack Israeli targets outside of the Middle East, while the

ANC leadership claimed it pursued a more restrained approach. From the early 1960s, South African guerrillas were supposed to concentrate on sabotage and military attacks, avoiding civilian targets. In a deeply segregated society, it would have been easy to kill large groups of whites: segregated white schools, segregated movie theaters, segregated shopping centers meant that if white deaths had been the only goal, potential targets could be found everywhere. But Oliver Tambo, the ANC's leader in exile, insisted that a Christian like himself could not condone a single unnecessary death. Only a handful of ANC attacks involved civilian deaths, white or black. For the most part, ANC guerrillas limited their targets to military installations and economic sabotage, aimed at facilities such as electric pylons and power plants.

While highly principled, this strategy was not particularly successful militarily: despite the rhetoric, most anti-apartheid activists concluded by the mid-1970s that in a highly urbanized, industrialized society, facing a well-equipped and sophisticated enemy army, a guerrilla insurrection could not succeed. Instead, anti-apartheid activists put their energy into political organizing, bringing people together around local issues, and looking for ways to protest which would not provoke immediate repression. In the 1960s, public protest had been effectively silenced; with leaders in jail and organizations outlawed, there was little open political discussion beyond university campuses, where students could at least discuss political issues in relative safety, and occasional protests by white moderates.

In the 1970s, black South Africans began to develop alternative tactics. By 1976, more than half of black South Africans lived in urban areas and worked in industrial settings—sites which offered new possibilities for organization. Especially as more experienced activists began to be released from the jail terms they began to serve in the early 1960s, they began to look at how black students could paralyze urban school systems, black workers could paralyze production, and black communities could demand better urban services. Like poor people elsewhere, anti-apartheid activists discovered the power of disruption: black South Africans learned that by mobilizing collective protests at school, at work, or in segregated black townships, they could disrupt the smooth functioning of apartheid, through boycotts, strikes and demonstrations—without exposing individual leaders to arrest, or provoking immediate police attacks.

Through the 1970s and 1980s, South Africa moved into a period of rolling insurgency. In 1973, a scattering of illegal wildcat strikes among black factory workers showed that some employers would rather negotiate than fire and replace striking workers; by 1985, South Africa had one of the world's most militant labor movements, and employers often begged police to release trade unionists so they could have someone with whom to negotiate. Similarly, the 1976 Soweto uprising revealed the capacity of high school students to disrupt township life; by the late-1980s, black high schools and universities were regularly disrupted by boycotts, to such an extent that employers and even white government officials expressed concerns about future shortages of skilled workers. From the early 1980s, township activists began to organize community groups around local issues, ranging from busfares to high rents; by the mid-1980s, these township "civic associations" organized rent and consumer boycotts, funerals for activists killed by police, and other forms of protest. In all these cases, activists focused on local issues; but beneath all the various demands and tactics was a common demand for political rights, democracy, and human dignity. As these community protests escalated, most ANC activists came to believe any real prospect of bringing down the South African government by force had been postponed indefinitely. By the early 1980s, the ANC was putting most of its resources and energy into supporting popular mobilization in townships, with clandestine networks linking activists across the country with the ANC leadership-in-exile.

Yet although most accounts treat these unions, community organizations, and student groups as strictly separate from the ANC's military efforts, the links between "above-ground" and clandestine guerrilla campaigns were far stronger than activists or researchers generally acknowledged at the time. Through the mid-1980s, the ANC leadership called its guerrilla attacks "armed propaganda," describing their aim in terms of raising black South Africans' morale, rather than a full-scale war. It is hard to overstate the symbolic importance of even small guerrilla actions — or even the way the well-publicized capture and trial of yet another ANC guerrilla often seemed to reinforce activists' determination. Archie Gumede, co-chair of the UDF who was also a veteran of the days when the ANC had been legal, said years later, "As far as effective attacks on the South African economy, [ANC's guerrillas] achieved what could only be called flea bites . . . [but] in my opinion, the armed struggle did have some effect in showing that people could resist oppression. It boosted morale. People . . . felt that the ANC has fought for them."[3]

Guerrilla attacks held a prominent place in the culture of the anti-apartheid movement. In the 1980s, although most ANC activists had abandoned the idea that a guerrilla movement would ever manage a military overthrow of the highly organized South African state, many township activists' commitment to supporting the idea of armed struggle — and respect for those who participated actively in it — was almost visceral. Almost certainly, at least some part of Nelson Mandela's extraordinary popularity stems from his role as first commander of "MK," as *Umkhonto we Sizwe*, the ANC's armed wing, was popularly nicknamed. Twenty-seven years later, Mandela garnered even more admiration in the townships when the government revealed that Mandela had repeatedly rejected government offers to release him from prison if only he would renounce armed struggle. Even when ANC resources had shifted to emphasize popular organization and protests over military attack, it retained its rhetorical commitment to armed struggle, describing its strategy as one that used "the hammer of armed struggle on the anvil of mass action." Indeed, in 1985, just as the anti-apartheid movement moved into a phase marked by popular unrest, the exiled ANC leadership announced it would intensify its guerrilla efforts, moving from what it called "armed propaganda" to "people's war"; even government data suggest that this announcement was in fact followed by a marked increase in attacks involving land-mines, hand-grenades or AK-47s.

Many black South Africans considered these categories intertwined: the struggle against apartheid, as activists often repeated, continued on many fronts. And the symbolic importance of the armed struggle even for those anti-apartheid activists who retained a strong moral commitment to non-violence should not be underestimated: even someone as explicitly pacifist as Archbishop Desmond Tutu avoided condemnation of those who had taken a different route. Throughout the 1980s, the ANC was regularly named by over half of black South Africans as the party they would vote for if allowed to vote, partly because of its history as the oldest anti-apartheid organization, but also, almost certainly, because of a popular perception in black townships that the ANC embodied the possibility of armed resistance to an oppressive regime.

But aside from the symbolic importance of the armed struggle, we do not yet have a clear picture of how far the clandestine guerrilla networks extended, nor of the role played by activists linked to clandestine ANC networks in coordinating mass mobilization. Many of the "non-violent" protests of the 1980s were coordinated by activists who were secretly linked to the ANC, and whose understanding of the anti-apartheid strategy embraced the armed struggle—even if they personally chose to focus on work in unions, community groups, or other forms of collective action. Many anti-apartheid activists actively avoided learning anything about guerrilla activities, hoping to protect peaceful protesters, and themselves, from the kind of repression invited by participation in guerrilla activities, and to protect clandestine guerrilla networks by reducing their visibility to the police. But some seepage was inevitable: a guerrilla needing help, including shelter or money, would frequently turn first to township activists whose statements suggested they might have ANC loyalties, even if they had no direct involvement in the armed wing, and frequently, those activists responded with support and aid.

Perhaps more importantly, ANC military strategists through the 1980s frequently planned attacks that would be popularly understood in terms of links to on-going mass mobilization. "Armed propaganda" boosted activists' morale, and reminded them that an army of clandestine guerrillas might already have infiltrated the country from their bases farther north on the African continent. As the popular uprising intensified after 1984, even smaller, less-dramatic attacks had an immediate impact on the conversations in union meetings, church groups, and student groups the following day, raising morale among activists, and providing proof that resistance would continue despite repression. Small attacks made large impressions when they were linked to popular struggles: where police had cordoned off a township, a post-office might be hit by a hand grenade; in the middle of a bus boycott, an empty bus might be bombed. Press censorship meant that these attacks were rarely reported in the national press, but activists' networks could spread the news rapidly, often adding exaggerated details for good measure. As white UDF activist Adele Kirsten put it,

> I think . . . it was effective in the sense that people did fear attacks by the ANC. Internally, people had the sense that the ANC's armed wing was much bigger and more effective than it was—even though they didn't see anything more than the SASOL bombing or blowing up of a few police stations. It was an effective strategy, it definitely did contribute.[4]

The strategy of disrupting apartheid from below required that nearly all black South Africans participate in campaigns entailing personal risk and daily difficulties. Such strikes, consumer boycotts, bus and rent boycotts, were generally called by groups affiliated to the UDF, but were often enforced by groups of young militants who identified explicitly with the ANC. Efforts to initiate and extend such campaigns often provoked violent conflict between black South Africans who thought ending apartheid was worth any sacrifice, and those who felt that in the short term at least, they had more to lose than to gain. While nationally visible leaders often dismissed acts like "necklacing"—placing a burning tire on a suspected informer—as the work of police provocateurs, such behavior was often widely condoned in townships. This kind of violent enforcement of mass mobilization was probably not centrally planned, but it reflected and reinforced the ANC's strategy of making the townships "ungovernable"—a coordinated strategy that underscores again the importance of reexamining the role of a clandestine network of activists linked across the country to each other and to the ANC leadership-in-exile.

THE IMPACT OF ARMED STRUGGLE

South Africa's armed struggle was important in shaping the "above-ground" anti-apartheid movement, and its legacies continue to play out in post-apartheid politics.

There is a great deal of evidence suggesting that activists' persistent support for the armed struggle played an important role in the associational networks of the anti-apartheid movement more broadly—not only in terms of recruiting young activists to leave the country for military training and supporting guerrillas when they returned, but also in terms of linking activists' strategies in different parts of the country to the overall ANC strategy. Often built around veteran ANC activists or prominent activist families, these clandestine networks were frequently involved in coordinating campaigns in different parts of the country—and, perhaps even more importantly, in coordinating guerrilla attacks with aboveground campaigns. Especially in UDF groups or in a few specifically ANC-linked unions, individuals' links to clandestine networks often gave a special status to their knowledge or suggestions.

In addition, material resources coming from clandestine networks may have affected the anti-apartheid movement as a whole. Obviously, the military resources provided by Eastern Europe to the exiled ANC played an important role in ideological discussions within the ANC; countries that provided military support and training became special allies for the ANC, strengthening the weight of the South African Communist Party within the ANC alliance. But we have very little understanding of how clandestine resources funneled to internal, above-ground groups may have shaped strategic choices and ideological debates within the open anti-apartheid movement. In impoverished black communities, the anti-apartheid movement struggled to find money to sustain protests: organizing in the townships required money not only for leaflets, gasoline and cars, and meeting spaces, but, especially in the repressive 1980s, for housing and feeding activists who were hiding from the police, for lawyers' fees to support detainees, and for sustaining families during consumer boycotts, strikes, and stay-aways. Through the early 1980s, the UDF received much of its funding from church groups and other international supporters. Some of these, like the prominent British anti-apartheid organization International Defense and Aid or the Dutch anti-apartheid movement, took advice directly from the exiled ANC about which South African groups to fund. But the UDF also received clandestine funding from the exiled ANC, sometimes smuggled into the country by the same methods used to smuggle guns and explosives.

How did access to donor funds and to smuggled cash alter the dynamics of debates within above-ground groups? What difference did it make to the strategies of above-ground groups that activists linked to clandestine networks could sometimes draw on additional resources, providing support for one kind of protest organization rather than another? In the early 1980s, for example, debates over whether activists should pursue "non-racialism" compared to a separatist black consciousness approach are frequently described in purely ideological terms; but clandestine resources gave greater visibility to ANC-backed, non-racial approaches—

and probably attracted new recruits more easily to non-racial organizations than might have otherwise been the case.

Neither networks nor resources alone would have sustained township support, however, if the idea of armed struggle had not retained a place at the symbolic core of the national liberation struggle. This strong symbolic role was neither natural nor accidental: ANC-affiliated activists worked hard through the 1980s to construct a culture of support for MK's guerrillas, in which those who chose to join the armed struggle—a choice that obviously involved enormous risks and sacrifice—were often considered heroes, even by activists who explicitly avoided clandestine work. Broad public campaigns like the 1981 campaign to "Unban the Freedom Charter," which used a loophole in South Africa's press censorship to discuss the ANC's goals and strategies, reflected conscious efforts to promote the ANC's visibility above ground. The ANC used a broad range of efforts to build community support for its armed struggle. Aboveground activists frequently traveled, legally and illegally, to neighboring states, where they met exiled ANC activists, sharing ideas and information, and discussing strategy. ANC supporters worked hard to reinforce a township discourse that treated the armed struggle as a legitimate, perhaps essential, part of the anti-apartheid movement.

At the beginning of the 1980s, the ANC was only one of several parties within the anti-apartheid movement; by 1990, it had emerged as the government's primary negotiating partner. The construction of community support for the ANC's guerrilla efforts involved a slow and painstaking project. The growth of support for the ANC's armed efforts did not reflect an innate black South African community consensus, but required movement resources and energy, and careful efforts to create a culture affirming the armed struggle.

Finally, it is worth noting that the armed struggle within the anti-apartheid movement is not important only for its historical symbolism: its legacy remains deeply embedded in Southern African politics, shaping collective memories and national aspirations as well as individual careers. Collective memories of nationalist struggles often give a special place to guerrillas, as heroes and martyrs whose commitment went beyond the ordinary. Such glorification of armed struggle lends legitimacy to particular political claims in the present. It could be argued, for example, that the ANC's popular commitment to a "non-racial" ideology, which welcomes white participation, was greatly shored up by the visible participation of several key whites in the guerrilla command structure, some of whom still serve in the ANC cabinet. Similarly, backgrounds in the ANC's armed wing bestow a unique credibility on individuals: histories of participation in guerrilla activities give activists a very different profile than even very visible leadership in "internal" groups, to such an extent that those histories, and the links and loyalties built up in the armed wing, help explain otherwise-opaque internal ANC power struggles.

Some of the legacies of armed struggle are more problematic for the new government. Questions of how to deal with existing guerrilla armies—how to disarm them, demobilize them, and reintegrate them into peacetime society—have been as difficult in South Africa as elsewhere. And in the longer term, there is the increased availability of guns, which poses a persistent threat to regional stability. Political schisms that emerged during armed struggle—often, conflicts over leadership, magnified by leaders' choices about alliances and sources of weapons—have repeatedly served as the fault-lines of Southern Africa's post-colonial civil wars, or provided an excuse for the repression of civil liberties as new governments try to extend their writ: networks of people who were mobilized, armed and trained during the "national liberation" struggle are all-too-easily re-mobilized after independence. Through-out the region, armed campaigns left behind widely dispersed caches of hidden weapons, as well as thousands of people with some military training who may feel displaced in the new order. In South Africa as well as its neighbors, the post-apartheid period has been marked by new flows of small arms and weaponry, as former guerrillas sell off hidden weapons; and by sharp increases in armed robberies and banditry, sometimes carried out by former guerril-las who draw on their military training to rob banks or armored vehicles, and who use the slogans of armed struggle to explain their actions when they are caught.

Armed struggle played an essential role in the multi-faceted campaign against apart-heid. But the armed society that remains in South Africa today—ironically, the legacy of centuries of white supremacism, brutally enforced, and of the armed struggle against racial oppression—could prove an obstacle to the peaceful and stable non-racial democracy to which so many South Africans aspire.

REFERENCES

1.   Kuper (1957), p. 94.
2.   Gordimer (1984).
3.   Quoted in Sutherland and Mayer (1999), p. 163.
4.   Quoted in Sutherland and Mayer (1999), p. 182.

The Palestinian "Intifada" Revolt

GLENN E. ROBINSON

Since its foundation in 1948, the state of Israel has faced primarily external threats: wars with surrounding Arab states and low-intensity conflict related to the efforts of the Palestine Liberation Organization to recover lands for Palestinians. Until the signing of the 1993 Oslo Accords, the PLO was always externally based, operating from its headquarters first in Jordan, then in Lebanon, and then in Tunisia. However, following the 1967 war with its neighbors, Israel occupied two areas—the Gaza Strip and the West Bank of the Jordan River—with large Palestinian populations. Over the next two decades, structural changes in those areas led to the emergence of an internal revolutionary challenge to Israeli authority: the Palestinian Intifada.

This case study of the Intifada—the uprising by the Palestinian people against the Israeli oc-cupation of the West Bank and Gaza, beginning in 1987—focuses on three central questions of revolutionary collective action. The first question I ask is fundamental: Why do people

From Building a Palestinian State: The Incomplete Revolution *by Glenn E. Robinson. Reprinted by permission of Indiana Uni-versity Press.*

rebel? I take up this question in the Palestinian case by asking what made the Intifada possible, given that Palestinians in the West Bank and Gaza had lived under Israeli military occupation for twenty years before the Intifada began without engaging in anything approaching this level of action. The question is not really what were the causes of the Intifada, since any people would chafe under military occupation, but rather what happened to transform individual anger into a revolutionary process.

The second question has to do with the revolutionary process itself. How is revolutionary collective action sustained in the face of overwhelming counterforce (as states almost always have over rebellious societies)? In this case, how could the Palestinians sustain collective action for years in the face of harsh Israeli measures meant to deter such action?

Third, and perhaps most interesting, is this question: How does the revolutionary process shape the political outcome in an emerging state? That is, when revolutions come to power, what can the dynamics of the revolution itself tell us about how the new state will look? What are the relationships between revolutionary causes, processes, and political outcomes? In the Palestinian case: How do the dynamics of the Intifada impact the state-building process of the Palestine Liberation Organization (PLO) in the West Bank and Gaza? What is the "logic" of Palestinian state-building?

ELITE CONFLICT AND STRUCTURAL CHANGE IN PALESTINIAN SOCIETY

The Intifada only became possible with the rise of a new and distinctive political elite in the West Bank and Gaza. Palestinian politics had long been dominated by an urban, landowning elite, which had its roots in nineteenth-century Ottoman policies. Ruling states had used this class, known as the notables, to maintain effective social control. The two bases on which the notables' authority rested were a web of traditional patron–client relations and ownership of land. Each pillar was undermined by the unintended consequences of Israeli policies: opening Israel's labor markets to mostly agrarian Palestinians weakened patron–client networks, and land confiscations attacked that which brought the notable class social power—control over land.

The new elite which rose to prominence in the 1980s came from a different social class than its notable counterpart. The new elite was not a landowning class, and its members were more likely to be from villages, refugee camps, and small towns than from urban centers. Because it came from a lower social class, the new elite was much more extensive than the old one. It largely coalesced at Palestinian universities—institutions that did not exist prior to 1972.

In large measure because it came from a different social class, the new elite promulgated an ideology different from that of the old elite. While the notables ultimately espoused political transformation—independence from Israel—the new elite sought not just political but also social transformation: to remake Palestinian society, thus undermining the social bases of notable power. It was this new elite that undertook a policy of popular mobilization in the 1980s. Grassroots organizations forged in this period—student blocs, labor unions, women's committees, voluntary works organizations—were the institutional expression of the new elite. Grassroots mobilization provided a means to both oppose notable power and build the social and political relations necessary to sustain the Intifada.

Structural change made the policy of mobilization possible. In this case, structural change—primarily changing patterns of employment, land tenure, and higher education—not only helped to eclipse the power of an old elite and create a counterelite but also produced a society in which the possibility of mobilization existed.

During the 1980s, fully 40 percent of the total Palestinian labor force (about 120,000 workers) worked daily in Israel. While the wages were low compared to the wages of the Israelis, they were high compared to what—if anything—could be earned in the occupied territories. This was particularly true for unskilled Palestinian peasants, or subsistence farmers, who could earn very little money by staying in agriculture. The cumulative effect of Israel's opening its labor markets to Palestinians was to eliminate the Palestinian peasantry and replace it with wage laborers. This diminished rural reliance on notable patronage, and it made the workers more open to recruitment to political action. In short, the changing labor market made peasants into Palestinians.

The second structural change which undermined the notables' power could be found in Israel's confiscation of land. On the eve of the Intifada, over half of the West Bank and one-third of Gaza had been confiscated or otherwise made unavailable for Palestinian use. This undermined the landowners; additionally, the inability of the notables to stop the seizures was not lost on other Palestinians.

The third important structural change was the development of the Palestinian university system, beginning in 1972. Prior to 1972 no Palestinian university existed in the West Bank or Gaza, although there were a small number of teacher training schools and vocational institutes. Those few Palestinians who acquired university degrees prior to 1972 were almost exclusively the sons of the notable elite, who were sent to study abroad. The growth of the Palestinian university system in the 1970s and 1980s meant that tens of thousands of Palestinians who otherwise would not have gone to a university now did. Moreover, the student body more closely resembled the larger Palestinian population, with about 70 percent of the university students coming from refugee camps, villages, and small towns. It was from this stratum that the new Palestinian counterelite was drawn. And it was this new elite that posed a direct political challenge to the notables.

It should be noted that after 1977, the Israeli government also engaged in a frontal assault on the notables, believing them to be too nationalistic. First it outlawed their organization, the Palestine National Front; then it dismissed and, in some cases, deported the mayors elected in the 1976 municipal Palestinian elections. It is ironic that the Israeli state under the Likud Party rejected a century of evidence—including that produced in Israel proper after 1948—about the necessity of supporting the notable social class in order to ensure political quiescence. Instead of politically decapitating the Palestinians, these actions, and other efforts to sever ties between the external PLO and the occupied territories, demonstrated to members of the new elite that the burden of resistance was on them, and actually energized their mobilization campaign.

The university students, graduates, and urban professionals all joined to create widespread organizations aimed at improving the health and welfare of Palestinian society. These included student political organizations; labor organizations; women's organizations; the Voluntary Works Program, which engaged in land reclamation, agricultural improvement, tree planting, road repair, water and sewage provision, and literacy campaigns; medical relief committees; health care committees; and agricultural relief committees. In effect, the modern organizations which the new elite built in the 1980s and with which they helped to politically mobilize Palestinian society were the "army" with which the new elite "took power"—i.e., became the dominant political elite within Palestinian society in the West Bank and Gaza.

The Intifada thus was made possible by the emergence of a new political elite, itself the by-product of structural transformations in Palestinian society. Sustained collective action could not be undertaken in the absence of the institutions and ideology of the new elite (in contrast to the nonmobilizational ideology of, and the absence of institutions built by, the notable elite). While the Palestinians always had a surplus of grievances living under military occupation, revolutionary collective action had to wait for a counterelite that could organize it. Not surprisingly, while the Intifada was primarily about confronting the occupation, it also contained a strong antinotable, transformative flavor.

SUSTAINING COLLECTIVE ACTION IN THE FACE OF OVERWHELMING FORCE

Central to understanding the Palestinians' ability to sustain the Intifada is the notion of *devolved authority*. With the rise of a new elite, authority had spread downward in society and become much more diffused within it than before. This was of critical importance. Earlier attempts to confront the Israeli occupation had largely failed because the authority in Palestinian society was concentrated in a small stratum at the top of society. Israel could cut off the metaphorical head of the beast and the nascent rebellion would collapse, deprived of leadership. In the Intifada, when one group of leaders was arrested another would immediately spring up.

The institutions of devolved authority numbered in the thousands. They included not only the extant grassroots organizations but also the popular committees, which virtually ran Palestinian society during the Intifada. Such popular organizations ranged from the ever-changing leadership of the Intifada (the Unified National Leadership of the Uprising, UNLU) to local branches of the UNLU to ad hoc committees that distributed food during curfews or taught neighborhood students while schools were closed. They included militant groups, which would enforce strikes, attack collaborators, and organize confrontations with Israeli forces. Such groups sustained collective action in spite of harsh Israeli measures to stop it— and in spite of attempts by the PLO in Tunisia to undermine autonomous political actions outside its control.

The political mobilization of Palestinian society in the 1980s was not limited to grassroots organizations established by elites and factions affiliated with the PLO. A parallel mobilization was undertaken by activists from various Islamist groups in the occupied territories, primarily the Muslim Brethren. The leadership of the Islamic societies was similar to that of the secular, nationalist leaders of the Intifada; both groups were from the emerging university-educated and professional elites. The prominence of Islamic movements in the Middle East in recent years is primarily attributable to the failures of secular regimes in their economic and political projects, including the devastating military defeat at the hands of Israel in 1967. In Israel the ascent to power in 1977 by the Likud Party, with its strong Jewish messianic ideological component, helped to shift the political discourse over the occupied territories from one of competing nationalisms to one of religious conflict. It is one of the great ironies of the conflict that the political hardliners among both Israelis and Palestinians essentially agree on the religious terms of the struggle, if on little else.

The growing influence of Islam in Palestinian society during the 1980s could be seen at a number of levels, including social practices, institution-building, student body elections at universities, and public opinion surveys. Gaza and the West Bank experienced a mosque boom, and a number of schools of Islamic learning were established in the years preceding the Intifada. Two Islamist factions in the occupied territories stand out in importance: the Muslim Brethren and the Islamic Jihad. The Muslim Brethren has traditionally been the oldest, biggest, and most influential of all Islamist groups in the Middle East, as it clearly was among the Palestinians. Islamic Jihad, more militant and aggressive than the Muslim Brethren, represented the small but growing confrontational nature of Islamist politics in the 1980s and was largely responsible for the onset of the Intifada.

For the Islamists, Palestine had been lost in large measure as God's punishment for turning away from Islam. They believed that Palestine was part of a larger God-given Islamic endowment; thus no human had the right to cede control of any part of such lands to non-Muslims. For these reasons, the Muslim Brethren never distinguished between the parts of Palestine occupied in 1948—Israel proper—and the lands occupied in 1967—the Gaza Strip, the West Bank, and East Jerusalem. While the PLO increasingly focused on gaining control of the lands occupied in 1967, a policy recognized formally in the Oslo Accords, the Muslim Brethren rejected any Israeli presence in the Middle East.

A campaign of daring strikes by Islamic Jihad in 1986, the year prior to the Intifada, demonstrated that Palestinian action against Israel was possible. Although the Jihad was subsequently targeted by Israeli authorities and largely suppressed, the Muslim Brethren reacted with an internal coup, in which the middle-stratum cadres came to the fore of the Palestinian Islamist movement and relegated the old, more conservative leadership to a more peripheral position. Adopting the name "Islamic Resistance Movement" (and popularly known as "Hamas") the new organization undertook an ideological campaign devoted to the idea that not one inch of Palestine should be ceded to Israel, and grew increasingly militant. Hamas also extended its political organization in the occupied territories, and competed with leaders of the PLO for local authority.

In sum, the revolutionary process was directly linked to the structural changes which preceded it. In this case, structural changes had weakened an old elite and brought a counterelite to the fore. This new elite mobilized a transformed society in order to better confront the occupation. By so doing, authority was pushed downward in society away from the notable elite and toward a much broader spectrum of individuals. The devolution of authority was seen directly in the Intifada by the emergence of thousands of popular committees and institutions which organized Palestinian society under emergency conditions and which Israel found impossible to eliminate. Sustained collective action, then, was directly linked to the reorganization of authority in Palestinian society by the mobilization efforts of the new elite.

While the Intifada was a social revolution, it remained incomplete. It was a social revolution precisely because of its social transformative element. In other words, it was not only an anticolonial political revolution but also a movement that sought to remake internal Palestinian society. The promise of social transformation was never entirely fulfilled. The new elite was never able to fully consolidate its position of power, largely because the Intifada was never able to throw off the yoke of Israeli occupation. Only by actually coming to power in a new polity would the new elite be able to consolidate not only the political changes, but also the social changes of the Intifada.

The new elite, however, would not have the chance to consolidate its position, because the political power in the post-Intifada polity was captured by an outside political force, one geographically and politically removed from the West Bank and Gaza: the PLO in Tunisia.

REVOLUTIONARY PROCESS AND POLITICAL OUTCOME

Compared to other cases of revolution or rebellion, the Palestinian case is exceptional in two significant ways. First, while all successful social revolutions create their own states, the Intifada produced its own polity without first enjoying success. Only after it was contained and largely defeated did the Intifada produce the political outcome of a new polity, as established and constrained by the 1993 Oslo Accords. Second, the political elite that came to power in the new "state" was not the same political elite that produced the revolution.

The Oslo Accords, so-named because they were first developed secretly in Oslo, Norway, by Israeli and Palestinian negotiators, had several components. The breakthrough document was the 1993 "Declaration of Principles," which was signed with great fanfare on the White House lawn. This was followed in 1994 by the "Gaza—Jericho" agreement, which allowed for the establishment of the Palestinian Authority (PA) in the Gaza Strip and town of Jericho on the West Bank. In 1995, the full, formal document governing the five-year interim arrangements was agreed to in Taba, Egypt. A host of other agreements were also signed which dealt with more specific issues, such as the Hebron and Wye River accords. What all of the Oslo Accords shared was a concern only for arrangements during a five year interim period, and purposely did not address the much more difficult issues at the core of the Israeli-Palestinian conflict. Nor did they result in significant transfers of land to Palestinian control. By the time the "Al-Aqsa Intifada" broke out in September 2000, the PA still only controlled about 15 percent of the West Bank. Frustration over the glacial pace of change—the peace process was criticized as all process and no peace—greatly contributed to the renewed outbreak of violence.

The Oslo Accords shaped the Palestinian state-building process in three fundamental ways. First and most obviously, Oslo made the possibility of actual Palestinian statehood much more likely. Indeed, one of the most consistent features of the Oslo process was recognition by both the political right and the left in Israel that a Palestinian state would be the end product (although they greeted that prospect in very different ways).

Second, the Oslo process focused exclusively on interim arrangements. The inability of subsequent negotiations to agree on the major contentious issues—the future of Jerusalem and of Jewish settlements in the West Bank and Gaza, the right of Palestinian refugees to return to the area, and eventual Palestinian sovereignty—increased Palestinian opposition to the peace process, not only by Hamas but also by mainstream politicians and former peace negotiators.

Third and most important, Oslo revived a fiscally bankrupt and politically dying PLO in Tunisia and put in power in Gaza and the West Bank a political elite quite removed from the realities of modern Palestine. The "outside" PLO which came to power in Palestine—epitomized by Yasir Arafat—did not have practical political experience with Palestinian society in the West Bank and Gaza, having spent most of the previous decades in exile, most recently in Tunisia. Put bluntly, the new "regime" did not trust its own society because it had so few connections with it. In particular, it did not trust the political elite that had produced the Intifada—a political elite largely consisting of leaders from inside Gaza and the West Bank. In fact, given the unusual circumstances under which it came to power in Palestine, the first political task of the outside PLO was to undermine the new elite through co-optation, coercion, and marginalization. The authoritarianism and the anti-institutional personalization of politics currently practiced by the Palestinian regime—the antithesis of the politics of the new elite—are largely aimed at consolidating the power of the Palestinian authority.

THE INCOMPLETE REVOLUTION

The political base of the new Palestine Authority under Arafat consists of four groups: security forces, "state" bureaucrats, the notable social class, and a reconstructed Fatah cadre system (Fatah is the largest faction of the PLO). Tensions continue with the popular Hamas movement, and politics are increasingly personalized and authoritarian under Arafat. However, as long as Arafat's government is maintained by external finance and support—in large part because Israel and other nations believe there must be a formal Palestinian leadership with whom to negotiate—the PA is likely to persist in its oddly disconnected, authoritarian control of the Palestinian territories.

Today, conflict continues on many levels in Israel and Palestine. The breakdown of the Oslo peace process has led to renewed violence and the polarization of public opinion. The political legitimacy of the "outsiders" or Oslo elite has been badly damaged in the eyes of most Palestinians by their inability to deliver a credible peace deal. This has permitted an opening for the Intifada elite, including its Islamist component, to reassert its own authority at the grassroots. In short, the future of Palestine's political leadership is currently under contestation because of the collapse of the peace process. Likewise, Israel is rethinking its entire relationship with the Palestinians. The only constant is that both Israelis and Palestinians will continue to share the same small piece of land between the Jordan River and the Mediterranean Sea. In all these respects, the Intifada remains an incomplete revolution.

The Afghanistan Revolutionary Wars

ANWAR-UL-HAQ AHADY

For more than twenty years, Afghanistan has been home to one of history's most brutal ethnic and political conflicts. Yet much of this struggle remained in obscurity until a band of terrorists, trained and evidently headquartered in Afghanistan, hijacked four commercial airliners and used them to destroy the World Trade Towers in New York and part of the Pentagon in Washington, D.C. Afghanistan's revolutionary wars were thus "globalized" both by the terrorists' attacks on foreign powers and by the ongoing efforts of foreign powers to shape Afghanistan's regimes.

Ahady describes the events that have divided Afghanistan for many decades. The country's devastation has come from coups and counter-coups, elite revolution, foreign invasion, and guerrilla wars of resistance, all fought for causes ranging from tribal loyalties to communism to support of Islam.

AFGHAN HISTORY: FROM TRIBAL STATE TO THE BEGINNINGS OF MODERNIZATION

Throughout the eighteenth and nineteenth centuries, the leaders of Pashtun tribes dominated Afghanistan. Tribal *jirgas* ("assemblies") resolved individual and communal conflicts in accordance with the Pashtun code of ethics, and the state intervened very little in the social life of the tribes. Afghan leaders depended on the tribes for their army and allowed considerable autonomy to the tribal leaders in return. From the 1880s to the 1950s, Afghan leaders who tried to abolish the privileges of the tribal chiefs met with rebellions that re-established the primacy of the Pashtun tribes in Afghan politics.

A combination of domestic and international political changes altered this situation in the 1950s. Within Afghanistan, the government of Prime Minister Mohammad Daud became strongly committed to rapid socioeconomic modernization. Internationally, from the 1950s the Soviet Union adopted a policy of seeking allies by helping developing countries in the Third World. Consequently, the Afghan government concluded an agreement with the Soviets in 1955 that provided for a $100-million loan to finance Afghan development projects and provide modern military equipment. Since then, foreign aid has become a major source of government revenues. In the period 1954–1978 the Soviet Union, Eastern Europe, and China provided over $1.3 billion in foreign aid to Afghanistan. Similarly, in competition with the Soviets, between 1946 and 1977 the United States gave a total of $515 million in aid.[1]

With foreign military assistance, the Afghan government was able to build a modern army 100,000 strong; with foreign financial aid, the government modernized and expanded national education and built the infrastructure for a modern economy. Consequently, school enrollment rose from 113,000 students in 1954 to 381,000 students in 1965, and major cities were connected by all-weather highways. Other industrial and commercial projects were initiated by the government, and these substantially increased the share of industry in the GNP. Government revenues increased from 188 million afghanis in 1952 to 1,500 million afghanis in 1958.[2] Government-owned industries, mining and natural gas, and foreign

---

Reprinted by permission of the author.

aid combined to provide 45 percent of government revenues in 1968 and about 50 percent in 1975.

These changes transformed relations between the state and rural society. By the 1960s the power base of the state had shifted away from the Pashtun tribes. The state was no longer dependent on the tribes to defend itself against internal and external challenges. The state provided social and economic services to urban as well as rural areas, including schools, hospitals, roads, transportation, and agricultural extension programs. The state also became the largest employer in the country.

In contrast to the declining relevance of the rural population and tribes, the cities became particularly important in Afghan politics in the 1960s and the 1970s, largely because of the success of the government's modernization efforts. The expansion of education in the 1950s and the 1960s created a relatively large professional middle class, which was mainly dependent on the state for its livelihood. About 90 percent of the professional middle-class jobs were positions with state economic, military, educational, and administrative institutions. Also, a disproportionate number of the middle class was concentrated in the capital, Kabul. Thus, Kabul dominated Afghan politics, and the state became the focus of professional and middle-class political activities.

THE ONSET OF STATE CRISIS

Although society experienced significant change during the 1950s and early 1960s, no serious incidents of political instability emerged. What triggered the beginnings of a state crisis was conflict within the royal family, as a consequence of which Prime Minister Daud had to resign and King Zahir Shah became a ruling monarch in 1963. To strengthen the legitimacy of his regime, Zahir Shah embarked on a policy of limited democratization. However, the policy raised hopes that were not satisfied. Discontent over this democratization policy, combined with conflicts over the role of Pashtun vs. other ethnic groups, and over economic development and modernization, undermined support for Zahir Shah's regime. After a decade of constitutional rule (1963–1973), former Prime Minister Daud returned to power by leading a coup to depose the King in 1973. Yet Daud's coup, far from bringing stability, initiated a violent spiral of further coups and civil war.

LIBERALIZATION UNDER ZAHIR SHAH

Until the 1950s, political participation in Afghanistan was largely confined to the tribal leaders, rural notables, and the leaders of the religious establishment, the *ulema*. The economic modernization programs of the 1950s and 1960s, however, produced a sizable middle class, mostly concentrated in Kabul, which demanded greater participation in politics.

Reportedly, Prime Minister Daud correctly analyzed the situation in 1962 and advised the king to replace the old system with a parliamentary democracy, which would dramatically reduce the decision-making role of the royal family and allow genuine participation by the people in the political process. Although the king responded by forcing Daud to resign and taking power himself, he nonetheless partially followed Daud's advice, and tried to rule as a constitutional monarch.

The constitutional decade (1963–1973) that followed saw a significant degree of liberalization and expanded participation. Although ultimate authority rested with the king, the parliament—based on the vastly expanded middle classes of Kabul and other cities—became an important element of government. The logical conclusion of expanded participation and democratization would have required a transfer of power to the people and their representatives, but the king was not willing to go that far. Instead, both political parties and parliament remained tightly restricted. The regime's refusal to fully implement its own policy of expanded participation hurt its legitimacy and weakened its support among the professional and middle classes.

Ethnic and Language Conflicts

Although Afghanistan originated as a Pashtun state, the ethnic composition of Afghanistan is a contentious issue. Most scholarly sources assert that the Pashtuns constitute at least half of the population; in recent years, at least one source believes them to be about 40 percent of the population. However, no one disputes that Pashtuns are the largest ethnic group in Afghanistan. Despite the numeric and political dominance of Pashtuns in Afghanistan, Pushtu has rarely been the language for official transactions. During the 1960s the issue of the status of languages became quite polarized. Many educated Pashtuns demanded the popularization of Pushtu in official transactions.

The liberal constitution of 1964 declared both Pushtu and Persian as official languages and Pushtu as the national language. However, the status of Pushtu in the 1960s and the 1970s alienated both Pashtuns and non-Pashtuns from the government. The non-Pashtuns considered the regime as fundamentally pro-Pashtun and resented their perceived inferior position in the polity. The Pashtuns, on the other hand, found the growing popularization of Persian a threat to the Pushtu language and Pashtun identity. Instead of seeking to resolve this conflict, the government simply ignored it. The language issue constituted one of the most explosive issues of Afghan politics and contributed significantly to political instability in the 1970s.

Economic Development and Modernization

During the 1950s, Prime Minister Daud had adopted a conception of modernization that included Westernization, and this policy remained in effect during the 1960s and the 1970s under the rule of Zahir Shah. Initially quite successful, state-led economic development began to slow in the late 1960s and early 1970s, as foreign aid no longer translated so easily into increased economic growth. Zahir Shah was then left presiding over a program of economic modernization that seemed ineffective, and that in its Westernization aspects was unwelcome to many Afghans.

This policy stimulated a strong Islamist movement that opposed Westernization because the Islamists considered Westernization as de-Islamization. The promotion and defense of Islam had been an essential element of the traditional Afghan theory of legitimacy. Thus, the Islamists' protest against Westernization added to the weakening of the regime.

The Emergence of Organized Political Groups

During the constitutional decade, the king allowed the de facto formation of political groups, but did not agree to laws that would have given political parties a formal role in the political system. This led to conflicts among these political groups, but no ability to manage these conflicts through elections. Three main political groups emerged: the Communists, the Islamists, and the nationalists.

The People's Democratic Party of Afghanistan (PDPA), the main Communist party, was formed in 1965. In line with its Marxist heritage, the PDPA preached class struggle and considered itself the representative of the workers and the peasants. It advocated close cooperation with the Soviet Union in both economic and political matters. It desired a more rapid development of the economy and more equal distribution of income, and considered land redistribution as essential to this purpose. The party refused to take a stand on the issue of languages. While the PDPA took advantage of the liberal political climate during the constitutional decade, it did not subscribe to liberal democracy as a permanent feature of the society it envisioned for the Afghans.

The Islamist groups largely arose as a reaction to the decline of Islamic culture and the rise of communism, and the government was blamed for both phenomena. The Islamists did not offer any coherent prescription for economic development; indeed, economic development and the distribution of income and wealth were not major political issues for them. The Islamists, however, took a clear stand regarding nationalism and the legitimacy of the government. They rejected the Pashtun-based conception of Afghan nationalism and believed that only Islam could provide a basis for national unity. The Islamists wanted close relations with Muslim Pakistan instead of the Soviet Union, and they considered it the religious duty of every Muslim to be politically active and to engage in *jihad* (holy war) for the defense or expansion of Islam.

The Afghan Social Democratic Party (ASDP), formed in 1966, was the main nationalist political group, and it advocated a truly representative parliamentary democracy. The ASDP favored a conception of Afghan nationalism in which Pushtu and the Pashtuns loomed large, believing that Pushtu was essential to the Afghan national identity. At the same time, it supported the modernization of sociopolitical and economic institutions.

The open competition for influence among these groups, and their conflicting views on the major political issues, combined with the indecisiveness of King Zahir Shah to add to the crisis of the state in the early 1970s.

Coup and Counter-Coup: Daud and the PDPA

For over 200 years, the foundation of any regime in Afghanistan was approval by the Pashtun tribal chiefs and the Islamic *ulema*. However, after the modernization and urbanization of the 1950s and 1960s these groups became far less significant in politics. Yet no other basis for the legitimacy of Afghan governments was fully accepted by the Afghan elites and populace. The regime of Zahir Shah was seen as too inclined to pursue Westernizing modernization to satisfy the populace, but not democratic enough to satisfy the urban middle classes. Moreover, its Pashtun-based conception of Afghan nationalism was not shared by the minorities. Finally, while the regime benefited from the good economic performance of the

1950s and early 1960s, the economic stagnation of the late 1960s and early 1970s under-mined whatever legitimacy the regime may have enjoyed. As a result, support for Zahir Shah's regime declined, while the communists, Islamists, and nationalists avidly recruited supporters and competed to see which group would shape Afghanistan's future.

In July 1973, with the help of personal friends, nationalists, and leftist officers, the for-mer prime minister Mohammad Daud conducted a successful coup, sent King Zahir Shah into exile, and declared Afghanistan a republic. Daud was a far more determined and ener-getic ruler than Zahir Shah, and he sought to play the three main political groups against each other while maximizing his own power.

In the first two years of Daud's administration, the communists (PDPA) had a strong presence in the new regime. Perhaps at the insistence of the PDPA, Daud, upon assuming power, launched an anti-Islamist campaign whereby a few Islamists were executed, some were arrested, and many sought refuge in Pakistan.

Yet after stabilizing his own position, Daud decided to curtail the leftists in his adminis-tration, for both internal and international reasons. Internally, Daud was a Pashtun (Afghan) nationalist who believed in modernizing Afghanistan without damaging its moderate Islamic character. Since he had previously attacked the extreme Islamists, he feared a close associa-tion with the PDPA would further damage his Islamic and nationalist credentials.

Internationally, Daud wanted closer relations with Iran, the Arab countries, and the West. With the rise of OPEC and the quadrupling of oil prices in 1973–1974, Iran and the Arab countries became potentially more generous providers of foreign aid than the Soviets. In return, the conservative Arab countries and the Shah of Iran, encouraged by the United States, wanted Daud to reduce his dependence on the Soviets. The PDPA opposed Daud's new policy, which led to their elimination from the government by 1975.

The PDPA saw Daud's ban on political activities, and his efforts to reduce Afghanistan's dependence on the Soviets, as a threat to the PDPA's survival. The PDPA resolved to act first against Daud. In April 1978, the PDPA instructed their supporters in the army and the air force to overthrow the Daud regime. Against daunting odds, the PDPA supporters were able to defeat the Republican Palace Guard units, kill President Daud and his family mem-bers, and transfer power to the PDPA.

The overwhelming majority of the people, rural as well as tribal, had become almost ir-relevant to national politics, and during the first few months of the change, they considered the PDPA coup as an interelite conflict in Kabul without any significance for rural life. How-ever, the situation changed dramatically when the PDPA attempted to transform its military coup into a social revolution.

THE PDPA'S ELITE REVOLUTION

The April 1978 transfer of power was not just a military coup but an elite revolution aimed at the destruction of the old social structure and the creation of a new order. Relying on gov-ernment decrees, the PDPA sought to transform Afghan society. Decrees No. 6, 7, and 8 of the PDPA government, announced in the summer and fall of 1978, have been described as the crux of the revolution. Decree No. 6 dealt with rural debt. It stated that land-mortgaged loans were to be reduced by 20 percent per year, and it canceled all interest. Thus, peasants who had mortgaged their land in return for a loan contracted in 1974 or before could re-possess their land without any payment to creditors. Peasants who had mortgaged their land after 1974 could repay the loan without interest, paying over a period determined by the length of the loan.

The PDPA believed that Decree No. 6 would help bring about the destruction of "feu-dal" social relations in Afghanistan and free the peasants from the devastating impact of in-creasing debt, which was one of the major factors responsible for their poverty. The PDPA also believed the benefits the decree conferred on the peasants would strengthen the posi-tion of the PDPA among them. Yet the actual impact of Decree No. 6 on the Afghan peas-antry is quite controversial. Fred Halliday has maintained that the impact of Decree No. 6 was quite minimal because the decree did not cover peasant debt contracted with bazaar merchants and moneylenders, and such transactions, according to Halliday, constituted the lion's share of rural debt. Furthermore, the decree destroyed the old rural credit system without providing an alternative. Thus, it seems that Decree No. 6 actually contributed to the economic hardship of the peasants, and consequently, it did not generate political sup-port among the peasantry for the PDPA.

Decree No. 7 regulated marriage and wedding expenses. It restricted wedding ex-penses and reduced the bride price from an average of 40,000 afghanis to 300 afghanis ($10.00). It also stipulated that marriages should not be contracted without the consent of the couple, and specified minimum ages of sixteen for girls and eighteen for boys. This de-cree was supposed to complement Decree No. 6. The PDPA believed that rural debt was contracted largely to pay for peasants' wedding expenses, so the cancellation of rural debt and a ceiling on wedding expenses, the PDPA believed, should improve the economic con-ditions of the peasants. The second measure was also aimed at changing centuries-old social customs that, according to the PDPA, had institutionalized the subservience of women in Afghan families. Although previous Afghan governments had also attempted to regulate marriage, the PDPA distinguished itself from the previous regimes by vigorously attempting to enforce Decree No. 7. This decree was considered by most of the rural population as an un-necessary government intervention in family life, and when the government supplemented the marriage regulations with a campaign for forced literacy of women, whereby male PDPA members taught Marxism to illiterate rural Afghan women, many rural communities rebelled against the PDPA's rule. Thus, once again, the PDPA attempt at reform backfired.

Decree No. 8 launched the most important program of the PDPA revolution—land re-distribution. Since its foundation, the PDPA had supported a radical land reform program, which, the party believed, was essential for the destruction of the old social order and for the promotion of social justice. The PDPA thought that land redistribution would strengthen the PDPA's position among the peasants, and thus contribute to the stability and viability of the PDPA regime.

However, the PDPA seems to have been badly mistaken about the rural situation. Due to mountains and lack of water, good-quality agricultural land is scarce in Afghanistan, and few if any landlords had accumulated large properties. The combination of a number of fac-tors—including the scarcity of land and the high density of population in most Afghan prov-inces; the impact of Islamic law, which requires division of inheritance among all family members of the deceased; and the practice of Afghan monarchs of confiscating the land of prominent people in order to prevent a potential threat to the royal family—had resulted in a relatively equal distribution of land.

The PDPA announced its land reform program in December 1978 and completed its implementation between January and July 1979. The PDPA expected to redistribute 5.4 million acres of surplus land to over 600,000 landless or land-hungry peasant households, but they were able to distribute only the equivalent of 1.3 million acres of first-quality land among 296,000 peasant families. The discrepancy between the PDPA expectation of surplus land and the actual distribution of land to the needy peasants indicates the inaccuracy of the PDPA belief about the inequality of land distribution in Afghanistan. The land redistribution program left many peasants still landless and land hungry, and even the beneficiaries of the reform did not receive adequate land to support a family of five people. Political considerations had loomed large in the initiation of the land reform program, the PDPA leadership believing that land redistribution would strengthen the party's support among the peasants. However, the incompetent implementation of the program instead strengthened rural opposition to the PDPA.

At the symbolic level, the PDPA attempted to reduce the influence of Islam and national traditions and to emphasize communist symbols. Thus, Decree No. 3 replaced the traditional black, red, and green Afghan flag with a totally red one, and PDPA teachers repeatedly denigrated Islamic symbols in the classrooms. To complete the destruction of the old dominant class, the PDPA government engaged in extensive purges within the state bureaucracy and the armed forces. Consequently, out of sixty-two generals, sixty were either retired or imprisoned. Similarly, most top-level bureaucrats were fired, and others were warned to either join the party or to expect dismissal. These measures caused upheavals that neither the PDPA nor its Soviet allies were able to suppress in subsequent years.

REVOLUTION AGAINST THE PDPA AND THEORIES OF REVOLUTION

The PDPA coup and revolutionary programs formed what Ellen Trimberger has called an "elite revolution," in which a military or bureaucratic elite seizes power and attempts a revolutionary transformation of society.[3] However, the PDPA revolution exhibited strong differences from other, more successful elite revolutions, such as those in Turkey under Attaturk and Japan in the Meiji era. In contrast to those cases, the PDPA leadership showed a complete disregard of those tactics that Trimberger says are essential for a successful elite revolution. The PDPA leadership engaged in the destruction of the old order before consolidating its power, launched socioeconomic and political changes simultaneously instead of one step at a time, and relied heavily on coercion instead of a selective use of force against opponents.

The PDPA regime thus created all the key factors that produce major social revolutions—a crisis of state effectiveness and justice, elite alienation, and popular discontent. It also committed the cardinal error of giving the lower classes reasons to unite with the old dominant class against the revolutionary regime.

State Crisis

Unlike many other regimes that have collapsed or faced major rebellions, the PDPA state did not suffer any financial crisis. Increased revenues from natural gas and foreign aid from the Soviet Union prevented any serious deterioration in the financial health of the state. Government revenues from natural gas increased from $39 million in 1977 to about $103 million in 1979 and $272 million in 1982. Similarly, foreign aid increased from 2.4 billion afghanis in 1978 to 7.2 billion afghanis in 1981 and 10.4 billion afghanis in 1982.

However, this aid did not produce economic development. Rather, the efforts at radical transformation of debt and credit relations and landholding appear to have damaged the rural economy. The regime thus looked seriously ineffective in its stated goal of lifting the Afghanistan economy to a higher level. In addition, the interference with marriage practices and the attack on Islamic symbols and practices by the PDPA severely damaged the regime's claims to be a "just" government in the eyes of most of the population.

Elite Alienation

The Islamists were determined enemies of the communist PDPA even before the PDPA revolution, and when the PDPA government assumed power it executed many Islamists, prominent *ulema,* and members of well-known religious families (e.g., the Mujadaddis). Furthermore, it launched a campaign to de-Islamize Afghanistan, and naturally, these developments intensified the old PDPA-Islamist enmity. Although the nationalists had some common objectives with the communists (e.g., rapid economic development and a more equal distribution of income), the oppressive nature of the PDPA regime combined with its insistence on monopolizing power forced the nationalists to resort to armed struggle against the regime. The PDPA had already purged top-level bureaucrats, military officers, and even non-PDPA members of academic institutions. Rural notables, tribal leaders, and religious leaders (mullahs) were considered the most dangerous enemies of the revolution and thus were persecuted.

By these actions, the PDPA antagonized all segments of the elite—right, left, center, modern, traditional, urban, rural, religious, and ethnic. Despite the considerable differences in their preferred vision of the future Afghan polity, all these alienated elites were united in their opposition to the PDPA regime. Consequently, each group of the alienated elites mobilized some segment of the society against the PDPA.

Popular Discontent

Widespread popular discontent provided an excellent opportunity for the alienated elites to fight the regime, although different grievances had differing importance in various regions of the country. For example, the regime's insensitivity to Islam was particularly important in the rebellion in Kunar Province. In Paktia Province, the government's intervention in social life, particularly the implementation of Decree No. 7 regulating marriage and wedding expenses and the forced literacy of women, was considerably more important in motivating rebellion against the PDPA government. Forced literacy for women and the insensitivity of the PDPA cadres to centuries-old customs and Islam were also important in the March 1979 uprising in the city of Herat. The uprising in Hazarajat coincided with the implementation of the land reform program, and the old dominant class, which owned large tracts of land, initiated the rebellion there. In many regions, although the land reform distributed small parcels of land to some landless peasants, it did not provide them with equipment, water, or seed; and cancellation of the land-mortgage system undermined the old rural credit system that might have helped them utilize their land. In the cities, the decline in business confidence, which reduced economic activities; the high rate of inflation; shortages of consumer goods; and, as a consequence of the PDPA purges, job insecurity for government employees, all resulted in widespread popular discontent. The brutality of the PDPA officials contributed even more to popular discontent and outrage, as they frequently resorted to severe beatings of landowners, mullahs, and ordinary peasants.

Thus, the PDPA government quickly and completely lost legitimacy with virtually all segments of the population. The regime was considered anti-Islamic, non-Afghan, utterly unjust, and brutally repressive. This situation led to a terrible cycle of violence. The people rebelled against the unpopular government, which led to disproportionately violent government reprisals against the dissidents, which only increased their defiance. By the summer of 1979, the rebellion had spread to fourteen out of the twenty-eight provinces. The government relied heavily on the armed forces, but the support of the army began to disintegrate in 1979.

SOVIET INVASION AND RESISTANCE

To prevent the further deterioration of the political and military situation, and to gain control over the PDPA, the Soviets invaded Afghanistan in late December 1979. The invasion, in turn, spread the rebellion to the entire country and turned the war in Afghanistan into a major international conflict.

The governments of Pakistan, the United States, Egypt, Saudi Arabia, Iran, and China actively supported the Afghan resistance against Soviet occupation. The escalation of the conflict forced the Soviets to send into Afghanistan an army of over 120,000 soldiers, at a cost of billions of dollars. Similarly, the U.S. opposition to the Soviet move resulted in the allocation of billions of dollars in military and economic aid to the Pakistan government and the Afghan resistance (known as the Mujahideen). Over one million Afghans lost their lives in the war, and another five million sought refuge in Pakistan, Iran, and the West. Although the Soviets withdrew their forces from Afghanistan in 1989, the upheavals of the previous decades created such a revolutionary situation that conflicts continued long after the Soviet departure.

THE ANTI-SOVIET RESISTANCE GROUPS

While initially dozens of different groups opposed the PDPA and Soviet occupation, foreign support for particular groups shaped the resistance. Pakistan emerged as the main base for the Afghan resistance and unilaterally decided to recognize only six (later seven) resistance groups. This development made it extremely difficult for other Afghan resistance groups to attract any military or financial foreign support, as Pakistan was the main conduit for foreign aid to the rebellion.

The seven resistance groups based in Pakistan were divided into two main camps: the Islamists and the traditionalists. The Islamist groups included those led by Gulbudin Hekmatyar and Burhanudin Rabani. They drew their support from graduates of government-operated *medresas* (schools for religious studies), secular schools, mullahs, Sufi orders, ethnic minorities, and some detribalized Pashtuns. They also attracted many dedicated individuals from Saudi Arabia, Egypt, Pakistan, and other Muslim countries who desired to participate in the "holy war" to expel the Russian invaders—including a young Osama Bin-Laden.

The traditionalist groups drew their support from a network of more conservative *ulema,* Pashtun tribes, the professional middle class, and bureaucrats of the old regime. Basically, the traditionalists desired a status quo ante (a pre-1978 situation) with minor reforms. They supported the return of ex-King Zahir Shah to the leadership position, though not necessarily as a ruling monarch.

The Islamists shared the traditionalists' desire to defend Islam and Afghanistan against communism and Soviet occupation, but they gave the anti-PDPA rebellion an ideological character that emphasized the abolition of the old monarchy and the creation of a revolutionary Islamic republic. The Afghan Islamists were united in their rejection of Westernization and any other element of modernization that might contradict Islamic values.

Success of the Resistance

The scope of the resistance was truly extensive, drawing on all the major social networks of Afghanistan (the *ulema,* Sufi orders, tribes, secular and religious schools) to exploit popular discontent and mobilize the population for the overthrow of the PDPA regime. Despite fundamental differences among organizations regarding the structure of a future Afghan polity, they united in their hatred of the PDPA regime and its Soviet backers. On this point, the Afghan guerrilla fighters had the support of the overwhelming majority of the people. The presence of about 5 million Afghan refugees in Pakistan and Iran immensely strengthened the resistance politically and provided it with an inexhaustible source of recruitment for fighters. The resistance also enjoyed certain strategic advantages. The low level of urbanization of the country and the thousands of villages scattered in some of the most inaccessible locations have helped the resistance to withstand the modern army and air force at the disposal of the PDPA and the Soviets. Perhaps equally important was the availability of sanctuaries in Pakistan.

The decision of international powers to oppose the Soviet invasion and to provide military, financial, and political support for the Afghan resistance nicely complemented the other strategic advantages of the resistance. Egypt and China provided very necessary weapons to the resistance in the early years of the war, 1979–1981, and the United States and Saudi Arabia subsequently became the major donors of weapons and financial aid. Furthermore, worldwide support for the resistance, especially in the United Nations, the European Community, the Islamic Conference, and the Non-Aligned Conference, increased the isolation of the PDPA regime and the international legitimacy of the Mujahideen.

Although the Islamists did not necessarily have the support of the majority of the people, they dominated the resistance. They were more organized, ideologically committed, militarily superior, and politically more often on the offensive than their traditionalist counterparts. Their dominance was also a result of their friendly relations with the government of Pakistan, which developed in the 1970s. President Mohammad Zia-ul-Haq of Pakistan, and much of the Pakistani military, consistently favored Afghan Islamists over other Afghan political groups.

With a nearly unlimited flow of small and medium arms from the United States and Saudi Arabia through Pakistan, and a nearly limitless supply of Afghan fighters from sanctuaries in Pakistan and Iran, the resistance was able to mount continuous raids on Soviet forces. Mines and shoulder-fired missiles inflicted heavy casualties on Soviet armor and patrols, while the Afghan guerrilla fighters took refuge in the country's many mountains and caves. After ten years of trying to pacify the countryside without success, the Soviet army withdrew in 1989, leaving the PDPA to its own devices.

The former PDPA regime, under President Mohammad Najibullah, survived for three years after the withdrawal of Soviet forces from Afghanistan. A combination of factors was responsible for their survival. First, the Soviet Union continued to subsidize Najibullah's regime. Second, using Soviet-supplied weapons and financial resources, Najibullah built up a number of militia units in various parts of the country that helped defend the regime against the Mujahideen. Indeed, some Mujahideen commanders defected to Najibullah's regime. Third, Najibullah abandoned the ideology of the PDPA, changed the name of his organization to the Watan Party, and advocated greater freedom for the people. And, fourth, the resistance organizations were very disunited in dealing with Najibullah. Some moderate resistance organizations advocated a negotiated settlement of the conflict while radicals insisted on a military resolution of the conflict. Amidst these divisions, the resistance lost its popularity, which helped the survival of Najibullah's regime.

The collapse of communism in the Soviet Union in 1990–1991 broke the stalemate in Afghanistan, as the disintegration of the Soviet Union undermined the financial basis of Najibullah's regime. Realizing that Najibullah no longer had weapons and financial resources to distribute, militia leaders such as General Abdul Rashid Dostam rebelled against Najibullah and sought autonomy in the Northern Alliance. The militia rebellions led to the collapse of Najibullah's regime in April 1992.

ANARCHY, CIVIL WAR, AND THE TALIBAN: 1992–2001

The collapse of Najibullah's regime at the hands of the Northern Alliance marked the beginning of several years of anarchy and disintegration in Afghanistan. Various resistance commanders and militia leaders gained control over different parts of Afghanistan. In Kabul, two radical Islamic groups engaged in heavy fighting for the control of the city. Because of the civil war, the Mujahideen government did not receive significant international support. In addition, Saudi Arabia withdrew its support for the radical resistance following the latter's declaration of support for Iraq in the 1990–1991 Gulf War. Furthermore, the rise of warlords throughout the country deprived the citizens of any kind of security, which delegitimized all resistance organizations and prepared the way for the rise of the Taliban.

The Taliban emerged in the southeastern city of Kandahar in late 1994, drawn initially from students in the religious seminaries, and Islamist groups among the former Mujahideen.

However, as the Taliban called for defiance of the warlords and construction of a new national regime, they gained support from fighters throughout the country. The primary reason for the emergence of the Taliban was the extreme insecurity that prevailed throughout the country, leading people to welcome any group that would restore security. The absence of security also frustrated the efforts of some Western oil companies to construct pipelines from Turkmenistan through Afghanistan and Pakistan. Thus, the West also saw some business opportunities arising with the rise of the Taliban. Among Pakistan's ethnic groups, the Taliban were particularly supported by the Pashtuns. Even before the collapse of Dr. Najibullah's regime, the war in Afghanistan had developed a strong ethnic dimension. Generally, the Pashtuns perceived the Mujahideen government in Kabul between 1992–1996 as anti-Pashtun. To end the dominance of non-Pashtuns in Kabul, the Taliban were enthusiastically supported by the Pashtuns. Furthermore, the strict interpretation of Islam that the Taliban favored was to the liking of many conservative Muslims in the Gulf. Thus, for different reasons, the Taliban acquired the support of the largest ethnic group in Afghanistan, the Pashtuns; Pakistan, the most influential regional power in Afghan affairs; Saudi Arabia, the wealthiest Persian Gulf country; and the United States, the only superpower.[4]

Of course, this combination of supporters made the Taliban very powerful. Thus, in less than one year, the Taliban gained control over all of southwest Afghanistan and captured two-thirds of the country, including Kabul, in less than two years. By 1998 the Taliban gained control over 90 percent of the country.

Initially, the Taliban were quite popular. Their major achievements were the restoration of security and the reintegration of the country. However, the Taliban lost popularity very quickly. Even though in economic matters the Taliban allowed the free market to rule, in socio-political matters the Taliban were Islamic totalitarians, controlling most aspects of socio-political life. Harsh punishments for religious infractions alienated the people, including the Pashtuns. The Taliban also lost popularity because they did not provide any social services to the people.

However, the Taliban's major problem was their isolation at the international level. The Taliban government was never recognized by international organizations; only three countries—Pakistan, Saudi Arabia, and the United Arab Emirates—recognized the government of the Taliban. The Taliban's disregard for international norms and women's rights were the main reasons for the Taliban's international isolation.

The Taliban also developed close ties with terrorist groups such as al-Qaeda, led by Osama Bin-Laden, who has resided in Afghanistan since 1996. Bin-Laden's group was implicated in the bombing of U.S. embassies in Kenya and Tanzania in 1998. The U.S. government asked the Taliban administration for the extradition of Bin-Laden, but the Taliban repeatedly rejected U.S. demands. Meanwhile, Bin-Laden continued his war through terror with the United States, culminating in the September 11, 2001, terrorist attacks on New York and Washington, D.C. After the attack, the Taliban once again refused to hand over Bin-Laden to the U.S. authorities. Consequently on October 7, 2001, the United States and the United Kingdom launched their air strikes against Taliban forces in Afghanistan.

In cooperation with remaining elements of the Northern Alliance, and supported by a broad international coalition against terrorism and states who harbored terrorists, resistance to the Taliban grew. By November, even Pashtun tribal forces in the South were turning against the Taliban, resulting in the complete collapse of the Taliban government on December 7, 2001.

REFERENCES

1. Lenczowski 1980, p. 245; Central Intelligence Agency 1997, pp. 112, 118.
2. *Statesman's Year-Book* 1953, p. 762; 1958, p. 796; 1960, p. 794.
3. Trimberger (1978).
4. Maley (1998), pp. 1–32.

A BRIEF GUIDE TO FURTHER READING

The following books further pursue the theory of revolutions and give more details on the particular revolutions discussed in this volume.

THE THEORY OF REVOLUTIONS

The Encyclopedia of Political Revolutions (Goldstone 1998) provides a large number of essays on theoretical issues relating to revolutions, on such topics as constitutions, democracy, socialism, communism, gender, and inequality. It also has an accessible introduction to theories of revolution.

Other excellent summaries of recent work on theories of revolution are *Theorizing Revolutions* (Foran 1997), *Debating Revolutions* (Keddie 1995), and *Revolution: International Dimensions* (Katz 2001). A highly comprehensive, but more scholarly, survey of recent trends in theories of revolution is offered by Goldstone (2001).

Of the major comparative studies of revolution that have advanced theoretical insights, most build on Moore's (1966) *Social Origins of Dictatorship and Democracy*—which presented a still-provocative analysis of how revolutions contributed to the political development of the United States, Europe, and Asia—and Tilly's (1978) *From Mobilization to Revolution,* which offered a path-breaking analysis of revolutionary mobilization. Skocpol's (1979) classic *States and Social Revolutions* focused scholars' attention on the role of the state in shaping both revolutions and their outcome through her comparative analysis of the French, Russian, and Chinese revolutions. Goldstone's (1991) *Revolution and Rebellion in the Early Modern World,* dealing with revolutions and rebellions in Europe, the Middle East, and Asia from 1500 to 1850, extended Skocpol's work by showing how the decisions of states and revolutionary actors were influenced by long-term social, economic, and demographic trends.

Whereas the above works concentrate on revolutions prior to World War II, the large number of revolutions in the Third World in the last fifty years has prompted a new round of outstanding comparative studies. Wickham-Crowley's *Guerrillas and Revolution in Latin America* (1992) provides a comprehensive guide to the causes and results of guerrilla movements in Latin America. More recently, Selbin's (1993) *Modern Latin American Revolutions,* Eisenstadt's (1999) *Fundamentalism, Sectarianism, and Revolution,* and Parsa's (2000) *States, Ideologies, and Social Revolutions: A Comparative Analysis of Iran, Nicaragua, and the Philippines* have emphasized the role of ideologies in revolutionary mobilization and its consequences. Skocpol's (1994) *Social Revolutions in the Modern World* surveys the many debates and issues surrounding comparative studies of revolution. Additional comparative works that cover a wide range of revolutionary conflicts are *Modern Revolutions (2nd edition)* (Dunn 1989), *Revolutions of the Late Twentieth Century* (Goldstone, Gurr, and Moshiri 1991), *European Revolutions 1492–1992* (Tilly 1993), and *No Other Way Out: States and Revolutionary Movements 1945– 1991* (Goodwin 2001).

Another area of rapid growth in theoretical studies of revolution is attention to issues of gender, both with regard to revolutionary participation and revolutionary ideology. A few of the major works in this sphere are *The Family Romance of the French Revolution* (Hunt 1992), *Women and Revolution in Africa, Asia, and the New World* (Tétreault 1994), *Women and Revolution: Global Expressions* (Diamond 1998), and *Women and Social Protest,* (West and Blumberg 1990).

SPECIFIC REVOLUTIONS

The literature on specific revolutions is enormous. The following suggestions cover only the major events discussed in this text. For suggested readings on the many dozens of other revolutions in world history, the *Encyclopedia of Political Revolutions* (Goldstone 1998) is again the best place to start, with coverage of over one hundred revolutions and revolutionary conflicts and bibliographies of recommended reading for each one.

For the English Revolution of the seventeenth century, Kishlansky (1996) offers an excellent survey of the causes and outcomes. Russell (1991) provides a more elaborate study with more detailed treatment of the Revolution's main events.

Classic works on the American Revolution include Wood (1969) and Greene (1986). More detail on matters of ideology is provided by Bailyn (1967) and Nash (1979).

The best short account of the coming of the French Revolution is still Lefebvre (1947). Doyle (1999) offers an excellent, up-to-date account of the Revolution's origins that incorporates recent research and controversies, and Schama (1989) provides a lively and detailed chronicle of events. Furet (1992) is a highly influential account of the place of the Revolution in French history. To continue the story of revolutionary France into the nineteenth century, Sperber (1994) covers the European revolutions of 1848, both in France and across Europe.

For the Russian Revolution, Trotsky's (1959) account is a literary masterpiece and a joy to read; Figes (1996) offers a more objective and up-to-date but still accessible history.

China's long history and recent revolution are both covered in lively fashion by Fairbank (1983) and Spence (1990). Heng and Shapiro (1983) offer a gripping firsthand account of life in revolutionary China, while the cultural revolution in Shanghai is examined by Perry and Li (1997). A valuable account of China's transformation in the countryside since the revolution is Friedman and colleagues (1991). The most comprehensive treatment of the background to the Tiananmen Revolt in 1989 is given by Zhao (2001).

Regarding Latin America, Womack (1969) has written a moving narrative of the Mexican Revolution; Knight (1986) provides a more analytical study. Dunkerly (1984) offers a fine account of the Bolivian Revolution, and Eckstein (1994) provides a thoughtful analysis of the course of the Cuban Revolution. The modern Haitian Revolution against the Duvalier dictatorship is covered in an excellent work by Dupuy (1997). Booth (1982) and Walker (1985) provide a fine introduction to the Nicaraguan Revolution, and Diskin (1984) offers an overview of Central America in general.

Among the many fine books on the Iranian Revolution, Abrahamian (1982) and Arjomand (1988) stand out; Keddie (1981) is also excellent and somewhat easier reading. Bill (1988) provides more detail on the U.S. role in these events.

Eastern Europe's anti-communist revolutions are superbly surveyed by Goldfarb (1992), Ash (1990), Stokes (1993), and Bunce (1999). The collapse of the U.S.S.R. is richly described in Dunlop (1993). Popular participation in the overthrow of Soviet communism is detailed in Urban and colleagues (1997).

In Southeast Asia, the Philippines' "people-power" revolution is well covered by Thompson (1995). The Vietnamese Revolution is thoughtfully examined by Kolko (1994), and the Cambodian Revolution by Kiernan (1996).

In Africa, the Algerian Revolution of 1962 is the subject of Horne (1977), while Kitchen (1987) examines the anti-colonial revolutions in both Angola and Mozambique. Keller (1988) gives an account of the Ethiopian Revolution. The struggle against apartheid in South Africa was many sided: the labor mobilization is examined by Seidman (1994); more recent and international developments are covered by Koelble (1998).

In the Middle East, the Palestine Intifada is given detailed coverage by Robinson (1997) and Hunter (1991). Ahmad (1993) examines the Kemalist Revolution in Turkey. For the Arab Nationalist Revolutions in Egypt, Iraq, and Syria, Katz (1997) provides numerous insights.

BIBLIOGRAPHY

Abrahamian, Ervand. 1982. *Iran Between Two Revolutions.* Princeton, NJ: Princeton University Press.

Adams, Richard N. 1966. "Power and Power Domains." *America Latina* 9:3–21.

Aganbegyan, Abel. 1989. *Inside Perestroika: The Future of the Soviet Economy.* Translated by Helen Szamuely. New York: Perennial/Harper & Row.

Ahmad, Feroz. 1993. *The Making of Modern Turkey.* London: Routledge.

Anderson, Perry. 1974. *Lineages of the Absolutist State.* London: NLB.

Appleby, Andrew B. 1975. "Agrarian Capitalism or Seigneurial Reaction? The Northwest of England 1500–1700." *American Historical Review* 80:574–94.

Applewhite, Harriet, and Darline G. Levy, eds. 1990. *Women and Politics in the Age of the Democratic Revolution.* Ann Arbor: University of Michigan Press.

Arendt, Hannah. 1963. *On Revolution.* New York: Viking.

Arjomand, Said Amir. 1988. *The Turban or the Crown: The Islamic Revolution in Iran.* London: Oxford University Press.

Ash, Timothy Garton. 1990. *We the People: The Revolutions of '89 Witnessed in Warsaw, Budapest, Berlin, and Prague.* Hammondsworth, UK: Penguin.

Aslund, Anders. 1991. *Gorbachev's Struggle for Economic Reform.* Updated and Expanded Edition. Ithaca, NY: Cornell University Press.

Bailyn, Bernard. 1967. *The Ideological Origins of the American Revolution.* Cambridge, MA: Harvard University Press.

Beissinger, Mark R. 1998. "Nationalist Violence and the State: Political Authority and Contentious Repertoires in the Former USSR." *Comparative Politics* 30:401–22.

Bill, James. 1978–1979. "Iran and the Crisis of 1978." *Foreign Affairs* 57:323–42.

———. 1988. *The Eagle and the Lion: American and Iran.* New Haven, CT: Yale University Press.

Blanning, T. W. 1986. *The Origins of the French Revolutionary Wars.* London: Longmans.

Booth, John. 1985. *The End and the Beginning: The Nicaraguan Revolution,* 2d ed. Boulder, CO: Westview.

Brinton, Crane. 1938. *The Anatomy of Revolution.* New York: Vintage.

Brown, J. F. 1991. *Surge to Freedom: The End of Communist Rule in Eastern Europe.* Durham, NC: Duke University Press.

Brysk, Alison. 1995. "'Hearts and Minds': Bringing Symbolic Politics Back In." *Polity* 27:560–63.

Bunce, Valerie. 1999. *Subversive Institutions: The Design and Destruction of Socialism and the State.* Cambridge: Cambridge University Press.

Burke, Peter. 1978. *Popular Culture in Early Modern Europe.* New York: Harper & Row.

Calhoun, Craig. 1983. "The Radicalism of Tradition." *American Journal of Sociology* 88:886–914.

———. 1998. *Nationalism.* Minneapolis: University of Minnesota Press.

Campeanu, Pavel. 1991. "National Fervor in Eastern Europe: The Case of Romania." *Social Research* 58:805–28.

Central Intelligence Agency. 1997. *CIA Factbook—Afghanistan.* Washington, DC: U.S. Government Printing Office.

Chamberlin, William Henry. 1965. *The Russian Revolution 1917–1921.* 2 vols. New York: Grosset and Dunlap.

Chinchilla, Norma. 1990. "Revolutionary Popular Feminism in Nicaragua: Articulating Class, Gender, and National Sovereignty." *Gender & Society* 4:370–97.

Chorley, Katharine. 1943. *Armies and the Art of Revolution.* London: Faber and Faber.

Christie, Pam. 1985. *The Right to Learn: The Struggle for Education in South Africa.* Johannesburg: SACHED/Ravan.

Clapham, J. H. 1969. *The Causes of the War of 1792.* London: Octagon Books.

Colburn, Forrest. 1994. *The Vogue of Revolution in Poor Countries.* Princeton, NJ: Princeton University Press.

Conroy, Michael E. 1990. "The Political Economy of the 1990 Nicaraguan Elections." *International Journal of Political Economy* 20 : 5—33.

Cornwall, Julian. 1977. *Revolt of the Peasantry 1549.* London: Routledge and Kegan Paul.

Davies, J. C. 1962. "Toward a Theory of Revolution." *American Sociological Review* 27 : 5—19.

Davies, Miranda, ed. 1983. *Third World/Second Sex.* London: Zed.

Davis, Christopher, and Murray Feshbach. 1980. *Rising Infant Mortality in the USSR in the 1970s.* Washington, DC: U.S. Department of Commerce.

Diamond, M. D. 1998. *Women and Revolution: Global Expressions.* Dordrecht, Netherlands: Kluwer.

Diskin, Martin, ed. 1984. *Trouble in Our Backyard: Central America and the United States in the Eighties.* New York: Pantheon.

Dix, Robert. 1983. "The Varieties of Revolution." *Comparative Politics* 15 : 281—93.

Dominguez, Jorge. 1978. *Cuba: Order and Revolution.* Cambridge, MA: Harvard University Press.

Doyle, W. 1999. *Origins of the French Revolution,* 3rd ed. Oxford: Oxford University Press.

Dunkerley, James. 1984. *Republic in the Veins: Political Struggle in Bolivia 1952—82.* London: Verso.

Dunlop, John B. 1993. *The Rise of Russia and the Fall of the Soviet Empire.* Princeton, NJ: Princeton University Press.

Dunn, John. 1989. *Modern Revolutions: An Introduction to the Analysis of a Political Phenomenon,* 2d ed. Cambridge: Cambridge University Press.

Dupuy, Alex. 1997. *Haiti in the New World Order.* Boulder, CO: Westview.

Eckstein, S. 1982. "The Impact of Revolution on Social Welfare in Latin America." *Theory and Society* 11 : 43—94.

———. 1994. *Back from the Future: Cuba Under Castro.* Princeton, NJ: Princeton University Press.

Edwards, L. P. 1927. *The Natural History of Revolution.* Chicago: University of Chicago Press.

Eisenstadt, S. N. 1978. *Revolution and the Transformation of Societies: A Comparative Study of Civilizations.* New York: Free Press.

———. 1999. *Fundamentalism, Sectarianism, and Revolution: the Jacobin Dimension of Modernity.* New York: Cambridge University Press.

Ekiert, Grzegorz. 1990. "Transitions from State-Socialism in East Central Europe." *States and Social Structures Newsletter* (Social Science Research Council) 12 : 1—7.

Elon, Amos. 1992. "In a Former Country." *New York Review of Books* 39 : 34—39.

Elton, G. R. 1974. *Studies in Tudor and Stuart Politics and Government: Papers and Reviews 1946—1972.* 2 vols. Cambridge: Cambridge University Press.

Emirbayer, Mustafa E., and Jeff Goodwin. 1994. "Network Analysis, Culture and the Problem of Agency." *American Journal of Sociology* 9 : 1411—54.

———. 1996. "Symbols, Positions, Objects: Toward a New Theory of Revolutions and Collective Action." *History and Theory* 35 : 358—74.

Everitt, Alan. 1967. "Farm Laborers." Pp. 346—465 in *The Agricultural History of England and Wales, Vol. IV: 1500—1640,* edited by H. P. R. Finberg. Cambridge: Cambridge University Press.

———. 1969. *Change in the Provinces: The Seventeenth Century.* Leicester: Leicester University Press.

Fainsod, Merle. 1953. *How Russia Is Ruled.* Cambridge, MA: Harvard University Press.

Fairbank, John King. 1983. *The United States and China,* 5th ed. Cambridge, MA: Harvard University Press.

Farhi, Farideh. 1990. *States and Urban-Based Revolutions: Iran and Nicaragua.* Urbana and Chicago: University of Illinois Press.

Fiddick, Thomas C. 1990. *Russia's Retreat from Poland, 1920.* New York: St. Martin's.

Field, Mark G. 1991. "Soviet Health Problems and the Convergence Hypothesis." Pp. 78—94 in *Soviet*

Social Problems, edited by Anthony Jones, Walter Connor, and David E. Powell. Boulder, CO: Westview.

Figes, Orlando. 1996. *A People's Tragedy: A History of the Russian Revolution.* New York: Viking.

Foran, John. 1993. "Theories of Revolution Revisited: Toward a Fourth Generation?" *Sociological Theory* 11 : 1–20.

————. 1995. "Revolutionizing Theory/Theorizing Revolutions." Pp. 112–135 in *Debating Revolutions,* edited by Nikki Keddie. New York: New York University Press.

————. 1997a. "Discourses and Social Forces: The Role of Culture and Cultural Studies in Understanding Revolutions." Pp. 203–226 in *Theorizing Revolutions,* edited by John Foran. London: Routledge.

————, ed. 1997b. *Theorizing Revolutions.* London: Routledge.

Friedman, Edward, Paul G. Pickowicz, and Mark Selden with Kay Ann Johnson. 1991. *Chinese Village, Socialist State.* New Haven, CT: Yale University Press.

Furet, François. 1992. *Revolutionary France, 1770–1870.* Oxford: Blackwell.

Garcelon, Marc. 1995. *Democrats and Apparatchniks: The Democratic Russia Movement and the Specialist Rebellion in Moscow 1989–1991.* Ph.D. Dissertation, University of California, Berkeley.

Gillis, John R. 1970 "Political Decay and the European Revolutions, 1789–1848." *World Politics* 22 : 344–70.

Gold, Thomas. 1990. "The Resurgence of Civil Society in China." *Journal of Democracy* 1 : 18–31.

Goldfarb, Jeffrey. 1992. *After the Fall: The Pursuit of Democracy in Central Europe.* New York: Basic.

Goldstone, Jack A. 1991. *Revolution and Rebellion in the Early Modern World.* Berkeley: University of California Press.

————. 1995. "Predicting Revolutions: Why We Could (and Should) Have Foreseen the Revolutions of 1989–1991 in the U.S.S.R. and Eastern Europe." Pp. 39–64 in *Debating Revolutions,* edited by Nikkie Keddie. New York: New York University Press.

————. 2001. "Toward a Fourth Generation of Revolutionary Theory." *Annual Review of Political Science* 4 : 139–187.

————, ed. 1998. *The Encyclopedia of Political Revolutions.* Washington, DC: Congressional Quarterly Press.

Goldstone, Jack A., Ted Robert Gurr, and Farrokh Moshiri, eds. 1991. *Revolutions of the Late Twentieth Century.* Boulder, CO: Westview.

Goldstone, Jack A., and Charles Tilly. 2001. "Threat (and Opportunity): Popular Action and State Response in the Dynamics of Contentious Action." Pp. 179–194 in *Silence and Voice in Contentious Politics,* by Ron Aminzade, Jack A. Goldstone, Doug McAdam, Elizabeth J. Perry, William Sewell Jr., Sid Tarrow, and Charles Tilly. Cambridge: Cambridge University Press.

Goodwin, Jeff. 2001. *No Other Way Out: States and Revolutionary Movements, 1945–1991.* Cambridge: Cambridge University Press.

Gordimer, Nadine. 1984. "Something Out There." *Salmagundi* 62 : 118–192.

Gordon, L., and A. Nazimova. 1986. "The Socio-Occupational Structure of Contemporary Soviet Society: Typology and Statistics," in *Social Structure of the U.S.S.R.,* edited by M. Yanowitch. Armonk, NY: M. E. Sharpe.

Greene, Jack P. 1986. *Peripheries and Centers: Constitutional Development in the Extended Politics of the British Empire and the United States 1607–1788.* Athens: University of Georgia Press.

Griffith, Samuel B., ed. 1966. *Peking and People's War.* New York: Praeger.

Gugler, Josef. 1982. "The Urban Character of Contemporary Revolutions." *Studies in Comparative International Development* 17 : 60–73.

Gurr, T. R. 1970. *Why Men Rebel.* Princeton, NJ: Princeton University Press.

Habibi, Shahla. 1995. Speech of Shahla Habibi, Presidential Advisor on Women's Affairs, presented at the Fourth World Conference on Women, Beijing (September 11, 1995).

Hall, John A. 1993. "Nationalisms: Classified and Explained." *Daedalus* 122 : 1–26.

Haynes, Viktor, and Marko Bojcun. 1988. *The Chernobyl Disaster.* London: Hogarth.

Heng, Liang, and Judith Shapiro. 1983. *Son of the Revolution.* New York: Vintage.

Hill, Christopher. 1980. "A Bourgeois Revolution." Pp. 109–39 in *Three British Revolutions: 1641, 1688, 1776,* edited by J. G. A. Pocock. Princeton, NJ: Princeton University Press.

Hirschman, Albert O. 1993. "Exit, Voice, and the Fate of the German Democratic Republic: An Essay in Conceptual History." *World Politics* 45 : 173–202.

Holderness, B. A. 1976. *Pre-Industrial England: Economy and Society 1500–1730.* London: J. M. Dent.

Horne, Alistair. 1977. *A Savage War of Peace: Algeria 1954–1962.* London: Macmillan.

Howell, Roger. 1979. "The Structure of Urban Politics in the English Civil War." *Albion* 11 : 111–27.

Hunt, Lynn A. 1992. *The Family Romance of the French Revolution.* Berkeley: University of California Press.

Hunter, Robert F. 1991. *The Palestinian Uprising.* Berkeley: University of California Press.

Huntington, Samuel P. 1968. *Political Order in Changing Societies.* New Haven, CT: Yale University Press.

Jelin, Elizabeth. 1994. "The Politics of Memory: The Human Rights Movement and the Construction of Democracy in Argentina." *Latin American Perspectives* 21 : 38–58.

Johnson, C. 1966. *Revolutionary Change.* Boston: Little, Brown.

Kandiyoti, Deniz. 1989. "Women and the Turkish State: Political Actors or Symbolic Pawns?" Pp. 126–49 in *Women-Nation-State,* edited by Nira Yuval-Davis and Floya Anthias. London: Macmillan.

Katz, Mark N. 1997. *Revolutions and Revolutionary Waves.* New York: St. Martin's.

————, ed. 2001. *Revolution: International Dimensions.* Washington, DC: Congressional Quarterly Press.

Kazemi, Farhad. 1980. *Poverty and Revolution in Iran: The Migrant Poor, Urban Marginality, and Politics.* New York: New York University Press.

Keddie, Nikki. 1981. *Roots of Revolution: An Interpretive History of Modern Iran.* New Haven, CT: Yale University Press.

————, ed. 1995. *Debating Revolutions.* New York: New York University Press.

Keller, Edmond J. 1988. *Revolutionary Ethiopia: From Empire to People's Republic.* Bloomington: Indiana University Press.

Kelley, J., and H. S. Klein. 1977. "Revolution and the Rebirth of Inequality: A Theory of Stratification in Post-Revolutionary Society." *American Journal of Sociology* 83 : 78–99.

Kelly, Linda. 1987. *Women of the French Revolution.* London: Hamish Hamilton.

Kiernan, Ben. 1996. *The Pol Pot Regime: Race, Power, and Genocide in Cambodia Under the Khmer Rouge, 1975–79.* New Haven, CT: Yale University Press.

Kishlansky, Mark. 1996. *A Monarchy Transformed: Britain 1603–1714.* London: Allen Lane.

Kitchen, Helen, ed. 1987. *Angola, Mozambique, and the West.* Westport, CT: Praeger.

Knight, Alan. 1986. *The Mexican Revolution.* 2 vols. Cambridge: Cambridge University Press.

Koelble, Thomas A. 1998. *The Global Economy and Democracy in South Africa.* New Brunswick, NJ: Rutgers University Press.

Kolko, Gabriel. 1994. *Anatomy of a War: Vietnam, the United States, and the Modern Historical Experience.* New York: New Press.

Kuper, Leo, 1971 [1957]. *Passive Resistance in South Africa.* New Haven, CT: Yale University Press.

Kuran, Timur. 1991. "Now Out of Never: The Element of Surprise in the East European Revolution of 1989." *World Politics* 44 : 7–48.

Labao, Linda. 1990. "Women in Revolutionary Movements: Changing Patterns of Latin American Guerrilla Struggles." Pp. 180–204 in *Women and Social Protest,* edited by Guida West and Rhoda Lois Blumberg. New York: Oxford University Press.

Lefebvre, Georges. 1947. *The Coming of the French Revolution.* Translated by R. R. Palmer. Princeton, NJ: Princeton University Press.

Lenczowski, George. 1980. *The Middle East in World Affairs,* 4th edition. Ithaca, NY: Cornell University Press.

Lenin, V. I. 1970. *Selected Works.* Vol. 1. Moscow: Progress Publishers.

Liu, Michael Tien-Lung. 1988. "States and Urban Revolutions: Explaining Revolutionary Outcomes in Iran and Poland." *Theory and Society* 17: 179–210.

Machiavelli, Niccolò. [1513] 1931. *The Prince.* Translated by W. K. Marriot. New York: E.P. Dutton.

Maley, William, ed. 1998. *Fundamentalism Reborn? Afghanastan and the Taliban.* New York: New York University Press.

Mann, Michael. 1986. *The Sources of Social Power.* Vol. I. Cambridge: Cambridge University Press.

Mao Zedong (Mao Tse-tung). 1961. "Cast Away Illusions, Prepare for Struggle." *Selected Works of Mao Tse-tung.* Vol. 4. Peking: Foreign Languages Press.

Marx, Karl, Frederick Engels, V. I. Lenin, Clara Zetkin, and Joseph Stalin. 1977. *The Woman Question: Selections from the Writings of Karl Marx, Frederick Engels, V. I. Lenin, Clara Zetkin, Joseph Stalin.* New York: International Publishers.

Mies, Maria. 1986. *Patriarchy and Accumulation on a World Scale.* London: Zed.

Migdal, J. S. 1974. *Peasants, Politics, and Revolution: Pressures Toward Political and Social Change in the Third World.* Princeton, NJ: Princeton University Press.

Milanovic, Branko. 1994. "Why Have Communist Federations Collapsed?" *Challenge* 37: 61–64.

Moghadam, Valentine M. 1993. *Modernizing Women: Gender and Social Change in the Middle East.* Boulder, CO: Lynne Rienner.

Molyneux, Maxine. 1986. "Mobilization Without Emancipation? Women's Interests, State, Revolution." Pp. 280–302 in *Transition and Development: Problems of Third World Socialism,* edited by Richard Fagan, Carmen Diana Deere, and José Luis Corragio. New York: Monthly Review.

Moore, Barrington, Jr. 1966. *Social Origins of Dictatorship and Democracy.* Boston: Beacon.

Nash, Gary. 1979. *The Urban Crucible: Social Change, Political Consciousness, and the Origins of the American Revolution.* Cambridge, MA: Harvard University Press.

Paige, J. M. 1975. *Agrarian Revolution: Social Movements and Export Agriculture in the Underdeveloped World.* New York: Free Press.

Palmer, R. R. 1959–1964. *The Age of the Democratic Revolution.* Vol. 1. Princeton, NJ: Princeton University Press.

Papanek, Hanna. 1994. "The Ideal Woman and the Ideal Society: Control and Autonomy in the Construction of Identity." Pp. 42–75 in *Identity Politics and Women: Cultural Reassertions and Feminisms in International Perspective,* edited by Valentine M. Moghadam. Boulder, CO: Westview.

Parsa, Misagh. 2000. *States, Ideologies, and Social Revolutions: A Comparative Analysis of Iran, Nicaragua, and the Philippines.* Cambridge: Cambridge University Press.

Perry, Elizabeth, and Li Xun. 1997. *Proletarian Power: Shanghai in the Cultural Revolution.* Boulder, CO: Westview.

Pettee, George S. 1938. *The Process of Revolution.* New York: Harper and Row.

Popkin, Samuel. 1979. *The Rational Peasant: The Political Economy of Rural Society in Vietnam.* Berkeley: University of California Press.

Reynolds, Siân. 1987a. "Introduction." Pp. ix–xvi in *Women, State and Revolution: Essays on Power and Gender in Europe Since 1789,* edited by Siân Reynolds. Amherst: University of Massachusetts Press.

————. 1987b. "Marianne's Citizens? Women, the Republic, and Universal Suffrage in France." Pp. 101–22 in *Women, State and Revolution: Essays on Power and Gender in Europe Since 1789,* edited by Siân Reynolds. Amherst: University of Massachusetts Press.

Rivera Cusicanqui, Silvia. 1990. "Indigenous Women and Community Resistance: History and Memory." Pp. 151–83 in *Woman and Social Change in Latin America,* edited by Elizabeth Jelin. London: Zed.

Robinson, Glenn E. 1997. *Building a Palestinian State: The Incomplete Revolution.* Bloomington: Indiana University Press.

Rostow, W. W. 1991. "Eastern Europe and the Soviet Union: A Technological Time Warp." Pp. 60–73 in *The Crisis of Leninism and the Decline of the Left: The Revolutions of 1989,* edited by Daniel Chirot. Seattle: University of Washington Press.

Rowbotham, Sheila. 1972. *Women, Resistance, and Revolution.* London: Allen Lane.

Rudé, G. 1964. *The Crowd in History: A Study of Popular Disturbances in France and England 1730–1848.* New York: Wiley.

Russell, Conrad. 1991. *The Fall of the British Monarchies, 1637–1642.* Oxford: Clarendon.

Russell, D. L. H. 1974. *Rebellion, Revolution, and Armed Force.* New York: Academic.

Schaller, Michael. 1979. *The United States and China in the Twentieth Century.* New York: Oxford University Press.

Schama, Simon. 1989. *Citizens: A Chronicle of the French Revolution.* New York: Knopf.

Scott, James C. 1976. *The Moral Economy of the Peasant: Rebellion and Subsistence in South East Asia.* New Haven, CT: Yale University Press.

———. 1977. "Peasant Revolution: A Dismal Science." *Comparative Politics* 9 : 231–48.

Seidman, Gay. 1994. *Manufacturing Militance: Workers' Movements in Brazil and South Africa, 1970–1985.* Berkeley: University of California Press.

Selbin, Eric. 1993. *Modern Latin American Revolutions.* Boulder, CO: Westview.

Selden, Mark. 1979. *The People's Republic of China: A Documentary History of Revolutionary Change.* New York: Monthly Review.

Sewell, W. H., Jr. 1980. *Work and Revolution in France: The Language of Labor from the Old Regime to 1848.* Cambridge: Cambridge University Press.

Sharp, Buchanan. 1980. *In Contempt of All Authority: Rural Artisans and Riot in the West of England, 1586–1660.* Berkeley: University of California Press.

Sharpe, Kevin. 1978. "Parliamentary History 1603–1629: In or Out of Perspective?" Pp. 1–42 in *Faction and Parliament: Essays on Early Stuart History,* edited by Kevin Sharpe. Oxford: Clarendon.

Shugart, Matthew Sobart. 1989. "Patterns of Revolution." *Theory and Society* 18 : 249–71.

Skocpol, Theda. 1979. *States and Social Revolutions.* Cambridge: Cambridge University Press.

———. 1994. *Social Revolutions in the Modern World.* Cambridge: Cambridge University Press.

Small, Melvin, and J. David Singer. 1982. *Resort to Arms: International and Civil Wars, 1816–1980.* Beverly Hills, CA: Sage.

Smelser, N. J. 1963. *Theory of Collective Behavior.* New York: Free Press.

Soboul, Albert. 1975. *The French Revolution, 1787–1799. From the Storming of the Bastille to Napoleon.* New York: Vintage.

Spence, Jonathan D. 1990. *The Search for Modern China.* New York: Norton.

Sperber, Jonathan. 1994. *The European Revolutions, 1848–1851.* Cambridge: Cambridge University Press.

Spufford, Margaret. 1974. *Contrasting Communities: English Villages in the Sixteenth and Seventeenth Centuries.* Cambridge: Cambridge University Press.

Stokes, Gale. 1993. *The Walls Came Tumbling Down: The Collapse of Communism in Eastern Europe.* Oxford: Oxford University Press.

Stone, Lawrence. 1965. *The Crisis of Aristocracy 1558–1641.* Oxford: Oxford University Press.

Sutherland, Bill, and Matt Meyer. 1999. *Guns and Ghandi in Africa: Pan-Africanist Insights on Non-Violence, Armed Struggle, and Liberation.* Trenton, NJ: Africa World Press.

Taylor, A. J. P. 1980. *Revolutions and Revolutionaries.* London: Hamish Hamilton.

Tétreault, Mary Ann, ed. 1994. *Women and Revolution in Africa, Asia, and the New World.* Columbia: University of South Carolina Press.

Thirsk, Joan. 1961. "Industries in the Countryside." Pp. 70–88 in *Essays in the Economic and Social History of Tudor and Stuart England,* edited by F. J. Fisher. Cambridge: Cambridge University Press.

Thompson, Mark R. 1995. *The Anti-Marcos Struggle.* New Haven, CT: Yale University Press.

Thompson, J. M. 1935. *Robespierre*. Oxford: Basil Blackwell.

Tilly, Charles. 1978. *From Mobilization to Revolution*. Reading, MA: Addison-Wesley.

———. 1993. *European Revolutions 1492–1992*. Oxford: Blackwell.

———. 1994. "In Search of Revolution." *Theory and Society* 23:799–803.

Tocqueville, Alexis de. 1955. *The Old Regime and the French Revolution*. Translated by Stuart Gilbert. New York: Doubleday.

Trimberger, Ellen Kay. 1978. *Revolution from Above: Military Bureaucrats and Development in Japan, Turkey, Egypt, and Peru*. New Brunswick, NJ: Transaction.

Trotsky, Leon. 1930. *My Life*. New York: Scribner's.

———. 1959. *The Russian Revolution*. Selected and edited by F. W. Dupee. Translated by Max Eastman. New York: Doubleday (Anchor Books).

Urban, Michael, Vyacheslav Igrunov, and Sergei Mitrokhin. 1997. *The Rebirth of Politics in Russia*. Cambridge: Cambridge University Press.

Urdang, Stephanie. 1989. *And Still They Dance: Women, War and the Struggle for Change in Mozambique*. New York: Monthly Review.

Van Ness, Peter. 1970. *Revolution and Chinese Foreign Policy*. Berkeley: University of California Press.

Verdery, Katherine. 1993. "What Was Socialism and Why Did It Fall?" *Contention* 3:1–23.

Vickers, George R. 1990. "A Spider's Web." *NACLA Report on the Americas* 24:19–27.

Vilas, Carlos M. 1990. "What Went Wrong." *NACLA Report on the Americas* 24:28–36.

Walker, Thomas. 1985. *Nicaragua: Land of Sandino*, 2d ed. Boulder, CO: Westview.

Wallerstein, Immanuel. 1971. "The State and Social Transformation: Will and Possibility." *Politics and Society* 1:25–58.

———. 1974. *The Modern World System I: Capitalist Agriculture and the Origins of the European World Economy in the Sixteenth Century*. New York: Academic.

———. 1980a. *The Modern World System II*. New York: Academic.

———. 1980b. *The Capitalist World Economy*. Cambridge: Cambridge University Press.

Walter, John. 1980. "Grain Riots and Popular Attitudes to the Law: Maldon and the Crisis of 1629." Pp. 47–84 in *An Ungovernable People? The English and Their Law in the Seventeenth and Eighteenth Centuries*, edited by John Brewer. New Brunswick, NJ: Rutgers University Press.

Walter, John, and Keith Wrightson. 1976. "Dearth and the Social Order in Early Modern England." *Past and Present* 71:22–42.

Watson, D. 1993. "Can Memory Survive the Storm?" *New Internationalist* 247:14–16.

West, Guida, and Lois Rhoda Blumberg, eds. 1990. *Women and Social Protest*. New York: Oxford University Press.

Wickham-Crowley, Timothy. 1992. *Guerrillas and Revolution in Latin America*. Princeton, NJ: Princeton University Press.

Womack, John, Jr. 1969. *Zapata and the Mexican Revolution*. New York: Knopf.

Wood, Gordon S. 1969. *The Creation of the American Republic, 1776–1787*. New York: Norton.

Zhao, Dingxin. 2001. *The Power of Tiananmen: State-Society Relations and the 1989 Beijing Student Movement*. Chicago: University of Chicago Press.

INDEX